to ALL NATIONS from ALL NATIONS

to ALL NATIONS from ALL NATIONS

A History of the Christian Missionary Movement

Carlos F. Cardoza-Orlandi
Justo L. González

Abingdon Press
Nashville

TO ALL NATIONS FROM ALL NATIONS
A HISTORY OF THE CHRISTIAN MISSIONARY MOVEMENT

This book is printed on acid-free paper.

Library of Congress Cataloging-in-Publication Data

Cardoza-Orlandi, Carlos F., 1961-
To all nations from all nations : a history of the Christian missionary movement / Carlos F. Cardoza-Orlandi and Justo L. González.
pages cm
Includes bibliographical references and index.
ISBN 978-1-4267-5489-0 (book - pbk. / trade pbk. : alk. paper) 1. Missions—History. 2. Church history. I. González, Justo L. II. Title.
BV2100.C27 2013
266.009—dc23

2013008609

13 14 15 16 17 18 19 20 21 22—10 9 8 7 6 5 4 3 2 1

MANUFACTURED IN THE UNITED STATES OF AMERICA

CONTENTS

PREFACE

To the authors of this book its history seems almost as long as the story it tells! It was over half a century ago, in the early 1960s, that one of us (Justo, for Carlos was still a toddler!) was teaching in Puerto Rico and received a request from Argentina that he write a history of missions. He acceded to that request rather reluctantly, for his actual training was in historical theology rather than in missiology or in the history of missions. The resultant book was published in Buenos Aires in 1970. A few years later, the Argentinean publisher ceased its operation, and the book went out of print. In spite of frequent requests from colleagues and friends in Latin America, that the book be reedited, Justo resisted such suggestions, for he was well aware of his shortcomings in the field of missiology. Then his friend Carlos F. Cardoza-Orlandi, having completed his Ph.D. in missiology at Princeton Theological Seminary, joined the faculty of Columbia Theological Seminary in Decatur, Georgia, the two became neighbors, and their friendship developed.

Out of that friendship emerged the idea for a book on the history of the missionary movement, using some of the material of Justo's earlier book, but bringing into the picture Carlos's expertise as well as new realities and the perspectives that both of us had developed in the intervening decades. The result was a book published in Spanish in Barcelona under the title of *Historia general de las misiones*, and in Portuguese in São Paulo as *História do movimiento missionário.*

It then remained to translate the material into English, at the same time rewriting and adapting some sections in view of the different audience for which this new book is intended. We are pleased that we are finally able to present this book to the English-speaking public. We do so in the hope that it will somehow contribute to the life of the church as it seeks to be faithful to its mission.

But there is another side to the story of a book such as this. We are grateful to the countless people who have contributed to it. Many of them are earlier scholars on whose research we have built. Others are present-day colleagues from whose work and comments we have benefited. Among them, we would be remiss not to mention Dr. James D. Smith III, of Bethel Seminary, San Diego, whose many comments, suggestions, and insights proved invaluable.

Carlos is also grateful for the support received from Columbia Theological Seminary (where he taught until 2010) and Perkins School of Theology, Southern Methodist University, where he now teaches.

Finally, our wives, Aida Lizzette Oquendo and Catherine Gunsalus González, besides supporting and encouraging us in the entire enterprise, read and reread our drafts, catching many an error, many an omission, and many an ambiguity that would otherwise have gone unnoticed.

Carlos F. Cardoza-Orlandi
Justo L. González

Chapter 1

INTRODUCTION

"Go therefore and make disciples of all nations." Few biblical texts are quoted as often as are these words, usually known as the Great Commission. Over the centuries, these words have inspired thousands of believers to take the gospel to the farthest corners of the earth. Some have simply crossed the street; others have crossed rivers, borders, and oceans. Some have given money; others have given their lives. Some were well received, and others died as martyrs at the hand of those whom they sought to evangelize. Churches have been built, schools and hospitals founded, injustice undone, and women liberated from the oppression of ancestral customs. Millions have learned how to improve their livestock, how to care for their health, and how to read. Hundreds of languages that only existed orally have been reduced to writing.

If that were the entire story, there would be ample reason for Christians to be proud of their work and their history. But there is the other side of the coin. Through the centuries, and even to this day, Christians have used the words of Jesus as justification for lucre and for imperialistic purposes. Christians have taken the missionary injunction as an indication of their own superiority, and with that sense of superiority, they have destroyed cultures and civilizations; they have established and supported despotic regimes; they have employed armed violence to force others to believe as they do. In brief, they have justified the unjustifiable.

Such havoc has not always been the result of hypocrisy, nor has it always been brought about by people consciously using the Christian faith for their own ends. It has also resulted from the work of sincere Christians convinced that the expansion of their faith justified their actions and that they were truly in the service of God. Convinced as they were of the truth of their belief, many took this to be a sign of the superiority of their culture and, with that sense of superiority, rode roughshod over cultures and identities and oppressed the defenseless.

More recently, however, the spread of the gospel comes from immigrants and refugees who become evangelizers in a strange land. Christian missionaries from Africa, Asia, and Latin America move across Southern Hemisphere boundaries to share the story of Jesus. Christian missionaries from Africa, Asia, and Latin America come to the United States, Canada, and Europe with extremely limited financial resources but with a deep zeal for sharing and embodying the gospel of Jesus Christ.

It is for these reasons that the study of the history of the missionary movement is both crucial and urgent. The history of the expansion of Christianity is at the same time both inspiring and terrifying. It is both a call and a warning. It calls us to join the shining legacy of those who witnessed to their faith. And it warns us of the danger of imagining that, because we are faithful Christians, we need not be concerned over the consequences of our attitudes and our actions.

At this point, it may be well to look again at the Great Commission itself. It begins with the words *go therefore.* The word *therefore* requires an antecedent, a reason for what follows. In this case, that antecedent is the word of Jesus, *all authority in heaven and on earth has been given to me.* In the final analysis, the reason why believers are to go to all nations is not that we feel sorry for those who are lost, or that our culture is superior, or even that we have something to teach others. The reason for our going is the universal lordship of Christ, who tells us that all authority in heaven and on earth has been given to him. There is no place where he is not present. There is no place where he needs believers to take him. The Lord who was at the beginning with God, through whom all things were made, the light that enlightens everyone, is already there. Christ is active in individuals and cultures, even though they may not be aware of it and even through an anonymous presence. Thus, the most that believers can do as they bear witness and invite others to believe is to present the name of Jesus, his teachings, his promises. But they are not taking him anywhere where he was not!

If Christ is already there before we arrive, this means that in the missionary enterprise we go out to meet not only those who do not believe but also the Christ in whom we believe. As Christians go to places over which his authority is real—even though unrecognized—we learn more of him and of his purposes. It was thus that Peter learned much as he met Cornelius, and the ancient church also learned much as it made its way through Greco-Roman culture.

This means that, properly understood, the history of missions is not only the history of the *expansion* of Christianity but also the history of its own many *conversions*—of what the church has learned and discovered as its faith becomes incarnate in various times, places, and cultures.

When the great historian of missions Kenneth Scott Latourette finished the seven volumes of his history, he was able to declare that the greatest event of the previous century—the nineteenth—was that for the first time Christianity had become truly universal, for it was now present in every region of the globe. Today, half a century later, we can say more. Not only is Christianity present in the farthest corners of the earth, but also many of those places that were previously considered corners have now become centers of vitality and numeric growth. In Latourette's time, Christianity, although present throughout the world, was still mostly the religion of the West, represented in the rest of the world by relatively small groups, many of them resulting from the Western missionary enterprise and still dependent on that enterprise. Today, although Christianity seems to be losing ground in its ancient centers in Europe and North America, it grows by leaps and bounds in Africa and in Asia. In Latin America, where in Latourette's time Christianity consisted mostly of a stagnant Roman Catholicism and a very small Protestant presence, today Catholicism is undergoing profound renewal, and Protestantism is growing to such a point that in several countries it embraces more than a quarter of the population.

These demographic changes point to the vitality of the Christian movement, the contextual nature of faith communities, the energy generated at the points of encounter among cultures and peoples, and the diversity of missionary theologies and practices that abound in the transmission and reception of the gospel. For this reason, it is our hope that this book will help its readers set aside a view of Christianity as a Western religion and rediscover its worldwide and cross-cultural nature. Thus, the vitality of Christianity in the global south becomes a prism through which one may reread and reevaluate missionary practice and theology. The study of the missionary enterprise reveals a multidirectional movement full of complexities and struggles that require a different frame of reference—*from all the world to all the world!*

However, if this history of the missionary movement is to serve as a tool for reflection for both the academy and the church, it is important to spell out what are the criteria, principles, and limits of the present work.

A. Missiology, Mission, and the History of Missions

Missiology is the discipline that studies all that relates to the mission of God and of the community of faith in a systematic and coherent fashion. It is a far-reaching discipline that relates to anthropology, economics, history, history of religions, systematic theology, and several other disciplines.

Strictly speaking, *mission* is the activity of God in the world. God is the protagonist of mission. By grace, God acts in the world to reconcile the world with God (2 Cor. 5:19). The church, as people of God, is born out of that mission and shares in it. The church is both the result and the co-protagonist of the mission of God. That is to say that the church discerns and shares in the activity of God in the world and thus becomes an active subject in that mission.

The term *missions*—in the plural form—is laden with a variety of meanings. This is not the place to discuss and analyze them, but it is the place to clarify what we mean by that term. Traditionally, this term has conveyed the image of a movement in one direction, from the Christian world to the non-Christian world. This has led to the association of *missions* with an ecclesiocentric enterprise in which the church is the main protagonist of mission.

In this book, *missions* refers to the movement of Christianity, including that movement within areas in which there is already a Christian presence. As we shall see throughout this history, Christianity—in its many forms—is introduced and reintroduced within a geographic area, thus creating varied and complex bodies and relations among those bodies. Therefore, missions are what the church has done—for good and not for good—in its effort to expand the faith both within and beyond the borders of its own context. This book is a "history of missions" and as such is part of Christian missiology. It collects data as well as critical reflection on the activity of the church. It is not a history of missiology (of the development of that discipline through the centuries); nor is it a history of the mission (of the activity of God and of the community of faith); nor is it a history of thought about mission (of the ideas, principles, and debates regarding the action of God and of the church in the world). *It is rather a history of the action of the church in its effort to communicate the gospel both within and beyond its borders, a history of the expansion of Christian faith in the world.* However, given the interdisciplinary nature of missiology, this history of missions is also shaped by the history of missiology and seeks to make a contribution to that discipline. It is part of a missiological and theological conversation on God's mission and on our own mission in the present days.

This history of the missionary movement (or of missions) also seeks to develop a "cartography" of missionary theology in various times and places. The relationship between the theology of mission and missionary practice is not unidirectional. Theology of mission informs and shapes missionary practice, and missionary practice informs and shapes the theology of mission. In this interdependent relationship, theologies and practices of mission clash and reciprocate, contest and accept, contradict and correspond, deny and affirm each other. The present history will show how both practice and theology evolve as historical circumstances modify them. It will also show that practices and theologies that had little success in one context had an entirely different result in another. For instance, as we shall see, what did not work in China was quite successful in Korea.

B. Church History and the History of Missions

Church history should not be divorced from the history of missions. Critical reflection on the life of the church—its worship, theology, and pastoral practice—should not be severed from equally critical reflection on the work of the people of God, both in expanding the outreach of the faith and in renewing the life of society and of the church itself. Unfortunately, the manner in which these two disciplines—church history and the history of missions—have been defined manifests a dichotomy, a bipolar perspective, that tends to eclipse the unity of church and mission and that implies that there are chapters in the life of the church that are part of its "history" and other chapters that are merely part of its "missions."

Such dichotomy reflects the Eurocentric perspective of both disciplines as they are traditionally defined. Thus, the conflicts of early Christians with the Roman Empire and its culture are part of church history, but the conflicts between Christians and the Persian Empire are studied—if they are studied at all—as part of a different discipline. What took place in Germany in the sixteenth century is part of church history; but what took place in Mexico at the same time is part of the history of missions. The Great Awakening in North America in the eighteenth century is part of church history, but the Pentecostal awakening in Chile early in the twentieth is not. Clearly, it is time to correct such perspectives or at least to try to do so.

We do not expect this book to undo such dichotomy between historical disciplines in the life of the church. But we do wish to move in the direction of a historiography that takes into account the complex relations and interdependency between the centers and the peripheries—between what church history has traditionally studied and what this history of the missionary movement conveys. To move beyond that, developing a church history that is also a history of the missionary movement will be the task of an entire generation of historians—of historians representing a wide variety of perspectives and contexts. Thus, the present book is offered only as a temporary remedy, as a reminder of the vast reshaping of church history that must still be done.

Since we are convinced that history needs to integrate "church history" with the "history of missions," we will repeatedly point to the complex interaction between missionary activity at the margins of the church and the life of the church at the center from which such activity emerges. An example may be found in the section on missions in later antiquity, which shows how missions among the Germanic and Celtic "barbarians" transformed the missionary practices that the church at the center had taken as normative. It is important to point out, however, that our emphasis will not lie on the manner in which the missional policies of the center are challenged and changed—which would turn this book into a history of missiological thought—but rather on the activities, conditions, and protagonists at the edges of Christian lands. In other words, this book is a history of the missionary movement mostly at the periphery of Christianity and not of missionary thought at the centers.

It is our hope that the day will come when it will not be necessary—or even feasible—to study or write the history of missions apart from the history of the church. Furthermore, the last chapter of the present history will show why we are convinced that such a day is dawning and that if some do not notice it, this is due to a certain myopia that is typical of every center. But at present most curricula and programs in theological education, as well as the academic formation of most professors, tend to study church history from the perspective of the center, as if only that which takes place at the center were significant. As long as this attitude is not overcome, the study of the history of missions will be necessary, at least to remind us that the center exists by virtue of the periphery, and that a good portion of the total picture is excluded when we look only at what takes place in the centers—centers of economic resources, of theological studies, and so forth.

A second consequence of this dichotomy in historical studies is an "exponential" understanding of the growth of Christian faith. In this view, one takes for granted that Christian faith grows and continues to grow in a single direction, as the center widens its outreach with little or no change in the center itself—much as a balloon grows and continues to grow as more air is blown into it.

In this book, we depart from such a view of Christian growth and join the growing number of creative voices throughout the world that propose: (1) Christian growth is, so to speak, "in series," so that the faith moves from a center to a periphery, transforming both and creating new centers that in turn move toward new peripheries—peripheries that may well be the ancient centers! (2) This movement affects both the theology and the practice of communities of faith, not only at the center, but also in the periphery. (3) The missional activity of the periphery shows great vitality, due in part to its intersections with cultures that are rich in religious, ethnic, and theological diversity, and in part to the struggles for justice by oppressed and suppressed groups such as social classes, women, children, and ethnic minorities. (4) We become aware that Christianity has always been and will continue to be global, cross-cultural, and contextual, and this in turn requires new perspectives from which to observe and write the history of the church.

Thus, the present history is written out of the conviction that, given the present situation, for some time it will still be necessary to discuss and to write the history of missions as if it were a different field, thus calling the entire field of church history to remember items, events, and challenges that it would otherwise tend to forget. We seek to meet the need for materials showing students, church leaders, and those engaged in various aspects of the mission the wide and varied mosaic that is the history of the transmission of the gospel. Most certainly, we cannot point to every detail in that mosaic. But we seek to help our readers: (1) discover the variety of tiles in this mosaic that is the totality of the church—of the church throughout the globe and through the ages; (2) understand and reflect on this variety; (3) take up the challenge to go beyond what is said in this book, widening their horizons by intentional experiences of contact and interchange with various sectors of world Christianity; and (4) discover other angles and perspectives from which to observe, study, and enjoy the glorious variety of the people of God, which reaches into every nation, people, tribe, and language.

C. Pastoral Theology, the History of Missions, and the People of God

Pastoral theology integrates several other disciplines into the pastoral task. Missiology, as well as church history and the history of missions, frequently needs to be integrated into pastoral theology. The latter is not limited to the activities and responsibilities of the ordained ministry. It refers rather to every action and reflection that seeks to integrate the knowledge and contributions of various disciplines into the life of the community of faith. Thus, in the context of the present book, pastoral theology asks questions such as, what contribution does this history make to the life of the church in its struggle to be faithful to the gospel and to be a sign of the reign of God? Some possible answers would be:

First, *the history of missions helps the people of God discover and accept that "missions" have taken Christian faith well beyond the borders of Christendom and beyond the former centers of that faith.* In this history, we shall meet believers—some officially known as "missionaries" and some not—whose faith placed before them an urgent imperative to share their experience of God. We shall see some of the challenges, ambiguities, struggles, victories, frustrations, and hopes that resulted from such a calling. We shall witness moments of triumph, but also of defeat; prophetic visions, but also twisted ones; great benefits, but also—we must confess—great damage.

Second, *the history of missions illustrates the rich diversity of "missions."* This history will show that missions are not, never have been, and never will be a homogeneous activity, moving always in the same direction and following the same pattern. On the contrary, this history bears witness to the sovereign will of the Holy Spirit and the discernment—or lack of discernment—of thousands of believers who, being away from the centers of ecclesial power, have sought to communicate the gospel where it was not known and to establish or renew the church within their own contexts.

Third, *the history of missions reminds us that the missionary activity of the people of God does not always measure up to the standards of the gospel of Christ.* As will be clearly seen in this book, on many occasions the history of missions is also a history of sin, of violence, of abuse of power, and even of genocide. This dimension in the history of missions will, on the one hand, counteract the triumphalist attitude that has often overcome the church in its mission and has allowed it to ignore and continue falling into the same errors and, on the other hand, call the church to critical and cautious reflection on its missionary activity.

Fourth, and at the other extreme, *the history of missions celebrates the legacy of missionary activities, critically recovering valuable elements in the strategies, styles, and theologies of healthy missionary work in the past, and thus developing a new generation of believers committed to the missionary task.* Just as it is important to question and reject practices that compromise the integrity of the gospel, so it is important to celebrate missions that have led to a historical consciousness, a critical attitude, a prophetic proclamation, and a quest for faithfulness to the gospel in the ongoing daily mission.

Finally, *the history of missions shows the diversity of the people of God, its presence over the face of the earth, and the promise that this faith will not be limited to a few cultures or geographic areas but reaches throughout the world as a living witness to its own vitality.* Missions witness to the activity of God in the world with all sorts of people and in every circumstance. They witness to God's risk-taking in sharing with the church the work of salvation and reconciliation. They witness to the diversity of the people of God and at the same time to their joint and constant struggle to discern the activity of God in the world—and to do so with humility and trust in God. They witness to the interdependence of the community of faith throughout the world, and to its full dependency on God, who is the main protagonist of every missionary activity.

D. The Structure of This History of the Missionary Movement

This book has been organized both chronologically and geographically. Thus, chapters 2 to 5 deal with different periods in the history of the church and its mission: the very early times, as depicted in the New Testament, antiquity, the Middle Ages, and the Early Modern Age. Since Late Modernity (from the nineteenth century to the beginning of the twenty-first century) is also the great period of Christian expansion—particularly Protestant expansion—five chapters are devoted to it: a general introduction (chapter 6), then specific chapters on Asia and the South Pacific (chapter 7), the Muslim world (chapter 8), sub-Saharan Africa (chapter 9), and Latin America (chapter 10). The book then concludes (chapter 11) with some consideration of the missionary movement in the postmodern or postcolonial age and of the manner in which the emerging world and the enormous demographic changes in its own constituency force the entire church—particularly the church in the United States, Europe, and other traditional centers of mission—to reconsider its general history, as well as its own understanding and practice of mission.

Chapter 2

BIBLE, MISSION, AND THE HISTORY OF MISSIONS

Paradoxically, the history of Christian missions, like every other aspect of church history, begins precisely at the point in which, according to Christian faith, the end has come—that is, with the advent and the resurrection of Jesus Christ. The fulfillment of all time in Jesus Christ is the point of departure and the very essence of the church's missionary message. This is why the biblical witness has to be both the starting point of any history of missions and the measure by which each moment in that history is to be judged, because it witnesses to Jesus Christ as both our starting point and our final criterion.

The biblical witness, particularly in the New Testament, attests to the fulfillment of God's purposes in creation itself and to the promises repeatedly given to humankind. In order to place that biblical witness within its own perspective, this chapter begins by discussing the use of Scripture in the history of missions (section A); second, it turns to a brief comment on translations of the Bible as interpretations and consequences of the missionary enterprise (section B); third, it deals with the importance and value of the Old Testament in the missionary enterprise (section C); fourth, on the basis of a missional reading of the New Testament, it expounds a number of important criteria for the mission of the church (section D); and finally, it briefly discusses the expansion of Christianity during the period of the New Testament (section E).

A. The Use and Interpretation of the Bible throughout the History of Missions

The purpose of this section is to outline four models of biblical interpretation that have been applied in the mission field. These four models do not exhaust the possibilities, nor do they include all the nuances of various interpretations. They do, however, offer a frame of reference that will help us understand the role of the Bible in this history.

(1) The first model is biblical interpretation *from the center.* This model limits the function of the Bible. First, the Bible is the book that justifies the work of the missionaries; and second, it is a sort of "recipe book" with clear steps to follow in order to fulfill the mission. Such an interpretation takes for granted that the Bible belongs solely to the church, particularly to the missionaries. Interpretation is exclusively a task of missionaries and sponsors of missionaries. An example of this model has been the way in which Matthew 28:16-20, the Great Commission, has been interpreted and used as the foundation for all missionary work, which is to make disciples, baptize, and teach, with no other theological or contextual consideration.

This interpretation from the center limits the missional task of the people of God. First of all, it tends to reserve the use and interpretation of the Bible to the missionaries and to the churches sending them. They already know what the mission is and then find references in the Bible to prove it. The accessibility, authority, and interpretation of Scripture are reserved to the culture and faith experience from which the mission proceeds. Second, such a biblical interpretation can become the justification for a single way of doing mission. As a consequence, the biblical witness is confused with dogma, and the vitality of interpretation of the Scriptures in the spirit of Christ is substituted with human and institutional prejudices, prescriptions, and directions. Finally, biblical interpretation from the center takes no account of the context of mission. There is no interchange between the biblical text and the context of the mission—its cultural, political, economic, and social setting.

(2) The second model is biblical interpretation *from the margin.* Even though a biblical interpretation from the center tends to ignore the context, biblical interpretation from the margin gives it a prominent place. Missionary personnel then analyze the cultural, economic, political, and social conditions of their setting, usually prioritizing situations of oppression, poverty, and marginality. Then one seeks in Scripture examples that (1) are similar to these situations and (2) justify acts and projects to alleviate these conditions. The main purpose of this model of biblical interpretation is to allow situations beyond the text of the Bible to select the biblical texts.

This model is often used in official denominational documents. Quite often such documents begin by describing the context in which the mission takes place. Then, by means of biblical texts, they establish the theological links between the context and the mission and justify missionary practice in a particular context.

Although this method overcomes some of the limitations of the model from the center, it still poses several difficulties: first, frequently the incorporation of the context into biblical interpretation is superficial, since it does not make use of the best scientific resources in analyzing both the situation and the text. In consequence, there is no real dialogue between the text and the context. What exists is a sort of combination of the two. Second, the analysis of the context becomes the absolute criterion for selecting and understanding biblical texts. Such a criterion does not allow a different interpretation of the text or the context. It is a one-way road. The biblical text only serves to illumine the context and to justify a particular course of action. Third, normally the analysis of the context is done by people who (1) are not part of the context or, in the best of cases, (2) are agents of mission and solidarity with the marginalize people. The participation of the people themselves who experienced marginality in their daily life is minimal. They serve as an example to justify the use of the biblical text. The people themselves, although with a sort of passive participation in the process of biblical interpretation and missional reflection, are still the object of mission defined by an interpretation that comes from outside their own marginality.

(3) A third model of interpretation is the *hermeneutical circle* (or circle of interpretation). This is typical of contemporary theology and particularly of Latin American liberation theology. It has been proposed by theologian Juan Luis Segundo, and it overcomes some of the limitations of the two methods previously mentioned. The hermeneutical circle takes the context seriously, but this is not the only criterion that determines the interpretation of the biblical text. Studying the context is joined to the interpretation of the text, which in turn leads to liberating action, all in the life of the people, who are the main actors in the interpretation of the text.

Essentially, the hermeneutical circle has four steps. One may begin with the analysis of reality. Using the social sciences, the oppressive conditions in which the people live are analyzed and their causes sought. There is an "ideological suspicion" that begins with the assumption that the situation of poverty and oppression is not God's will. The next step is reading the Bible in relationship to that analysis of reality. At this point, one makes a political reading of the biblical text. This text and reality speak to each other in a dialogue from which an imperative emerges, a liberating and transformative action. This liberating *praxis* is the third step, and it is the missional action that the community will undertake. The fourth step is the experience of transformation that is born out of the liberating practice. The missional and liberative action produces a new reality, which in turn has to be evaluated and studied, so that the hermeneutical circle begins again, and the Scriptures are a subject of continued conversation with the context and with the liberating praxis.

One of the most important contributions of this model in the field of missiology is the consciousness of God's accompaniment. Mission and the biblical reflection on it become dynamic and fluid, demanding discernment and growth in the faith. The first two models tend to limit God's actions to the past. The hermeneutical circle challenges any static understanding of God's grace and manifests God's continuing action and presence. The missionary God invites us to join in mission and to discern God's saving action in the world. Another important contribution of the hermeneutical circle is that the people who experience oppression and marginalization have an active role in missionary reflection and action. The people are in partnership with God in liberating and reconciling action; they are agents rather than mere objects of mission.

However, this model of biblical interpretation also has its limitations. The hermeneutical circle tends to reduce biblical interpretation in the context of mission to social, political, and class struggles. This reduction often does not allow for the inclusion of themes and realities that, besides having a political context, also have to do with matters of culture, religion, family, and so on. Any reduction in the way in which we understand the presence, mission, and accompaniment of God limits our vision of God's encounters with human beings in their contexts.

(4) A fourth model of biblical interpretation results from the theological and biblical dialogue between Bible scholars and missiologists. This model reflects a certain maturity, for Bible scholars then take the biblical testimony regarding mission quite seriously, and missiologies

overcome the limitations of the models previously described, discovering in the Scriptures, with the help of biblical scholars, great missiological riches. Both disciplines then show interest in the Bible itself and identify criteria and questions that will help a biblical theology of mission.

This model leads the reader of the Bible to find in it thematic lines having to do with God's mission. This tends to leave behind the selection of texts, the exclusive dependency on the context, and the reduction of missionary themes to sociological categories. Consequently, one discovers the far-reaching scope and the power of God's mission throughout the biblical witness. As Catholic missiologist Robert Schreiter has indicated, without ignoring the context and sociological categories, the text now begins a conversation on the followings questions: (a) Why mission? (b) How is mission? (c) What is mission?

(a) The first question deals with God's missionary nature. Schreiter calls this biblical reflection "the Bible *for* mission." In other words, the church seeks in the biblical witness the missionary nature of God, the call of mission, the divine command, and the origin of the relationship between the missionary God and the missionary people. The church examines and studies the spirit of the well-known text: "As the Father has sent me, so I send you" (John 20:21).

(b) The second question deals with the "how" of mission. Still centering attention on this text, it serves as a bridge between the why of mission and missionary action itself. As we study the nature of the "sending" in John 20:21, the question "how is mission?" finds a significant answer in Philippians 2:5-8:

> Let the same mind be in you that was in Christ Jesus, who, though he was in the form of God, did not regard equality with God as something to be exploited, but emptied himself, taking the form of a slave, being born in human likeness. And being found in human form, he humbled himself and became obedient to the point of death—even death on a cross.

The how of the church's mission must reflect the mission of the Triune of God.

(c) The third question, "what is mission?" evaluates our missional action. Still dealing with the texts from John and Philippians, we now ask: what contents, what praxis, give witness to the fact that Jesus made God known by emptying himself, that he took the form of a servant, that he humbled himself and made himself obedient even to death on a cross? This third question underscores the historical nature of God's mission, the contextualization of that mission by God's people, and the importance of the Holy Spirit in the discerning of mission.

These three questions are not independent of one another. It is not a matter of answering one and then moving to the next. On the contrary, they are intertwined in a biblical reflection that allows for creativity in the light of the diverse circumstances of each community in mission. Thus reflection seeks to discover God in mission and to discern the church's task in witnessing responsibly and in the freedom of the Spirit to the God of mission.

Missional biblical interpretation is constantly developing. It faces serious challenges when communities of faith have to deal, for instance, with the dynamics of transcultural mission, the presence and vitality of other religions, the growing distance between rich and poor, the demographic changes in the church, violence among ethnic groups and against women and children, and the environmental and ecological crises. A missional community of faith needs to overcome those models of biblical interpretation that limit it to inflexible and archaic proposals that cannot respond to the challenges of the twenty-first century.

Still, no method of interpretation will ever exhaust the riches of the biblical text or the complexity of reality. Thus one needs to keep biblical interpretation open to the breath of the Spirit, hence the significance of missional questions and the importance of learning to "read"

Scriptures missionally, taking into account that mission is first of all God's activity in all of creation.

B. Translation and Interpretation

Christianity is a religion of translation. It has no official language. The Christian Scriptures are the most evident and eloquent example of this religious characteristic and, moreover, of the never-ending process of biblical interpretation in missionary work. Throughout history, Christian missionaries have worked to make the Bible accessible in mother tongues. Recent historical and linguistic studies prove that translations generated vitality and grounding of faith in unexpected ways. Oral languages became written languages providing longevity and stability to different cultures. Yet, translations also domesticated the oral reception and fluidity of the Christian story by imposing a translation—an interpretation—over oral and fluid interpretations of the Bible.

Christian groups that do not have the Bible in their mother tongue continue to practice their Christian life and discipleship. The story of the gospel flows within an oral cultural world. Among many groups in Africa, Asia, and Amerindians in Latin America, these oral cultures interact with one another. Linguistic groups have their translators who have multi-language skills and serve as interpreters among the groups. These translators have "natural" cross-cultural linguistic skills. When the Bible has been translated into one group's language, these translators bring the Bible and translate for their community, generating a cross-cultural communication event between the translated Bible and the oral language of their group. The flow of languages and images is abundant as oral and literal worldviews overlap in the translations and interpretations of these cross-cultural dynamics. Frequently forgotten, some of the most important Christian missionaries are those cross-cultural translators and interpreters in a particular region. Many Bible-translating missionary organizations depend on the intuitive and linguistic knowledge of these nationals and locals who know the Christian Scriptures in more than one language!

C. The Old Testament and the Mission of the Church

The concept of "missions," such as it is found in the New Testament, does not appear in the Old. But this does not mean that there is no understanding in the Old Testament of the universal lordship of God and God's significance for Israel's mission. This concept shaped and still shapes the church's understanding of mission.

1. Universality in the Old Testament

Often the Old Testament is interpreted in exclusivist terms, as if it were simply the story of a people who considered themselves God's favorite. When the Old Testament is thus understood, it is difficult to see how it can be the point of departure for the missionary views of the New Testament. However, the Old Testament is much wider in its vision than many generally think. The book of Genesis, whose high point is the election of Abraham and Sarah and their descendants, begins with a long prologue or introduction of eleven chapters that stresses the universal lordship of the Creator over all creation and all humankind. The history of Israel, as it begins in chapter 12 of Genesis, can be understood within the general context of the history of humankind, and particularly within the purpose of God for us, as it is also found in the first eleven chapters of the book. The very election of Abraham, which opens chapter 12 in Genesis, expresses the universal purpose of the divine election: "and in you all the families of the earth shall be blessed" (Gen. 12:3).

All of this means that although Israel is the chosen people of God, such election is not a sign of favoritism; but it is rather a sign of obligation, the result of people who must live in covenant with God. Also this responsibility on Israel's part requires that it announce its own election in the midst of people who have other religions and therefore hold to other histories of salvation. The encounter of the faith and the election of Israel with other people resulted in new understandings of how to live and express God's election. On one hand, there were strong confrontations such as that between Elijah and the prophets of Baal, and on the other hand, there were interesting interpretations of the action of God beyond Israel itself, as when Isaiah announces the liberation that is to come in the form of the Persian king, Cyrus (Isa. 44:28–45:7).

In any case, Israel has been called by God to be a people of blessing for all the nations of the earth, which is expressed in multiple ways. It is clear that on many occasions God intervenes in order to clarify to Israel what its election means. God uses the particular situations of the people to communicate the divine will. At the same time, the people of Israel face the challenge of discerning the will of God. It is within this constant dynamic that the people come to understand the meaning of their election and therefore of their mission.

2. Israel's Universal Mission

(a) The centripetal dimension of Israel's mission

In the Old Testament, the mission of Israel is understood "centripetally" rather than "centrifugally." It is not a matter of Israel going to all nations, preaching the message of salvation, but it is rather that all the nations of the world will find in Israel their salvation. For this reason, Israel's mission is to witness to the salvation of God throughout creation. Psalm 2 shows the centripetal nature of Israel's mission:

> Now therefore, O kings, be wise; be warned, O rulers of the earth.
> Serve the LORD with fear, and rejoice with trembling,
> Kiss the Son, lest he be angry, and you will perish in the way,
> for his wrath is quickly kindled.
> Blessed are all who take refuge in him. (Pss. 2:10-12 ESV)

(b) From exclusivity to inclusivity: The case of Jonah

The missionary nature of the book of Jonah is well known and debated. Quite often, we miss the central message of the book because we are engaged in sterile discussions regarding the authenticity of the document itself. However, the book of Jonah is one of the most eloquent texts having to do with the mission of Israel and later of the church.

A careful reading of Jonah will provide significant insight into God's purpose and Israel's universal mission. First of all, the purpose of the book is not to call Israel to go to all the world preaching the lordship of Yahweh, but rather is to call Israel itself to acknowledge that this lordship of God is universal. The acknowledgment of the lordship of Yahweh beyond geographic and ethnic borders requires the people of God to open its borders and to acknowledge the grace of God in other people who accept the call to repentance.

Second, this openness on the part of Israel, illustrated in the story of Jonah, indicates how mission transforms faith and our thoughts regarding the will of God. Jonah's main difficulty was in accepting the scope of God's mercy. To go to Nineveh as a missionary implied trusting exclusively in God, not in prejudice regarding Israel's election. In other words, the mission in Nineveh required Israel to think of its election in a different way, acknowledging its particular place and responsibility in the history of salvation, which is a place of compassion, but without confusing this with exclusivity and privilege.

(c) "Remember that you were a slave in the land of Egypt; therefore I am commanding you . . ." (Deut. 24:22)

The faith of Israel centers on the experience of liberation from Egypt. The entire Pentateuch refers continuously to the experience of slavery in Egypt and of liberation as the ethical and missional criterion for the life of the people. The memory of the liberation from the yoke of slavery in Egypt is the announcement of God's reign of justice and peace.

Justice and peace are central themes in the history of Israel and its mission. The prophets remind both the people and the leaders of the importance of God's *shalom*, peace and justice. The prophet Micah expresses it quite eloquently:

> He has told you, O mortal, what is good;
> and what does the LORD require of you
> but to do justice, and to love kindness,
> and to walk humbly with your God? (Mic. 6:8 ESV)

(d) The eschatological nature of mission

There are certain texts in the Old Testament, particularly in Second Isaiah, that have a markedly missionary character, referring to the salvation of the nations. But it seems best to interpret these texts eschatologically. They point to the day when God's salvation will reach to the ends of the earth. Within the context of the Old Testament there is no place for the idea of an "evangelization" of the world that is to take place through Israel's efforts. That "evangelization" in which the chosen people are to be employed as God's instrument is eschatological and will take place in the last days and only on the basis of God's sovereign decision. In the Old Testament, mission or missions are not an obligation imposed on Israel throughout all its history as part of its task as God's chosen people, but rather a sign of the end times.

D. The New Testament and Theological Criteria for the Mission

The New Testament offers abundant criteria for the mission of the church. All of its books deal with themes of mission. Furthermore, when we reflect on it, we realize that practically all of the New Testament was written in a missionary context, and in good measure in order to respond to questions and difficulties that the context itself posed. Thus, for instance, in Paul's epistles, the subject of the inclusion of Gentiles and their relation to Israel is paramount. There are other missionary themes in the Gospels, Acts, and the rest of the New Testament.

What determines the missionary tone of a text is not its literal reading or its traditional interpretation, but the manner in which it is read from the perspective of mission. For instance, the passage of the foreign woman (Matt. 15:21-28 and Mark 7:24-30) becomes a "missional paradigm" with several variants: the encounter of Jesus with a woman (gender paradigm); the encounter of Jesus with someone who is not Jewish (interreligious paradigm); the encounter of Jesus with a foreigner (intercultural paradigm); and so on.

In this particular section, our purpose is to show three basic criteria that emerge from the New Testament and serve as central themes on which to reflect regarding the Bible and the mission of the church. They certainly do not exhaust what the New Testament tells us regarding this matter. But they do represent great missionary challenges for the church of Jesus Christ in the new millennium that has begun.

1. Jesus and His Ministry

Any reflection on the New Testament needs to take quite seriously the ministry of Jesus as it appears in the Gospels. The ministry, death, and resurrection of Jesus show how he related to men, women, and children; to Roman and Jewish authorities; to sinners; to the social institutions; to people of other cultures; to his disciples; and to the Father.

In the history of Christianity, the Jesus event has often been reduced to the cross and the salvific benefits of his death. Such a perspective needs to be enriched by a consideration of Jesus' life and ministry. This will lead the Christian people to a wider understanding not only of salvation but also of what it means to live out that salvation in history.

2. The Church: Community of Mission in the Spirit

It is the Holy Spirit who enables the church for mission and discipleship. It is also the Holy Spirit who impels and surprises the church, as was the case with Peter in his encounter with Cornelius (Acts 10). Furthermore, it is the Spirit of Christ who effects within the community of believers the reconciliation of Christ, breaking down cultural, ethnic, economic, and religious barriers. It is the Holy Spirit who is "doing mission" long before our word and action, preparing hearts and minds for the message of Christ.

The work of this Spirit, both in the church and outside of it, requires serious and profound reflection. The mystery of the presence of the Spirit in both spheres is a bridge allowing the church to discern its mission and discipleship, its witness to the world, and its life as a community. Being a community of mission in the Spirit allows the church to be both a sign and an agent of God's mission.

3. The Option for Life

The witness of the New Testament points to life. The ministry of Jesus does not end with death. His ministry and fidelity to the Father give Jesus power over death, which is his resurrection. The missionary activity of the disciples comes after the resurrection of their Lord. It is the resurrected life that marks the beginning of the mission of the church and of the new age that leads to the coming of God's reign.

Between this new age and the end of history, God is working for life: "I came that they may have life, and have it abundantly" (John 10:10). The mission of the church is to announce the good news not only of life after death, but also of life against death that so threatens all the world. The biblical witness, in both the Old and the New Testament, announces that the God of mission is the God who grants life, the God of life.

E. The Expansion of Christianity during the Period of the New Testament

There are very few surviving documents telling us of the origins and the first expansion of Christianity. Most of those documents deal with Paul's life and missionary activities. This may lead us to think that he was the most important of the first Christian missionaries. However, we must remember that there is no certainty of this and that there is no doubt that at the same time Paul was on his missionary journeys, there were many others taking their faith from one place to another.

The book of Acts tells us about the beginning of the Christian church in Jerusalem. But it also speaks of Christians in Galilee, Samaria, and Damascus. Acts itself claims that Philip baptized an Ethiopian eunuch but does not tell us what the eunuch did upon his return to Ethiopia. It is about the church in Antioch and its missionary work that we have more data. However, even the origin of the church in Antioch, like that of the other main Christian churches, remains hidden in the shadows of history. Acts tells us that it was the disciples who were dispersed as a result of the persecution after Stephen's death who took the gospel to Cyprus and Antioch (Acts 11:19); although we are also told that it was Cypriots and people from Cyrene who took the gospel to the Gentiles in Antioch (Acts 11:20). In any case, the church in Jerusalem learned of the newly formed community in Antioch and sent Barnabas to inquire about events there. He remained in Antioch and continued working in that church. It was in Antioch that believers in Jesus Christ were first called "Christians." It was also the church of Antioch that sent Paul and his companions on their missionary journeys. (Perhaps it is worthy of note that according to Acts, the call did not come to Paul and Barnabas privately but rather from the Spirit through the church.)

The journeys of Paul are well known, and it is not necessary to summarize them here. It will suffice to say that the apostle Paul took the gospel to Cyprus, to several cities of Asia Minor, to Macedonia, to the main cities of Greece, to Rome, and, according to some, even to Spain. About his methods, it is necessary to point out that, although Paul considered himself sent to the Gentiles, according to the book of Acts, he would normally begin working in the synagogue of each city, where he would teach and preach the gospel. In some cases, such as in Athens, he tried to find points of contact between his message and the local culture. He also took care of the churches he had founded—particularly of healing the divisions that appeared in them. His tendency to travel rapidly from one place to another, leaving small groups of disciples in each city, was not so much a missionary strategy, which left to those new disciples the task of taking the gospel to the countryside, but was rather due to the understanding that Paul had of his own mission, leading him to think not so much in terms of individuals as in terms of place. Once the gospel had been planted in a particular place, his task was to move on.

We know that Paul was not the only Christian missionary during the New Testament times, because the book of Acts and Paul's own epistles mention several episodes concerning other missionaries. Barnabas and Mark went to the island of Cyprus. Paul's first epistle to the Corinthians speaks of the Alexandrian Jew, Apollo, who worked in Corinth. Also, even before Paul reached Rome, there was already a Christian church in that city. Even more, in the relatively small Italian port of Puteoli, there were already Christians who went to receive Paul when he arrived there on his way to Rome. All of this should serve as a reminder that Paul is only one—even though perhaps the most important—of the many Christians who, during the first century, took their faith to various parts of the known world.

Finally, one should mention legends claiming that the apostles preached the gospel in various parts of the earth. Most of these legends are quite fantastic, but even the most believable ones cannot be confirmed.

It is only in the case of the apostle Peter that one can assert that there is reason to believe that he actually was in Rome, as tradition claims. Actually that tradition is so old that it is reflected already in the New Testament, and most ancient Christian writers echo it. As part of the same tradition, Peter's martyrdom in Rome should be considered quite likely. This does not mean, however, that Peter founded the church in Rome, for Paul's epistle to the Romans seems to imply that there was already a church there long before the visits of either Peter or Paul.

At any rate, the fact is that toward the end of the first century there were already Christians throughout the northeastern regions of the Mediterranean basin and that this expansion had taken place without a concerted missionary plan or strategy. It was also clear that this missionary task was transcultural, for it did not identify the gospel with a particular ethnicity or race. Thus, from its very beginning, the church was crossing cultural boundaries and growing roots in various contexts.

Chapter 3

MISSIONS IN ANTIQUITY

A. From the End of the New Testament to the Conversion of Constantine

Although very little is known about the expansion of Christianity during the apostolic period, even less is known about the period immediately following. This is not surprising, since this was precisely the time of the great persecutions, and a persecuted church finds it difficult to preserve and transmit the history of its origins. Furthermore, much of the expansion of Christianity during this time was not so much the work of missionaries completely devoted to evangelization, as it was the result of the witness of merchants, soldiers, slaves, and others who traveled for a number of reasons. Christianity would then make its entrance into a new area in a quiet and unnoticeable way, and when the church there was sufficiently mature to produce its own literature or some other monument that would let us know about its history, it had often forgotten much of its own origins. Inquiry into the origins of Christianity in various cities and regions is made even more difficult by the inclination of many in those ancient times to idealize the apostles and to try to attribute the beginning of Christianity in every particular city to an apostolic figure. This gave origin to many a legendary tradition that is not always easy to distinguish from historical fact.

Yet, on the basis of existing documents and archeological evidence, it is possible to discover sociological dimensions that help us interpret the growth of Christianity during this apostolic period. Existing data lead us to two significant conclusions: the first is that most converts to Christianity seem to have come from the religious traditions that were commonly accepted in society—that is, what today we call paganism—and not from marginal religions or sects. A second conclusion is that many conversions took place through direct personal contact with family or other connections. These two conclusions must always be kept in a dialectical tension. On the one hand, Christianity was attractive precisely because it proposed a way, a faith, and a lifestyle that were different from those of society at large. On the other hand, that faith was communicated through direct contact with that very society. Ideally, Christian growth takes place when the church, while asserting the contrast between itself and society at large, retains its human contact with that society.

In order to understand the geographical expansion of Christianity within the Roman Empire, some characteristics of life within the empire should be kept in mind. It is important, first of all, to recognize that Greco-Roman civilization was primarily urban. Certainly, rural life went on, for without its produce cities could not subsist. But the Greeks as well as the Romans were convinced that the greatest invention was the city. Thus the very word *civilization* originally meant "citification." One of the goals of the conquests of Alexander at an earlier date, and later of the Romans, was to "citify" the world. For this reason, most human and economic resources were concentrated in the cities. Roads, rather than ways into the interior of the land, were means of communication among cities. Therefore it is not surprising that Christianity, developing within such an environment, was for a long time mostly an urban religion.

This empire that saw itself as a network of cities subsisted through trade and other communication among those cities. It was to this end that Rome built its famous roads. Along those roads, and even more along sea and river routes, many peoples traveled: merchants, artisans seeking employment, students in quest of wisdom, pilgrims inspired by their faith, and many others. It was mostly through that constant mix that Christianity expanded from one region to another.

In its religion, the Roman Empire mingled the ancient religions of Rome with those of the conquered peoples. Whenever possible, links and connections were made among the gods from different areas and cultures. Thus, for instance, it became common to affirm that the Roman Neptune was the same as the Greek Poseidon and that the Greek Artemis was the same as the ancient goddess of the Ephesians and the Roman Diana. To these were added the mystery religions, whose followers partook in rites through which they were united to their gods, as well as a multitude of teachings that are usually given the generic name of Gnosticism. These offered salvation to those who learned their secret knowledge (gnosis). And, as a link connecting all of this, emperor-worship was encouraged and in some cases required as a sign of loyalty to this very diverse Roman Empire.

1. Geographic Expansion of Christianity

Although all these reasons make it impossible to provide a detailed narrative of the names and methods of missionaries who took Christianity to each area, it is possible to gain an approximate view of the geographical expansion of Christianity in the years between the apostolic age and the conversion of Constantine. That expansion is so astounding that it is particularly unfortunate that we do not have the exact data on how the new faith entered each region of the empire.

At the end of the New Testament, Christianity had already expanded beyond Palestine and Syria to Asia Minor, Greece, and Rome. There are no reliable data regarding the presence of Christianity beyond the imperial capital. Although there is some reference of a possible trip of Paul to Spain, nothing is known about its results, and it may not even have taken place. However, by the end of the second century—and particularly by the middle of the third—there is ample evidence that Christianity had expanded throughout the Mediterranean, particularly in the major cities, in which there were significant Christian communities.

(a) Egypt

In Egypt, particularly in the city of Alexandria, there soon was a growing church that some claimed had been founded by Mark, although there is no historical evidence for such claims. At any rate, by the middle of the second century, the Christian community in Alexandria had important thinkers such as Pantenus and, slightly later, Clement and Origen. A further sign of the intellectual and religious attraction of Christianity in the area is that it was precisely in Alexandria that Gnosticism made some of its most serious attempts to assimilate Christianity within itself.

(b) North Africa

In the region that the Romans called Africa, along the northern coast of that continent, and particularly in the city of Carthage, Christianity also appeared toward the end of the second century. However, at the point when Carthagenian Christianity first appears in historical records, it was already so mature that one may safely assert that it was founded several decades earlier. It was in Carthage, and not in Rome, that the earliest Christian literature in Latin was produced—in the work of Tertullian—and that area was also, with both Tertullian and Cyprian, the center of Western theological thought during the entire period we are studying and even later, with St. Augustine.

How did Christianity arrive in North Africa? Who took it there and from where? It is impossible to know. The traditional view is that Rome was the center from which Christianity was taken to Carthage. However, more detailed study indicates that the origins of North African Christianity came from the east and perhaps from the region of Phrygia. It was later that political and cultural circumstances led the African church to develop closer ties with Rome and to forget its ancient link with the Greek-speaking world.

(c) Spain

The origins of Christianity in Spain, as well as the history of the church there during the second century, are completely unknown. Apart from the possibility that Paul may have visited the Iberian Peninsula, some legends affirm that the apostle James worked there, and others affirm that Peter sent seven bishops to the area. The truth is that the Spanish church, which probably existed at least by the end of the second century, has left no written or other record that would allow us to think that there was a strong Christian presence in the Iberian Peninsula before the middle of the third century. However, the list of participants at the Synod of Elvira, about the year 300, is proof that by that time Christianity existed as far north as Asturias and as far east as Zaragoza, even though its strongest presence seems to have been in what today is known as Andalusia.

(d) Gaul

Christianity was already present in Gaul during the second half of the second century, and perhaps even earlier. In the year 177, persecution broke out in the cities of Lyon and Vienne which shows that there were already Christian communities there. Shortly thereafter, the writings of Bishop Irenaeus of Lyon, perhaps the greatest theologian of his time, witness to the strength of Christianity in that area, both numerically and intellectually. It would seem that Christianity reached Gaul brought there by Christian immigrants from Asia Minor or at least from the east, and that for some time it was particularly strong among the Greek-speaking population. However, Irenaeus himself indicates that Christians in Lyon—or at least Irenaeus himself—were attempting to evangelize their Celtic neighbors. In one of his books, written in Greek, Irenaeus explains that he has difficulty writing that language elegantly because he spends much of his time evangelizing the Celts. When a synod gathered in Arles in 314, there were people present, not only from all of Gaul, but even from as far as the British Isles. Therefore, before the opening of the fourth century, Christianity had extended along the entire Mediterranean basin and was present in all of the major areas of the empire.

(e) The areas where the apostles had labored

In those parts of the empire that are already mentioned in the New Testament as places where Christianity reached during the apostolic age, the church continued its missionary work, expanding now into lesser cities and towns. Thus, by the middle of the third century, there were already in Italy approximately a hundred bishops. Growth seems to have been slower in Greece, as well as along the Semitic nations of Syria and Palestine. However, in Asia Minor there was surprising growth, and there were soon churches in remote regions, as well as large Christian communities in major cities. This may be seen in the letters of Pliny, governor of Bithynia, to Emperor Trajan. According to Pliny, in the region of Bithynia—where no apostle had ever reached—the pagan temples were "practically deserted." Fortunately, more is known about Christian missionary activity in Asia Minor thanks to the records referring to Gregory of Neocaesarea and his work.

2. An Outstanding Missionary of This Period: Gregory of Neocaesarea

Although little is known of the many believers who must have contributed to such expansion, there are some whose lives and work are better known. These provide us a glimpse into the Christianity and missionary methods of the time. One of these outstanding missionaries was Gregory of Neocaesarea, better known as Gregory the Wonderworker.

Gregory was born in Pontus into a pagan family. His true name was Theodore, and it was at his baptism that he took the name of Gregory. He was fourteen years old when his father died, but even so, he was able to study in the best schools, for his family had means. For a number of reasons, Gregory and his brother, Athenodore, visited the city of Caesarea in Palestine. There they met Origen, who, according to Gregory's biographer, so captivated them that they were "frozen" at his feet. The great Alexandrian teacher taught them, besides logics, physics, geometry, and astronomy, the "true philosophy" of Christianity. This was typical of Origen and his teacher Clement of Alexandria, for both believed that Christianity was the "true philosophy" and as such proclaimed it to the cultural elite.

After remaining in Caesarea some five years, Gregory and Athenodore returned to Pontus, where they soon became known as active promoters of their new faith. Eventually Gregory was made bishop of Neocaesarea. Athenodore became bishop of a nearby city and collaborated with Gregory throughout their life.

The position of bishop of Neocaesarea did not seem to involve much responsibility, for, according to Gregory's main biographer, the Christian community at the time had only seventeen members. But Gregory took this responsibility very seriously and devoted himself to preaching the gospel in the city itself and in the surrounding areas with such zeal and success, that we are told—with a measure of hyperbole—that at the time of his death there were only seventeen pagans remaining in the city.

The missionary methods of Gregory—insofar as we know them—illustrate the means by which Christianity was expanding. There is no doubt that he had an attractive demeanor and that he used his personal charisma at the service of his ministry. He also declared in *Panegyric to Origen* that whenever he was able to do so, he employed the same method of theological persuasion that had been so successful in his own case. He always held that Christianity was the true philosophy, but this did not mean a specific set of doctrines, but rather a practical philosophy in which speculation must always be joined to virtue.

Yet, in the area of Pontus, far away from the main thoroughfares of thought and study, and particularly among uneducated people, Origen's method was not always practical. Therefore, his biographer says:

> Behold an important trait in this man's great wisdom: he needed to lead an entire generation into new life. As a coach driver who knows how to direct human nature, he held them firmly with the rein of faith and the knowledge of God. But at the same time he allowed them to have, under the rule of faith, a measure of freedom and joy. He noticed that this childish and illiterate people were grossly tied to their idolatry by sensual pressures and therefore, seeking first of all to stress the essential, and to draw them away from vain superstition and towards God, he allowed them to celebrate the memory of martyrs with the same joy and happiness. He knew that with the passing of time their lives would become more sober and orderly, for faith itself would lead them to this. And this was indeed what happened with most of them: their joy was transformed and leaving aside the bodily pressures they turned to those of the spirit. (Gregory de Nisa, *The Life of St. Gregory Thaumaturgos,* 1)

This method of adapting a message to the intellectual, moral, and religious conditions of the people to be evangelized has been widely used not only by Gregory but also by a long series of missionaries throughout all times and has led to long and bitter controversies.

In any case, this did not mean that Gregory allowed his converts to remain in their old practices and beliefs or that he was content with a mere verbal confession of Christian faith. On the contrary, first the persecution under Decius, and then the invasion of Pontus by the

Goths and others, gave him opportunity to show what was expected of true Christians. Apparently many who claimed to be Christians at the time of the Gothic invasion acted in ways that Gregory felt he should condemn, as may be seen in his *Canonical Epistle.* In this writing, Gregory excommunicated those who at the time of the invasion were "so daring that they took the time that brought destruction to many as the precise moment for their own profit" (Canon 2). Those who have taken or even found what does not belong to them must return it immediately; those who have made captives must let them go free; traitors who supported the barbarian invaders, and shared in their crimes, are to be excommunicated under a synod, under the direction of the Holy Spirit, that decides what to do with them; and those who helped restore order by returning to others what belonged to them must not expect any reward or payment for this service. Thus, Gregory's missionary and pastoral method was a combination of sensitivity and integrity: flexibility in adapting to the customs of the people and integrity in demanding that they behave as Christians.

Finally, it is important to note that one of Gregory's methods was the practice of miracles, and for this reason he came to be known as "the Wonderworker"—or *Thaumaturgos.* However, in the stories about these miracles, history and legend are so intertwined that it is impossible to distinguish between them.

3. The Methods

In seeking to study and to describe the missionary methods of this period, once again we are faced by the lack of exact records and by the fact that those that have remained represent only a privileged sector of the total Christian population. We do have extensive apologies written in defense of Christianity, as well as the stories of some individual conversions. But basically all these witnesses only tell us how the more cultured and privileged people became Christian, and very little about the conversion of slaves, artisans, and women.

(a) Polemics against Judaism

The conflict between Christians and Jews has left a profound stamp on several of the writings of the New Testament, as well as in later Christian literature. However, before studying the actual contents of those polemics, it is important to clarify the nature of the conflict itself. The common notion that Christianity soon ceased to be a religion or a movement within Judaism in order to become almost completely Gentile does not seem to be quite correct. In recent times, sociological studies of the ancient church and Judaism have shown that the process of Jews joining Christianity continued for much longer than was originally thought. Many of the Gentiles whom Jews had early called "God-fearers," people who were attracted by Israel's faith but did not become Jews, now joined the church. But also many Jews of the Diaspora, that is, Jews living among Gentiles, seem to have seen in Christianity a way of retaining the tradition of their ancestors and at the same time adapting to their new circumstances. This practice continued for at least three centuries, and therefore many of the Christian writings of today that we read as polemical were not really addressing Jews themselves as much as addressing those Jews who had become Christian. These documents reveal the tensions found in the quest for a Christian identity between Jewish and Gentile Christians. Thus, in reading these documents we must remember that they provide us only with a partial vision of the actual relationship between Christians and Jews.

The method that appears frequently in the surviving documents is theological argument and polemics. This sort of argument was already employed during the period of the New Testament, particularly in trying to convince Jews that Jesus was the fulfillment of the promises of the Hebrew Scriptures. During the period we are now studying, this anti-Jewish polemic continued, but attention increasingly turned to polemics against paganism. This is a sign that the church, becoming convinced that most Jews would not convert to Christianity, was turning its missionary impetus toward the Gentiles. By the end of this period, the church had clearly become a Gentile community, and by then its polemic with Judaism was no longer an attempt to convince Jews, but rather to crush a rival religion.

The basic arguments of Christian writers facing Judaism concerned the fulfillment of certain prophecies in the person of Jesus, particularly in his birth and his death. Also, like many of the writers of the New Testament, Christian polemicists made use of typology, claiming that certain events in the Old Testament were signs, "types" prefiguring what would happen in the New Testament. Finally, other Christian writers, particularly those connected with Alexandria, made use of allegory, often denying the historicity of the narratives of the Old Testament and turning them into allegories that were compatible both with the teachings of the New Testament and with the moral teachings of society at large.

Still other Christians—such as Marcion—denied the validity of the Hebrew Scriptures, claiming that Christianity was so radically new that it could not be the fulfillment of the ancient promises made to Israel. But the majority of Christians rejected this view, which was considered heretical.

(b) Polemics against pagan worship

When facing paganism, Christian polemics had to struggle on two fronts: pagan worship, and pagan philosophy. Rejecting pagan worship, Christians followed the teachings of Judaism by insisting on a moral monotheism and thus made use of many of the objections that for generations pagan philosophers had been raising against the plurality of the pagan gods, as well as of their criticism of the apparent immorality of the gods. By the time Christianity appeared, for centuries Greek philosophers had been expressing doubts about the Olympic gods and particularly about the stories told about them. Following the lead of those pagan philosophers, Christians criticized these gods, first, because they were powerless human creations, and second, for the immoral acts attributed to them. An example of this sort of argument may be found in the writings of Aristides, who in the middle of the second century wrote,

> Seeing that their gods were sewn by their craftsmen, and polished and cut, and shortened, and burned, and shaped, so that these artisans can change them into all sorts of things, and seeing also that these gods grow old as time passes, or are melted or break into pieces, how could they not understand that these are not true gods? If such gods cannot save themselves, how can they save humans? (*Apologia* 13.1)

And then, pointing to the immorality of the Greek gods:

> The Greeks, having established their own legal systems, did not notice that their own laws condemn their gods. If their laws are just, their gods are perverse, for they have transgressed the law, killing one another, practicing magic, committing adultery, looting, and sodomy, among other things. If their gods have been right in doing these things, as the Greeks themselves describe them, their laws must be unjust, for they have not been established following the will of the gods. In this manner, the entire world errs. (*Apol.* 13.7)

(c) The encounter with pagan philosophy

Regarding the manner in which they should relate to pagan philosophy, Christians were not in agreement among themselves. They did agree that Christianity was a higher truth, revealed by God, which no philosopher would have been able to attain. But they disagreed on the value that should be attributed to philosophy, for some saw it as the handmaiden leading to Christ (Justin Martyr, Clement, and Origen), while others insisted on a radical opposition between Christianity and philosophy (Tatian, Hermias, and Tertullian). Some were convinced that philosophy was a helpful and even necessary instrument for biblical hermeneutics, while others saw it as the source of every heresy.

Some claimed that Jesus was Lord both of Athens and of Jerusalem, while others agreed with Tertullian's famous words: "What does Athens have to do with Jerusalem? What does the Academy have to do with the church?" (*Prescription against Heretics,* 7). On these matters, most of the writings that have survived support the position of Justin and Origen. But one should always remember that such writings do not necessarily reflect the opinions of the majority of Christians.

A good and illuminating example of the positive attitude of many Christians toward philosophy is the work of Justin Martyr, who wrote in the middle of the second century. In order to show the more cultured among the Gentiles that Christianity is not opposed to Hellenistic civilization and philosophy, but rather complements and surpasses them, Justin made use of the doctrine of the *logos* or word. This was very useful, for one of the central themes of pagan philosophy at the time was the notion of *logos,* and this was also the term that the Gospel of John applied to Jesus. Besides, the much earlier Jewish philosopher Philo of Alexandria had used the notion of *logos* as a bridge between Greek philosophy and Jewish religion.

Following the tradition of Greek philosophy, Justin agrees that all knowledge humans have is the result of the *logos,* the rational principle of the universe. But turning then to the Fourth Gospel and its use of the term *logos,* Justin also claims that this logos or word of God, which is the rational principle of the universe, was incarnate in Jesus Christ. Therefore, the truth that philosophers knew is none other than Christian truth, even though Plato and his colleagues knew the word only "partially" whereas Christians know the word "wholly." Philosophers only knew the truths that the word revealed to them, but Christians know the word itself. Therefore, whatever there is of good and truth in pagan culture and philosophy actually belongs to Christianity! Thus Christian polemics, in facing both Judaism and paganism, sought ways to affirm the universal lordship of Jesus Christ—in these two cases, lordship over culture and over the Hebrew Scriptures—without compromising the fundamental affirmation that the one who is the Lord and eternal Word of God has come to us in Jesus Christ in a unique and concrete manner.

(d) Personal contact among intellectuals

However, all these arguments seem to have served for the propagation of the gospel only when they were connected with the personal witness of Christians. There is no record of anybody accepting Christianity by reading Justin's *Dialogue with Trypho* or his *Apologies*—which is particularly remarkable since there are many cases of philosophical conversions resulting from reading the philosophers—but there are a number of cases in which personal intellectual discussions led someone to Christianity.

Justin himself showed the importance of this method, combining intellectual discussions with direct witness, by relating that his own conversion was the result of such an encounter, when a venerable older man taught him the "true philosophy." We have already seen the case of Gregory the Wonderworker and his brother, Athenodore, whose conversion was the result of their contact with Origen. Something similar seems to have occurred in the cases of Clement of Alexandria, who was converted through the witness of Pantenus, and of Cyprian of Carthage, through the testimony of Caecilian. And, if the *Octavius* of Minutius Felix is the report of a historical event, then it shows another attempt to gain converts through direct and personal discussion of the ideologies and doctrines of Christianity as compared with paganism.

(e) Christian schools

Quite frequently such encounters were not left to chance, for Christians founded schools whose functions were mainly catechetical but at the same time could address cultured pagans wanting to learn more about Christianity or simply seeking to debate the most distinguished

Christian teachers. As examples of such schools following the pattern of the ancient Academy of Athens, one may look at the one founded by Justin in Rome, later led by his disciple Tatian, and the very famous school of Alexandria, connected with the names of Pantenus, Clement, Origen, Heraclas, and others. The latter was sometimes attended by the highest representatives of pagan nobility and intelligentsia. These schools had an important role in the expansion of Christianity, for many pagans who attended them were converted, and the schools also evolved as centers out of which Christians emerged in order to teach and expand the knowledge of the gospel—as may be seen in the case of Gregory the Wonderworker coming out of Origen's school in Caesarea. Furthermore, literature produced in these schools helped less-educated Christians in expressing their arguments against paganism and thus holding their own in controversy.

(f) The witness of common folk

Such direct and personal witness, led by an ardent desire to convert others, was not limited to the higher levels of philosophers and rhetoricians but actually seems to have been much more frequent among slaves, artisans, and women—in a culture that took for granted that such people were not capable of profound thoughts. This may be seen in the following quotation, in which Celsus, a pagan philosopher attacking Christianity, accuses Christians of being ignorant:

> We see, indeed, in private houses workers in wool and leather, and fullers, and persons of the most uninstructed and rustic character, not venturing to utter a word in the presence of their elders and wiser masters; but when they get hold of the children privately, and certain women as ignorant as themselves, they pour forth wonderful statements, to the effect that they ought not to give heed to their father and to their teachers, but should obey them; that the former are foolish and stupid, and neither know nor can perform anything that is really good, being preoccupied with empty trifles; that *they* alone know how men ought to live, and that, if the children obey them,

> they will both be happy themselves, and will make their home happy also. And while thus speaking, if they see one of the instructors of youth approaching, or one of the more intelligent class, or even the father himself, the more timid among them become afraid, while the more forward incite the children to throw off the yoke, whispering that in the presence of father and teachers they neither will nor can explain to them any good thing. (Quoted by Origen, *Against Celsus,* 3.55; *Ante-Nicene Fathers,* 4:486)

It is a great misfortune that, precisely because of their own nature, the work and witness of such Christians are not better known, for we would then see that their contribution to the expansion of Christianity was significant and probably even greater than the contribution of schools and of the more learned defenders of the faith.

Seen in this context, three points must be underlined which have not been sufficiently studied by historians. The first of these is the role of women in the expansion of ancient Christianity. There is no doubt that during the early centuries, the church had more women than men. This may be partly due to Christian teachings regarding gender. Although usually indirectly, such teachings called for a respect for women that contrasted with the practices of society at large. As a result, cases in which women converted to Christianity and then brought their husbands and the rest of their family to church were much more frequent than those cases in which Christianity entered a family through its male members—and even more so, than cases in which Christianity entered a household through the head of the family, the *paterfamilias.* The network of communication among women in their daily chores was one of the main channels through which the word of the gospel spread.

A second point worthy of mention is the effect of plagues on the population of the Roman Empire and the manner in which the church responded to the plagues. In and around the middle of the second century, there was a series of epidemics that decimated the population.

This contributed to the growth of Christianity in at least two ways. First, since Christians took care of other believers, the rate of survival among them was greater than among the rest of the population. Second, in those difficult times there was a sharp contrast between the majority of the population, fleeing the cities and caring only for their own health, and Christians, who took care not only of their own sick but also of many others in the community at large. As a result, there are numerous records of people whose first attraction to Christianity came as they noticed the charitable work of believers, even at the risk of their own lives.

A third factor that should be mentioned is the demographic growth among Christians, due to their opposition to both abortion and infanticide—both practices that were common and acceptable in pagan society. Although the attitudes of early Christians toward other methods of birth control are not entirely clear, the rejection of abortion and infanticide, as well as insistence on limiting sexual relationships to those taking place within marriage, led us to a positive index of demographic growth even amid a society in which population growth was negative—in other words, a society in which more people died than were born.

(g) Miracles

Miracles seem to have been an important factor in the growth of Christianity, both among common folk and among the more cultured. Although it is impossible to ascertain how many of the wonders told about Gregory the Wonderworker are based on historical fact, it is clear that all who undertook the task of retelling his life believed that his miracles were one of his most powerful instruments for the conversion of pagans. Toward the end of this period, there began to appear Gospels and books about the acts of various apostles, all stressing the miraculous as one of the main guarantors for the truth of Christianity.

(h) Martyrdom

Among all miracles, none was as remarkable and fruitful in conversions as martyrdom, which was relatively frequent during the second and third centuries. Children and women, elderly people, and slaves who normally bent before their master's will were seen to confront authority with unexpected vigor and to face death with an inexplicable joy. For a world seeking for truth that would give meaning to life and death, such acts pointed to a commitment, a certainty, and a joy that other people lacked. For the martyrs themselves, what seemed madness to an outsider was actually a rational decision to sacrifice life and undergo a short time of pain in exchange for an everlasting life of joy and peace. This made martyrdom so attractive that the church had to speak out against the "spontaneous"—who offered themselves voluntarily for martyrdom—and to insist that martyrdom was a crown to be attained only by divine election. Many ancient texts refer to a pagan being profoundly moved upon seeing the sufferings of a Christian martyr. This reality stood behind Tertullian's famous dictum that "the more we are destroyed, the more we grow; the blood of the martyrs is seed" (*Apology, 50*).

(i) Worship

Another factor that must be mentioned, but not because it was a direct means of conversion but for the opposite reason, is divine worship. The Eastern cults invading the empire at the beginning of the Christian era—those of Attis and Cybele, of Isis and Osiris, of Dionysius, and many others—offered a fascinating and moving liturgy. In contrast, Christian worship—which those who were not baptized could not even attend—was rather simple. It is clear then that, in contrast to what would come to be expected by many churches in more recent times, worship in the ancient church did not usually result in the conversion of nonbelievers. What we would call "evangelism" took place outside of worship, in places where common life provided for contact between Christians and others.

(j) Missionaries

Something similar is true regarding the practice of sending missionaries; although in this case it is true that the ancient church did send missionaries to carry the gospel to new areas. The case of the church in Antioch sending Paul and his companions on a mission is well known. In the period that we are studying, the case of Pantenus should be mentioned, for we are told that he traveled to the east—probably to Arabia, although some claim that he went as far as India—as a "herald of the Gospel of Christ." Documents such as the *Didache* and Origen's *Against Celsus* imply that there was a good number of people devoted exclusively or almost exclusively to traveling while preaching the gospel, as Paul had done earlier. On the other hand, much of the work of these people seems to have consisted in visiting already-existing churches, supporting them, and strengthening them in the faith, rather than in seeking converts and planting new churches.

Most of the expansion of Christianity in the centuries before Constantine was not the result of the work of people exclusively devoted to that task, but rather the result of the constant witness of hundreds and thousands of merchants, slaves, and exiles who carried their witness for Jesus Christ wherever life took them and thus founded Christian communities in places where the "professional" missionaries had not yet reached. And once the seed was sewn, most of the work was not done by itinerant preachers visiting the community in order to preach and teach for a few days, but rather by those who, as in the case of Gregory the Wonderworker, lived among their people and felt responsible not only for the body of believers but also for their community at large.

(k) Sociological factors

In the preceding pages, several sociological and demographic factors contributing to the expansion of Christianity have already been mentioned. However, since these are often forgotten, it is important to note that recent sociological studies remind us of the importance of factors such as the network of relationships in urban society, the role of women, the demographic effect of epidemics, the support system binding believers, the practice of charity for those beyond the community of faith, and so on. It is important to stress all of these factors, for Christians planning missionary work tend to forget them, without realizing how important they have been throughout the history of the expansion of Christianity.

(l) Summary: Christian attitudes toward paganism

It may be said that Christianity spread rapidly throughout the Mediterranean basin thanks to the factors and witnesses mentioned above. But all of this would have had scant results were it not that the church and its members combined a surprising sensitivity to their surroundings with a firm loyalty to the tradition that was being formed. Had Christianity been completely insensitive to culture, as if truth were to be found only in the church and the tradition of Scriptures and as if all pagan truth were necessarily falsehood, it would have made it impossible for a Hellenistic pagan to become a Christian without immediately abandoning every trace of Hellenistic culture and learning to think as a person of Hebrew extraction. It was its sensitivity, born partly out of its desire to reach others, that turned the church into a powerful instrument for the expansion of the gospel. By contrast, there were limits to such sensitivities. While it was acceptable to acknowledge some truth in pagan culture, not all of that culture was equally acceptable. For instance, any who offered sacrifice to the emperor or to one of the gods were by that very act declaring themselves to be beyond the pale of the church.

By placing itself between an extreme flexibility and an extreme legalism, being firm on what it considered essential and yet open to the cultures and traditions of the Greco-Roman world, the church avoided the risk of losing the integrity of its faith, as well as the opposite risk of becoming completely alienated from its surrounding culture. The life of the church in that early period shows a clear commitment to proclaim the gospel in new cultural and social contexts and at the same time to remain faithful to the proclamation of the central events of the gospel. By living within this difficult tension, that early church became a powerful instrument for the expansion of the gospel, and at the same time it reflected, albeit imperfectly, the love of the Lord who "being in the form of God" took "the form of a slave" out of love for humankind.

B. The Christian Empire and the Suppression of Paganism

1. The Conversion of Constantine

The conversion of Constantine is a landmark in Christian history, opening new pathways and creating new conditions for the church. For that reason, it is also one of the most debated events in the history of the church. Some see in it the beginning of a corruption of Christianity that would eventually require the reformation of the sixteenth century. Others point out that the victory of the persecuted church over its persecutors is the greatest expression of the impetus of Christianity in its early centuries. Both of these views are partially correct, for an event of such magnitude as Constantine's conversion would necessarily have important consequences for the church—some positive, some negative, and some positive yet involving great dangers.

Undoubtedly, Constantine's conversion was quite different from what most of us understand by a conversion and also different from what was then the usual conversion. Normally, the means leading to the conversion of pagans was a Christian whose witness the converts credited for their new faith; then the converts would place themselves at the disposition of the church in order to be instructed in Christian faith and practice; finally, through baptism they joined the church, which from that point on would determine much of their life. Constantine's case is radically different. According to Eusebius of Caesarea, Constantine himself claimed that his conversion was not the result of conversations or discussions with a believer, but rather of a direct vision from God. According to that vision, Constantine's mission had been given him by the Lord of the church and therefore was related to the mission of the church; but since it had been given directly, it did not depend on the church, nor was it subject to guidance from the church. Furthermore, for Constantine the Christ he now served was not so much a savior from the power of sin and death, as he was the conqueror who gave Constantine victory over his enemies. In exchange for that support, Constantine was to honor Christ and contribute to the growth of his church.

How did all of this affect the expansion of Christianity? There is no doubt that the prestige connected with the emperor himself turned many toward Christianity. Places of worship soon became too small to hold the great number of converts. At first, the church kept its earlier custom of preparing converts for baptism through a long period of testing and catechetical instruction. But now there were not enough teachers for the masses joining the church. As years went by, the period of preparation for baptism became shorter, and instruction more superficial, eventually leading to mass conversions early in the Middle Ages. This tended to undermine the personal commitment of believers, particularly in matters having to do with Christian life, for on doctrinal issues the church did develop means to retain the almost absolute adherence of the faithful.

By contrast, Constantine's conversion did not have only negative consequences. On the contrary, the century immediately following is the golden age in the history of the early church. Leaders such as Athanasius, Basil the Great, Ambrose, Jerome, and Augustine witnessed to the intellectual power, literary output, and spiritual discipline of the church when it was freed from the threat of persecutions. The great basilicas that were then built, and the art that decorated them, show that Christians were ready to take the best elements of the culture that now accepted them and place it at the service of their Lord. Ecclesiastical organization was developed and improved thanks to imperial protection and means of communication. And that organization turned out to be the only power capable of preserving and developing the remains of Greco-Roman culture after the Germanic invasions. Finally, it was also the century of Constantine's conversion that produced missionaries such as Wulfila and Martin of Tours.

The emperor's conversion also raised issues that the church had not encountered before. Should the emperor be subject to the church or vice versa? Should the emperor employ his power in order to promote Christian principles? What was his responsibility to his pagan subjects? Should the church use its influence on the emperor in order to produce a more just social order? Should Christians accept privileges from the state? Was the church betraying its own principles when it ceased being persecuted and became the recipient of imperial favor? All of these questions the church had to face in the fourth century and those that followed. They are also difficult issues, for in every case there are arguments that could be adduced in one direction or the other. Were the emperor to use his power to promote Christian principles, there was the danger that the church would come to trust in the emperor's political and economic power rather than in God. If, however, the emperor kept his faith apart from his office as a ruler, this would imply that his faith was only one aspect of his life, that it was a personal faith that could be limited to the religious sphere and kept apart from the rest of life. Therefore neither solution was adequate, and it was difficult to determine what the relationship of church and state should be. However, there was one point that could not be doubted: the emperor's conversion, as anybody's conversion, should be received with joy by all Christians no matter what the consequences could be for the church.

2. Constantine's Sons and the Pagan Reaction

Although Constantine was always tolerant toward paganism, his three sons and successors—Constantine II, Constantius, and Constans—followed an ever more rigid policy against the old religion. In 341, sacrifices were forbidden, and in 354, Constantius ordered that all pagan temples be shut. Although these laws were not fully enforced throughout the empire, they did result in violent actions against pagans by overzealous imperial functionaries. Also, under the shelter of such laws, some Christians began destroying pagan temples and building churches on their ruins. Given that situation, a pagan reaction would not be surprising.

That reaction materialized when Julian came to the imperial throne. Although it is traditional among Christian historians to refer to him as "the apostate," the truth is that Julian never seems to have been a convinced Christian. The only Christianity that Julian seems to have known was a highly intellectualized Arianism whose main defender, Constantius, had ordered that all Julian's family be slaughtered. (For more on Arianism, see chapter 4.) Being convinced that he had been chosen by the gods to restore their worship, Julian enacted a series of laws against Christianity and also reorganized the ancient pagan religion following the pattern of the church. All the privileges that Constantine and his children had granted Christians, and particularly Christian clergy, were revoked. Christians were forbidden from teaching classical literature and philosophy. Although Julian did not order that Christians be persecuted, in several regions of the empire the populace did persecute Christians. By copying the organization of the church, Julian hoped to renew paganism. He retook the old title of *Pontifex Maximus*, which made him head of pagan worship, and in each province he appointed a high priest who would lead the religious life of the area. Under the direction of these high priests, all other priests must lead strictly moral lives, and besides celebrating the traditional worship, they should also teach universal love among all human beings. Finally, Julian himself took the time to write against Christians, whom he called "Galileans."

In spite of all this, Julian's project was doomed to failure. Although it was true that Christianity had not yet developed deep roots among the population, it was also true that ancient paganism was declining. The populace in Antioch scoffed at Julian's religion and his stoic morality. The religious ideal of the time was no longer the temperate and wise person of Marcus Aurelius and the Stoics but the Christian monk with his ascetic life. Christian worship proved much more meaningful and effective than the animal sacrifices that Julian ordered. Finally, the church produced thinkers, writers, and preachers who proved to be vastly superior to those whom Julian was able to recruit among pagans. When in 363 Julian fell victim to a Persian lance, the unavoidable happened. The brief pagan reaction was followed by a period of uninterrupted advance of Christianity over paganism.

3. The Christian Empire

Julian's immediate successors, Jovian and Valentinian I, restored the previous policy of supporting the church while at the same time tolerating pagan worship. Their successor Gratian, partly following the guidance of Bishop Ambrose of Milan, began a policy of placing paganism under more difficult conditions. But it was the advent of Theodosius to the imperial throne that spelled the doom of paganism.

Theodosius was convinced that he had been called by God to defend orthodoxy against heresy and Christianity against paganism. Therefore, in 391, he banned all sacrifice to pagan gods and ordered that the ancient temples be closed down or turned to secular uses. The following year another edict went much further, prohibiting not only public pagan worship but also the private practice of paganism. Furthermore, under Theodosius's guidance, local authorities tended to be indifferent and even sometimes supportive toward the violence of Christians against pagans. In Alexandria Bishop Theophilus, well known for his lack of scruples and charity toward his adversaries, provoked the pagans to an unequal confrontation whose result was the destruction of the ancient and monumental temple of Serapis. Similar events in other regions of the empire deprived paganism of some of its most cherished centers of worship.

4. The End of Antiquity

After Theodosius's death in 395, the western and eastern sections of the Roman Empire followed different routes. In the east, the Roman Empire continued existing for another thousand years, and while the church was closely related to the state, normally civil authority took precedence over religious. In that area, paganism continued its decline both because of its own inner weakness and because of pressures from both church and state. The final bulwark of ancient paganism was the Academy of Athens, shut down in 529 by order of Emperor Justinian. After that date, the ancient religions seem to have survived only in some small and very isolated communities. It was at that point that the ancient religion came to be called *paganism*, a term derived from "paganus," which traditionally simply referred to an uncouth person from the countryside.

In the west, the advance of Christianity was suddenly threatened by the invasions of the Germanic peoples whom the Romans called "barbarians," who broke into the empire taking advantage of the decline that followed the death of Theodosius. The vast majority of these invaders were pagans, and almost all those who were Christian were Arians. This presented a great challenge for the church in the lands conquered by the Germanic peoples, for no matter whether they were pagans or Arians, the church was convinced that its mission was to bring all to orthodox faith. How this was done will be discussed in chapter 4.

5. Missionary Work after Constantine's Conversion

It would be an error to think that once the authorities began supporting Christianity the church left the task of evangelizing pagans in the hands of the state. Certainly, much more is known about the official measures to weaken paganism and promote "conversions" to Christianity than about the work of believers seeking such conversions by means less spectacular or violent. We do know, however, that at the same time when the emperor sought to destroy paganism by means of edicts and prohibitions, there were Christians working to the same end by other means. Ambrose of Milan, while certainly seeking to have imperial pressure applied against paganism, did himself preach to the pagans, and there are records of several conversions that resulted from his preaching. Others continued the long tradition of earlier Christian apologists, writing defenses against pagan accusations or prejudice. Among them stand such illustrious names as Lactantius, Eusebius of Caesarea, Augustine, and John Chrysostom. Still others worked in places far removed from the centers of thought and of government and sought the conversion of pagans through preaching and polemics. Two examples of such people are the Arian Wulfila and the orthodox Martin of Tours.

(a) Wulfila

Very little is known of the childhood and conversion of Wulfila, for the few data that are recorded are mostly legendary. We do know that when he was thirty years old he was made "bishop to the Goths" and that after some time, with imperial permission, he settled just south of the Danube with a group of Christian Goths. In order to translate Scripture to the Gothic language, Wulfila developed an alphabet that was able to express the various sounds of that language. There are still remains of an ancient Gothic Bible, which may be the result of the work of Wulfila. It is important to point out that this is one of the earliest examples—perhaps the earliest—of an aspect of missionary work that has continued throughout the centuries, that is, developing the means to write a language in order to translate the Bible into it.

Tradition also claims that Wulfila was the main instrument for the conversion of the Goths to Arian Christianity. Most probably, although Wulfila may have been an important contributor to the process, the Goths were converted to Arian Christianity not so much through the work of a particular missionary as through their constant contacts with the Roman Empire at a time when its rulers were mostly Arian. During the reign of Constantius, and later under Valentinian II and his mother, Justina, Arianism was much favored in the imperial court, and it was precisely during those times that the Goths had most contact with the empire.

(b) Martin of Tours

There are several ancient biographies of Martin of Tours. As could be expected, these become increasingly legendary as time goes by. Even the most ancient, written by Sulpicius Severus, seems to combine history with legend. Even though from a historical point of view this may be unfortunate, it is also a sign of the impact that Martin's life made on his contemporaries and successors.

Martin was born in Pannonia—probably in what is now Hungary—around the year 316. His long and checkered career took him first to the army, then to Poitiers, back to Pannonia, and finally to Tours, in what today is France. He became a Christian when he was in the army. Therefore, by the time he reached Tours, where he eventually became bishop, he already had vast experience as a Christian and as a witness to his faith.

As bishop of Tours, Martin surrounded himself with a group of monks whom he directed in an unceasing work of preaching the gospel and destroying ancient pagan temples. On the ruins of those temples, churches were built, so that the demons who had resided there would not be able to return. At times Martin was able to convince the pagans themselves that their temples should be destroyed. The story is told of a community that worshiped an old tree. In order to show the power of his God, Martin had himself tied on the precise spot where the tree would fall if it were cut, and he then dared the people to cut the tree so that it would fall on him. Challenged by such daring, the pagans cut down their ancient sacred tree, expecting it to crush Martin. Inexplicably, the tree fell in the opposite direction. In the face of such a miracle, several pagans were converted, and even those who were not converted offered no resistance when Martin destroyed their nearby temple and built a church on its ruins.

However, Martin's methods were not always as violent. He became known for his undaunted courage, and the story soon circulated that when he was attacked by a group of pagans, he himself bared his neck so that he could be decapitated. Shocked by such behavior, the pagans did not dare hurt him.

Whatever the truth in these stories, there is no doubt that Martin, by means of both violence and persuasion, contributed to the expansion of Christianity in the environs of the city of Tours. Most likely when he was made bishop there was only a relatively small Christian community in the city itself, and in the surrounding areas paganism was dominant. By the time of Martin's death, the church had expanded into the countryside, and paganism had lost much of its power.

These are two of the many missionaries who worked for the expansion of Christianity among the pagans at the same time when civil authorities were seeking to complete the christianization of the empire. Undoubtedly, if the passing of centuries had not dimmed our knowledge, we would know of hundreds of Christians whose work was similar to that of these two.

Still, it is important to stress that Constantine's conversion and the policies of his successors had consequences that may not have been as noticeable immediately but that would affect the entire history of missions. Christianity, which until then had been ready to dialogue with new cultures and traditions, now became less tolerant toward such differences. Trusting its political power, it took a route that eventually would make it more difficult for it to adapt to new cultures and circumstances.

C. Christian Expansion beyond the Roman Empire

Although usually most attention is paid to the development of the church within the confines of the Roman Empire, Christianity also expanded eastward into regions not belonging to that empire.

1. Christianity in Edessa

The independent city of Edessa, at the border between the Roman and Persian empires, witnessed the first conversion of a ruler. This was Abgar IX, who ruled toward the end of the second century and early in the third. Later, in an attempt to establish a direct link between Jesus and Christianity in Edessa, the legend appeared of a supposed correspondence between Abgar IV, a contemporary of Jesus, and the Savior himself. It seems that Christianity actually reached Edessa around the middle of the second century, coming from Antioch. At any rate, Christianity in Edessa took root in Syriac culture and was much less influenced by Hellenism than was its counterpart within the empire.

Something similar happened in the very small state of Adiabene, east of Edessa, from which soon missionaries went into the heart of Asia.

2. Christianity in Armenia

Of all these lands, it was in Armenia, particularly thanks to the work of Gregory the Illuminator, that Christianity achieved its most notable and permanent expansion. For centuries the geographic position of Armenia, as a border state between the Persians and the Romans, subjected it to repeated invasions from one or the other of these two great powers. In that constant struggle, Roman policy generally consisted in granting Armenia a measure of autonomy and protecting its legitimate rulers as a buffer against Persian advance, while Persian policy sought to annex the region. The result was that popular sentiment was more inclined toward Rome than toward Persia.

An important episode in that constantly fractured history is the struggle of King Tradt III (also called Tiridates and Tirdat) to recover the throne that the Persian troops of Sapor had taken from him. The Persians had profited from the death of the Armenian king, who had been murdered by Persian emissaries and at that juncture Persia invaded Armenia. The young heir to the throne, Tradt, had to seek asylum in the Roman Empire. Armenia remained under Persian power until the young Tradt, with Roman support and after many vicissitudes, managed to recover his throne. This struggle for a throne and for the independence of a nation was quite important for the history of Christian expansion, for the result was the earliest conversion of an entire country—excluding the case of much smaller Edessa. While Tradt was in exile, many of the nobility and the military leadership who accompanied him into exile, particularly in Syria and Asia Minor, made contact with Christianity. A number of them became Christians and upon returning to their land took their faith with them. Others, although not immediately converted, at least took with them a certain knowledge of Christian doctrines and lives.

Among the Armenian nobility who was forced to seek shelter in the Roman Empire, there was a young relative of Tradt who eventually became known as "Gregory the Illuminator," or "Lusarovich." Gregory became a Christian in Caesarea of Cappadocia, and when the political situation in his country allowed it he returned to Armenia, where he devoted himself to spreading his faith. At first Tradt opposed Gregory's preaching, and as a result Gregory was imprisoned for fifteen years—probably for both political and religious reasons. Eventually, however, Tradt accepted the faith of his relative, and he as well as his family and the nobility of the land were baptized around the year 302.

A mass conversion followed. Ancient temples became Christian churches. Even many priests of the old religion, or at least their sons, became Christian priests, with the result that just as the ancient priesthood was hereditary, so was the Christian priesthood of Armenia—and this to such an extent that for centuries the church in Armenia was headed by the descendants of Gregory the Illuminator.

The first years of Christianity in Armenia were difficult. But by the time Tradt died the new faith had developed such roots among the people that, even though the land was once again invaded by the Persians, and although the conquerors made every effort to implant Zoroastrianism, Christianity continued being the faith of most of Armenia. Furthermore, what had begun as a mass conversion soon became a profound movement, especially after, thanks to the work of Christian scholars, the Armenian language was reduced to writing, and Christian literature was translated from Greek and Syriac.

When the Council of Chalcedon gathered in 451, the Armenian church was not represented, because the land was being invaded by the Persians. The Armenians fully expected help from Rome, and when this did not arrive, they felt betrayed. As a result, they rejected the decisions of Chalcedon and accepted the doctrines of Emperor Zeno's *Henoticon*, thus breaking communion with Orthodox Christianity and becoming Monophysite.

3. Christianity in Georgia

From its base in Armenia, Christianity expanded toward Georgia and throughout the Caucasus. Although it is possible that there had been some Christians in Georgia before that time, the first account of the arrival of Christianity to the area is to be found in the *Church History* of Rufinus, who claims that the conversion of Georgia took place when King Miriam and his wife were converted to Christianity, approximately at the same time that Constantine was doing likewise. According to Rufinus, Queen Nana was converted when the prayers of a Christian slave resulted in healing, first for Nana's son and then for Nana herself. Shortly thereafter, and due to another miracle, the king was also converted. There followed a mass conversion similar to what had taken place earlier in Armenia. The new church established links with the church in Constantinople, from which it received its leadership.

If this account is correct, it would seem that, as in so many other cases, several factors contributed to the conversion of this land: the sincere and simple faith of a captive Christian, the commonly held belief in the miraculous, the desire of the king to establish cultural and political contacts with the Roman Empire (apparently because he feared it less than he feared Persia), the active support of the king for the new religion, and the agreement of the masses.

4. Christianity in Mesopotamia and Persia

In its expansion toward the east during this early period, Christianity made use of the Syriac language and culture. First in Antioch, and then in Edessa, an entire body of Christian literature was being produced in Syriac. Since this language was widely used for international trade throughout the Middle East, Christianity found in it a channel for its expansion. Through merchants and other travelers of Syriac culture, Christianity entered regions such as Mesopotamia. Soon Christians in Mesopotamia were able to found their own theological schools, of which the most famous was in Nisibis, by the Euphrates.

When the church first made its appearance, Persia was ruled by the Parthians, who did not impede Christianity's progress. There are indications that by the year 225 there were churches in several regions of the Persian Empire. Among the missionaries who worked in those areas, ancient chroniclers repeatedly refer to Thaddeus, Haggai, and Mari, who apparently took Christianity to the very borders of India. But in 226, the Sassanid Dynasty came to power, and it was tenaciously opposed to Christianity. After Constantine's conversion the situation worsened, for now the Persian rulers, who had been traditional enemies of the Roman Empire, feared that Christians would sympathize with their enemy and serve as its agents. By repeatedly declaring themselves defenders of Christians within the Persian Empire, Roman rulers did not make the situation any easier. For these reasons, among others, the church within the Persian Empire tended to stress its difference and its distance from the church within the Roman Empire. This led to a permanent breach when the churches in Mesopotamia and Persia rejected the christological decisions of the rest of the church and became Nestorian. (For more on the Nestorians, see chapter 4.)

Christianity continued expanding in the region following the routes through which Syriac culture was also expanding. There seems to have been in the capital city of Seleucia-Ctesiphon a fairly large church that worshiped in Syriac and was composed mostly of immigrants and merchants from Syria. That church gained a number of converts among the Persians themselves, and soon there were at least small Christian communities in all the main cities of the Persian Empire, and even as far as Turkestan. Much Christian literature was translated into Syriac and then also into the language of Persia, and soon there was also original literature in these languages. As has already been stated, Christians were persecuted by the Sassanids, who sought to employ Zoroastrianism to bind their empire together—just as Roman emperors made use of Christianity to the same end. Christians were seen as allies of Rome and were therefore subject to persecution whenever relationships between the two great empires became tense. This situation improved when the church in Persia distanced itself from the church in the Roman Empire, first by developing its own organization and then by adopting a different theological stance.

The Persian church became an independent organization in 410, when a council gathered in Seleucia-Ctesiphon gave the bishop of that city the title of "patriarch" and made him the head of the church throughout the empire. On its theology, the Persian church broke away from its counterpart within the Roman Empire by accepting the christological doctrine that is usually called Nestorianism. Since that doctrine had many adherents in Antioch and Edessa, it is not surprising that, when it was rejected by the Council of Ephesus in 431, many of these adherents sought refuge among Syriac-speaking Christians beyond the borders of the Roman Empire. Thus many Nestorians settled in Nisibis, where the theological school that they organized became a center for Nestorian theology. As a result, the Persian church eventually made Nestorianism its official doctrine and rejected the Christology of the rest of the church.

5. Christianity in India

According to an ancient tradition, Christianity was taken to India by St. Thomas the Apostle. This is not absolutely impossible, but the tendency of many churches to try to attribute their origins to an apostolic figure has led many to doubt the truth of this tradition. There is also another tradition claiming that it was St. Bartholomew who took Christianity to India.

At any rate, there is no doubt that the new faith was present in southern India from an early date. Since its earliest remains are written in the language of the Persians, one may well suppose that Christianity came to India through Persia and that some of its first followers were themselves Persians—perhaps even refugees fleeing the persecution of the Sassanids. There are also indications that there were also Christian immigrants of Syriac origin.

Nothing is known about the missionary methods of the first Christians who reached India. The fact that many of its converts belonged to the higher castes would seem to indicate that those early missionaries addressed primarily the higher echelons of society.

6. Christianity in Arabia

Christianity was present also in Arabia during this early period. Since Arabia had the Roman Empire to its west, the Persian Empire to the east, and Abyssinia to the south, missionaries entered the Arabian Peninsula from all three sources. However, the number of converts does not seem to have been great.

7. Christianity in Abyssinia (now Ethiopia)

Finally, Christianity in Abyssinia merits special attention, for during the early period that we are now studying, a church was founded there that would last until the present day. There are legends attributing the early evangelization of Abyssinia to the evangelist Matthew and the apostle Thomas. However, such legends are hardly credible. Even so, the church in Ethiopia claims very early origins, and connects them with the Judaism that is said to have existed there since the times of Solomon and the Queen of Sheba.

In any case, Christianity in Ethiopia dates at least from the middle of the fourth century, when two Christian brothers, Frumentius and Edessus, were shipwrecked on the Red Sea and reached the shores of the kingdom of Axum. Although at first they were imprisoned by the people of that kingdom, soon their ability gained them not only their freedom but also the esteem of the rulers of Axum. Frumentius began gathering Christian traders who came to Axum and creating a community among them. Soon there were converts among the Abyssinians themselves. Edessus returned to Tyre, but Frumentius decided to continue his evangelizing work and went to Alexandria to be consecrated bishop of Axum by the famous church leader Athanasius. A hundred years later, around 450, the early work of Frumentius and his successors finally led to the conversion of King Exana. As in many other cases, a mass conversion followed. Since Exana was an able politician and warrior, his kingdom rapidly expanded to the shores of the Nile and became the nucleus of modern Ethiopia. At the same time that he was expanding his kingdom, Exana was forcing the conversion of those among his subjects who would not willingly accept the Christian faith. The Bible and other literature were translated into the language of the land, which also began producing its own devotional literature. Eventually the Ethiopian church became autonomous, although it was always connected with the church in Alexandria. In the sixth century, since the Copts of Egypt had become Monophysites, the Ethiopians did likewise.

D. General Considerations

Although the scarcity of surviving data makes its study difficult, the period whose history we have outlined is one of the most interesting in the entire history of the expansion of Christianity.

It is interesting, first, for the almost incredible expansion that took place. At the end of the apostolic period, the Christian church consisted of small minorities scattered throughout the main cities on the eastern half of the Mediterranean. Now, after only four centuries, Christianity had become the official faith of the Roman Empire as well as of the lands of Edessa and Armenia and had expanded toward the east as far as India, and toward the south as far as Abyssinia. The only periods that would outdo those early centuries in the expansion of Christianity would be the sixteenth and nineteenth centuries.

Second, this period is interesting because of the missionary methods that were employed. These methods reflect a genuine interest in sharing the faith in various circumstances and places, frequently making use of the cultural and social structures of each group or society as channels for communication. One of the most remarkable characteristics of this period is the almost total absence of "missionaries"—that is, people sent by the church to teach the faith elsewhere. One must also note that preaching and worship were not the main means for the conversion of pagans. Perhaps all of the above indicates that a truly missionary church does not seek to discharge its responsibility by placing it on the shoulders of missionaries or by limiting it to a particular moment of its life but itself becomes an instrument of its missionary vocation.

Third, the encounter between Christianity and the surrounding cultures quickly resulted in the need to translate the Bible, as well as Christian teaching and worship, into new languages. Such translations have been a sign of the best periods in the history of missions, and they are an indication of the openness of the new faith and its spokespersons to the traditions and values of new audiences.

Fourth, the "Christianization" of philosophical idiomatic language and pagan religious expressions, on the one hand, and the polemical and confrontational approach to philosophy and pagan religion, on the other hand, demonstrate a creative missionary reflection and practice quickly forgotten. Christians searched and discovered contextual connections to ground the faith and yet developed distinctive features to make Christianity a vital alternative in the already-diverse religious contexts of antiquity.

Fifth, one must not forget the importance of the conversion of rulers and other members of the social and political elite in various lands and regions—people whose conversion was soon followed by the rest of the population.

Finally, this period interests us because it poses the question of the relationships between church and civil society in its own creative ways, and this is one of the main issues of our time. The church is not an agency of political power or social pressure. But if the church believes in the lordship of Jesus Christ for the entire world, it must also expect that this lordship will be served even by the agencies of political power and social pressure. These two poles in the life of the church present a paradox that becomes particularly perplexing in times of rapid social and political changes, such as ours.

This paradox forces Christians to discern when political power serves the purposes of Jesus Christ and when not. Such discernment is never absolute or infallible, and therefore the missionary task is always complex and risky. It may well be that study and reflection on Constantine's conversion and its implications for the church will help us face our missionary responsibility today.

Chapter 4

MEDIEVAL MISSIONS

We now turn to a period that has often been described in negative terms, as a time of superstition and obscurantism. However, the Middle Ages witnessed rich and creative exchanges between Christianity and the various Germanic cultures as well as Islam. The story of those exchanges is valuable for our reflection on the mission of the church and the evangelizing task. Although the church found itself in an ambiguous and fragile situation, the missionary practices of the times show the birth of new methods and a creative missional reflection that may well serve as a guide for our response to the challenges facing the church today as it relates to different cultures, traditions, and religions. What others might call the "Dark Ages" can also be seen as a period of creative transformation in the life of the church and its understanding of its mission.

A. From the Germanic Invasions to the Advance of Islam

1. The Reconquest of the Ancient Roman Empire

From its very beginning the Roman Empire was constantly challenged by the presence at its borders of peoples, mostly Germanic, whom the Romans called "barbarians." In Europe, the Danube and the Rhine were the natural limits holding back the Germanic and Slavic impetus. In Great Britain, where there were no such natural borders, an entire system of fortifications was built to prevent the invasion of Roman lands by Scots and Picts. In North Africa and Egypt, there were frequent battles with Moors and Nubians. Toward the east, the great enemy of Rome was the Persian Empire, apparently more to be feared than the barbarians, but not so in fact. Persia might invade the Roman Empire and take two or three of its provinces, as it did repeatedly, but its population would not move en masse into Roman territory, leaving behind their place of origin, as many of the barbarians were ready to do. For these reasons, the eastern portion of the Roman Empire was not as seriously threatened as the west until other nomadic people, in this case the Arabs, would rise and conquer both the Persian Empire and a good part of the eastern Roman Empire. In the western portion of the empire, in contrast, there was the constant menace of an enemy whose final goal was to establish itself within the empire.

Although a series of small border wars that weakened the empire began during the second century under the reign of Marcus Aurelius, it was actually in the late fourth century—particularly after the death of Theodosius—that the Roman legions were no longer able to hold back the successive Germanic waves that entered the western empire through all its borders. After years of prosperity and relative security, the empire and its inhabitants had become accustomed to a life of comfort and security. Since the ancient inhabitants of the empire would rather not go into war, Roman authorities began enrolling into the Roman legions large numbers of barbarians who were ready to take arms on behalf of the empire. Soon the defense of Rome against the supposed barbarians was in the hands of other barbarians. Thus, some as defenders of Rome and others as invaders—and in many cases alternately first one and then the other—a number of Germanic peoples began settling and establishing their own kingdoms within the borders of the empire. The process was slow and—although there were important moments, such as the sack of Rome by Alaric in 410, or the deposition of Emperor Romulus Augustulus by Odoacre in 476—most of those living at the time did not realize their enormous significance.

2. The Germanic Challenge to Christianity

From the point of view of the history of civilization, the Germanic invasions posed a great challenge. Through centuries of cultural development, the Roman notion of *romanitas* had come to express the cultural inheritance that its beneficiaries believed had resulted in the greatest civilization that Europe had ever known. It was precisely this *romanitas* that had made possible the accumulation of wealth that the barbarians coveted, for one of their main motives in moving into Roman territory was to take possession of that wealth and to participate also in *romanitas* itself. However, the same people, with alien customs and their lack of understanding of the true foundations of *romanitas*, threatened to destroy that which they sought to possess.

The Germanic invasions also posed a challenge from the point of view of missions. The invaders brought with them their traditions and their gods. Since the various Nordic peoples who invaded the Roman Empire shared some common origins and traditions, it is often difficult to distinguish among the religions of the various invading peoples. Also, since our main sources for knowing those religions date from several centuries after the invasions themselves, they may well reflect later influences and interpretations. However, in general one may say that all of the invading nations believed in life after death, at least for valiant warriors, who would share in feasts in the hall of the god of war—a god that had a name among the Goths, another among the Slavs, and still another among the Scandinavians. To this god as well as to many others, it was customary to offer as sacrifice animals, crops, and sometimes even humans. In some cases a practice was followed similar to that of the Israelites of old when they took Jericho, sacrificing to their gods all the booty of a particular conquest, including all captives. Other important elements of the religion of these various peoples were the sacred places where the gods and other supernatural spirits supposedly dwelled, in particular sacred forests and trees.

Their societies comprised three major social classes: chieftains and priests, warriors, and farmers and herders, for war represented a higher form of morality than peace, while the concepts of sin, salvation, and humility were considered reprehensible. In contrast, the Christian notion of honor stemmed from a desire to avoid the guilt and fear of sin, an honor that was essentially world-rejecting. Consequently, significant obstacles existed in the world-accepting worldview of the Germanic tribes that would have prevented their ready acceptance of Christianity. Unlike earlier Christians in the Roman world, who usually came to Christianity as individuals, the Germanic tribes converted in mass at the behest of their chieftains—who themselves tended to convert out of political expediency rather than a true change of heart. Also, while earlier Christians underwent years of catechesis before baptism, now the Germanic tribes experienced little education in their newfound religion, merely incorporating Christ into their existing roster of gods. Post-baptismal catechesis remained sparse, leading to a situation in which church leaders accommodated and appropriated pagan practices. As a result, many of Latin Christianity's ethical expectations were transformed to emulate Germanic notions of honor and war. Honor led to wealth, power, and prestige, while shame resulted in the opposite. The Latin form of Christianity that spread north from Italy after 400 underwent a substantial transformation as it encountered the socially cohesive Germanic tribes of northern Europe. Through this process of syncretism a Germanized version of the Christian religion evolved, took hold, and held firm throughout Europe for centuries.

The vast majority of those who settled in the ancient imperial lands were pagan, and their religion and social organization was as we have just described. Those who were Christian had been converted through their contacts with Arians and were therefore themselves Arians, considered heretics by other Christians. Some of the regions where Christianity had been able to spread most effectively—Gaul, Italy, Spain, and North Africa—were now populated by new people among whom a new missionary task was necessary.

For those Christians who had been formed under the influence of *romanitas,* the challenge to civilization and the challenge to Christianity were one and the same thing. For them, the Roman Empire had been created by God, whose providence had established it as a means for the transmission of the gospel. If now God allowed that empire to be threatened, this was also part of the divine plan for the redemption of the world, for by invading Roman lands the barbarians were also gaining access to the faith. But God's plan also included the opportunity for these barbarians to gain access to the faith by participating in *romanitas.* It is for this reason that throughout this entire period the missionary work of the church is conjoined to a "civilizing" effort, so that the mission of the church was understood as both the conversion of the barbarians and their Romanization. Furthermore, some Christian writers, such as Paulinus of Nola, claimed that one of the reasons why the conversion of the pagans should be sought was that, were they to become Christian, they would no longer threaten the empire and its civilization.

This does not mean, however, that all Christians believed that their religion was simply a means to save *romanitas,* for some were ready to see the entire structure of civilization destroyed if it was God's will to do so for the evangelization of the barbarians. Thus Orosius, a disciple of Augustine, declared:

> If the only reason why the barbarians have been sent within the confines of the Roman borders was that throughout the east and west the church of Christ will be full of Huns and Suevi, of Vandals, and Burgundians, of diverse and innumerable believing peoples, then the mercy of God is to be praised and exalted, because so many

> people have attained a knowledge of truth that they would never have had without these events, even though it may be through our own destruction. (*History*, VII: 41)

Thus, the efforts of the church to regain the territory lost through Germanic invasions began the very day when it became necessary. The pagan peoples established in Roman territory soon began adapting to and transforming the customs and beliefs of their conquered neighbors. At the same time, the new missionary methods and the shape that the encounter between these cultures took transformed the Christian faith, making it more Germanic and less Latin. The conversion of those invaders who were Arian before crossing the borders into the empire—Goths, Lombards, and Vandals—took longer. But eventually their tendency to accept the customs of their Roman neighbors led all Arians to embrace Catholicism.[1]

3. The Conversion of the Pagans

The process of conversion of the Germanic invaders shows how a non-Christian majority, impressed by the "Christian" culture and civilization of a minority, will progressively accept the faith of that minority. Naturally, the result of that process is an intermingling of both cultures, so that the resulting Christianity bears the stamp of both the earlier Christian tradition and the culture of the recently converted peoples.

The leaders of the church thus found themselves living in a tension that would continue throughout the history of Christianity. On the one hand, it seemed necessary to have converts abandon as much as possible of their ancient religion. On the other hand, such religions had profound roots in the traditions and customs of the people whose conversion was sought. This tension may be seen in the policies of Gregory the Great, bishop of Rome, toward converts in England. Gregory had received news of the conversion of King Ethelbert of Kent and sent missionaries to that land with instructions that they were to destroy all pagan temples. But shortly thereafter he sent other instructions:

> When therefore, Almighty God shall bring you to the most revered Bishop Augustine, our brother, tell him what I have, upon mature deliberation on the affair of the English, determined upon, viz., that the temples of the idols in that nation ought not to be destroyed; but let the idols that are in them be destroyed; let holy water be made and sprinkled in the said temples, let altars be erected, and relics placed. For if those temples are well built, it is requisite that they be converted from the worship of devils to the service of the true God; that the nation, seeing that their temples are not destroyed, may remove error from their hearts, and knowing and adoring the true God, may the more familiarly resort to the places to which they have been accustomed. For there is no doubt that it is impossible to efface every thing at once from their obdurate minds; because he who endeavors to ascend to the highest place, rises by degrees or steps, and not by leaps.[2]

Although the conversion of the pagan invaders began as soon as they settled within the Roman Empire, and there were soon many Christians among the Suevi and the Burgundians, most often the decisive step was the conversion of a king and his nobility, which was then followed by a mass conversion. The most important of these events was the conversion of the Frankish king Clovis in 496. The consequences of that event would be felt for centuries.

Clovis became king of the Salian Franks in 481. This was not a great or powerful kingdom, and for five years Clovis seemed content with ruling it. But in 486, he began a series of military campaigns that rapidly expanded his holdings. In 493, he married the Catholic princess Clothilde, a daughter of the king of the Burgundians. Although already by that time Clovis had shown great respect toward Christianity and its bishops, it was apparently Clothilde who eventually led him to accept Christianity. Clovis first agreed to have his children baptized, and sometime later he himself accepted baptism. The ceremony took place in Rheims on Christmas Day of 496, and many of the nobility—and eventually the entire nation—followed the king to the baptismal font.

There were a number of political reasons that may have contributed to the Frankish king's decision. He apparently was already planning further expansion of his lands, and in that effort the church could be an important ally. The church could also help him organize the growing Frankish kingdom. In order to achieve that, it was necessary for the king to be a Christian so that his actions could be seen as inspired by his faith. In accepting baptism, and calling on his subjects to do the same—although he did not use violent means—Clovis was accepting and inviting the support of the church, and particularly of its bishops, for his political purposes. However, had Clovis not decided to be baptized, there is little doubt that eventually the Franks would have become Christian, as was the case with all the surrounding nations.

The baptism of Clovis is important because it marks the beginning of the great Frankish kingdom that would eventually become a new empire. By the ninth century, the Frankish kingdom claimed to be a reincarnation of the then-defunct western Roman Empire, and it was through its influence that Christianity achieved some of its most significant gains in northern Europe. The history of that Frankish Empire and of its significance for Christian expansion belongs elsewhere in the present chapter.

4. The Conversion of the Arians

Although it too was destined to disappear, Arianism proved more resistant to the Catholic faith than did the ancient pagan religions. Aside from the Vandals, who soon crossed the Strait of Gibraltar and settled in North Africa, and whose Arian convictions lasted until they were conquered first by the Byzantines and then by the Muslims, the main Arian peoples who settled in the former territories of the western Roman Empire where the Ostrogoths, the Lombards, and the Visigoths. The Ostrogoths ceased being a challenge for Catholic Christians when they lost their power to the Lombards. Ruling over a Catholic population, trying to learn its ways, and often considering that marriage to Catholic princesses was an important asset for kings, the Lombards soon abandoned Arianism and became Orthodox. This is one more reminder that throughout history, family links, with the cultural and religious exchanges that follow from them, have always been an important factor in evangelization. Both the Ostrogoths and their cousins the Visigoths, who settled in Spain, were generally tolerant toward the Catholic population. Even so, there were sporadic persecutions and various forms of coercion seeking the conversion of the Orthodox to Arianism. This policy did not succeed, and finally in 589, King Recared—whose deceased father had persecuted the Orthodox—embraced the Nicene faith. Even then Arianism did not disappear in Spain but actually remained in existence until the Muslim invasion ended Visigothic rule in the year 711.

This process of converting the Arians, who already considered themselves Christians, is an example of another issue that would appear repeatedly in this history: the evangelization of those who already bear the name of Christ. The Catholics were convinced that the Arians must abandon their persuasion in order to be true Christians and therefore sought their conversion. Centuries later in the Near East, Roman Catholics tried to convert the Eastern Orthodox, and even later in Latin America Protestants sought the conversion of Roman Catholics.

5. Missions in the British Isles

The Roman Empire had reached only into the southern sections of Great Britain—what today we call England. By now, however, these lands were the possession of several Angle kings. More to the north and west, what are today Scotland, Wales, and Ireland were still inhabited by ancient Celtic peoples whose religion was very similar to that of the

Germanic peoples of the continent. Missions in the British Isles deserve special attention because the church that was founded there soon became a center for missions to the continent. Also, in the case of missions in Great Britain there are four points to be noted: (1) the expansion of Christianity to lands beyond the borders of the ancient Roman Empire, with the work of Patrick, discussed below, and others; (2) the expansion of Christianity from Ireland through monastic institutions such as the one in Iona; (3) the first mission on record organized by the Roman see, which is that of Augustine to England; and (4) the development of a missionary methodology sanctioned by Rome that took seriously the religions and cultural contexts of the evangelized—for this was the setting of Gregory's letter regarding pagan temples quoted above.

(a) Patrick

This missionary, generally known as St. Patrick, and who is now the patron saint of Ireland, was born near the end of the fourth century in what is today England. His father, a Roman decurion, was a Christian, as had been his grandfather. But young Patrick did not take his faith very seriously until his own misfortunes led him to it. He was still an adolescent when a band of raiders from Ireland took him captive to that land. There he spent several years as a slave, mostly working as a shepherd. He was eventually able to escape to the continent thanks to the connivance of the captain of a ship. But even there he again faced difficulties, for now those who had helped him escape sought to enslave him again. Finally, after a long series of adventures that led him as far as the Mediterranean, Patrick returned to his home, taking with him a renewed faith forged in his many misfortunes.

Back in Great Britain, where he had hoped to settle for the rest of his life, Patrick had a dream calling him to missionary work in the land of his former captivity. He said that he saw a man coming to him from Ireland with many letters, one of which claimed to be "the voice of the Irish," inviting him to return to the island:

> I saw in a vision of the night a man coming apparently from Ireland whose name was Victoricus, with an uncountable number of letters, and he gave me one of them and I read the heading of the letter which ran, "The Cry of the Irish," and while I was reading aloud the heading of the letter I was imagining that at that very moment I read the voice of those who were by the Wood of Voclut which is in the Western Sea, and this is what they cried, as with one voice, "Holy boy, we are asking you to come and walk among us again," and I was struck deeply to the heart and I was unable to read any further and after that I woke up. God be thanked that after several years the Lord granted them according to their cry.[3]

Having returned to Ireland in obedience to his vision, Patrick seems to have employed various methods to obtain the conversion of his former masters. Generally he would first approach the leadership of a community and then, through their influence, achieve the conversion, or at least the baptism, of the masses. In doing this, Patrick was following a profoundly Celtic tradition, which insisted on unity in a community, so that important decisions, once made by the leaders, were also the decision of the entire group. In the field of religion, this meant that, if the leaders decided to embrace Christianity, the rest of the population would follow them. It was therefore this leadership that Patrick addressed most directly. In order to reach kings and other influential people, he would often make them presents. At times not even this resulted in a friendly reception, and Patrick's biographer tells us that he looked on the dangers upon his life as someone who was convinced that martyrdom was the crown of faith.

Through these means Patrick was able to baptize thousands. One may question how profound was the faith of such converts. However, one must point out that it was precisely out of a recently converted Ireland that a great missionary movement arose that would eventually extend throughout most of northern Europe. One factor contributing to this result was that at the same time that Patrick was baptizing multitudes, he was also ordaining priests who would nourish and guide the recently converted. Quite likely, at first these priests were almost as ignorant as their flock, but soon the influence of monasteries founded thanks to Patrick's work made itself felt, for these monasteries were centers of study and devotion. This reminds us of the often-forgotten fact that quite often the greatest challenge to mission is not the expansion of faith but rather its deepening. Making disciples requires more than making converts.

As a result of Patrick's work—and undoubtedly of many others whose names history does not record—an autonomous church was established in Ireland, and that church came to be part of the lifeblood of the Irish people. Through a process that is not entirely clear, but that reflects elements of ancient Celtic culture, that church came to have certain characteristics regarding its organization, the date on which it celebrated Easter, and several other such matters. Thus, for instance, ecclesiastical authority was vested not in the bishops but rather on the abbots of monasteries, whose authority was similar to that of the ancient Celtic bards. Later this would lead to conflicts between the Irish missionaries and those who followed the customs of Rome and of the rest of Western Christianity.

(b) Columba and the Iona Community

Shortly after Patrick's missionary endeavors, Ireland became an important center of missions. Irish pilgrims traveled throughout Europe, preaching and calling Christians to a life more in accord with the principles of the gospel. They often founded monasteries that they then left behind in order to continue their wanderings. Often their customs and their interests clashed with the local ecclesiastical hierarchy, and in those cases they would normally simply continue their wanderings, seeking a place more fitting to their purposes.

In general, these pilgrims did not consider themselves missionaries, nor were they moved by a missionary purpose. Rather, they saw their pilgrimage as a way of making their monastic life more demanding. They had abandoned their possessions and ambitions in order to lead an ascetic life, and now they undertook extended pilgrimages as another way of giving up what they most loved: their land and their kindred. Often they were wandering in lands that were already Christian, and the local authorities were wary of them. This reminds us that missionary activity, precisely because it takes place at the borders between peoples and cultures, frequently challenges ecclesiastical structures that are quite accustomed to their place in their own culture. It is probably for this reason that many church histories written "from the center" pay little attention to missionary work. Also, these missionaries from Ireland pose again the difficult question of the evangelization of those who already call themselves Christian. At other times the wanderings of these Irish pilgrims led them to places where the population was not Christian, and then a pilgrimage born out of an ascetic goal led to an evangelistic task. As in many cases, discipleship led to witness, and vice versa.

The best known among these Irish pilgrims is Columba. Born within Irish aristocracy, Columba was educated in one of the many monasteries that had preserved some of the knowledge of antiquity. He then founded several monasteries in Ireland. But when he was forty-two years old—apparently as an exile seeking to atone for homicide—he crossed the sea with twelve disciples and settled on the island of Iona, off the coast of Scotland. This was a small island on which, according to an ancient chronicle, only five families lived. There he founded a monastery that would eventually become quite important for the expansion of Christianity. He then traveled repeatedly to Scotland, where he made a number of converts, thus founding the church in that area.

However, the influence of Columba and of the Iona community was not limited to Scotland or to his generation. It was a mission from Iona that resulted in the conversion of Northumbria. The king of that area, Oswald, had been forced into exile and during that time was baptized. When he regained his kingdom, he asked the community in Iona to send a bishop who could teach the Christian faith to his subjects. The second bishop that Iona sent to that area was Aidan, a true representative of Columba's spirit. Following the example of Columba, Aidan established a monastery on the island of Lindisfarne. From that center, Aidan and those who succeeded him made repeated trips in which they preached, taught, and administered the sacraments. As a result of this work, even when a pagan reaction followed after Oswald's death, Christianity remained firmly rooted in the hearts of these new converts. Aidan died nine years after this reaction, but his successor, Finian, continued his work, so that from Lindisfarne, Christianity reached into the kingdoms of Mercia, Essex, and Wessex.

In the work of Columba and his successors—in Iona, Lindisfarne, and other similar centers—we encounter a new sort of missionary work. We have seen that in earlier centuries Christianity expanded in various ways. Sometimes churches would send missionaries; at other times, the bishop himself would visit the areas around his cities; at others, the new faith was propagated through the work of people traveling for various reasons, such as merchants, slaves, and others; finally, at still other times, it was cultural interchange among nations as well as the establishment of new family ties that resulted in conversions. By the fourth century, monastic centers of community life had appeared whose members sought to live out their lives in a particularly devoted fashion. Now, at Iona, the monastic ideal and missionary work were fruitfully joined. The Iona community was both monastic and missionary. Through study, discipline, and prayer, the residents of monasteries such as Iona and Lindisfarne were seeking not only to strengthen their own spiritual life, but also to train for missionary work. From that point on, the best of the monastic ideal and of its quest for a deeper faith would become part of the missionary enterprise. Later on in this history we shall see various ways in which medieval Christians sought to harness monastic ideals to the missionary task. Much later, during the sixteenth century, we shall see that in rejecting monasticism, Protestantism relinquished an important missionary instrument and that this was one of the main reasons why it took Protestantism several centuries before it was able to match Roman Catholic missions.

(c) Augustine of Canterbury

According to legend, at about the same time Columba was working among the Picts of Scotland and setting the foundations for what would eventually become a vast missionary movement, a young man who would later be known as Gregory the Great was ambling along the slave market in Rome when his attention was drawn by a group of young blond men who were up for sale. He is said to have asked, "To what nation do these young men belong?" When he learned that they were Angles, he commented, "That must truly be their name, for their faces are like angel faces. What is the name of their province?"

"They are from the province of Deiri," he was told.

"They must truly come from that province, for they have been called from wrath [*de ira*], to the mercy of God. Who is their king?"

"Aella."

"Alleluia! The creator God must be praised in that land."

Gregory himself tried to go as a missionary to the land of the Angles, but an angry mob would not allow him to leave. By the year 590, he had become pope, and nine years later he turned once again to the land of the Angles—England. He chose a number of monks from a monastery that he had founded and charged them with the task of evangelizing the Angles. He named a former abbot of the monastery as their leader, Augustine (not to be confused with Augustine of Hippo, the much earlier North African theologian).

Augustine and his companions landed in the kingdom of Kent, where they were well received by King Ethelbert, whose wife was a Christian. Although they were permitted to preach and teach freely, it was some time before the missionaries were able to report their first conversions. But finally the king himself—and much of his kingdom after him—descended into the waters of baptism. From that point on the missionary enterprise progressed rapidly. Augustine himself, who became Archbishop of Canterbury, the capital of Kent, named and consecrated other bishops who helped spread the gospel throughout the kingdom. By the time Augustine died, less than ten years after his arrival at Kent, most of the population was Christian.

It was in connection with this mission that Gregory wrote the letters to Ethelbert mentioned earlier, telling him first that pagan temples should be destroyed, and then reversing his decision.

Although there was a brief pagan reaction after Ethelbert's death, soon the new king also became a Christian. From that point on, Christianity continually expanded throughout the south of the island, moving from Kent to Northumbria, and then from Northumbria to East Anglia.

Clearly, Augustine and his companions were not the only missionaries seeking the conversion of the Angles, and it is quite likely that the Iona community led to more conversions than Augustine's mission. However, that mission left an indelible mark on English Christianity by introducing it to Roman customs and establishing the authority of the Roman hierarchy and thus tending to obscure the unique characteristics of Celtic Christianity. As a result, to this day the Archbishop of Canterbury heads the hierarchy in the Church of England.

One should also note that Augustine's mission to England was the first indisputably recorded occasion in which a pope directly and officially sent a mission to a distant land. Until that moment, most Christian expansion had been the result of circumstances having little to do with a missionary strategy or with the interests or decisions of the ecclesiastical hierarchy. Thus, in Augustine and Gregory we have an important new development in the history of missions. Now the missionary task would become the responsibility of the entire church, and particularly of its leadership, which became responsible for missionary planning and strategy. This is to an extent a result of the crisis that the church was facing at that time throughout Europe, so that geographic expansion through missionary work became a light in what seemed to be very dark horizons.

As is well known, the British Isles continued serving as a missionary center for centuries. After the Protestant Reformation, England and Scotland would be the main centers for the expansion of Protestant Christianity. What is often forgotten is that this form of Christianity still contained traces of its ancient Celtic traditions. Thus, for instance, the celebration of Halloween in countries of British descent is simply the continuation of ancient Celtic practices, when people would lock themselves up in their homes with the belief that demons were loose upon the world. Also belonging to that tradition were ancestral customs of celebrating spring with rabbits and eggs and winter with mistletoe, a sacred plant among the ancient Celts.

6. Eastern Missions

(a) Orthodox Christianity

During the period between the fall of Rome and the advance of Islam, the eastern Roman Empire, now known as the Byzantine Empire, was one of the great powers of the world, whose only dangerous rival seemed to be nearby Persia. That empire included much of North Africa, the eastern Mediterranean, and the southeastern regions of Europe. This Byzantine Empire served as a center of missionary activity in the Near East.

It was during Justinian's reign that Byzantium regained the lands of North Africa that had previously been conquered by the Vandals. The task was immediately begun of rebuilding Orthodox Christianity, which had been almost smothered by the Arian faith of the Vandals. It was also during Justinian's reign that Christianity expanded south of Egypt, into Nubia, which saw the activity of a number of Orthodox missionaries as well as others of Monophysite faith. Toward the north, Justinian achieved the conversion of most of the peoples in the Caucasus and of some among the Heruli. Finally, following the policy of his predecessors, Justinian also enacted laws against paganism, with the result that conversions to Christianity became numerous, although often superficial.

(b) Nestorians and Monophysites

Although Christian expansion toward the east included the establishment of some Orthodox communities in Persian lands, the bodies that gained the most followers beyond the borders of the Roman Empire were the Monophysites and the Nestorians—two groups resulting from the christological controversies of the fourth century.

The Nestorians were named after Nestorius, a patriarch of Constantinople who had been condemned by the Council of Ephesus in 431. They insisted on the distinction between the divine and the human natures of Jesus, for they feared that otherwise the Savior's humanity would be eclipsed. Thus, instead of the Orthodox formula, which affirmed that Jesus exists "in two natures"—the divine and the human—"and one person," the Nestorians would rather speak of "two natures and two persons." From the Orthodox perspective, this seemed to render Christ asunder and therefore deny the true incarnation of God. After the condemnation of Nestorius, many of his followers moved to the Persian Empire, where they soon became numerous. To this day, there are relatively small Nestorian communities in Iraq and Iran.

At the opposite christological extreme from the Nestorians, the Monophysites rejected the formula "two natures in one person" established by the Council of Chalcedon in 451 and preferred to speak of "one nature and one person." They thus underscored the union of divinity and humanity in the Savior. But from the point of view of the Orthodox, this seemed to deny the true humanity of Jesus, which was then absorbed and eclipsed by his divinity. The Monophysites established strong churches in Egypt, Ethiopia, and Syria—churches that still exist.

Nestorian Christianity expanded mostly among Syriac-speaking people who were scattered throughout Persian lands and even beyond—in Central Asia, India, and Arabia. Given the traditional connection between Antiochene theology and its exponent Nestorius, on the one hand, and Syrian culture, on the other, it is not surprising that much of Syrian Christianity became Nestorian. Christianity continued expanding through the work of these Syriac-speaking Nestorians, who also achieved a number of conversions among the Persians. Among the latter, the best known is Mar Aba, who became "Catholicos" of Seleucia-Ctesiphon and therefore head of the Nestorian church throughout Persia.

The Monophysites also expanded throughout the Middle East during this time. The origins of the Coptic Church in Egypt and of the church in Ethiopia, both of which became Monophysite, has already been discussed. However, the Monophysite body that gained greatest expansion during the first years of the Middle Ages was the Jacobites. Although they claimed that their name came from Jacob, the brother of the Lord, it was apparently the result of the very active missionary work of Jacob Baradacus, who lived in the sixth century and traveled along the routes from Nisibis to Alexandria, strengthening, organizing, and promoting Monophysite Christianity. Before the advance of Islam, the Jacobites were particularly numerous in Syria, Mesopotamia, Persia, and Egypt.

At any rate, the most remarkable and far-reaching missionary expansion during this period was the arrival of Nestorian Christianity in China, taken there by Alopen, a missionary from Syria. His work is described in an inscription from the year 781 usually called the "Nestorian Monument," in which we find the following information about his arrival in China in 635:

> When the illustrious emperor Tai-tsung inaugurated his magnificent career of glory and splendor . . . there was in the kingdom of Ta-ch'in a man of great virtue called Alopen. Led by signs in the blue sky, he decided to take with him the true oracles, and following the movements of the winds, after many difficulties arrived at Chang'an. The emperor sent his minister, Duque Fahn Hsuan-ling, with an honor guard to this western suburb, in order to meet the visitor and take him to the imperial palace. The oracles were translated in the imperial library. His majesty inquired about "the way" in his private apartments, and after being convinced of their truthfulness gave special orders that the message be announced.

When Alopen arrived in China during the Tang Dynasty, in the year 635, he followed the silk route, which connected China with Europe. Nestorians, noted for their mercantile enterprise, would follow that route to China and carry their faith with them. There are indications that the first Nestorian church in China was founded by the Mar Sergis immigrant family. It is important to stress at that time the Tang Dynasty was opening a period of religious tolerance and of educational revival that allowed openness both to Christianity and to Zoroastrianism. The first Christian church in China was built under imperial auspices in 638, which was also the date of an important edict of tolerance.

Alopen was well received by the reigning house and devoted himself to translating the Scriptures and founding monasteries. Although there is no doubt that soon there was a good number of Christian converts, it is almost certain that most of the members of the Nestorian church in China were foreigners—most likely Nestorian merchants—and for this reason Christianity had a small effect among the Chinese, which was felt mostly among those in the intelligentsia who had contacts with Nestorian merchants. At a later time, a dynastic change brought about persecution, to the point that Nestorian Christianity in China was obliterated.

7. The Advance of Islam

The seventh and eighth centuries mark one of the most difficult periods in the history of Christianity in the Middle East and North Africa. It was a time of great territorial losses, with the result that many of the most ancient and important Christian churches either disappeared or became small enclaves within the surrounding society. It was also a time that gave birth to enmities that would continue for centuries.

The beginning of the Muslim era is usually marked by the Hegira, in 622. When Mohammed died in 632, his followers controlled only a fairly small area on the western coast of Arabia, and their influence had not reached beyond that peninsula. His successor, Omar (634–644), with the help of his very able general, Khalid, and profiting from the weakness of both the Byzantine and the Persian empires, directed the conquest of Syria, Mesopotamia, Egypt, and much of Media and Persia.

The conquest of Syria was made easier by the conflicts between the Monophysite and the Orthodox. Furthermore, most of the people of the area were of Semitic origin and therefore were not completely opposed to the Arab invasion. This began in 634, and by 636, the entire area was under Arab control—except Jerusalem and Caesarea, which surrendered in 638 and 640, respectively. As a consequence of the conquest of Syria, the Roman portion of Mesopotamia, severed from its Byzantine capital, soon fell too. In 634, at the same time when they were invading Syria, the Arabs also invaded Persia and Mesopotamia, and, in spite of some initial setbacks, by 637, the city of Ctesiphon surrendered. They then continued their eastward march, first into Media and then into Persia itself—although the complete conquest of these lands did not take place until 649, after Omar's death. Even then, the ancient Iranian culture continued existing and was able to leave its imprint on the form that Islam took there. In 640, Omar's troops, commanded by General Amr, invaded Egypt. There was little resistance, for Patriarch Cyrus, whom the Byzantine emperor had made both patriarch and governor, quickly capitulated. When Alexandria surrendered in 642, all of Egypt was under Islamic rule.

Caliph Othman (644–655) was not able to continue Omar's conquest. His fiscal policies as well as his inclination to nepotism soon resulted in discontent, and all that he was able to conquer was eastern Persia and the island of Cyprus. Othman was assassinated, but his successor Ali was not able to gain full control. Soon there was civil war, with a long succession of pretenders to the caliphate, until Abdalmalik established the caliphate of Damascus in 692.

In spite of internal dissension, Islam continued its advance, and by 698, all of North Africa was under its rule. The conquest of this particular area was difficult due to Berber resistance. But the Berbers soon embraced the religion of their conquerors, to the point that by 711, the Islamic force that invaded Spain was mostly Moorish in origin. The conquest of Spain was easy. The entire peninsula, except the region of Asturias, was soon under Muslim rule. In 720, and then in 725, the Islamic armies invaded the kingdom of France, reaching the edges of Tours and also advancing along the Rhone even beyond the city of Lyon. The battle of Tours (or of Poitiers) in 732, when Charles Martel defeated the Muslims, stopped the advance of Islam into western Europe. Most Christian historians see in this victory the end of Muslim advance and the beginning of the ideology of the Crusades, but many Muslim historians claim the defeat was not as serious. While the importance of the battle itself may to be subject to debate, there is no question that after that date Islam did not continue its advance into Europe.

Though there were still repeated Islamic invasions of various provinces in Anatolia, and the armies of Islam even threatened the city of Constantinople in 716 and 717, the border between Islam and the lands under Christian rule was generally fixed by the year 720. By then, Islam had conquered the entire Persian Empire, Armenia, Mesopotamia, Syria, Arabia, the north coast of Africa, and almost the entire Iberian Peninsula.

The Abbasid caliphate began in 650, and its capital eventually became Baghdad, which was founded in 762. The Abbasids did not achieve great military conquests but did manage to develop a civilization that brought together Western science and philosophy and Muslim religion. The period of the initial expansionist thrust of Islam had come to an end.

Christianity continued existing in the lands conquered by Muslims. Under the leadership of Mohammed, Christians could continue professing their faith as long as they paid a tribute; but even so, many became Muslims. The Koran allowed a special place for Christianity as one of the peoples of the book—jointly with Judaism. As a result, Muslims did not always seek the conversion of Christians by force, and in many cases there were Christians who shared in government. Furthermore, many of those Christians who did not accept the decisions of the Council of Chalcedon—that is, the Monophysites and Nestorians—accepted the new order as putting an end to the former injustice that they suffered in the lands controlled by the Byzantine Empire. Quite a few Monophysite writers in the seventh century saw in the advance of Islam a sign of the judgment of God against the churches that followed the doctrines of Chalcedon. In general, although with some very serious exceptions, Christians were not persecuted in Islamic lands.

However, the new conditions did place Christianity and its followers in a condition of disadvantage. Although there was religious tolerance, Christians were considered second-class citizens. Even those who converted to Islam were often considered inferior to their Arab conquerors. There were also obligations and restrictions that Christians were forced to follow, such as dressing in particular ways and avoiding any external sign that could be a means of announcing or promoting Christianity. This included ringing church bells as well as raising pigs where Muslims could see them. Although there was tolerance for those who had been Christians at the time of the Muslim conquest, as well as for their descendants, there were severe penalties—including death—for any Muslim who would convert to Christianity.

The religious and political relationships of Christians and Muslims can be described with four different "conditions of coexistence." The first condition existed when Muslims ruled yet were suspicious of Christians and other non-Muslims who were the majority of the population. In this case Muslims sought religious differentiation in order to foster power over the majority. Although many Christians hoped to return to power, conflict was minimized unless the subjects rebeled, and church life and mission were restricted.

Second, there were conditions in which Muslims ruled peacefully even though Christians were the majority, yet Muslim rulers used Christians pragmatically, with no stress on social or religious differentiation. Muslims and Christians shared social and cultural customs, making daily coexistence respectful. Muslims declared that their religion led them to protect Christians and non-Muslims but encouraged conversion to Islam and penalized conversion to Christianity. Christians had to wrestle between accommodation and strong differentiation. Missionary work was twofold: it turned inward, to help the Christian population keep its spiritual and theological integrity, and it turned outward, to an interreligious dialogue between the Muslim and Christian elites.

A third condition existed in which Muslims ruled but were politically and religiously divided and violent among themselves. Here again Christians and non-Muslims were in the majority. Hence, Muslim rulers employed Islamic doctrinal interpretations to protect Christians. Yet Christians emphasized religious and political differentiation and resisted Islamic domination. This was a condition of tension and ambiguity. Missionary activity was restricted and was limited to sustaining resistance to Muslim rule.

The fourth condition of coexistence was one in which Muslims were challenged by external non-Muslim forces. Under these conditions, Muslims used Christians for their political organization and frequently as scapegoats. Christian groups were divided between the path of accommodation and peaceful coexistence with Muslims and the risk of alliances with outside non-Muslim forces. Missionary work was limited and, at times, dangerous.

Similar "conditions of coexistence" could very well describe the relationship of Muslims when Christians ruled, though history is witness to the fact that often Christian treatment of Muslims was more violent than Muslim treatment of Christians.

The life and work of John of Damascus serve to illustrate the second condition of coexistence described above, at the time immediately following the Muslim conquest. John's father, Mansur ibn Sarjur, was a Jacobite Syrian Christian who served the Omayyad Dynasty in Damascus, which in 661 became the first center of Muslim government outside of Mecca. John of Damascus became an Orthodox Christian and is best known by his extensive work, *On the Orthodox Faith.* But just as important is his *Dialogue Between a Saracen and a Christian.* In this latter treatise, John offered an apology that characterized eighth-century Christian missiology within an Islamic context. Even though he was convinced that Islam was a heresy, John of Damascus also provided a model for understanding the methods and views of Muslims and also sought to enable Christians to discuss matters of faith with Muslims. The entire treatise illustrates the concerns of Christians and their confrontations with Islam. Such confrontations, which during John's time were relatively mild, would become increasingly violent in later centuries.

Another example from the ninth century is the Christian treaty *Summa Theologiae Arabica.* According to Sydney H. Griffith, Professor of Semitic Studies at the Catholic University of America, this document shows two missionary strategies in the context of a long-standing Islamic rule. First, the author appropriates the Arabic language and style of the Koran to clarify Christian theology, particularly trinitarian theology. It is an apologetic document in the *lingua franca* of Arabic. Second, the treaty reveals the processes of adaptation of Christian communities to the language and ethos of Muslim faith in its day-to-day relationship, yet it demonstrates the concern of the Christian leaders for the church population and its Christian formation. The *Summa Arabica* is an example of the translation and use of idiomatic expressions in order to ground the Christian faith in a context in which a new religion and a new language displace the Greek Christian tradition.

Christianity—in its Orthodox, as well as its Nestorian and Monophysite, form—continued existing in Persia, Syria, and Egypt. These churches continued their missionary task, resulting in churches and bishoprics in distant regions such as Tibet, India, China, and other areas in central and Southeast Asia. Catholicos Timothy I reports of requests from regions in the East asking for missionaries and bishops. The monasteries in the East provided significant support for these missionary efforts. They also provided training in the field of medicine. Thanks to their work, some of the monks were considered to be holy people by the population of the region. Regretfully, they did not have the same success with their Muslim neighbors and rulers.

As Egypt was conquered by Islam, the churches in Nubia and Ethiopia were severed from the rest of Christianity, which in turn made them more conservative and undermined their missionary engagement.

In North Africa, Christianity continued existing for some time, but after a few centuries it had completely disappeared. A possible reason for this is that Christianity never really penetrated the heart of the earliest inhabitants of the area and also that many Christians simply left for Italy or France.

In the Iberian Peninsula, however, Christianity continued existing, not only in the northern regions of Asturias, but also in all the lands ruled by Islam. As is generally known, this was the largest area that Christians were finally able to wrest from Islam, mostly through armed force. However, the discussion of those events belongs elsewhere in the present chapter.

B. From the British Missionary Thrust to the Crusades

Two parallel events—the advance of Islam and the conversion of the British Isles—completely changed the picture of the geographical distribution and expansion of Christianity. Until that time, the center of Christianity was a wide strip of land running east to west along the Mediterranean coast, from Rome and Carthage in the west to Constantinople, Antioch, and Alexandria in the east. One result of the Muslim conquests was that Antioch, Alexandria, and Carthage ceased being missionary centers, and Constantinople was limited to expansion toward the north, for the south and the east were ruled by Islam. At roughly the same time, the conversion of the British Isles was so thorough that soon these islands became missionary centers. As the Carolingians came to power, and the Frankish kingdom flourished, there was a new axis of Christian vitality in the west, now running from the British Isles on the north to Rome in the south, with the Frankish kingdom at its center. Constantinople, standing almost alone at the edge of Islam, continued being a center of Christian mission toward central and eastern Europe. That western European axis and the Constantinopolitan nucleus would be the two centers of missionary endeavor during the rest of the Middle Ages.

1. Missions in Northern Europe

(a) The first missions to the Low Countries and to Germany

Although the first attempts to take the gospel to the Low Countries came from the Frankish kingdom, it was English missionaries who were first able to establish Christianity in that area. The first of these missionaries was Wilfrid, who visited the region twice and baptized large numbers of converts. He was followed in 690 by Willibrord, also English, who went to Frisia with eleven companions, as Irish pilgrims had done before. When King Radbod opposed him, Willibrord turned to Charlemagne's ancestor Pippin of Heristal, whose support he gained. He continued to Rome, where the pope blessed his enterprise. Thanks to the military prowess of Pippin, which Radbod feared, Willibrord was able to penetrate into the Low Countries and settle in the city of Utrecht, from where he directed the expansion of Christianity throughout the southern regions of the area. Although after Pippin's death there were struggles in the Frankish kingdom that allowed Radbod to regain some of the land he had lost, soon Charles Martel gained control of the Frankish kingdom and forced Radbod to withdraw.

The most important of the English missionaries who sought the conversion of the Frisians was Boniface, whose true name was Winfrid. He joined the venturesome and wandering spirit of many British monks of his time with a burning passion for the conversion of pagans. Boniface's first visit to the Low Countries coincided with the period of unrest after Pippin's death, and Boniface had to leave the area, but he did not abandon his missionary commitment and soon returned to the land. On this second occasion, he went directly to Rome, where after some hesitation Pope Gregory II blessed his work and armed him with relics that were to accompany him in his mission and aid him in it.

However, this mission was not so much preaching to the pagans as organizing and reforming churches that were already in existence. This was not particularly attractive to Boniface himself. From Rome, he went to Thuringia, where he undertook the task that the pope had entrusted to him. But when he learned that Radbod had died, he decided to return to Frisia, where he worked for several years under Willibrord's guidance. He then returned to Germany, where he would spend most of his life. There, as in Frisia, other missionaries—mostly Franks and Irish—had preceded him, but even so, it was Boniface who attained greatest success in the conversion of the area. After working for some time in Bavaria, he went to Hesse and then back to Rome to be consecrated a bishop before returning to Thuringia. In this latter region, Irish missionaries had already established Christianity, although this particular form of Christianity carried some of the traits of Celtic Christianity that we have already mentioned. Therefore, Boniface's main task was seeking the uniformity of the church throughout the region and joining it more closely with Rome and other churches patterned after it. After a third trip to Rome, Boniface went to the Frankish kingdom, where the authorities entrusted him with the task of reforming the church. Finally, after so many wanderings, he returned to his first love in Frisia, where he was killed by pagans in 754, when he was some eighty years old. By then, Christianity had already developed roots in the Low Countries, and Boniface's death did not stop its growth and expansion.

(b) Charlemagne and the conversion of the Saxons

Although many others before him had employed the force of arms in support of missionary work, Charlemagne far outdid them. His armies contributed to the final conversion of the Frisians after

Boniface's death. But it was particularly in the case of the Saxons that Charlemagne used the power of the sword mercilessly. He fought the Saxons from the beginning of his reign in 771 to his death in 814. Through repeated campaigns, Charlemagne was able to force his rule and his religion over the lands of the Saxons. Rebellion was frequent, and Charlemagne crushed them with his superior military power. After each campaign against the Saxons, Charlemagne forced those who had surrendered to accept baptism, thus turning Christian faith into an instrument for his political purposes, and his policy into an instrument for the expansion of Christianity. Each victory of Charlemagne was followed by the settling of missionaries in the newly acquired regions, with the support of the Frankish authorities, and there they began teaching the recently baptized.

Although the Saxons accepted baptism under coercion, and it is difficult to believe that there was a genuine conversion before they did so, it is remarkable that soon they became some of the staunchest defenders and promoters of Christian faith. Some of the Saxons who were coerced into baptism became convinced Christians and then spread their new faith among other Saxons. Possibly one of the reasons for this is something we will find repeatedly in the history of Christian expansion: although pagans, the Saxons believed that there was a certain power in baptism. In being baptized they were swearing allegiance to the Christian God, and their own gods would henceforth abandon them. This left them with no other option than being faithful to Christianity—no matter how little they understood of their new faith. At any rate, this clearly shows that forced conversion does not always lead to an ephemeral acceptance of Christianity.

One must note that missionary methods affect the content of the message being communicated. In the case of the Saxons, the violent methods of Charlemagne and his Frankish armies were combined with the warlike traditions of the Saxons in order to produce a version of the Christian message full of violent imagery. This may be seen in the anonymous poem *Heliand*, a long piece of almost 6,000 lines, written by a Saxon bard a few years after the forced conversion of the Saxons by the Franks. In this poem, Jesus is the warrior par excellence, the leader of a band of twelve daring adventurers. In the story of his birth, rather than sheep and shepherds, there are warhorses and those who guard them. Given such a reading of the Christian message, it is not surprising that soon the Saxons themselves sought to convert their neighbors by force of arms.

(c) The conversion of the Scandinavians: Ansgar

Shortly after Charlemagne's death, a new series of invasions threatened European civilization. The invaders were the Norse or Scandinavians, a warlike people of Germanic background who would raid neighboring coasts in order to acquire loot. Since they were Germanic people, their religious worldview was similar to that of their closest neighbors. At first, the Norse only conducted rapid raids in which they looted an area, particularly its churches and monasteries, and immediately withdrew, carrying off captives into slavery. Then they began establishing colonies in some of the lands that they had invaded repeatedly and thus settled on eastern England, Ireland, Iceland, and even Greenland. As they settled in Christian lands, they brought ruin to the churches there, but eventually they would accept the faith of those they had conquered and would be baptized.

Since the Norman invasions coincided with the decline of Carolingian power, it was not possible to organize among them a mission such as Boniface had earlier conducted among the Frisians. At first, the only Christians reaching Scandinavian lands were those made captive by the Vikings—as they called their raiders—or an occasional Norseman who had accepted Christianity in his travels.

An outstanding figure early in the ninth century is Ansgar or Askar, a Saxon monk who devoted his life to missionary work among the

Scandinavians. Due to political circumstances, first a Danish king and then a Swedish one requested missionaries from the court of the Frankish king, Louis the Pious. After several unsuccessful attempts to find among the Franks people willing to undertake such a task, Louis decided to send Ansgar, a monk whose monastery represented the ancient tradition of Iona. Ansgar established his center of operations in the city of Hamburg and from there traveled repeatedly to Denmark and Sweden. Thanks to the influence of Louis the Pious, Rome established an archbishopric in Hamburg and named Ansgar as its first occupant. Besides traveling in person to the lands entrusted to him, Ansgar sent missionaries to continue working among the Scandinavians. Also, as he found Danish boys on sale as slaves, he would buy them in order to train them as missionaries. In presenting the gospel, Ansgar depicted Christ as a powerful god who was able to give victory in battle to his followers. Since such a message agreed with the religious and cultural worldview of the Scandinavians, many accepted it. Although there is no record of the continued existence of the Christian communities established in Scandinavia by Ansgar and those working under him, there is no doubt that through this work the Scandinavians began hearing about Christianity, and this prepared the way for future missions. At any rate, the see in Hamburg, founded by Ansgar, continued to serve as a center for missionary work into Scandinavia for a long time, and its role in the conversion of the entire area was remarkable.

(d) The conversion of Scandinavia: Denmark

Just as earlier Carolingian power had played an important role in the conversion of the Saxons, now the newly risen Saxon power became crucial for the conversion of Scandinavia. Early in the tenth century, under the rule of Henry the Fowler, the Saxons began expanding and forming what would eventually become the Holy Roman German Empire, whose first emperor was Otto I, a son of Henry the Fowler. Given the prestige of this nascent empire, which had already turned to Christianity and had begun making that faith less Latin and more Germanic, its Danish neighbors, and eventually other Scandinavians, began feeling the presence of Christianity along their borders. Thus, we shall repeatedly find Scandinavian kings who, partially for reasons of their cultural affinity with Germanic Christianity and partly for other reasons that are not completely clear, accepted the Christian faith and sought to spread it and even impose it in their lands.

The first of these kings was Harald Blaatand (Harald Bluetooth), a powerful king of both Denmark and Norway, who made every effort to establish Christianity in his domains. However, his son Svend I opposed the policies of his father and led a rebellion in which he killed Harald and took over his throne. This led to a pagan reaction.

But then the grandson of Harald Blaatand and son of Svend, whose name was Knud or Canute, returned to Christianity and established it throughout Denmark. Canute began by taking possession of those sections of England that were under Danish rule and later expanded his rule so as to cover Denmark, England, and Norway. He was a convinced Christian, and it is clear that his policies promoted Christianity, although there is no record that he tried to impose baptism on his subjects by military force. His profound faith led him to undertake a pilgrimage to Rome, as well as to ask the Archbishop of Canterbury to consecrate three bishops for Denmark—much to the chagrin of the Archbishop of Hamburg—and to take measures for the Christian instruction of his subjects. Some seventy years after Canute's death, Denmark had its own ecclesiastical hierarchy, headed by an archbishop in the city of Lund—which now belongs to Sweden.

(e) The conversion of Scandinavia: Norway

Although there were earlier Christians in Norway, the conversion of that land was a result of policy and coercion on the part of some of its Christian kings. The first of these was Haakon the Good, whose father had founded the kingdom of Norway, and who had been baptized in England. Haakon sought the conversion of the Norse, but most rejected baptism and insisted on their king's obligation to partake in the ancient pagan rites and sacrifices. Eventually Haakon yielded, partaking of the sacrificial meat and drink of the religion of his ancestors. It is said that shortly before his death he returned to Christianity. There followed a period of unrest after which Harald Blaatand of Denmark gained control of Norway. However, Harald's efforts to establish his Christian faith in these territories did not have great success. The two Norwegian kings who finally implanted Christianity in their territories were Olaf Tryggvason and Olaf Haraldson.

Olaf Tryggvason, who was born in exile and spent his youth in Russia and England, tried to impose Christianity when, late in the tenth century, he managed to take possession of the kingdom of Norway, founded by his great grandfather, Harald Haarfager. His methods were violent, and those who refused to receive baptism were often sent into exile or received physical punishment. He would also make concessions to the members of an assembly that was responsible for the government of a particular region, on condition that the assembly would decide that the region would become Christian. It was also under his leadership that Christianity entered the Scandinavian colonies in Iceland and then in Greenland, so that eventually it reached the coasts of North America with Leif Ericson—in the region that Leif called Vinland. However, this was followed by a strong reaction to his policies. This reaction was supported by King Svend I of Denmark and resulted in a battle in which Olaf lost both his kingdom and his life. Norway then passed into the hands of Svend and the pagan reaction.

Nineteen years later, Olaf Haraldson reestablished Norwegian independence and continued the work of conversion begun by Olaf Tryggvason. His methods were not quite as violent as those of his predecessor, although on occasion he coerced his subjects into baptism. Once again there was a rebellion against his policies, with the result that Olaf lost the throne and Norway was added to the possessions of the Danish king Canute. But Canute himself was also a Christian, and the conversion of the Norse would continue.

(f) The conversion of Scandinavia: Sweden

As in the cases of Denmark and Norway, the conversion of Sweden took place through the support of a number of rulers. Although one must remember that Ansgar had traveled through the area much earlier and that there were Christian communities of which little is known, the first Christian king seems to have been Olov Skotkonung. He and most of his successors were Christians and sought to lead their subjects to accept their faith. There does not seem to have been much physical coercion in this enterprise. Since the conversion took place approximately 100 years after the conversion of Denmark and Norway, it was favored by a movement for religious renewal that had begun to flourish under the leadership of Hildebrand, better known as Pope Gregory VII, and later of Cistercian monasticism. As a result the conversion of Sweden was both more rapid and more profound. It is important to note that the method that was followed in the conversion of Scandinavia reflected the sociological, cultural, and political structures of the region. It was customary for Scandinavians to take all-important decisions to an assembly of the leaders of the area. In that assembly, known as the *Thing*, decisions made were expected to be accepted by all. Repeatedly—and particularly in the case of Iceland, which has not been discussed here, but whose conversion was simply a decision of the general assembly or *Althing*—the kings or missionaries who sought the conversion of the community posed the matter before the *Thing*, and the assembly would debate and decide for the entire community whether it would accept Christianity. This missionary method has been used in other parts of the world and at different times. In that method, what is sought is not the individual conversion of people who are used to more collective thinking. In this case, what is done is to accept the cultural, political, and sociological views and practices of the people whose conversion is sought, and the gospel is presented as a message, not to individuals, but to the community as a whole.

2. Missions in Central Europe

As the Scandinavians accepted Christianity, the conversion of the Germanic peoples who had begun invading western Europe at the end of antiquity and the beginning of the Middle Ages was practically complete. There were, however, other non-Germanic groups in Europe who had come there as part of the great migration that pushed the Germanic nations toward the Roman Empire. Most of these were Slavs, although there were also others such as the Avars and the Magyars or Hungarians. During the period we are now studying, Western Christianity began moving into the lands held by these various peoples. Naturally, this geographic expansion was later and slower than the movement into Germanic lands, for these other regions were more distant from Western Europe, culturally as well as geographically. Thus, during the period we are now considering, the conversion of these various nations did not reach the same levels as the conversion of those of Germanic origin. Also, since borders in eastern Europe were even more fluid than in western Europe, it is difficult to organize a detailed study of the expansion of Christianity in these areas. Finally, the process of conversion of the various regions in eastern Europe so repeats itself that it suffices to offer some general comments and to say a word about the main missionaries into that area.

The first Christian missions among the people who had settled in eastern Europe took place during the great flourishing of Carolingian power. Later, as the Carolingian Empire was dismembered, the growing power of Saxony and eventually of the Holy Roman (by this time Germanic) Empire came to occupy the vacuum left by Frankish decline. It is also important to note that given its geographical position, between Rome and Constantinople, this area received missionaries from both sees, which vied for authority over the newly opened missionary lands. For this reason, in studying the expansion of Christianity into central Europe, three factors must always be remembered: first, the political and imperialistic policies, earlier of the Carolingians and then of the Holy Roman Empire; second, the rivalry between Rome and Constantinople; and finally, the expansionist interests of the Byzantine Empire.

The most numerous among the various peoples that settled in central Europe were the Slavs. Christianity first appeared among the Slavs as a result of their contacts with their Christian neighbors—the Saxons to the west and the Byzantine Empire to the south. However, the most remarkable missionary effort in that area was led by two brothers, Constantine and Methodius, in the ninth century. These two brothers began their work under the aegis of Byzantine Christianity but in the end worked under Roman auspices. We shall look at the history of these two brothers both because of the importance of their work itself and because it illustrates several of the general characteristics of work among Slavs that have already been mentioned. Constantine—whom history knows as Cyril—and Methodius already had some experience as missionaries. Cyril had debated with Muslims, and he as well as Methodius had been part of a mission in Crimea. It is also possible that they both knew Slavonic before leaving for Moravia, for they were raised in Thessalonika, where there were many Slavic inhabitants.

The missionary work of Cyril and Methodius among the Slavs began when Moravian prince Ratislav asked Byzantine emperor Michael III to send Christian missionaries. It is difficult to know the reasons behind such a request. Perhaps Ratislav was trying to counterbalance the influence of his western neighbors, whose combination of Christian mission and political imperialism seemed to endanger his independence. Perhaps he was simply attracted by the prestige of Patriarch Photius, one of the most erudite men ever to occupy the Constantinopolitan see. At any rate, Emperor Michael III sent Cyril and Methodius in response to Ratislav's request. Although the two brothers worked for the conversion and the Christian instruction of the people to whom they had been sent, the most important part of their work was the development of an alphabet whereby it was possibly to reduce Slavonic to writing and therefore translate the first Christian books. Apparently, even before they set out in their mission, Cyril had already begun translating the Bible into Slavonic. Once they were in Moravia, both he and Methodius continued that task. This is one of hundreds of examples in which missionary commitment has led Christians to develop the necessary means to reduce a language to writing and to establish an intercultural dynamic whose effect on the contextualization of Christian faith has not always been understood.

Besides the Bible, Cyril and Methodius translated the liturgy of the church. This is important because the resulting debate illustrates the growing tension between Western missionary enterprises and those coming from Byzantium. In the church of the East it was customary to celebrate the liturgy in the language of each different population. In contrast, the church of the West had become accustomed to celebrating the liturgy only in Latin. For these reasons, joined to political rivalry, the Germanic bishops who were beginning to work among the Slavs opposed the work of Cyril and Methodius—even though Rome itself had authorized the use of a translated liturgy. The result of that tension was a series of vicissitudes that need not detain us here, but that placed Cyril and Methodius within a constant maelstrom of rivalry between Rome and Constantinople and between the political interests of Byzantium and those of the Holy Roman Empire. The brothers themselves sought to lessen this tension by traveling repeatedly to Rome and securing papal support for a mission that had originally come from the church of the East. But this did not prevent the Germanic bishops of neighboring areas to continue opposing Cyril and Methodius both openly and through political intrigue.

Cyril and Methodius died before the conversion of the Slavs had been completed. However, their translations and particularly the alphabet that they had prepared, known as the Cyrillic alphabet, were instruments that would long serve to take Christianity to Slavs. The Cyrillic alphabet is still employed by several languages of Slavic origin, such as Russian.

After the deaths of Cyril and Methodius, missionary work among the Slavs continued being a bone of contention between the Byzantine church and its western counterpart. It was particularly in Russia that the eastern church succeeded in its missionary work—but the story of how that came about belongs elsewhere in this chapter. In the western regions of Slavic territory—what is today Poland, Estonia, Lithuania, and Latvia—it was the West, making use of the power of the Holy Roman Empire, that achieved the formal conversion of the population.

It is interesting to note that the Saxons, who a century earlier had been forcibly led to Christianity by the arms of Charlemagne, were now applying the same method to take Christianity to their neighbors to the east. Beginning in the time of Henry the Fowler, but particularly with the great flourishing of Saxon power under Otto I, the various Slavic peoples were forced to accept Christianity by the superior military might of their Germanic neighbors. In vast areas, particularly along the coast of the Baltic Sea, conversion took place in a way that simply repeated what had happened to the Saxons under Charlemagne.

There was, however, another factor that contributed to the conversion of the Slavs. This was the joining of nationalist sentiment with Christianity. Poland offers a particular case in which Christianity played a central role in the unification of the country. The same may be said about the Hungarians, although they are not a Slavic people. Christianity played an important role in the development of Hungarian national sentiment, particularly under the leadership of kings Geisa and Stephen.

3. The Expansion of Byzantine Christianity

As a result of the advance of Islam, the expansion of Byzantine Christianity was limited to its northwest, in the Balkans, and to the north into what is today Russia.

(a) The conversion of Bulgaria

The first remarkable episode in the expansion of Byzantine Christianity during the period we are now studying was the conversion of Bulgaria. Although the land had already seen Latin and Byzantine missionaries, Christianity there received its greatest impulse when King Boris accepted baptism. Since Bulgaria stood geographically between Western and Byzantine Christianity, both had sought to bring Bulgaria into their sphere of influence. At a point when the Bulgarians were engaged in war along their western borders, the Byzantines took advantage of the opportunity in order to invade Bulgaria and demand that King Boris accept baptism and declare himself a subject of Emperor Michael III. Boris took these conditions seriously and promoted Christianity throughout his lands. Perhaps part of his purpose was to undercut the power of the Bulgarian nobility, who opposed monarchial centralization and defended the ancestral pagan customs of the Bulgarians. Not unexpectedly, the nobles rebelled, but Boris crushed the uprising. From that point on, baptisms were numerous, while Byzantium and Rome vied for hegemony over the new Christian land. After many ups and downs, Boris opted for Eastern Christianity, which in turn responded by consecrating a Bulgarian archbishop. This sealed a close relationship between Bulgaria and Constantinople. When Boris abdicated in order to withdraw to a monastery, he was succeeded by his son Simeon. Although at first Simeon had to face a civil war, he was able to consolidate his power and proceed with the conversion of his subjects. Since Simeon himself had been a monk and had a profound understanding of the nature of Christianity, the conversion of Bulgaria was more thorough than was the case in other nations that also converted en masse. Simeon saw to it that Christian books were translated into Bulgarian, and he had recourse to some disciples of Cyril and Methodius who helped him in the conversion and instruction of his Slavic subjects. He also established and defended the independence of Bulgaria, proclaiming himself emperor and claiming for the head of the Bulgarian church the title of patriarch, which made the church in that land autocephalic—that is, having its own head.

(b) The conversion of Russia

The most remarkable Byzantine expansion during the period that we are studying took place toward the north into what is today Russia. This region was populated by Slavs, but these were under the rule of Scandinavian invaders who had settled first in Novgorod and later in Kiev. At roughly the same time their relatives in Scandinavia were accepting Christianity, the lords of Kiev were doing likewise, although their Christianity was related to Byzantium rather than to Rome.

It is impossible to know how Christianity first entered the kingdom of Kiev. In Constantinople were Russian soldiers serving the emperor, and it is quite likely that some of these accepted Christianity while living in Byzantine territory and later took it back with them as they returned to the land of their birth. Also Patriarch Photius and later Emperor Basil I sent missionaries to the Scandinavian kingdom of Kiev. At any rate, it was in the middle of the tenth century that Queen Olga converted to Christianity and began a policy of seeking the conversion of her subjects. Most of her contacts were with Western Christians, particularly through Emperor Otto I, and the results of her work are not known.

It was Olga's grandson Vladimir who first turned Kiev into a Christian kingdom. This was toward the end of the tenth century, but it is impossible to know the reasons that led Vladimir to accept Christianity and even less to know why he opted for Byzantium rather than

Rome. There is also little agreement as to how Vladimir sought the conversion of his subjects. Some sources claim that, like the Scandinavian kings of Norway, Vladimir made use of force in order to coerce his subjects into accepting baptism. According to other sources, his work was more pacific, consisting above all in founding monasteries, establishing ecclesiastical courts, importing relics and icons, and promoting missionary work. We are told that he ordered the destruction of a statue of the god Perun which sat atop the highest mountain in Kiev with a shining silver head and golden whiskers. Later his son Jaroslav continued his work, taking particular interest in the production of Christian literature in the language of the people. From that point on, Eastern Orthodox Christianity became the religion of Russia and was supported by the state until 1917.

Important in the evangelization of the Finnish tribes in northern Russia were the "colonizing monks." Once again, monasticism became a vehicle for evangelization and the expansion of a cultural influence. Some Orthodox historians point out that these colonizing monks practiced a spirituality in which one abandons the pleasures of the world in order later to return to that world bearing the gospel. One should also mention the work of Tryphon, a layman who brought the gospel to the Lapps in northern Russia.

Although at first the conversion of Russia seems to have been quite superficial, one must point out that when the Mongols invaded the land in the thirteenth century, Christianity had become one of the pillars of nascent Russian national identity and that after the period of Mongol rule it was even more entwined with Russian identity than it had been before.

As time went by, Russian Christianity became stronger than its mother church in Byzantium, to the point that Moscow began claiming for itself the title of "the Third Rome of Christianity" after Rome and Constantinople.

4. Christianity in the East

During the period we are studying, Christianity remained relatively stagnant in the areas that had been conquered by Islam. However, Nestorian Christianity continued expanding northward into central Asia. There are records of a Turkish king who accepted Christianity late in the eighth century and also of Christian penetration during the eleventh century among the nomads of Chinese Turkestan.

In China, an emperor who favored Taoism ordered a persecution that destroyed the small Christian communities that had resulted from the work of Alopen and probably other missionaries.

At any rate, the scarcity of concrete data about the expansion of Christianity in these areas shows that, even though there was some expansion, this was not sufficiently lasting to leave a record of its existence.

5. The Offensive against Islam

During the time we are studying, Christians did little in order to try to convert Muslims through pacific means or through verbal persuasion. There were, however, three important attempts to recover by military means the land that the Muslim invaders had taken. These are three: the Spanish Reconquista, the establishment of the Norman kingdom of Sicily, and the Crusades.

(a) The Spanish Reconquista

Although the Muslim armies were able to conquer almost the entire Iberian Peninsula, there were always small centers of resistance in the Cantabrian Mountains and the Pyrenees. Those who resisted in the Cantabrian Mountains were descendants of the ancient Visigoths. Scarcely ten years after the Moorish invasion, Asturias entered the picture as a center of resistance against the Moors. In the Pyrenees, opposition to Muslim rule was due mostly to the influence of the neighboring Frankish kingdom. From the mountains of Asturias, Christians descended into Leon, where they established a new center of resistance. Later, when Castile became independent from the monarchy of Leon, this would give rise to the most important Spanish state. On the foot of the Pyrenees, the origins of Navarre, Aragon, and Catalonia show Frankish influence.

The first battles of the Reconquista took place north of the river Douro. Apparently, most of these battles were much smaller than some chroniclers would have us believe. The first of these was the Battle of Covadonga, which took place early in the eighth century, and which Muslim chroniclers completely ignore. Shortly thereafter, dissension spread among the Muslims, and their Christian enemies made use of the moment in order to advance toward the south. Also the Franks, for various political reasons, crossed the Pyrenees in a campaign that history remembers mostly because of the massacre of Roncesvalles, in which the Franks fell into a Basque ambush, and which was commemorated in the *Chanson de Roland.*

It was beginning in the eleventh century that the most important battles of the Reconquista take place. In 1085, Christians took the ancient capital of Toledo. After that disaster, the Moors were reinforced by the Almoravids, who crossed from Africa and repeatedly defeated the Christian armies. But their own inner disagreements made it impossible for them to put an end to the Spanish Reconquista. Late in the twelfth century, a new invasion from Africa, this time by the Islamic militants known as Almohads, once again threatened the small Christian kingdoms. At that point, King Alfonso VII of Castile responded by organizing a great crusade against Muslim power. Although few crossed the Pyrenees in response to what he had hoped would be a call to all Christendom, Alfonso did gain the support of the kingdoms of Navarre and Aragon. On July 16, 1212, in the Battle of Navas de Tolosa, the Muslims were completely defeated. From that point on, Christian victories would follow one after another, being interrupted only by disagreements among Christians, who often fought among themselves. Cordova was taken by King San Fernando in 1236, and then he took Seville in 1248. But it was only on the second of January in 1492, when Granada finally surrendered before the forces of Isabella and Ferdinand—known as the Catholic monarchs—that the Reconquista of the Iberian Peninsula was complete.

So goes the official and traditional narrative. However, the story is much more complex than that, for the Reconquista was neither as direct nor as purposeful as it is frequently described. On the contrary, in most of the wars within the Iberian Peninsula at that time, religion played only a secondary role, and there were frequent alliances between Christian and Muslim rulers—sometimes to make war on a neighbor who might be either Christian or Muslim. El Cid, the legendary hero of the Reconquista, did on occasion join Muslim armies fighting against Christians.

Although eventually Spain came to be known for the religious intolerance of its government and citizenry, during the period of the Reconquista, Christians and Muslims alike showed a high degree of tolerance. There were Christians living among the Moors (the Mozarabs) as well as Moors living among Christians (the Mudejars). In most of the lands conquered by Christian rulers, Muslims were allowed to keep their mosques and their ancient customs and traditions. There was a similar policy regarding Jews. In spite of such apparent tolerance, there certainly was frequent pressure on both Jews and Muslims to embrace Christianity, and there were numerous Moors and Jews abandoning their ancient faith and accepting baptism. It was toward the end of the fifteenth century, when the Catholic monarchs ruled in Spain and when Cardinal Ximenes de Cisneros led the church, that Spain became intolerant in religious matters and that the expulsion of Jews and Moors was decreed. By then many of the Muslims who had accepted baptism—usually called *moriscos*—had assimilated into the general Spanish population and had become constituent elements.

Furthermore, after the expulsion of the Moors—and even to this day—many signs remained of Moorish effect on the Spanish culture, architecture, and language.

(b) The Norman kingdom of Sicily

During the first half of the ninth century, Sicily had been taken by Muslim forces from Tunisia. In the eleventh century, it was conquered once again for Christianity, although that was not the actual purpose of those who retook the island. The constant Norman search for lands to explore and conquer took them to southern Italy, where they established a Scandinavian county in the region of Calabria. Later in the eleventh century, when the Muslim rulers in Sicily were fighting among themselves, Calabrian Norman Count Roger I seized the opportunity to invade the island. The campaign lasted eleven years and ended with the fall of Palermo, which made Roger master of Sicily. His successor, Roger II, was crowned king by a pope who was vying with another rival for the Roman see and coveted Roger's support. This gave rise to the Kingdom of the Two Sicilies, which would subsist until the modern age. The Normans did not invade Sicily in order to implant Christianity in it, and for over a hundred years the island included Western and Byzantine Christians, Muslims, and Jews, all living in relative harmony. In the thirteenth century, Sicily fell into the hands of Emperor Frederick II of Germany, and this brought to the island religious intolerance and political decline. It took less than a century for all religions except Roman Christianity to be expelled from the land.

(c) The Crusades

The Crusades were the most important of all attempts to recover through the use of arms the lands that the Muslims had conquered before. Their importance does not lie, however, in their direct results, which were ephemeral, but rather in the persistence of the crusading ideals through the centuries and especially in their tragic effect on relations between Christians and Muslims.

Although there were many other factors contributing to the Crusades, the starting point for the movement is usually placed on the call that Pope Urban II issued in the city of Clermont, that a Christian army should march eastward in order to retake the holy places from the hands of Muslims: "I declare it to those who are present; I order that it be proclaimed among those who are not: Christ commands it!" This eloquent call took place in 1095. A series of events and movements had awakened western Europe's interest in the Holy Land. Pilgrims returned, bringing home stories and relics of the holy places. Devotion was inclined toward the contemplation of the humanity of Christ, a humanity that had lived in the Holy Land. Constantinople, the ancient Christian bulwark in the east, was threatened by the Seljuk Turks. In the West, landless young noblemen expressed their warlike spirit in constant warfare. Why not vent that warring impulse toward the East, joining it with the mystical interests that the Holy Land aroused? In all of this, the missionary thrust had no role. Urban's call seemed to be confirmed by a series of signs and wonders, and soon all of Europe was afire with the notion of a crusade. There was first a series of popular crusades in which disorganized mobs whose only purpose was to reach Jerusalem began marching eastward. Along the way, they ransacked the lands where they traveled, massacring the local population, and particularly any Jews they found. Most of these groups vanished before reaching Constantinople, as a result of their own disorder and of the difficulties of the land to be traversed. What was left of that early popular movement eventually joined the First Crusade, which came shortly thereafter under the leadership of several European noblemen.

It is not necessary to retell here the entire history of the Crusades. Let it suffice to say that the First Crusade consisted of various groups that joined in Constantinople, then crossed the Bosporus (today known as the Istanbul Strait) and followed a long trek through Asia Minor.

The ambitions of the various leaders of the Crusade became ever more pronounced, to the point that one of them, Baldwin, finally left the rest of the expedition and marched on Edessa, which he took in 1098 and founded a Christian state under his rule. The same year, after a long siege that finally ended through the betrayal of an Armenian who lived in the city, Antioch fell to the crusaders. A year later they reached Jerusalem, which was taken after a siege of slightly over a month. With the conquest of that city and the creation of the Christian Kingdom of Jerusalem under the rule of Godfrey of Bouillon, the First Crusade accomplished its purpose of reconquering the holy places of Christianity. Along the road to Jerusalem, it had also created the Christian states of Edessa, Antioch, and Tripoli. All of this was done through much bloodshed and cruelty, with repeated massacres among the civilians and other atrocities.

The seeming success of the First Crusade was due partly to the internal weakness of the Turks and partly to the rivalry between them and the Fatimite Arabs. The crusade convinced Christendom that it was possible through military force to regain the territories lost to the armies of Islam. It was for this reason that the notion itself of a crusade became so tantalizing for medieval mentality. It was also the reason why Western Europe continued sending expeditions toward the east, even though none of them had the success of the first. The fall of Edessa in 1144 prompted the Second and Third Crusades. The second was a total disaster. The third only managed to retake the city of Acre. The Fourth Crusade was also disastrous, for instead of following its initial purpose of attacking Saladin in his headquarters in Egypt, it took and sacked the Christian city of Constantinople.

Since the Fourth Crusade imposed a western emperor and a western patriarch in Constantinople, this seemed to have healed the longstanding schism between Rome and Constantinople. But in truth all that it accomplished was to continue weakening the Byzantine Empire, which had long served as Europe's bulwark against eastern invasions.

When Constantinople managed to regain its independence from Rome and the West, the breach between it and the papal see had become even deeper, and its political, economic, and military power had been irreparably damaged, with the eventual consequence of the disappearance of the Byzantine Empire.

Although the crusading ideal captivated the mind of Christendom for centuries, it was only the First Crusade, and to a very small degree the Third Crusade, that achieved their military objectives. At any rate, the Crusades were an absolute failure as an attempt to expand Christianity into Muslim territories. All the states that the Crusades established in the Middle East soon disappeared. The Crusades also increased the hostility and even hatred between Muslims and Christians, to the point that even in the twenty-first century their consequences are being felt.

Even so, in other areas the ideal of the Crusades was employed in the process of evangelizing non-Christian lands. This was true in Finland, Spain, and, in a way, the Western Hemisphere. But the latter events belong elsewhere in our narrative.

C. From the Renaissance of the Twelfth Century to the End of the Middle Ages

1. Western Europe

For reasons that need not be discussed here, the twelfth century witnessed a revival in the life and religion of western Europe. Ironically, contacts with the Muslims in Spain and in the Near East through the Crusades were one of the factors that helped widen the horizons of Western Christians. Trade increased and so did the cities and the rate of mobility of the population. New currents of thought were penetrating the Christian world—particularly the philosophy of Aristotle, which first arrived through translations made in Spain. It was the time of the early flourishing of Gothic architecture and of the first scholastics. The power of the papacy was rising. All of this was joined to the profound piety that we find in persons such as St. Bernard of Clairvaux. This led to the flowering of the thirteenth century, which is the golden period of the Middle Ages. This was the time of the great scholastics and of Innocent III. It was the time that saw the rise of universities of Paris, Oxford, and Bologna. But it was above all the age of the mendicant orders of St. Francis of Assisi and of St. Dominic.

(a) St. Francis and the Order of Friars Minor

Saint Francis, whose true name was John, was born late in the twelfth century in the Italian town of Assisi. He showed profound sensitivity from his early youth. His devotion focused mostly on the contemplation of the sufferings of Christ. He was almost thirty years old when he felt called to marry "Madame Poverty" and to devote his life to itinerant preaching. He began this task in his own hometown of Assisi, and it is interesting to note that in this case the saying was not fulfilled, that one cannot be a prophet in one's own land, for soon some of his friends joined him. They, like him, sold all that they had and gave it to the poor in order to be absolutely free for the task of preaching that they were undertaking. Shortly thereafter, Francis and some of his followers went to Rome, where they obtained the approval of Innocent III and thus became the Order of Friars Minor.

In the new situation in Europe in the thirteenth century, with cities whose growth put great stress on the traditional system of parishes, the Order of Friars Minor filled an urgent need. Their flexibility and their zeal allowed them to meet needs that the hierarchical and territorial structure of the church could not. Fifteen years after its founding, the new Order had reached practically every region of Europe and even beyond that continent. It is also important to point out that because the Franciscans—as the members of the Order of Friars Minor were popularly known—took vows of poverty, this allowed them to work among the poor and the dispossessed and to understand some of their woes and penuries. This was one of the reasons why some Franciscans, and later also some Dominicans, became defenders of the poor and the oppressed, as would become clear centuries later, during the European conquest of the Americas.

Preaching to non-Christians was always one of the main interests and goals of St. Francis. He repeatedly visited Muslim territories and gained interviews with their leaders, particularly the Sultan Ayyubid saultan al-Kamil, whom he met in 1219. His simple faith and loving attitude inspired many Muslim leaders to listen to him with respect. With similar respect, reflecting his own personal meetings with Muslim leaders, Francis proposed approaching Muslims through pacific means. This may be seen in his *Rule*, which he gave his followers in 1221, and whose last chapter deals with "those who go among the Saracens and other infidels."

In a few years, Franciscan missionaries could be found from Morocco in the west to Beijing in the east. Among Muslims, Franciscans continued work in the Holy Land long after the failure of the Crusades. Through the centuries, this work in the Holy Land has produced more than 2,000 martyrs. Also, in Morocco and in southern Spain, which was then under Muslim rule, many Franciscans spilled their blood in witness to the Lord. Other Franciscans traveled toward the east—among them John of Plano Carpino, Odoric of Udine, and, above all, John of Montecorvino. In 1275, John of Montecorvino began a series of missionary attempts into the east that would continue until his death. He served as papal legate before the sultan of Persia, who after the Mongol invasions ruled the lands that had formerly belonged to the Abbasid caliphs of Baghdad. He was also a legate before the emperor of Ethiopia. Later he went to India, where he founded a Christian community in the area of Madras. He moved on to Beijing, in China, which was the stage for the rest of his life as a missionary.

In Beijing, John of Montecorvino was granted some freedom of action, as well as a measure of respect from the civil government. Given the success of his work, he was soon followed by Arnold of Cologne and others, and the pope founded an archbishopric of Beijing, which he entrusted to John of Montecorvino. The missionaries that followed were mostly Franciscans who had been consecrated as bishops for various areas, and through them John extended his work to other regions of China. It is said that his work was so expressive of love and respect that after his death he was venerated both by those who were Christians and by those who were not.

Raymond Lull never became a Franciscan, but he was inspired by the spirit of St. Francis, and therefore this may be the best place to discuss his work and his missionary views. Although there is much legend woven around his life, it seems safe to say that Lull was born in Majorca around the year 1235. He grew up among the aristocracy of that island and was slightly over twenty years old when he married a member of that aristocracy. Even after his marriage, Lull continued leading a libertine life, as he himself tells us in his *Liber de contemplacio en Deu,* until he was converted when he was thirty years old. He was writing a love poem when he had a repeated vision of the crucified Christ. This made him repent of his ways and undertake a new life whose main purposes would be missionary work among nonbelievers, the production of books refuting their views, and founding monasteries for the training of missionaries. He spent nine years studying Latin and Arabic, thus preparing for his mission. Then he went to Mt. Randa, where we are told that he received much of his wisdom through a direct illumination from God. For this reason he is often called "The Illumined Doctor." Then followed several visits to the main capitals of Europe, especially Paris and Rome, trying to convince the authorities to establish centers for the study of Eastern languages that could serve for the training of those who would later be missionaries. He spent the rest of his life in this endeavor, which he interrupted only to visit Africa in order to preach to Muslims. He was expelled on two occasions, and on the third occasion he was stoned before being sent back to Majorca. It is said that he died in the ship that was taking him home, as a result of the wounds he had suffered. Although Lull never saw the fulfillment of his dream of having centers of study for mission, his work would still bear fruit as such centers were founded throughout Europe.

(b) Saint Dominic and the Order of Preachers

Although during this period it was the order founded by St. Francis that obtained greatest geographic expansion, the Order of Preachers founded by St. Dominic of Guzman also made a significant contribution to missionary work. Saint Dominic had been born in Castile and was an Augustinian monk before feeling called to found the order that is commonly named after him. This call came when, in the company of his bishop, Don Diego de Acevedo, he traveled in southern France. The heresy of the Cathars was then flourishing in the area, and in order to stop it, the church and powerful states in northern France had declared a crusade. The cruelty of the crusaders, whose motives were political and economic more than religious, did little to convert the Cathars. Don Diego and Dominic decided that the only way to face heresy with success was persuasion and that this should be the task of monks of profound devotion and vast erudition. When Don Diego returned to his diocese, Dominic remained in charge of this endeavor and began organizing and extending it to such a point that, in 1215, Pope Innocent III acknowledged his followers as a legitimate order within the Roman church.

In contrast to the Franciscans, the Dominicans—as members of the Order of Preachers are commonly called—from the very beginning underscored the importance of study as a means to carry forth their mission. They therefore became known by their work in the universities—although one must also note that Franciscans soon established their presence in those centers of study. Some of the most distinguished theologians of the thirteenth century, such as Albert the Great and St. Thomas Aquinas, were members of this order. However, in spite of their interests in study and erudition, the Dominicans always kept their missionary goal in mind. Thus, for instance, it is quite likely that the *Summa contra Gentiles* of Thomas Aquinas was written as a manual of theology for missionaries in Muslim lands.

The Dominicans became particularly known for their missionary work among Jews and Muslims. Obviously, such work called for strong intellectual and theological training. One of the best-known Dominican missionaries among Muslims was William of Tripoli, who preached in that city and managed to convert many Muslims—a success that was partly due to the presence of the crusaders in Tripoli.

It was among Jews, and particularly in Spain, that the Dominicans proved most successful. One of their earliest missionaries among Jews was Raymond of Peñaforte; but he was far surpassed by St. Vincent Ferrer. Vincent was born in Valencia in 1350, and he joined the Order of Preachers when he was eighteen years old. He soon stood out for his gifts as a preacher and as a student, and in 1385, he was already a respected leader in his native town. His work as a preacher among Jews began in 1390, when Cardinal Pedro de Luna, who later became pope, took Vincent with him in a sojourn across the Iberian Peninsula. Beginning at that point, Vincent undertook the task of preaching to Jews and seeking their conversion. Among his converts was a rabbi who eventually became a bishop.

The biography of St. Vincent is full of visions that he repeatedly understood as new calls from God. One of those visions, in 1398, ordered him to preach the imminence of the final judgment. From that date until his death in 1419, he traveled all over Europe, preaching his message of the immediate return of Jesus. Shortly after his death, he was declared to be a saint and came to be known as "the apostle to the Jews."

(c) Women as agents of mission

The important contribution of women to the mission of the church during this period deserves particular attention. That contribution is frequently ignored, in part because mission is understood in terms of traveling to distant places, which was not a possibility for most women at the time. However, if mission is understood also in the sense of fully living out the gospel, showing the love of Christ particularly among people who have been marginalized and dispossessed, medieval women did play an important role in mission.

An example of this is the work of the "Beguines," women who, with no official ecclesiastical backing, would gather in order to share a common life of voluntary poverty, devotion, ascetic discipline, and service to the needy. Their extra official convents, or "beguinages," frequently became centers for feeding the hungry, places of medical attention for the poor, hospitals for lepers, and so on.

The earliest beguinages were founded before the orders of St. Francis and St. Dominic. Furthermore, there are strong indications that their practice of poverty, simplicity of life, and service to the needy influenced both St. Francis and St. Clare—who would found the feminine branch of the Franciscan order.

The Beguines were increasingly recognized by the church hierarchy, until Gregory IX, in the thirteenth century, acknowledged them officially. However, that papal endorsement also began sapping the originality and flexibility that had characterized them in earlier times.

A woman who was influenced by the Beguines, as well as by St. Francis and St. Clare, was St. Elizabeth of Hungary (1207–31), whose father was king over that country, and who married the Landgrave of Thuringia. Her acts of charity were such that when her husband died, the new landgrave expelled her from court, claiming that she was spending too much on charity. She then sought refuge in Marburg, where she turned all her possessions over to the poor and devoted herself to the care of the sick and the dispossessed. There are several feminine organizations providing social and medical services that see her as their forerunner or even distant founder.

Beyond such famous cases, there are also hundreds of other women who could be cited as proof that, through their commitment to the gospel and obedience to it, women became outstanding participants in mission within their own communities.

(d) The continuation of the crusading ideal

The crusading ideal continued playing an important role in European life throughout the Middle Ages and well into the Modern Age. Of the true Crusades—that is, those that went to the Holy Land—only the first one achieved military success. But the crusading idea had become so rooted in the medieval mind that it would repeatedly sprout again. We have already seen that in Spain the war of Reconquista took on the nature of a crusade, even though the Reconquista itself had begun before the First Crusade was proclaimed. Later another crusade was launched in France, although no longer against Muslims, but now against the Cathars or Albigensians in the south of that land. During the period we are studying, crusades were employed to expand Christianity toward central Europe, particularly along the shores of the Baltic and as far north as Finland. Various crusades conquered Livonia and then Prussia, Lithuania, and part of Estonia. These were led by a military monastic order known as the Teutonic Knights. Although this order had some monastic characteristics, its members were soldiers who would invade an area, conquer it in the name of Christ, and then rule and exploit it for their own benefit, usually ignoring the interests of the original inhabitants. King Eric the Good of Sweden conquered Finland by means of a crusade. There were also crusades against other Christians, some apparently without premeditation, as in the case of the Fourth Crusade, which took and sacked Constantinople, and others quite intentionally, such as the one against Emperor Frederic II.

2. The Expansion of Eastern Christianity

One should not be surprised that the occupation of Constantinople by the crusaders, and then the constant pressure of the Turks, did not allow that ancient Christian city to undertake a far-reaching missionary task. Constantinople was now surrounded by Muslims on one side and Western Christians on the other. Therefore, it was the Russian church that now continued expanding Orthodox Christianity. Although at first the conversion of Russia was rather superficial, Christianity slowly penetrated the life of the nation, from its highest nobility to the common people. When the area was invaded by the Mongols in the thirteenth century, Christianity became a symbol of national unity and of Russian resistance. Since the Mongols tolerated Christianity, it was able to expand under the relative calm that the conquerors had imposed on the surrounding lands. Toward the east, Russian Christianity reached the Mongolian capital of Sarai. Toward the north, it reached the Finns and Lapps. At first, most of this expansion was not the result of a conscious missionary impulse. It was mostly a matter of some Russian Christians who, seeking not to live under Mongolian rule, migrated toward the north, where they established hermitages that would then become monasteries and eventually became also centers of population. This promoted contact between Russian Christians and those who had not been converted, thus resulting in a new missionary thrust.

The best known of Russian missionaries among the Finns was St. Stephen of Pema. Stephen was a scholar who left his books behind with the purpose of taking the good news of the gospel to the Finns living north of Russia. Like so many before him and also after him, Stephen reduced the language of the Finns to writing. He also sought the economic and social improvement of his flock, defending it from foreign invasion, and helped it to find food in times of scarcity. His prestige grew as miracles were attributed to him, and he was soon able to baptize many Finns. Among them he founded monasteries and trained and established a native clergy. After his death, his disciples, St. Jerome and St. Pitirim, continued his work, which they both sealed with martyrdom. But in spite of these deaths, Christianity continued expanding in the area thanks to the memory of St. Stephen and his earliest companions.

Although few details are known, Russian Christianity also expanded among the Lapps and toward the shores of the White Sea. Christian Orthodoxy was established in Lithuania through Russian conquests in the thirteenth and fourteenth centuries, but when the Lithuanians became part of the kingdom of Poland, the Orthodox Church that had been founded there became Roman Catholic.

D. General Considerations

As we come to the end of our quick review of Christian expansion during the Middle Ages, some general remarks about that expansion are in order. It was during the Middle Ages that Christianity took root in northern Europe and extended as far as China and Russia. It was also during this time that Christianity lost to Islam some of the lands in which it had originally flourished. All of this points to the complexity of the thousand years that are commonly bundled together under the title "Middle Ages" and that should not be simplified as if they were a monolithic reality.

However, it is possible to draw from the foregoing pages some general observations that may help us understand the nature of Christian expansion during the Middle Ages.

First, it is interesting to note that the mass conversion of an entire people or nation, rather than the exception, was the rule throughout most of the Middle Ages. Naturally, most often this meant that the new converts lacked a profound understanding of the gospel and that in order to provide such an understanding a long process of education was required—a process that was not always possible. The modern mind, accustomed as we are to thinking in individualistic terms, is loath to grant any value to conversions in which individuals did not decide about their own religion. But at this point we must remember that in medieval society it was customary to come to decisions collectively, and it would not have been realistic to expect individuals to be converted quite apart from their communities.

Second, such mass conversions often took place through the action of a ruler, perhaps of the nation itself (as in the case of the kings of England), or perhaps of an invader who used Christianity as a tool of his expansionist policies (as in the case of Charlemagne and the Saxons). Most often rulers who were converted simply promoted their new faith by means of their prestige; but there were also many cases in which a ruler coerced his subjects into baptism. There were also cases in which, seeking to protect his borders, a ruler sent missionaries to neighboring lands—as in the case of Charles Martel and Boniface.

Third, one must underscore the importance of monasticism in the expansion of Christianity. There were many cases of monks who abandoned their homeland, who sought solitude, and, even without intending to do so, became forerunners and founders of Christianity in regions where it had not yet reached. In other instances, such as in the case of many Irish monks, those who went into pagan lands did this quite consciously following a missionary calling, but with the primary purpose of turning their work among the unconverted into one further act of monastic renunciation. Finally, in the case of Franciscans and Dominicans, these monks were primarily interested in mission from the very beginning of their orders and used monastic discipline partially as a tool for mission.

Fourth, one may be surprised to note that the papacy and the Roman hierarchy in general were not a predominant factor in medieval missions. Actually, before Augustine's mission to England, there is no trustworthy report of any pope sending missionaries to other lands and then directing their policies. Later Boniface and Willibrord did establish relations with Rome, but it was not the papacy that sent them out as missionaries. Although the Crusades received part of their initial impulse from the papacy, they should not really be considered a missionary enterprise. Nor did the orders of St. Francis and St. Dominic result from papal initiative, although their founders did place themselves and their followers under the authority of the Roman see and believed that a central aspect of their mission was to bring all humanity to papal obedience. This does not mean that Rome did not enjoy great prestige, influence, and authority, particularly during the high point of the Middle Ages; but it does point out that, in spite of its enormous power, the role of the papacy in the expansion of Christianity was relatively minor. In fact, it was not until the Modern Age that Catholic missionary work began to be organized so as to place all of it under Roman supervision and direction.

Fifth, although it is impossible to measure to what extent, the response of Christians and of church leaders to the physical needs of people had a great effect in obtaining conversions and in promoting the prestige of the church. In their service to the needy, the Beguines and other women were a practical demonstration of Christian love. Already during antiquity one of the facets of Christianity that had most affected pagans was their care of the ill during times of epidemics. At the very end of antiquity, Constantine himself had declared that this had impressed him profoundly even before he became a Christian. Pagan emperor Julian also pointed to the contrast on this score between Christians and pagans as shaming the latter. But exactly the opposite was the case by the end of the Middle Ages, when the bubonic plague swept through Europe and many priests and prelates fled from possible contagion. This was one of the many factors that eroded the prestige of the church toward the end of the Middle Ages and prepared the way for the Reformation of the sixteenth century.

Sixth, the presence of Islam, much more than any other religion before, forced Christians to face the variety of contexts in which mission takes place. The result was the beginning of discussion and experimentation as to various ways to understand and to structure mission itself.

Finally, a word must be said about the message of medieval missionaries. Most of the medieval sermons addressed to nonbelievers begin with an attack on pagan gods and pagan religion. Sometimes the gods are accused of being powerless, and some other times their power is attributed to Satan or his followers. But in all cases hearers are invited to abandon their ancient gods and follow the only true God. This true God has sent his Son Jesus Christ to save the world, and those who do not accept and follow him will suffer the torments of eternal fire. Then, some missionaries also pointed to the prosperity of Christian lands and promised their hearers similar blessings. If the king was preparing to do battle, or if there was danger that a crop could be lost, a missionary would often promise that God would help the faithful. And, if these arguments did not suffice, there were also missionaries who had recourse to threats and coercion.

Such were the message and methods of Christian missionaries during the Middle Ages. No matter how ill-advised or mistaken those methods may seem today, one must admit that within their own goals they were successful and that the peoples who were converted from them remained faithful Christians for centuries. Repeatedly, people converted by the most inadequate methods became a center of strong missionary movements, although one must also note that some of them—the Saxons, for instance—soon began using against their neighbors violent methods similar to those employed in their own conversion.

Chapter 5

MISSIONS IN THE EARLY MODERN AGE

The second half of the fifteenth century, and the first half of the sixteenth, brought about a series of changes in the religious, cultural, political, and economic life of Europe. Although many of these changes had their roots in earlier events, the fact that they all converged in a relatively brief period justifies historians in claiming that a new age was dawning in European history. In 1453, the Ottoman Turks took the city of Constantinople and thus put an end to the long history of the Byzantine Empire. Although for several centuries Constantinople had been losing its importance as a missionary center, from that date on, that importance was practically nil. At the same time, explorers from western Europe, particularly from Portugal and Spain, began discovering new lands and new routes to lands that were already known. In 1492, Christopher Columbus reached what is now called the Americas. In 1497 and 1498, Vasco da Gama reached India by sailing around Africa. It was only twenty-four years before Ferdinand Magellan and his successor, Juan Sebastián del Cano, completed the circumnavigation of the Earth. These voyages opened new horizons for Europe, and particularly for Spain and Portugal. Such new horizons, joined with the fall of Constantinople, completely changed the geographic picture of

Christian expansion, which would now set out from the Iberian Peninsula toward both the Americas and Africa.

In Europe itself, there were social and theological changes that could have led one to believe that Christianity would not be able to undertake the vast missionary task that these new discoveries placed before it. The ancient political unity of Europe was being eroded as nationalism grew. The philosophical unity of the high point of scholasticism had disappeared under the attacks of nominalism. Ecclesiastical unity itself had suffered the consequences of a series of events that weakened the authority of Rome. First came the papacy's exile in Avignon, then the Great Western Schism, and finally the Conciliarist movement. The moral life of many of the leaders of the church was questionable, as many reforming voices in the fifteenth century had repeatedly stated. As a result, there were many in the universities and other centers of study and reflection asking themselves whether the church was being faithful to the gospel or, on the contrary, its theology and practice had perverted the Christian message.

All of this came to a head in the Protestant Reformation of the sixteenth century, when leaders such as Luther and many others arose in protest against Roman theology and practice. The ensuing division is well known, and one would have wondered whether this would not weaken the missionary thrust of European Christianity as it faced new geographic horizons.

This was the time of the Renaissance in Italy and the growth of humanism in northern Europe. The Italian Renaissance tended to focus on classical antiquity, with the result that the period in European history during which Christianity had been dominant was often seen with disdain—for which reason it was dubbed the "Middle Age," as if it were an irrelevant time between antiquity and modernity. The work of humanists such as Erasmus and his many colleagues showed that the ancient Christian documents, including Scripture, had been corrupted by the manuscript tradition and misinterpreted by the theological tradition. With the invention of the movable type printing press, it was easier for all of these new ideas to penetrate much farther than they could have done at an earlier time.

These changes in European life posed a great challenge for Christianity: would it be able to face the opportunities opened by the new discoveries and geographic horizons, or would it simply become a relic of times past?

During the early years of the Modern Age, most Christian missions were the work of Roman Catholics. Protestant missions came onto the scene later. Therefore, one could say that the time between the sixteenth and the eighteenth centuries is characterized by Roman Catholic geographic expansion and theological reflection on mission. As for Eastern Christianity, it continued existing in the same areas where it was already present, and it was only Russian Christianity that managed to extend into new areas.

A. Catholic Missions

1. Reasons for Catholic Preponderance and Protestant Limitations

The missionary task takes place within the geopolitical, economic, cultural, and religious conditions of nations. In the case of the Modern Age, several factors contributed to Roman Catholic preponderance:

(a) The geographical advantage of Catholicism

As a result of the Reconquista, in Spain and Portugal, the national identity of Catholic countries was closely related to Roman Catholicism. These two were the dominant naval powers during the early Modern Age. When they began losing some of that power, it was France that took the lead in Catholic missionary advance. It is not surprising that in countries that had constant exchanges with distant areas in the Americas and the Far East, missionary interests would be awakened. Furthermore, both Spain and Portugal considered that the expansion of Christianity was one of the main reasons justifying their military and economic conquests. Protestantism, in contrast, was born in the center of Europe, in areas with no coasts or with very limited naval power. When it made headway in Holland, England, and Scandinavia, these were not naval powers. The high point of Scandinavian maritime expansion had past, and the time had not yet come for the British or the Dutch.

(b) Military and political advantage

The sixteenth century marked the beginning of the great colonial expansion of Portugal and Spain, which became rich with the gold and other products imported from their new colonies and therefore gained hegemony in Europe. Thus, although the colonial enterprise required vast human resources, these two Catholic powers were able to face wars of religion in other parts of Europe without their own existence being threatened and never saw the wars of religion as a matter of survival. In the case of Spain, the recently achieved national unity had a strong dose of a sense of mission, of a historic destiny to defend and expand the Catholic faith. The other great European power that by that time had achieved national unity and vied with Spain for hegemony over the continent was France, also a Catholic country.

In contrast, during its early years, Protestantism was threatened with annihilation by military and political pressure coming from all the great powers of Europe. Germany and Switzerland, the early centers of the Protestant movement, were not yet unified. At the beginning of the Reformation, the emperor was His Catholic Majesty Charles I of Spain, also known as Charles V of the Holy Roman Empire. The Netherlands had yet to gain their independence from the Spanish crown. The Scandinavian countries, which soon became Protestant, were too far away to intervene actively in the struggle, and it was only Sweden, under the leadership of King Gustavus Vasa, that eventually was able to bring its military power to bear. As for England, the very survival of Protestantism in the kingdom was in doubt for a long time, and in any case, England was not yet one of the great European powers. For these reasons, Protestantism was constantly threatened by the wars of religion, while Roman Catholicism was able both to participate in those wars and to employ resources for missionary and military intervention in distant lands.

(c) Catholic unity

There is no doubt that one of Catholicism's advantages over Protestantism was its own inner unity. Although Catholicism was not the monolithic body that sometimes Protestants seem to believe, it did have the capacity to coordinate its action. Thus, on several occasions, Rome became the arbiter between Catholic powers seeking to establish their influence in one of the new territories. Also, although missionary expansion took place mostly through the work of the religious orders and of military conquerors, Rome was able to offer certain general directions and also to establish organisms such as the *Sacra Congregatio de Propaganda Fide*. The *Propaganda*—as it is usually known—founded in Rome in 1622, continued existing into the twenty-first century. Its function was to serve as an instrument overseeing all missionary work, addressing not only non-Christians but also Protestants and other non-Catholics. It soon developed a college where young men from various countries were trained as missionaries, and its printing press published books in a multitude of languages. This organization contributed much to the missionary work of the Roman Catholic Church.

In contrast, for centuries Protestants were not able to develop a coordinated approach to missionary work, for they were deeply divided among themselves. Furthermore, many Protestants were convinced that their mission consisted in reforming the church as a whole and therefore devoted their energies to combating Roman Catholicism and often even to debating among themselves the nature of the reformation that the church as a whole needed.

(d) The continuation of an ongoing thrust

For Roman Catholicism, missionary work was simply the continuation of a movement that had existed throughout all its history and had gained impetus with the founding of the mendicant orders in the thirteenth century. There were many treatises showing the need and urgency of missionary work, and some dealing also with its methods. In contrast, Protestantism, in its eagerness to return to Scripture, was often forced to question all that it had received from earlier tradition and to rebuild all of its theology and practice. In consequence, the ancient arguments for missionary work were questioned. Luther himself even declared that the commandment of Jesus to preach the gospel throughout the world was given only to the apostles, who had already fulfilled it. It is true that as Protestantism began feeling more secure in Germany, Luther began thinking about missionary work among neighboring non-Christians, that is, the Turks and Jews. But even so, Luther believed that the Great Commission no longer applied. This greatly hampered the missionary task of Protestantism, until the political and religious situation in which Protestants lived began to change, and other leaders began offering a different interpretation of the Great Commission.

(e) Monastic orders

Luther and almost all Protestants rejected monasticism as a perversion of the gospel. Since Protestants insisted on salvation by grace and not by works, the very notion of the monastic life as a particular work for one's salvation was abhorrent to them. However, in flatly rejecting monasticism, the Reformation deprived itself of one of the most useful and tried missionary instruments. Throughout the entire history of the church, and particularly during the Middle Ages, monastics had been the main agents in preaching the gospel to nonbelievers. Even in the case of those areas where Christianity was imposed politically or militarily, it was always the monks who followed the soldiers and who, with their instruction and preaching, turned what had been a forced conversion into a genuine one. By ridding itself of monasticism, Protestantism found it necessary to discover and create new instruments for mission. This would take centuries, and the eventual result would often show certain affinities with monasticism itself.

2. Spanish Missions

(a) The religious unification of Spain

Although the last area in Spain under Muslim rule disappeared in 1492 with the capitulation of Granada, this does not mean that all the population of the land was Christian. There were still large Jewish and Muslim minorities. That very year, 1492, the monarchs ordered that all Jews who refused to be baptized must leave Spain. Although many did accept baptism, this immediately raised the question of the sincerity of their conversion. This in turn increased the power and activity of the Inquisition, whose main task was to discover among the "new Christians" those who were still Jewish in their faith. The hatred of the Spanish Christian population for the *marranos*—literally, "pigs"—as Jews converted to Christianity were commonly called, increased and therefore many left for other countries in Europe or in North Africa.

The Muslim population was concentrated in the southern areas of Spain. According to the terms of the surrender of Granada in 1492, Islam would be tolerated. For some time this agreement was followed, but Cardinal Ximenes de Cisneros, convinced that these concessions were an unforgivable weakness, began demanding the conversion of the Muslim population. Rebellions were mercilessly crushed. Finally, in 1524, Charles V expelled from Spain all Muslims who were not ready to accept baptism. Even so, the *moriscos*—as converted Muslims were called—posed a similar problem to that of Jewish converts, and soon the Inquisition intervened. In 1567, Philip II issued an edict forbidding the moriscos to keep their particular customs, clothing, and language, and ordering them to adapt to Spanish custom. Furthermore, the Spanish crown issued laws prohibiting former Jews or Muslims from traveling to the Americas. After a series of rebellions and massacres, in 1609, those moriscos who clung to their traditional ways were expelled from Spain. Thus the kingdom was religiously unified, although the imprint of Jewish and Muslim culture would still be felt in the art and customs of the Spanish population, and this would often lead to suspicion and persecution from the Inquisition.

(b) The Americas

Surprisingly, even before the last Jewish and Muslim residues in the country were assimilated, Spain undertook the task of taking its power, faith, and culture to lands several times more extensive than Spain itself. The first half of the sixteenth century witnessed an unprecedented migration in which the Spanish population poured into the Western Hemisphere. The various factors leading to this are still debated among historians, but one may affirm that Spain moved into the New World under the impulse of three intertwined motivations that made it possible for the most dissimilar spirits to join in a common venture: glory, gold, and God. For those who sought glory and renown, the New World offered an opportunity to conquer empires never before imagined. Those who simply wished to become rich found in the "Indies" legends of great treasures. Finally, the existence of vast lands where the gospel had not been preached attracted those for whom religion was the main motivating force, and particularly members of the monastic orders—Franciscans, Dominicans, and others.

The speed and far-flung outreach of Spanish expansion into the New World during the sixteenth century are surprising. Columbus arrived for the first time to these lands in 1492. In 1496, he founded the city of Santo Domingo de Guzmán on the island that he named Hispaniola. By 1500, Juan de la Cosa published the first map of the new lands. At the same time, the north of South America and a good part of North America were being explored. In 1508, Sebastián de Ocampo circumnavigated Cuba, thus showing it was not part of the mainland. The expedition of Vasco Núñez de Balboa, between 1509 and 1515, discovered the Pacific Ocean. In 1513, Juan Ponce de León landed in Florida, and two years later Juan Díaz de Solís reached the River Plate. There were numerous expeditions to the coasts of North America and into the interior of that land, but foremost among them is that of Álvar Núñez Cabeza de Vaca, who between 1527 and 1536 traversed the entire continent from Florida to Mexico. Hernando de Soto went from Florida to the Mississippi in 1539 to 1541. At the same time, Francisco de Orellana was exploring the basin of the Amazon. These various explorations were inspired by the hope of finding a route to the East and also by the rich treasures that the native population was said to possess.

The irony of the early stages of the process is exemplified in the life of Christopher Columbus, who thought he had reached the "Indies." His was a "discovery" by means of serious navigational errors. For this reason, the continent does not carry his name but that of Americo Vespucio, who proposed that these lands were a new continent, thus changing the entire worldview of the times.

The explorers were followed by conquistadores. The Greater Antilles did not offer much resistance to Spanish conquest, and soon the entire population of these islands was subject to new rulers. Eventually, most of that population disappeared. As centers of operation for future conquest, the Spanish founded cities that still exist: besides Santo Domingo, which has already been mentioned, in 1508, they founded the city of Puerto Rico (now known as San Juan); in 1514, they established Santiago de Cuba; and a year later, Havana was founded. In 1519, Hernando Cortez landed on the coast of Mexico, and two years later the conquest of the Aztec Empire was complete. After several failed attempts, Francisco Pizarro and Diego de Almagro undertook the final conquest of Perú. After two years, they had taken the capital city of Cuzco. Although there was soon a civil war between the supporters of Pizarro and those who took Almagro's side, the conquest of the Incan Empire was already complete. By then, all the major centers of pre-Columbian culture and civilization, except the Yucatan, were in Spanish hands. The conquest of Central America and the Yucatan began in 1523 and took less than twenty years. This, and similar conquests in the River Plate, Paraguay, and North America, completed the vast process of Spanish expansion in the New World. Yet, all this did not take place without resistance on the part of the native population nor without philosophical and theological debate among Christians.

The discoverers and conquistadores were followed by the colonizers. These did not seek to find new lands, but rather to settle in population centers where they could benefit from trade, agriculture, and especially mining. It was the process of colonization that made the vast Spanish expansion permanent. Had Hernando Cortez and Francisco Pizarro not been followed by many men—and later women—who were willing to settle permanently on the conquered lands, one may well imagine that soon the indigenous population would have managed to cast off the Spanish yoke.

This colonization of the New World by the Spanish was one of the most significant events in the entire history of Christian expansion. The church was already represented in Columbus's second voyage. From then on, as was to be expected given the religious convictions of the Spanish crown and people, there were always priests present in the various exploring and conquering expeditions, as well as in the new colonies. Some of these priests—particularly those who did not belong to monastic orders—felt that their mission was limited to ministering to the spiritual needs of the colonizers. Some even wondered whether it was possible to convert the native population—whom they called "Indians" because

Columbus had thought that he had arrived at the Indies. But soon others responded by declaring that such conversion was not only possible but also the obligation of the Spanish church and crown and that the main purpose of the conquest and colonization of the New World was precisely the conversion of the indigenous population.

In order to fulfill this task, Spain counted above all on its profound religious spirit, grounded in an understanding of the Reconquista that gave the historic task of Spain almost messianic proportions. That religious spirit combined with the quest for riches and adventure to produce and support the vast missionary enterprise of the sixteenth century. At the beginning of that century, the mendicant orders, particularly Franciscans and Dominicans, were numerous in Spain. Spain was also the cradle of Ignatius Loyola, and the Society of Jesus—the Jesuits—had gained many members in that land. These orders—jointly with the Mercedarians—would be the main instrument of mission in the New World. Furthermore, from the very beginnings of the conquests, the Spanish crown had almost absolute control over the life of the church in its new possessions. The rights of the Spanish crown in this regard are called *Patronato Real.* In 1493, Alexander VI issued a series of five papal bulls granting the rulers of Spain religious and political authority over all lands that had been discovered or might be discovered beyond a line of demarcation that was drawn a hundred leagues west of the Azores, and as long as Spain would be sailing west and the discovered lands were not already in the possession of a Christian prince. This was not only a privilege granted to Isabella and Ferdinand and their successors—and, in a similar series of bulls, to the rulers of Portugal, as long as they remained east of the line of demarcation and sailed eastward—but also a missionary obligation that the pope decided to avoid by placing responsibility on the crowns of Spain and Portugal. The popes of the Renaissance who ruled at the time were more interested in politics and arts than in religion and had no time or energy to spare on distant lands.

Beginning in 1501, the Patronato Real allowed the Crown to receive all the benefits and tithes of the new churches but also made it responsible for all the expenses of the missionary enterprise. When the first episcopal sees were established, Pope Julius II gave the Crown the right to propose the names of those who would occupy them as well as other high ecclesiastical positions. Although the papal bulls spoke of a right of patronage over the new lands, soon Spanish theologians, both in Iberia and in the New World, began speaking of a *Vicariato Regio*—a royal vicariate—by which the king was the pope's vicar in the New World.

This merger between the interests of the state and the expansion of Christianity eventually proved to be problematic. Missions were employed as a means to extend Spanish culture and power. On occasion, a mission was founded not so much for the conversion of the indigenous population as with the purpose of preventing colonization by another European power.

Even so, for the Spanish crown, this union between church and state seemed so natural that the question was never asked, as it would be today, of whether the state was making use of the church or vice versa. For the Spanish crown, European culture—particularly Spanish culture—was a synonym for Christian faith. Therefore, the Hispanization of the original American population was for them the same as its Christianization. Nor should we leave aside the issues and debates that the Crown had to confront in the tasks of evangelizing that population. Repeatedly the Crown defended the rights of the Indians against those who sought to exploit and enslave them. If such official policies lacked success and if massacres of the native population went unpunished, this was due to the complex relationship between Spain and its representatives in the Western Hemisphere and to the enormous distance that made it difficult for the Spanish authorities to enforce their laws in the colonies.

Many Dominicans, Franciscans, Jesuits, and other friars opposed the exploitation of the indigenous population by the Spaniards and sought the support of the Crown for more justice. It was frequently the secular or diocesan clergy that supported the inhumane practices of the conquistadores. We shall see some examples of this as we look at the life and work of people such as Fray Bartolomé de Las Casas and Fray Antonio de Montesinos.

Some of the greatest abuses were committed against the original inhabitants of the Greater Antilles, whose culture was relatively primitive. The Spanish did not come to these lands in order to cultivate or farm them with their own hands, and therefore they needed the labor of the native population. Although legally other names were employed, the new order turned out to be a form of slavery. All of this was covered by the mantle of a missionary goal, so that native people were "entrusted"—*encomendados*—to the colonizers so that, as they worked for the Spaniards, they would also be instructed in the Christian faith. The resulting institution, called *encomienda*, was a veiled form of slavery, made worse because the *encomenderos* (the colonizers) did not even have a financial investment that would encourage them to care for those who were entrusted to them. The encomenderos did not even try to learn the native languages and simply sought to force the Indians to produce to the maximum.

Although the encomiendas were established with the approval of the Spanish crown, they soon led to debates on the nature of evangelization, on the humanity of the indigenous population, and on their freedom. Unfortunately, the Crown was not always aware of the manner in which the encomiendas were abused. As far as we know, the first to protest against them was Father Antonio de Montesinos, of the Order of St. Dominic. Realizing that his preaching in the New World was ineffectual, Montesinos made certain that his complaints reached the Spanish court. The result was the Ley de Burgos, issued in 1512, which tried to guarantee justice for the indigenous population.

Although not abolishing the system of encomiendas, this law tried to make it clear that the encomendados were not to be used as slaves, that people entrusted to a particular colonizer could not be sold or given to another, and that Indian labor should be fairly paid.

As could be expected, the Ley de Burgos was never fully applied in the New World. Even so, it showed that authorities in Spain paid heed to the efforts on the part of the friars to humanize the colonial regime. Once again we are faced by the complex relationship between evangelization and conquest, for it is clear that the interests of the conquistadores, the colonizers, and some in Spain who were being enriched by the entire enterprise outweighed the efforts on the part of some religious leaders to develop a more just form of evangelization. This may serve as a warning that the missionary enterprise can be polluted by destructive ideologies.

Another defender of the Indians, better known than Father Montesinos, was Fray Bartolomé de Las Casas. Moved by the preaching of Montesinos, Las Casas decided to join the Dominicans. After giving up his own encomienda, he sold all his properties in the New World and returned to Spain, seeking more just laws in favor of the indigenous population. In Spain, he was granted the official title of "General Protector of the Indians," and armed with it he returned to the Antilles. There he was seen as a dreamer who believed that the Indians were people like the rest and that they could be pacified by loving means. Seeing that it was impossible to enforce the laws defending the native population, Las Casas returned to Spain, thus beginning a long series of comings and goings, constantly seeking to improve the life of the colonized. In the New World itself, he traveled to Mexico and Perú, always intervening to protect the native population. Finally, in 1542, the Consejo de las Indias—the body in Spain in charge of all colonial matters—issued a series of "New Laws" which granted certain rights to the indigenous population. Desperately seeking to defend the native population against an economic system that made its exploitation practically inevitable, Las Casas suggested that slaves be brought from Africa so that the indigenous could be free. Serving as bishop of Chiapas, where his work was exemplary, Las Casas returned to Spain, where he recanted from his earlier suggestion that slaves be brought from Africa and wrote a series of treatises on the evangelization and colonization of the New World until he died in 1576.

The case of Las Casas—far from being unique in the history of the New World—is an example of an attitude that was relatively common. In Mexico City, Bishop Juan de Zumárraga, a man of vast humanistic culture, worked for the education and religious instruction of the indigenous population. It was through his efforts that the first printing press was established in the New World. Some other outstanding names that have survived among the hundreds who sought to ameliorate the life of the original inhabitants of the New World are Bartolomé de Olmedo, Eusebio Kino, Luis Cancer, Luis Beltrán, and Francisco Solano. There were also some civil authorities who followed similar policies regarding the indigenous population—foremost among them the famous Cabeza de Vaca.

Although the encomiendas continued, the main missionary method for the expansion of Christianity among native populations of nomadic customs was the *reducciones*. In some areas, the population lived in very small communities in the countryside and jungles—communities that were sometimes limited to a single family. This made their evangelization very difficult, and even more difficult was any attempt to supervise their morality, which the missionaries also felt was part of their responsibility. For these reasons, with the support of the Crown, the friars began bringing these families together into a larger community that they called a "reduction" or a "mission."

A reduction was a small village built around the church and the plaza in front of it. There the work was supervised by the friars, who taught their charges crafts and new methods of agriculture. At the same time, they were instructed in the Christian faith, and their customs were supervised in order to bring them closer to what the friars considered Christian. There is no doubt that these missions were better than the encomiendas, whose only true result was exploitation. But the missions also left much to be desired, particularly because of their excessive paternalism and their attempt to Hispanicize people, uprooting them from their old means of life and not fully preparing them to survive independently in the new order that was being imposed. This left them in a cultural, existential, and religious vacuum that eventually became a form of genocide. The result was that most of the missions disappeared when the friars were no longer present to care for them. This was particularly true in Paraguay, where the Jesuits had established a vast network of missions reaching from the north of Argentina to some regions in southern Brazil. When the Jesuits were expelled from all Spanish lands in 1567—another instance of the complex relationships among the Crown, the colonies, and the Roman church—and the Franciscans, Dominicans, and other friars proved insufficient to fill the vacuum left by the Jesuits, the vast majority of the Paraguayan missions disappeared.

Before beginning that practice in Paraguay, friars from various orders—Franciscans, Dominicans, and Jesuits—established similar missions in various lands where the native population had nomadic or seminomadic customs. Sometimes the missionaries were escorted by small groups of soldiers who protected their lives, but also on occasion missionaries went beyond the reach of Spanish power, for which then they served as a beachhead. Many of these missionaries died as martyrs, killed either by those whom they sought to serve or by others who invaded their lands and took their missions.

The theory was that once these missions were sufficiently established, the friars would leave them in the hands of the secular or diocesan clergy and would move on to new lands and found new missions. In practice, this rarely happened, for the friars were not ready to abandon their missions, and the diocesans were not often inclined to take up parishes whose material benefits were minimal.

When conquering lands of high civilization such as Mexico or Peru, the Spanish followed a different missionary policy. The very act of conquest consisted mostly of taking the place of the ancient lords of the land—who often were also conquerors who oppressed and exploited those whom they ruled. When this was possible, the new rulers simply took the place of the old, and the already-established system of production and authority was continued. From the point of view of politics and economics, this sort of conquest had the great advantage of not disturbing the structures of production and administration that were already in existence. For missionaries, it also had the advantage—although perhaps a superficial and false advantage—that the conquered people, accustomed as they were to following the orders of their superiors, now seemed to be ready to accept baptism without major resistance.

First in Mexico, and then in Perú, hundreds of thousands received baptism without having the slightest notion of the meaning of the rite. At first very few Spaniards bothered to learn the native languages of America. But beginning with the work of Bishop Zumárraga in Mexico and Bishop Toribio Alfonso de Mogrovejo in Lima, Christianity began taking root among the earlier inhabitants of these two vast empires. The printing press established by Zumárraga published books in several of the native languages in order to teach the true meaning of Christianity. Universities were also founded in Lima and Mexico, as well as a number of seminaries whose purpose was to train mission workers among the native population. Still, vestiges of the ancient religion would subsist and eventually be revived late in the twentieth and early in the twenty-first century. As we shall see, today it is clear that the interaction between the native religions and Christianity was rich and complex. This has led historians and missiologists to reevaluate the history of the evangelization of the native peoples in Latin America, discovering that the process of evangelization and Hispanization was also a process of religious and cultural interchange. This includes resistance as well as the creation of new religious symbols and practices.

African slaves were brought to the Americas in order to provide the labor that the Spanish colonizers refused to undertake. The tragedy of slavery is well known. Apparently, in spite of the growing number of African slaves brought to the New World, the church does not seem to have realized the importance of mission work among them. Very few made it their business to preach the gospel to slaves. This may be related to the overwhelmingly geographic understanding of mission that was then prevalent, which led many to think that what had to be done was simply to go to lands where the gospel was not yet known. There were, however, some Christians who were moved by their faith to work among slaves and people of African descent. In this regard, the work of Alfonso de Sandoval is significant, for he wrote an extensive book, *Instauranda Aethiopium Salute*, on the methods, problems, and challenges connected with the evangelization of people of African descent.

Most remarkable, however, was the work of Pedro Claver, a Jesuit born in Catalonia who went to the New World and in the city of Cartagena made it his particular mission to visit slaves as they were arriving from Africa. His work, besides preaching and instruction, included the physical care and the nurture of recently arrived slaves who were frequently ill as a result of the Atlantic crossing and the anguish of their captivity. His work was not grounded in any sense of condescension toward inferior beings, for he was convinced that Africans should be considered as equal in every respect to Europeans, and as able to take within the life of the church the same place as white believers. There is no doubt that his work alleviated many sufferings. But there is also no doubt that he and the handful of other Christians who became actively involved in the lot of African slaves were isolated within a sea of incomprehension as well as of political and economic pressures. If eventually the descendants of the original slaves accepted Christianity, this was not due to any particular missionary work among them, but simply to the tendency of slaves to adopt some of the customs and faith of their masters. As in the case of the native population, the Christian faith exists in many communities of African descent and still bears the mark of ancient and of new African religious practices, with the result that even in the twenty-first century Christianity was searching for its identity within Afro-Latin American cultures.

Although the foregoing summarizes the main missionary methods employed by the Spanish in the New World, we must also look at the development of Christianity in each of the main regions of Latin America and the Caribbean.

The Antilles were the first lands "discovered" by Columbus, and therefore it was there that the colonization and evangelization of the Western Hemisphere began. The result was that the native population of the Antilles suffered the worst consequences of the Spanish presence, and it was there that the regime of the encomiendas was first implanted and most extensively employed. Since the original inhabitants of the West Indies were not accustomed to such a life, and since the colonizers did little to make it any easier for them, the result was the almost total disappearance of the original population, which survived almost exclusively in the descendants of Spanish men and the native women whom they forcibly took. Therefore, the Spanish presence in the West Indies, more than elsewhere in the Americas, was limited to the colonization of the area and had little to do with evangelization or enculturation. Generally, the African slaves who began arriving as soon as the native population declined posed a greater problem for the church than did the conversion of the Indians. But by then Spanish control of the islands was such that the slave population was converted simply through a process of adaptation to the Christian faith while at the same time preserving many elements of African religions.

In a territory as thoroughly colonized as were the Greater Antilles, an ecclesiastical hierarchy was quickly established. The first three dioceses were founded in Hispaniola in 1508. Similar steps were taken in Puerto Rico in 1511 and in Cuba in 1517.

From the Greater Antilles the conquistadores—as well as the missionaries—moved on to Florida, which had been "discovered" by Ponce de Leon in 1513. The first attempts to conquer the land were unsuccessful, and it was only much later, when the nearby presence of the French caused the Spanish to worry about the area, that the effective conquest and colonization of Florida took place. The Jesuits' encounter with the Calusa—sedentary hunter-gatherers who developed negotiation skills to face the Europeans—served as a starting point for a missionary strategy. Jesuit missionaries were dependent on the hospitality of the Calusa. The Calusa negotiated religious practices with Jesuits but never understood themselves as recipients of a new faith. While Jesuits Juan Rogel and Pedro Martínez taught and attempted to explain the mysteries of the faith to the Calusa, these took a "what fits we take" approach to the transmission of the Christian religion. Missionary work seemed to be a process of religious negotiation and persuasive conversation, with little success given the pragmatic spirit of the Calusa.

The story with the Franciscans is quite different, and yet it shows the expectations that the Calusa had in their religious negotiations. Under the Franciscans, some of the Calusa allowed their children to be baptized. However, frustration overwhelmed the Calusa, as they did not receive any benefits from their children's baptisms. As tensions increased, the Franciscans decided to destroy the native "idols," and the Calusa put an end to the missionary work. Documents show that the Calusa had knowledge of Christian concepts, ideas, and argumentation. It is evident that their hesitation toward the Christian faith developed as missionaries imposed the Catholic structures and attempted to destroy the Calusa's spiritual worldview.

During the time between the initial explorations and the final conquests, many Dominicans, Jesuits, and Franciscans who went to Florida as missionaries died as martyrs. From Florida, and as part of the same enterprise, the friars moved into what is now called Georgia and even as far as Virginia. Throughout these areas, missionary work was very difficult and came to an end in 1763 when Florida became British.

It was also from the Greater Antilles that Christianity reached into Mexico. Cortez, the conqueror of Mexico, was profoundly devoted to Christianity—as his Spanish contemporaries understood it. During the early years, mission activity in what was then called New Spain was led by the Franciscans, who settled in Mexico City and Puebla in 1524. From those two centers and during the next forty years, Franciscan missions expanded first westward and then northward, reaching as far as Durango. The Dominicans arrived in 1526 and at first were working also in Mexico City and Puebla, but then they moved south to the region of Oaxaca. The Augustinians came seven years after the Dominicans (1533) and settled in Mexico City, from which they also moved toward the north and the west, mostly occupying the spaces that still remained between various Franciscan and Dominican settlements. The Jesuits were the other great order that worked in Mexico, but they did not arrive until 1572. Then they became known for the many educational institutions they founded and for their missions in the north of New Spain. As in other parts of the world, they were expelled from Mexico in the eighteenth century. The Mexican hierarchy was established in 1530, when Fray Juan de Zumárraga was made bishop of Mexico. The diocese of Antequera, in Oaxaca, was founded in 1534, and soon thereafter there were also bishops in Michoacan, Chiapas, Guadalajara, and Cozumel.

Completing the transplantation of the Spanish church to New Spain, in 1569, by royal action, the Inquisition was established in Mexico as well as in Perú. Although before that date there had been inquisitorial processes in Mexico, the official establishment of the Holy Office brought a new wave of repression both for the indigenous people and for the Spanish, but even more so for foreigners. Three years after it had been established, the Holy Office had more than 400 people under investigation or on trial. Even in spite of the Inquisition, and sometimes with the acquiescence of church authorities, the ancient religious practices continued under the mantle of Christianity. The most notable example may be traced back to the fertility goddess Tonantzin, whose devotion was closely connected with the Virgin of Guadalupe.

It was from Mexico, and only two years after Montezuma's empire had been overrun, that the Spanish, led by Don Pedro de Alvarado, began the conquest of Central America. This region was organized as a "General Captaincy" whose capital was Guatemala and included the provinces of Chiapas, Salvador, Honduras, Nicaragua, and Costa Rica, besides Guatemala itself. The area saw the labors of Franciscans, Dominicans, Mercedarians, and Jesuits. The first bishoprics founded were in Guatemala, Nicaragua, Comayagua, San Salvador, and Verapaz. The Inquisition in the area was under the jurisdiction of its offices in Mexico and included representatives in all the main towns in Central America. In general, the conversion of the native population was slow, and as late as the twentieth century there were still communities in Guatemala that practiced the ancient religion and followed the Mayan calendar. Late in that century, and into the twenty-first, there was a revival of some of the ancient religious practices.

The first Spanish settlements in what eventually became the Viceroyalty of Nueva Granada were Darién—in what is today Panama—and Urabá. The early expeditions of Ojeda and Nicuesa included Franciscan friars. The first colony was established in San Sebastián de Urabá, and later moved to Darién, where in 1513, the Episcopal see of Santa María del Darién was founded. This was the center for missionary work among the native population. This work was superficial, and sometimes the conquistadores themselves, without even awaiting the arrival of missionaries, baptized the "converts." Throughout the colonial period, Catholic missionaries from various orders continued working in the area, but even so by the twenty-first century there was still much work of evangelization to be done in Urabá.

Colombia was the center of the Viceroyalty of Nueva Granada. Besides Urabá, the Spanish settled in the area of Cartagena, which had been conquered by Don Pedro de Heredia in 1533. A year later, the Dominican friar Tomás del Toro arrived in Cartagena, where he would serve as its first bishop. From that point on, supported by Dom Tomás and his successors, intensive missionary work was carried out mostly by Dominicans and Franciscans. The Jesuits did not arrive until 1598, but at that point they too undertook extensive missionary work.

From Cartagena, the Spanish moved toward the south, where they founded the city of Santa Fe de Bogotá, which became a bishopric in 1562 and an archbishopric in 1564. From a very early date, the Colombian church began producing its own clergy, which was an indication of its deep roots in the area. However, this clergy was recruited only among people of Spanish or mixed descent, and the ordination of the first person of pure Indian blood was long postponed.

Venezuela was also part of Nueva Granada. The first attempts to bring Christianity into the area ended in martyrdom. It was in the seventeenth century, thanks to the daring of Francisco de Pamplona, that the Capuchins finally settled in Venezuela. Six years later the Observant Franciscans followed them, while the Jesuits were entering from Colombia in the west. The work of the Jesuits was quite successful, but when they were expelled from the region, the other orders did not have sufficient resources to continue their work, which rapidly went into decline. The episcopal see of Caracas was founded in 1530.

The conquest of Ecuador, which eventually became part of the Viceroyalty of Nueva Granada, was undertaken from two different directions: by Pedro de Alvarado from the north and by Diego de Almagro from the south (Perú). Although at first there were rivalries between these two groups as they vied for the possession of the much-vaunted treasures of Quito, they eventually joined in order to take the city. Almost immediately a Franciscan convent was established there and shortly thereafter a Mercedarian one. Four years later, in 1541, the Dominicans also settled in the area. As throughout all of Spanish America, the diocesan or secular priests also accompanied the conquistadores and almost immediately established parishes in the conquered areas but paid little attention to the task of evangelizing the native population. In the kingdom of Quito, as throughout all the lands that had previously belonged to the Incas, missionary work was hampered by the conduct of the Spanish conquistadores—a conduct even worse than in other areas of the continent. The destruction of the Incan Empire through deceit and treachery, followed almost immediately by civil war among the Spanish, inspired in the native population a profound hatred and contempt for anything that had a connection with the invaders. This sentiment was particularly deep among the nobility of the ancient empire, for the subjects of the Incas were mostly people whom they had conquered before the arrival of the Spanish and for whom the Spanish Conquest was little more than a change of masters. Once again, it was the mendicant orders that did the most extensive missionary work in the interior of the country. One of the most notable missionary enterprises was led by the Jesuits in the area of Mainas. Ecclesiastically, Quito was dependent on Perú until the bishopric of Quito was established in 1545. As in the other Spanish colonies, the church built hospitals and schools, which, although insufficient, were the only attempt at social aid in the area.

The conquest of Perú is one of the darkest pages in the history of the Americas. The destruction of the ancient Incan Empire and its highly developed civilization is inexcusable. Francisco Pizarro, who in his native Extremadura had tended pigs, became a knight and conquistador, and he bears much of the responsibility for what took place. But much of the responsibility must fall also on the church and its representative, Vicente Valverde, who became infamous as a central figure in the incident of Cajamarca. There, Pizarro hid his troops around the central square. When the Incan emperor Atahualpa entered the city, Valverde invited him to accept the Catholic faith and swear allegiance to the Spanish crown. When, as was to be expected, Atahualpa haughtily refused, Valverde declared that the Spanish were justified in attacking him. Pizarro and his men opened fire, a great slaughter ensued, and Atahualpa was made a prisoner. Pizarro then offered Atahualpa his freedom in exchange for a huge ransom in gold. When this was gathered from throughout the Incan Empire, Pizarro broke his word and ordered Atahualpa killed—although as an act of kindness, because Atahualpa had accepted Christian baptism, he was strangled rather than burned alive! After Atahualpa's death, civil war broke out among the Spanish, who would not be satisfied with the vast treasures they had taken from the Incas and now sought to despoil one another. It is not surprising, therefore, that there were numerous rebellions against Spanish rule and against the Christianity they represented—the last of which took place in the eighteenth century under the leadership of Tupac Amaru.

In spite of the high degree in which Spanish behavior hampered their work and even of the fanaticism and greed of the first Dominican in Perú—Fray Vicente Valverde—the mendicant orders did extensive work in the region. The Dominicans arrived with the earliest conquistadores in the person of Valverde, and by 1539, there was already an independent Dominican province known as the Provincia de San Juan Bautista del Perú. They were followed almost immediately by the Franciscans and the Mercedarians and by the Jesuits in 1567. At first, most missionary work took place within the confines of the ancient Incan Empire, but by the beginning of the seventeenth century, Spanish missionaries were going beyond the ancient empire and into the Amazonian jungle. Among the most distinguished missionaries were Fray Francisco de San José, Fray Pedro González de Agüero, Fray Manuel de Sobreviela, and Fray Narciso Girbal y Barceló.

The first episcopal see established in Perú was in Túmbez, and this was soon followed by the see of Cuzco. It was not until 1543 that Lima received its first bishop, but three years after that, it was made the metropolitan see with jurisdiction over the entire area. The most famous archbishop of Lima during the sixteenth century was Toribio de Mogrovejo, later canonized by the Catholic Church. The Inquisition was introduced in Perú in 1529 and continued working there until 1821, a year before the nation declared its independence.

The conquest of Chile, in which Diego Almagro failed and Pedro de Valdivia lost his life, was much slower than the conquest of Perú, for the resistance of the Araucanians forced the Spanish to remain north of the Bio-Bio River. Where the soldiers could not go, the missionaries went, and the church existed south of the Bio-Bio long before Spain was able to rule that land. Meanwhile, in 1561, Santiago de Chile had become an Episcopal see, although it was only in the nineteenth century that it became a metropolitan see with jurisdiction over the rest of the country. As throughout Spanish America, most of the missionary work was conducted by Dominican, Franciscan, and Mercedarian convents. But it was the Jesuits who must be credited with most of the work among the Araucanians, whose language they learned and whose trust they earned. As elsewhere, the Inquisition was also brought into Chile and continued functioning there until 1820.

The first permanent Spanish settlement in what later became the Viceroyalty of La Plata was in Asunción, in 1537. The conquest of the area proceeded both from Asunción and from Perú. During the second half of the sixteenth century, forces from these two areas founded the cities of Santiago del Estero, Tucumán, Córdoba, and Buenos Aires—the latter for a second time.

Although other orders labored in the area, once again it was the Jesuits who did outstanding work in the region of Paraguay. In 1607, the Jesuits of the area became the province of Paraguay, and by then they were present in most of the cities. Besides their establishment of schools, which has always been a mark of their work, the Jesuits established reducciones, or missions among the native peoples, particularly the Guaranis, who were the most numerous. These missions were similar to those organized elsewhere, except that they had no military presence. Rather, the priests armed the natives, and even took arms themselves, in order to defend the missions. It is estimated that at their height there were fifty-seven such missions, with approximately 113,000 residents. Both because of their size and because of their high degree of independence, these missions were seen with suspicion by civil functionaries, and this suspicion was supported by colonizers who saw the Jesuits and their missions as an obstacle to their plans for expansion. Opposition to the missions increased when, after Spain and Portugal signed a treaty determining the limits between Portuguese and Spanish possessions in South America in 1750, it was ordered that a number of these missions move elsewhere. In response to that order, the native population rebelled. Some blamed the Jesuits for the rebellion and started speaking of the "Jesuit War"—all of which was part of a long-standing campaign in Europe to discredit the Society of Jesus. In 1761, the treaty between Spain and Portugal was annulled, and the population was allowed to return to its missions. But the harm had been done. The residents of the missions were still trying to undo the damage that had taken place during their absence when the order expelling the Jesuits from all Spanish possessions arrived in 1767. Although members of other orders tried to fill the vacuum left by the Jesuits, the task was too great for them, and decline set in. This was the end of a missionary experiment that, in spite of its paternalism—which was still better than the treatment that the indigenous people received from "Christians" elsewhere—was the most serious and lasting attempt on the part of Catholic missionaries in the New World to organize the native population into Christian communities.

In Bolivia, convents were established in every major city almost at the very time when the cities themselves were founded. Missions were organized by the Jesuits from Paraguay, mostly in lands that eventually would be disputed between Bolivia and Paraguay, and also by the Franciscans. The first diocese to be established, in 1551, was Charcas—now known as Sucre.

Christianity penetrated the River Plate region both from the coast and from the north. The first attempts to settle on the shores of the estuary failed, and the colonizers, who had arrived by sea hoping to begin a new colony, had to go northward and join those in Asunción. The first Franciscan missionaries reached Tucumán coming from Perú. Among them were Fray Juan de Rivadeneyra and Francisco Solano, to whom we have already referred, and who was the first great missionary among the indigenous populations in the north of what is now Argentina. The Mercedarians were also present in the area, moving beyond the reach of Spanish protection, and several dying as martyrs. Dominican work in the River Plate was under the supervision of the Dominicans in Chile and does not seem to have progressed as rapidly as the Franciscan enterprise. The first Jesuits arrived in 1585, and two years later, they were followed by another contingent of missionaries from Brazil. Although they landed in Buenos Aires, their most permanent work took place in the northern reaches of Argentina, in a series of missions that at that point were part of their enterprise in Paraguay. The see of Tucumán was established in 1570 and that of Buenos Aires in 1620.

In brief, one may say that the conquest of Latin America by Roman Catholicism was possible through a series of factors and circumstances. The evangelization of Latin America was at the same time a history of abuse, injustice, jealousy, and unrestrained ambition, and a history of daring missions that quite often resulted in martyrdom. The presence of the colonizers was a constant threat to the well-being of the native population. Together with the colonizers and sometimes ahead of them, missionaries arrived. In many cases, these missionaries opposed the abuse to which the colonizers subjected the native population. In some cases, military might was employed to protect the missionaries and even to force people to accept baptism. But in general, the distinction between missionaries and soldiers was kept more clearly than it had been in Europe during the last centuries of the Middle Ages.

It is also important to point out that the Christianization of Latin America and the Caribbean was never completed, not only in geographic terms, but also and particularly in terms of the effect of Christianity on the customs and beliefs of the people. Perhaps this failure was more frequent in Latin America and the Caribbean than in other areas, but it is certainly not a new phenomenon in the history of Christian missions. This is not very different from what happened in the earlier history of Christianity, when missionaries as well as mission theory expected from the new converts that they would completely abandon their earlier religious traditions and that conversion would produce a radical discontinuity with their ancestral cultures.

(c) The Philippines

These islands, named after Philip II of Spain, were visited by Magellan in 1521. As is well known, the great Portuguese sailor, whose expedition was under Spanish auspices, lost his life in the Philippines. It was half a century later that the conquest of the Philippines began. Still, most of those who arrived at the Philippines from Mexico came for a purpose different than had taken the conquistadores and colonizers to the Western Hemisphere. The Philippines were too distant from Spain to become a center of trade with Europe. Following the policy that the Spanish would normally sail westward from Spain, and the Portuguese eastward, the normal route to reach the Philippines was across the Atlantic, overland through Mexico, and finally across the Pacific. This meant that from the point of view of Spain, these islands, rather than a land to be colonized and exploited, tended to be a center for the establishment of colonies and missions in the Far East. This in turn meant that the role of missionaries was more dominant than it had been in the Americas. For this reason, the abuse of the local population, although always present, was not as extensive as it had been in the Americas. Still, the missionary policy that was first implanted was the old system of the encomiendas, which were a means of forcing the population to work for the Spanish. It was toward the end of the sixteenth century that vast numbers of Augustinians, Franciscans, Dominicans, Jesuits, and others arrived. As in the Americas, these friars centered their attention on founding missions or communities in which the Christian faith and European customs were taught. These missions were relatively successful, and by the end of the eighteenth century, most Filipinos called themselves Christian.

Still, missionary work in the Philippines met several obstacles. Foremost among these was the presence of Muslims in the southern islands. The missionaries were able to convert very few among them. There were also Japanese and Chinese on the islands, and many of these had arrived long before the Spanish. Apparently they did not oppose the preaching of the missionaries, but the latter feared that their growing numbers would undo their work and might turn the Philippines into a Chinese colony. The end result was a series of massacres of the Chinese. Meanwhile, the Dutch were disputing Spain's right to rule over the Philippines. Also, the expulsion of the Jesuits during the second half of the eighteenth century resulted in the disappearance of many of the missions they had created.

However, the greatest obstacle to missionary work in the Philippines was the constant dissension among Christians. Civil authorities vied with ecclesiastical ones. The secular clergy tried to take possession of the missions founded by the friars, and the latter resisted. Various orders competed among themselves in spite of royal directives forbidding two different orders to work in the same province. This, aggravated by the paternalistic and condescending attitude of Spanish authorities, civil as well as ecclesiastical, meant that the Philippines never became a center of missions to the Far East, as the earliest missionaries had hoped.

(d) Other Spanish missions

The Spanish did attempt some missionary work west of the Philippines. There were Spanish missionaries in Indonesia, Japan, Southeast Asia, and China, but their work never had the effect that other Spanish missionaries had in the Americas and the Philippines.

3. Portuguese Missions

Hemmed in as it was within the Iberian Peninsula by neighboring Spain, Portugal began its seaward expansion long before Spain. Under Henry the Navigator (1394–1460), sailing and exploration became one of the most important Portuguese endeavors. During the first half of the fifteenth century, the Portuguese reached the Azores and the islands of Cape Verde. In 1453, the fall of Constantinople made communication with the east by the overland route ever more difficult, and therefore it was natural for the Portuguese to seek a route to the Orient by sailing around Africa. In 1486, Bartolomé Diaz reached the Cape of Good Hope, and eleven years later, Vasco da Gama reached India. On the basis of these discoveries, the Portuguese crown obtained several papal bulls granting it sovereignty over all lands to be discovered. When the voyages of Columbus introduced Spain into the competition for new lands, the pope had to determine which new territories would belong to each of the two Iberian kingdoms. The pope at that time was the Spaniard Alexander VI, one of the worst popes of all time. After long negotiation and repeated protests by the Portuguese, the pope set an imaginary line 370 leagues west of the islands of Cape Verde. Though the exact line was never fully respected, eventually Portugal would establish colonies on the eastern tip of South America, the African coast, and the Far East. Spain was granted authority over the rest of the Americas and most of the Pacific. Although the Philippines were technically in Portuguese territory, an agreement was eventually reached, placing them under Spanish jurisdiction.

After exploring the routes to the East, steps were taken for establishing colonies. The basic structure of Portuguese colonization in the East was developed by Alfonso de Albuquerque between 1510 and 1516. In order to control trade with the East Indies, Albuquerque took possession of several strategic points along the sea routes. In the Arabian Sea, the Portuguese made themselves strong in Socotra, Ormuz, and Aden, thus controlling navigation along that route. In India, they took and fortified Goa, and they did likewise with Colombo in Ceylon. By taking possession of the Straits of Malacca, they closed the easiest route to the Far East to all competitors, while they then settled in Macao and other Chinese ports. Since all these lands were occupied by large populations that could not easily be conquered, the Portuguese were content with gaining control of these strategic points that allowed them to benefit from trade with the Orient without having to attempt the conquest of all the land.

By contrast, in South America and Africa, the Portuguese settled in areas where population was sparse and not highly organized, and therefore they followed policies similar to those adopted by the Spanish in the colonization of the Americas and the Philippines.

Although the papal bulls granted Portugal lands as extensive as those that were meted out to Spain, Portuguese colonization was never as extensive as the Spanish. In the richer and more populated territories allotted to Portugal, such as China, Japan, and India, there were ancient cultures whose religions offered greater resistance to Christianity than did the religions of those conquered by the Spanish. Areas such as the eastern tip of South America and the African coast could not vie with the riches of China and the East for Portuguese attention.

(a) Portuguese colonization in America

The Portuguese had long known that it was easier to sail south and around the Cape of Good Hope if they steered far away from the

African coast, where the prevailing winds and currents ran northward. It was in one such attempt to sail out to sea far enough to be able to round the Cape of Good Hope that the Portuguese discovered the eastern tip of South America. Although the papal bulls and then the Treaty of Tordesillas did not confer to Portugal more than a very small area in the east of what today is Brazil, soon Portuguese colonization began moving westward far beyond what were supposed to be its legal limits. The area eventually became known as "Brazil" after a tree by that name that grew there and was highly valued as a dye for textiles.

The colonization of Brazil was slow, since the Portuguese crown was much more interested in trade with the Orient. To colonize the land, "captaincies" were established in Brazil. These were basically a transplant into the New World of the ancient feudal system. Each captaincy was granted to a poor member of the Portuguese aristocracy who sought lands to colonize and rule. They were usually measured only by their extension along the coast, which varied between 50 and 100 leagues. It was taken for granted that the interior of the land was open to those who owned the coast. Originally twelve such captaincies were established, but only two had a measure of success. In order to grant the system more stability, in 1549, fifteen years after the establishment of the first captaincy, the Crown decided to establish a "general captaincy" in the city of Bahia, from which the entire area would be ruled.

The indigenous populations that the Portuguese met along the Brazilian coast were enslaved, sometimes quite openly and sometimes under legal pretense similar to the Spanish encomiendas. According to the law, Indians captured in "Just War" could be enslaved. The main missionary work was carried on by friars, mostly Jesuits and Franciscans, who moved inland to establish missions similar to those we have already seen when discussing Spanish colonization, and which were known as "doutrinas." These missions were often attacked by Portuguese colonizers seeking slaves for their plantations. In spite of the work and protest of missionaries such as José de Anchieta and António

Vieira, it was not until 1755 that the law prohibited enslaving the native population. Although not promoting the abuse of that population, the Portuguese crown did even less than its Spanish counterpart to protect it from injustice and exploitation.

In general, missions in Brazil did not develop as well as or as rapidly as they did in Spanish America. Although the Jesuits founded several schools, for a long time there was no university, and those wishing to continue their studies had to go to Coimbra, in Portugal. Nor was there in Brazil a church leader comparable to Zumárraga in Mexico, with his concern to bring the advantages of the printing press and of reading to the colonies. Furthermore, the Catholic Church was even less successful than in Spanish colonies in the task of assimilating the population brought from Africa to serve as slaves when Indian labor became scarce. Therefore, the ancient African religions persisted. Part of the reason was that Portugal had other colonies that attracted its best missionaries.

The first bishopric in Brazil was established in San Salvador de Bahia in 1551 or 1552. San Sebastián de Rio de Janeiro (now known as Rio de Janeiro) was made an apostolic vicariate in 1575 and became a bishopric in 1676. On this latter date the bishopric of Pernambuco was also founded, and this was followed a year later by San Luis de Maranhão. By the eighteenth century, three others were added: Belem, São Paulo, and Mariana.

(b) Portuguese expansion in Africa

As has already been stated, Portugal had begun exploring the African coasts long before Christopher Columbus sailed across the Atlantic. During the fifteenth century, the Portuguese had settled on several islands along the western coast of Africa, particularly in Cape Verde and Fernando Poo. Some limited missionary work on the African mainland was undertaken at that time. But it was only in the sixteenth century that the true process of establishing colonies in Africa began. At first the interest of the Portuguese was simply in establishing stopping places along their route to the Indies. But those who settled in those areas were followed by priests who at first came to serve the settlers but soon began doing missionary work. Such work at first took place mostly along the western coast of Africa, particularly in Angola and in the kingdom of the Congo, whose capital, Baji, was a few miles from the mouth of the Congo River. In this latter zone, missionary work attained remarkable although ephemeral success. We are told that a king of the Congo whom the Portuguese called Alfonso accepted baptism and that this resulted in many conversions in the area. Shortly thereafter a son of Alfonso was consecrated bishop of Baji, thus becoming the first black bishop consecrated by the Roman church. Some students of African Christianity during this period affirm that many visitors regarded the Congo as Christian and never as pagan. There, Christianity was a faith shaped also by the religious worldview of the Africans. Regretfully, political conditions in the Congo changed, and the church in the area disappeared. The church in Angola, whose beginnings had not been as auspicious as in the Congo, still exists. After colonizing parts of the western coast of Africa, the Portuguese began establishing maritime bases on the east coast. Islam was already present there, and this made missionary work more difficult. In spite of this, the Portuguese and the church they represented took firm root in areas such as Mozambique and Mombasa.

The presence and activity of Luso-Africans were critical to missionary work, particularly in the islands of the Atlantic coast, but also in the eastern coast of the continent. Jesuit documents show that there were well-trained Luso-African priests who served as missionaries all over the region. In Sierra Leone, Balthasar Barreira, a layperson, established the first mission in 1604. His work was such that a Capuchin mission, which arrived in 1669, found among the Susu people the memory of Barreira's mission work. Documents also suggest that some of these

Luso-African priests served their communities better than some white priests who had arrived with the Portuguese. This reminds us of the importance that nationals have always had as missionaries.

Of all the Portuguese missions, those that drew the least attention were the ones in Africa. One reason was that the Portuguese authorities, civil as well as ecclesiastical, saw Africa not so much as an area to be converted or colonized, but rather as an obstacle along the route to the East. Furthermore, soon the Portuguese began a very active slave trade, taking people from Africa across the Atlantic to the Americas, and this seriously hampered missionary work. In the late seventeenth century a black Luso-African Catholic layperson, Lourenço da Silva, strongly confronted slavery and petitioned the Vatican to eradicate it as well as the mistreatment of black people.

During this period it is evident that Africans received Christianity with an Iberian garb. A fundamental dimension of the missionary work of Luso-Africans and Africans was to take the transmitted faith and make it African.

Before the Portuguese even attempted to enter the heart of Africa, other powers arose that vied with them for the conquest and colonization of that vast continent. Yet at the end of the period we are now studying, most of Africa was still an unknown continent for Europeans and virgin land for Christian missions.

(c) The Far East

Although the pope had placed the responsibility of colonizing the entire East on the shoulders of the Portuguese, this was not a task that Portugal alone could fulfill. The Far East was the most densely populated region of the globe, and it included some of the most ancient civilizations. It is not surprising that the ancient Oriental cultures, with their long-standing religions, would respond to European culture and to the religion that came with it with a much more vigorous resistance than the Europeans met in the Americas or in Africa. Such ancient cultures required a different missionary method than that employed elsewhere.

All that Portugal was able to achieve in the Far East was to establish small colonies along the coast, by which they controlled the oceans and trade, but certainly not the lands where they were established. Having strongholds in India, in Ceylon, and in the Straits of Malacca, the Portuguese controlled trade with the East and particularly with China, where the small colony of Macao served essentially as a trading post.

Naturally, the first churches that the Portuguese built in the East were in these small colonies they had founded there. Their ministry was mostly addressed to the Portuguese, although attempts were also made to convert those among the original population who lived within the colonies. In such cases, Christianity was often identified with Portuguese culture, and converts were required to accept, jointly with baptism, a Portuguese name and lifestyle. Not surprising, this method alienated people who loved their culture and who became convinced that they would have to abandon it in order to become Christians.

It is not possible to follow here the entire narrative of the manner in which Christianity moved from one to another region in the East. Therefore, we shall center our attention on the most notable Portuguese missionary of the sixteenth century, St. Francis Xavier, and a lesser-known but important missionary, Catharina de Farão. We will then show how a second generation of missionaries such as Roberto di Nobili and Mateo Ricci began developing more daring missionary methods.

Francis Xavier was born in Navarre in 1506. He was not yet twenty years old when he went to study at the University of Paris, where he remained until 1530. Shortly thereafter, he befriended Ignatius Loyola. Francis, Ignatius, and five other companions were the original nucleus that gave birth to the Society of Jesus, finally approved by Pope Paul III in 1539.

From its very beginnings, the Society of Jesus was committed to missionary work. One of the first Jesuit missionaries was Francis Xavier himself, who left for India in 1541, taking with him a letter of recommendation from King John II of Portugal as well as the title of papal nuncio for the East Indies. This began a life of constant travel throughout the East, preaching the gospel, organizing and strengthening churches, and instructing Portuguese as well as native converts.

After spending approximately four months in Goa, Francis Xavier went to southern India, to the Fishery Coast, where after six or seven years he had baptized more than 20,000 people. He centered his work there until 1545, although during that time he also traveled to Goa and Cochin. In 1544, he served as a mediator to settle a local armed conflict, and as a result 10,000 people were baptized. He worked mostly with children, teaching them prayers and the catechism—in Latin!

In 1545, he went to Malacca where he remained several months before moving on to Amboina, in the Moluccas. In these latter islands, he found seven villages whose residents had accepted baptism sometime before, but there was no priest. He made an effort to instruct them and to give them the pastoral care that they lacked. After four months, he went to the Moluccan capital, Temate, where he continued his work of evangelization and catechesis, and from where he also wrote letters asking that other Jesuits be sent to work in the Moluccas.

In 1547, he left these islands with the purpose of returning to India, where his presence was needed in order to supervise and organize the work of other Jesuits. Along the way, he stopped in Malacca, where he met three Japanese people, and this led him to consider working in Japan. However, he continued his voyage to India, where he once again visited Cochin, the Fishery Coast, and Goa. In all of these places there were already other Jesuits, and his work consisted mostly in supervising and organizing them. By 1549, there were more than thirty missionaries working under his direction.

Finally, Xavier felt free to undertake the mission to Japan. With two other Jesuits and the three Japanese people whom he had met in Malacca, he began the Japanese mission, and he remained in the land for slightly over two years. By the time he left, there were signs that the nascent church in that country would be one of the most remarkable successes in the Orient. He had no way of knowing that shortly after his death, for reasons that are not quite clear, a persecution would break out and Japanese Christianity would almost completely disappear.

When he returned to Malacca, Xavier learned that a new province of the Society of Jesus had been formed, that this province included all lands east of the Cape of Good Hope except Ethiopia, and that Xavier himself had been named its superior. This delayed his dream of undertaking the evangelization of China, for now he had to devote most of his time to reorganizing and supervising the work of Jesuit missionaries throughout the East. His supervisory responsibilities took him back to Cochin and Goa, from whence he finally left for China in 1552. The Chinese government, however, opposed all entry of foreigners into its territories, and therefore Xavier had to remain on the island of Shangchuan to await an opportunity to enter the mainland. It was there that he died in 1552.

Xavier's missionary methods were typical of his time. He and many other Jesuits were ready to baptize people en masse, without much Christian instruction. His constant moving from one land to another made it difficult for him to establish contacts that would really allow him to understand the cultures in which he was working, so that he was always forced to use interpreters. While such a method may work among people who for whatever reason are seeking to adopt the culture of the missionary, it falls far short of the mark when applied within cultures of long tradition, whose members have no interest in adapting to European ways. Furthermore, from the perspective of most Portuguese missionaries, pagans who became Christians also became subjects of the

Portuguese crown. They were given Portuguese names and expected to dress and behave in the same manner as their new countrymen.

Recent scholarship has uncovered the missionary work of many women who worked with the Jesuits in Asia. Among them, one important and yet little known missionary was Catharina de Farão. Catharina was a "very active Abyssinian Christian matron," who actively worked as a missionary among Muslim and Hindu women. Sixteenth-century scholar and professor of church history at Columbia Seminary Haruko Nawata Ward describes Farão as a missionary who engaged and persuaded Hindu women in their own mother tongue. She also is known as a healer and a liberator of women from oppressive customs and practices. Catharina de Farão is an example of the many women who converted to Christianity through the Jesuits and engaged in missionary work. The Jesuits themselves did not know what to make of many of these missionary women working at the fringes of the Jesuit order.

It was other Jesuit missionaries toward the end of the sixteenth century and early in the seventeenth who first began taking into account the cultures in which they were working and trying to develop a form of Christianity that would not be alien within that culture. This they did through a process of cultural adaptation. Most notable among this new generation of missionaries were Roberto di Nobili in India and Mateo Ricci in China.

The story of di Nobili, Ricci, and those who worked with them points to the importance of the cultural and social transformation of the missionaries themselves. Both di Nobili and Ricci were Italians living at a time when there was great discussion in Italy of items such as the nature of beauty and the function of a culture in shaping a community. Furthermore, their own original context meant that they were not part of the imperialist project of their Portuguese forerunners—a project that very often led to paternalistic and condescending attitudes, which in turn hampered missionary work.

Although an Italian by birth, Roberto di Nobili was sent to India by the Society of Jesus with the approval of the Portuguese crown. After spending some time in the Fishery Coast, he went to Madura, also in India, where he began his new experiment in missionary work. He sought to adapt to Indian custom as much as possible. He studied the languages of the area, as well as Sanskrit, which he thought should be the liturgical language of Christians in India. He also adopted the Hindu vegetarian diet and took for himself the respected title of "teacher." He adapted to Indian culture to such a point that he believed Christians could accept caste distinction as a sociological rather than a religious phenomenon. In di Nobili's own church, only those people of the higher castes were allowed. For others Indians, di Nobili thought special churches should be created. Following his advice, other Jesuits began working with separate castes, keeping them separate. Di Nobili accepted not only the caste system, understanding it to be a sociological and cultural phenomenon, but even the custom of *satee,* that is, burning the widow of a Hindu of high caste on the funeral pyre of her husband.

It is not surprising that di Nobili's methods were severely criticized. This led to the "Controversy of the Malabar Rites." We shall see that in China Mateo Ricci followed a similar method and that this led to an even more bitter controversy. In 1704, after great hesitation, Rome agreed to the practices of the Jesuits. It seems that this was done on the basis of inexact or incomplete information. Still, the debate continued for another forty years, until finally a papal bull prohibited the continuation of the methods that di Nobili had introduced. The entire controversy hindered missionary work in India.

Mateo Ricci is more remarkable than di Nobili. As we have already seen, St. Francis Xavier died while seeking access to China. A few years later, a Spanish leader said, "With or without soldiers, to try to penetrate into China is like trying to reach the moon." Alessandro Valignano, who was a superior of Jesuit missions in the East Indies beginning in 1573, seems to have been the first to realize the need for a new missionary method in order to be able to enter China. It was Valignano who ordered Michele Ruggieri to devote himself to the study of Chinese so that some day he would be able to work as a missionary in China. Fully understanding Valignano's intentions, Ruggieri studied not only the Chinese language but also the culture and customs of the land. His knowledge of Chinese culture gained him great prestige among the Chinese in Guangzhou (Canton) and later in the provincial capital of Shaoxing. After political changes made his first attempts unsuccessful, Ruggieri was able to settle in Shaoxing, where Mateo Ricci, another Jesuit, was appointed to work with him. Like di Nobili, Valignano, and Ruggieri, Ricci was Italian by birth. He had entered the Society of Jesus in 1571, and in 1578, after studying in the University of Coimbra, in Portugal, he set out for the Orient with the approval of the Portuguese crown. His first experiences in Goa convinced Valignano that Ricci would be a good companion for Ruggieri. Once he learned that China was to be his mission field, Ricci made every effort to understand and appreciate the civilization in which he hoped to work.

At that point, China was ruled by an elite group of scholars. Since he was convinced that it would be impossible to carry out permanent work among the common people, Ricci decided to join the ranks of those scholars. In this, he was aided by his knowledge of mathematics, astronomy, and geography. European clocks caused great amazement among visitors whom Ricci received at his home. His world map soon became known throughout China, thus bringing recognition both to its author and to the cause he represented. The respect and interest that Ricci showed for Chinese culture led some among the erudite class to approach him and his message with a similar respect and interest. Ricci was a careful student of the Chinese classics, and he wrote in Chinese a *Treatise on Friendship*, which soon circulated among the philosophers of that land, showing them that also in the West and among Christians this virtue that the Chinese prized was admired. At the same time, one must point out, although Ricci appreciated the Confucian culture of China, he showed contempt for the religious practices of the country, tied to Buddhism and Taoism. In this, he shared the attitude of the ruling intellectual elite of China, which was also quite critical of these religious expressions.

Ricci never established open churches in Chinese territory. One reason for this was that he did not wish to arouse suspicion among the authorities. Another reason was that he feared that the common people would follow the practice that had become common in Buddhist temples, which had often been turned into recreation centers and places for public banquets. Nor did Ricci seek to have great numbers of converts, but rather he limited his work to personal contact and conversation with the scholars who ruled the land. For himself, he claimed to be no more than a wise man from the West and therefore a colleague of the wise men with whom he met.

Ricci's methods allowed him and his followers to enter a country that was practically sealed against foreigners. From Shaoxing, he moved to Nanjing, and eventually to Beijing, where he worked for nine years until he died in 1615.

Although Ricci did not gain many converts, in each of the places where he resided, he left other Jesuit missionaries to continue his work; and in Beijing itself, he and his fellow Jesuits were officially in charge of all astronomical research.

When, in the middle of the seventeenth century, the Ming Dynasty was forced by the growing power of the Manchus to move south, the Jesuits had such prestige that they were able to continue working both among the Ming and among the Manchu. At that point also their scientific knowledge became useful, for one of the ways in which the Jesuits gained the support of the Manchus was by helping them in the casting of cannon to be used against the Ming. Thus the Jesuits were actually allies of both sides.

Less than a century after Ricci's death there were already several thousand Christians in China. However, just as in the case of di Nobili in India, the work of Ricci and his successors was weakened by the opposition of other Catholic missionaries—particularly Franciscans and Dominicans—who opposed the methods of Ricci and his companions as an unwarranted accommodation of the Christian faith. The Jesuits claimed the veneration of Confucius and of his ancestors was not religious, but rather social, and that it could therefore be continued after baptism. Another point of controversy had to do with how to translate the name of God. One side tried to use the traditional name for the supreme being, which seemed to be rather impersonal, and the other preferred a more personal way to refer to God. The controversy was heated and prolonged. Eventually, Rome followed the same policy that it had eventually followed in India, forbidding the veneration of ancestors and of Confucius and declaring that the word that the Jesuits were employing to refer to God was not adequate. Quite understandably, this provoked the ire of those Chinese who were interested in the matter, and particularly of the emperor, who is said to have demanded how a "barbarian" who had no notion of the Chinese language dared determine how it should be spoken. From that point on missions in China faced ever-increasing difficulties.

The story of the Portuguese missions in the Orient helps illustrate one of the most serious considerations in missionary work: how does one determine the right degree and the appropriate methods of adapting to a given culture? On the one hand, an attempt to proclaim the message with no adaptation leads to an undesirable confusion between the Christian message and the culture of those who proclaim it. On the other hand, there is always the danger that in an attempt to adapt to a new culture, something essential to the Christian message may be lost. Furthermore, it is interesting to note that it was not the Portuguese, but rather Italian missionaries working under Portuguese sponsorship, who most clearly understood the need to establish the distinction between

Portuguese culture and power on the one hand and the Christian faith on the other. Probably the very fact that they were not Portuguese helped them see the senselessness of trying to "Portugalize" converts.

4. French Missions

Although not to the same extent as Spain and Portugal, France also contributed to the expansion of Roman Catholicism during the period we are now studying. A significant part of that expansion was simply the result of conquest and colonization, while some of it was also the result of the Société des Missions Étrangères de Paris.

(a) French expansion

Following the lead of Spain and Portugal, and in competition with them, France launched a process of conquest and colonization of new lands. In that enterprise, it was hampered both by the inner conditions of France itself and by the papal bulls that granted all newly discovered lands to Spain and Portugal. However, during the Modern Age, France was able to establish colonies in North America (where it occupied a vast section of the eastern coast of Canada and also of the Mississippi basin), in some of the islands of the Caribbean, and in the north of South America (what became known as French Guyana or Cayenne). In all these lands, there was sparse native population, and their civilization was no match for French colonization. Thus, the French could not follow in these areas a policy similar to that of the Spanish in the vast Inca and Aztec empires. Rather, they had to emulate the policies of the Spanish and Portuguese in areas where the indigenous population lived in conditions similar to those in the newly established French colonies. The most important missionary work carried on by the French in the Americas took place among the Hurons in the St. Lawrence basin. Although the work was quite successful, it disappeared in the middle of the seventeenth century when the Iroquois coalition invaded the area and annihilated the Hurons.

From the point of view of our history, the most important event was the establishment in the Americas of new Christian communities formed mostly by European immigrants and by African slaves who eventually became Christian. During the eighteenth century, France had to cede to England and Spain most of its territories in North America; its only permanent foothold in that continent was in the region of Quebec. Even after Quebec itself became British, the influence of French Catholicism did not disappear but became even more marked as the identity of the French-speaking Canadians became associated with their traditional faith. As to the Mississippi basin, French influence could long be felt near the mouth of the river, particularly in New Orleans. In the Antilles and French Guyana, the European population was soon joined by a large number of slaves brought from Africa. The French church, and particularly its friars, were very much interested in the conversion of the slaves, and there were soon Christian communities among them.

(b) The Société des Missions Étrangères de Paris

The purpose of this society was to develop a native clergy in mission lands. According to its founders, as long as these newly established churches had to continue receiving their clergy from Europe, they would be totally dependent and would be unable to undertake missionary work on their own. For this reason, the Société des Missions Étrangères was especially interested in sending diocesan clergy to mission lands, where their task was to train a native diocesan clergy. Among its leaders and founders were distinguished missionary and ecclesiastical leaders, such as François Pallu and François Xavier de Laval-Montmorency, who was bishop of Quebec and in 1668 founded in that city a seminary for the training of diocesan clergy following the principles established by the society.

Much of the work of this society of foreign missions took place in the Orient, particularly in India, Southeast Asia, and China. The presence of the society in these areas was extremely valuable, particularly after the Jesuits were expelled from all Portuguese lands in 1759. The resulting disaster for missionary work would have been much worse had there not been a diocesan clergy already provided by the society. Frenchman La Motte Lambert settled in Siam in 1662, and two years later was joined there by Pallu himself. There they worked in the training of a diocesan indigenous clergy for Cochinchina and other regions of Southeast Asia. The institution they founded was eventually moved to India.

The presence of the Société des Missions Étrangères in missionary work in the East created friction with Portuguese and Spanish authorities, who held that the papal bulls granted them monopoly over missionary work in the area. Those who represented the Portuguese and Spanish empires feared that French missionaries would provide a beachhead for French colonial expansion. This was what in fact happened, although it is also necessary to point out that, without French missionaries, Roman Catholic work in much of the East would have disappeared jointly with Portuguese and Spanish might.

5. The Beginnings of Catholic Missiology

The vast outreach of Roman Catholic missions during the Modern Age awakened interest in missiology within some Roman Catholic theological circles. This was true both of missionaries themselves and of some among the theologians who remained in Europe. Spanish Dominican Francisco de Vitoria, who is credited with establishing the basis for modern international law, devoted himself to the study of what was then called *Derecho de Indias*—meaning the laws and the ethic to be applied in the new lands—and strongly criticized the policies of his countrymen in the Americas. Carmelite Tomás de Jesús, another Spaniard who at first opposed the participation of his order in missionary work, eventually wrote a treatise, *De procuranda salute omnium gentium*, which sought to gather in a single volume the best missiological theory and knowledge of his time. But, even though some claimed that Tomás de Jesús was superior, the great theologian of missions during this time was the Spanish Jesuit José de Acosta.

Acosta combined many years of academic and professorial work with a direct experience of mission among the inhabitants of the Americas—particularly in Peru, where he worked for sixteen years. His main work is *De procuranda Indorum salute*, published in six books in 1588. There Acosta tries to justify the evangelizing work among the native population but also offers numerous methodological and theological considerations.

Acosta believed that the foundation for mission is the saving will of God, who does not wish the indigenous population to be lost. Thus the purpose of mission is preaching the gospel and saving souls—in which he contrasted with many Catholic theologians in the twentieth century, who claimed that the object of missions was the establishment of the church in various areas, what they called *plantatio ecclesiae*. It should also be noted that, although Acosta was convinced that the original inhabitants of the Americas should be converted and baptized, he was also convinced that they were inferior human beings whose intellectual and moral deficiency disqualified them for the priesthood.

B. The Expansion of Orthodox Christianity

During the period we are now considering, Orthodox Christianity was not able to expand from Constantinople due to the constant Turkish pressure. However, Russian Orthodox Christianity did expand eastward at the same time that Russian power moved in the same direction. In the sixteenth century, Russia expanded beyond the Urals, and by the seventeenth, it had reached the Pacific Ocean. Early in the eighteenth century, Russia began colonizing the Aleutian Islands and Alaska. This political expansion was accompanied by the expansion of a church that was closely tied to the state. However, the expansion of the church was not limited to the Russian population that moved eastward. There were also missionaries who sought to carry the gospel to the ever-increasing population that was now subject to the czar. A special mention must be made of missionary Philotheus Leszcynskij, metropolitan of Tobolsk, who devoted himself to organizing missionary work in the areas where the Russian Empire reached. Shortly after Leszcynskij's death, a seminary was founded in Irkutsk for the training of missionaries. There the languages of the subjected peoples were studied, as well as Chinese. During this time there also was a Russian mission in Beijing, although this was limited to providing church services for the very small Russian colony and to serve as a diplomatic representative of Russian interests.

Besides the preaching of priests and monks, the main instrument employed by the Russians in order to lead people to accept baptism was an offer of tax exemption for converts. Many of those who were converted under such conditions did not have a very clear idea of the meaning of the step they were taking. However, one must note that, except in the Russian lands of North America, the Russian Orthodox Church developed roots that would continue at least until the twenty-first century.

C. Early Protestant Missions

1. The Opposition of Orthodox Protestantism to Missions among Nonbelievers

We have already noted that during the entire period we are studying, Catholic expansion overshadowed all Protestant efforts in this direction. This was due to a series of political and theological factors. The first reformers, who lived mostly in lands that had no contact with the recently "discovered" territories, did not feel the same missionary responsibility that Christians in Spain and Portugal felt. But those early reformers also justified their lack of interest in missions to other lands with theological arguments, and therefore many of their successors felt compelled to take the same position.

(a) Martin Luther

Martin Luther's interest in missionary work was always marginal. It was not that he opposed such work, but rather that the task of reforming the church and converting the "heathen" that clung to ancient doctrines and traditions took all his time and attention. Led by the heat of controversy, Luther even declared that the commission to go throughout the world preaching the gospel was given only to the apostles and that later Christians should not take that commandment as addressed to them. Rather than that, they should remain where God has placed them and there work for the cause of the gospel. At any rate, Luther adds, there are always Christians who are taken to lands of nonbelievers as captives or for some other reason, and God uses such people to witness to their faith in those places.

This does not mean that Luther completely rejected all missionary work among nonbelievers. On the contrary, in his writings one finds references to the hope that the pagans and Muslims will be converted. Furthermore, in some of these texts he speaks positively about Jews and Muslims, although as time progressed he tended to emphasize both the hope that they would be converted and also his contempt for their religions. Finally, although Luther himself never employed it to that end, his own insistence on the priesthood of all believers would eventually result in an added interest in missionary work on the part of Protestants.

(b) Philipp Melanchthon

Philipp Melanchthon followed Luther's lead on the matter of missions. He agreed that the Great Commission was given only to the apostles, who fulfilled it, and therefore the church need not be concerned about work in other lands. He does affirm that civil authorities in Christian lands have a responsibility for expanding the Christian message.

(c) Ulrich Zwingli, John Calvin, and Martin Bucer

These three reformers, the fountainheads of the Reformed tradition, generally agreed with Luther and Melanchthon on the matter of missions to distant lands, although they would say that the preaching of the gospel to every creature throughout the world has not yet been fulfilled. Calvin held that apostleship was an extraordinary office granted only to the first disciples of the Lord and that the expansion of the gospel to other lands is the responsibility of civil authorities. On the other hand, Bucer and Zwingli did believe that the office of apostle continued throughout history. God calls specific persons to different parts of the world so that the gospel may be proclaimed. But this call is given to a very small number of people, and any who claim that they are to take up that task must first of all make certain that God has called them to it. As to the responsibility for the church to organize and plan missionary work in lands other than its own, all of these reformers say very little.

(d) Hadrian Saravia and Theodore Beza's response

Among all Protestant theologians in the sixteenth century, only Hadrian Saravia argued openly and decisively for the responsibility of Christians to do missionary work in lands other than their own. Although born in the Netherlands, Saravia spent most of his life in England, where in 1590, he published a work in which he dealt with, among other subjects, the missionary task and the apostolic ministry: *De diversis ministrorum gradibus, sic ut a Domino fuerunt instituti.* Here Saravia claimed that, just as the promise "I am with you until the end of the world" was given to the entire church and not only to the apostles, so also the commandment to go throughout the world and preach the gospel has been given to all Christians. Furthermore, the apostles themselves, in appointing companions and successors, made it clear that their work had to be continued after their death, and this the church has done throughout its history. Finally, it would be absurd to think that the task of evangelizing the entire world could be accomplished by a small number of apostles in a few years of ministry. For all these reasons, it is necessary for the church to take upon itself the task of proclaiming the gospel throughout the world, for it is precisely for this reason that it has been given the keys to the Kingdom.

Theodore Beza, Calvin's successor in Geneva, responded to this in 1592 with his treatise *Ad tractationem de ministrorum evangelii gradibus ab Hadriano Saravia.* In this work, he refutes much of what Saravia had to say, particularly referring to offices within the church. In that which concerns missions, Beza follows Calvin's position, although he claims that there are two parts to the Great Commission. The first, "go throughout the world," applied only to the apostles. The second part, "preach the gospel," is valid for the church throughout all times. Even so, Beza did accept Saravia's principle that the churches do have the obligation to seek to expand God's reign, although he did not offer any indications as to how this was to be done, nor is it clear that this had anything to do with preaching the gospel among the unconverted.

(e) Johan Gerhard

This famous theologian in Jena published early in the seventeenth century his *Loci theologici*, in which he developed an entire system of Protestant theology. His position regarding missions is the same as that of the reformers. According to Gerhard, the apostles preached to all the nations, although some did not accept the message that was preached to them. From those early nations where the apostles proclaimed the gospel, all the nations of the earth are derived; and therefore if some do not know the gospel today, this is not due to the negligence of the church nor to an injustice on God's part, but simply to the fact that their ancestors did not accept the preaching of the apostles. According to Gerhard, this is true, not only of the nations in the Mediterranean basin, but also of the natives of the Americas, for in Mexico, Perú, and

Brazil European settlers have found signs of an almost-forgotten Christianity. The same is true of the various Eastern civilizations.

As to the ministry of proclaiming the gospel elsewhere, Gerhard affirms that the present ministers of the church have authority to preach the gospel and to administer the sacraments, but they differ from the apostles in that these ministers do not have a direct calling from God, cannot do miracles, are not infallible, and have not seen Christ in the flesh, and their ministry is limited to a particular place. This is followed by a detailed refutation of all the arguments that could be used to claim that the church still has a missionary obligation. These sections are directed mostly at Saravia's arguments.

(f) Justinian von Weltz

During the second half of the seventeenth century this Austrian nobleman undertook the task of calling the Lutheran communion to its missionary obligation. In 1664, he published his first treatise in defense of missions, and this was soon followed by two others. In these works, von Weltz was the first to try to respond to the Roman Catholic claim that Protestantism's lack of interest in creating a worldwide church through missionary work showed that it was not truly a catholic and apostolic church. Before von Weltz, Protestant theologians tried to respond to this accusation by claiming that it was not true that the church should be concerned about worldwide mission. Von Weltz saw the value of the accusation and decided to respond to it, not with simple arguments against missions themselves, but rather calling "all Christians of the right faith of the Augsburg Confession" to organize a society for missionary work. This society would include people whose task would be to collect the necessary funds for missionary work, others who would direct the society itself, and finally others who would go to nonbelievers in order to preach the gospel to them. For the training of the latter, a *Collegium de propaganda fide* should be created, for it was important for missionaries to know the language and the customs of the lands where they would be working. This appeal by von Weltz was not well received by church authorities. But von Weltz himself sealed his teachings by giving up his life as a missionary in Dutch Guyana (Surinam).

As an example of the reaction of orthodox Protestantism to von Weltz's proposals, one may cite the following works from the Ratisbone theologian Ursinus, who claims that, in order to make von Weltz's project work:

> it would be necessary for pagans not to be positively savages, lacking in all human characteristics. It would also be necessary for them not to be ferocious and warlike, people who do not allow foreigners to live among them. Certainly it would be necessary for them not to be obstinate blasphemers, persecutors of Christians, destructors of the Christian religion that their ancestors lost because of their hateful ingratitude. . . . The holy things of God are not to be cast before such dogs and swine. (Quoted by G. Warneck, *Abriss einer Geschichte der protestantischen Missionen* [Berlin, (Martin Warneck), 1905], 36–37)

2. Protestant Expansion through Political Expansion

As we have seen, most early Protestant theologians claimed that the missionary task should be the state's responsibility. However, it is important to point out that, with a few exceptions, most Protestant governments were much less interested in fulfilling that responsibility than were Catholic governments. At any rate, the dawning of the expansion of Protestant nations was one of the main reasons for the emerging Protestant interest in world missions. Leaving aside the failed Huguenot attempt in Brazil under the leadership of Nicholas de Villegaignon, and the work of Swedish king Gustavus Vasa to carry his faith to the Lapps, Protestant colonial expansion was mostly the result of the growing power of Great Britain, the Netherlands, and Denmark. This took place mostly in the seventeenth and eighteenth centuries, which was also the time when Spanish and Portuguese power was declining. After the destruction of the Spanish Armada in 1588, the British began filling the vacuum left by the maritime decline of Spain and Portugal. In this, they were soon joined by the Dutch and the Danes. This would eventually lead to the great Protestant missionary expansion of the nineteenth and twentieth centuries.

(a) Dutch expansion

As soon as it became independent from the Spanish crown, the Netherlands emerged as a growing maritime power. Dutch sailors began crossing the seas, competing for the trade that had previously been held exclusively by the Spanish and the Portuguese. This resulted in the founding of the Dutch East India Company. From its very beginning, this company claimed to have a missionary purpose among others. Following the teachings of the early reformers, the Dutch believed that the civil authorities should be responsible for missionary work, and for this reason it was the company and not the church that organized such work in Dutch colonies. Although it was the church that ordained missionaries, their work was supervised by the Dutch East India Company. Since there were not too many people trained to do this sort of work, in 1622, a *Seminarium Indicum* was founded in Leiden. This was to be a center for the preparation of missionaries to the Indies. But this institution disappeared after twelve years of existence. Most of the missionaries working under contract with the East India Company did not work as much in the preaching to nonbelievers as in the spiritual edification and pastoral care of Dutch settlers. Even so, there were regions where many converts were made.

It was in the Orient that Dutch missions had their greatest success. In Java, Ceylon, the Moluccas, and Formosa, Dutch missionaries were able to create strong churches. In those areas, there were mass conversions such as we have already found in other chapters of this history. We are told, for instance, that a king of Timor joined the church, bringing with himself all his subjects. It was also customary to pay missionaries on the basis of the number of baptisms they performed, and therefore some tended to offer baptism without requiring much training for those who were to receive it. It is important to take this into account in order to understand that originally Protestant missions did not always seek the conversion of individuals, nor did they insist on catechetical instruction before baptism.

The Dutch also settled in South America. Besides a short attempt to settle in Bahia, they established in 1630 a colony in Pernambuco, which lasted slightly over thirty years. In neither of these cases were there permanent results in terms of churches or communities being founded. As to the Dutch colony of Surinam, the Dutch themselves did not seem to have paid much attention to the work there among the native population or among African slaves, and it took the Moravian impulse later on to begin missionary work among them. There are no records of any permanent results of Justinian von Weltz's work in that area.

The effect of Dutch colonies in North America was greater. It was the Dutch who founded New Holland, which later became the British colony of New York. Its purpose was mercantile rather than religious, and therefore there were not many missionaries in New Holland. The most distinguished among those missionaries was Johannes Megapolensis, who in 1643 began working among the Mohawks, whose language he learned. Although most of the settlers in New Holland belonged to the Dutch Reformed church, there was always religious tolerance, which allowed other Protestants to settle there. When New Holland passed into British hands, Dutch influence began declining.

Probably more important than the actual founding of missions was the beginning of a missionary interest in the Netherlands. This may be seen in the work of Justus Heurnius's *De legatione evangelica ad Indos capessenda admonitio.* This was soon followed by others, in which various Dutch theologians showed that they had been influenced by contact with the Far East and the Americas. This new interest would lead to a Protestant missionary awakening in the nineteenth century.

(b) British expansion

At approximately the same time as the Netherlands, and also mostly at the expense of Spain and Portugal, Great Britain began developing its naval power to found colonies, particularly in North America. The first British attempts to settle there took place in the sixteenth century, and from the very beginning one of its avowed purposes was the propagation of Christianity, although in truth political and economic interests were much more important than any missionary concern. At any rate, when Sir Walter Raleigh established the colony of Virginia, the preaching of the gospel to the natives of the area was begun. Sir Walter Raleigh himself provided funds so that the Virginia Company could preach the gospel among the natives. The charter of the Virginia Company declared that it was to proclaim Christianity "to such people as yet live in darkness and miserable ignorance of the true knowledge and worship of God," and we are told that in 1587, the first Native American convert to Protestantism was baptized.

The most important missionary in early Virginia was Alexander Whitaker, who preached the gospel and also sought to teach the native population—among whom was the famous Pocahontas. His work was destroyed when Indians were massacred in 1622. Another attempt to evangelize and educate the original inhabitants of Virginia was the founding of the College of William and Mary, whose explicit purpose was to instruct both white and indigenous people. However, there were not many of the latter ever enrolled in that institution.

There was also a lively missionary interest among the New England pilgrims. They had left England and traveled to the Netherlands in quest of a respite from the pressure to which they were subjected in England because they would not submit to the religious norms of that nation. Then similar reasons led them to leave Holland and settle in the New World. Although the call to preach the gospel among nonbelievers was not central to their thought, it was always present. One of the early settlers was Roger Williams, who is credited with much of the early evangelization of the native inhabitants of New England. Also, several pastors in Plymouth did similar work.

The best known among the New England missionaries was John Eliot, who began working among the Mohicans in 1646 under the auspices of the Massachusetts Bay Company. His work as a missionary lasted almost half a century, and during that time he not only preached to the Mohicans, but also translated the Bible into their language and taught them how to read. There was an eschatological dimension to his missionary enterprise, for Eliot thought that perhaps the natives of America were the ten lost tribes of Israel, and that in that case their conversion would be a fulfillment of ancient prophecy. It was probably also for that reason that he applied the law of Moses among those who received the gospel. Converts lived in fourteen villages organized according to that law. At the center of each village stood a common building that served both as a church and as a school. Besides religious instruction, people also learned new means of subsistence, particularly in agriculture.

Although Eliot's work did not last because of the violence perpetrated against the people among whom he had worked, it did have great effect in England. The news that arrived there about Eliot's work was one of the main reasons that led to the creation of the Society for the Propagation of the Gospel in New England in 1649. This society had a long history of missionary service, and it was the forerunner of many others that we shall meet later.

Another interesting experiment was conducted by the Mayhew family in Martha's Vineyard. This land was granted to the Mayhews in 1642, and they immediately showed a special concern for the education and evangelization of people living within their domain. This enterprise was passed from parents to children during five generations, ending with the death of Zachariah Mayhew in 1806.

As a sign of the importance of missionary motivation in the early years of New England, one must remember that Harvard University, founded in 1636, declared that one of its purposes was the training of English and Indians in both knowledge and piety.

Also important was the work of Dr. Thomas Bray, ecclesiastical commissioner for Maryland beginning in 1696, whose reports were widely read in England. This led to the creation of several societies to support missionary work. The Society for the Promotion of Christian Knowledge was founded in 1698, the Society for the Propagation of the Gospel in Foreign Parts in 1701, and "Dr. Bray's Associates" in 1723. All of these groups, but most particularly the second, did extensive work among both the indigenous and the African populations of North America. However, since many of the white settlers in the New World feared that the work of missionaries sent or supported by these Anglican societies would serve to strengthen the power of the official Church of England, this work met many obstacles.

The Society in Scotland for Propagating Christian Knowledge was founded in 1709. It was similar to those that the Anglicans had founded in England, but it had the advantage that the Scottish church was better received among the settlers in the New World because the Church of Scotland was Presbyterian rather than Anglican. The Scottish society founded corresponding boards in America, particularly one in New York that played an important role in missions not only in New York, but also in New Jersey and Pennsylvania. The best known among the missionaries who worked under the direction of the Scottish Society was David Brainerd, who worked in several of these colonies. His work was of short duration, for he died when he was twenty-nine years old. His method consisted mostly in founding schools and in encouraging the native population to live in areas where it was possible to provide religious instruction for them. The main reason making Brainerd's work important is that in 1749, Jonathan Edwards published *Life of Brainerd* based on the missionary's diaries. The effect of this work was enormous, and it may be seen in the work and thought of important figures in the history of the Christian missionary movement such as William Carey and Francis Asbury.

The foregoing refers only to some of the many missionaries who worked among the natives and among people of African descent in the British colonies of North America, but they suffice to show that from the beginning of British colonization there was a genuine interest in the conversion of the people in the areas where colonies were established. It is also important to point out, however, that this missionary concern was not shared by the church as a whole, but rather was the work of individual Christians who undertook that task and who created societies to support it.

Besides the colonies established in North America, Britain also occupied several islands in the Atlantic, particularly in the Caribbean, as well as a section of the eastern coast of Central America—mostly along the Mosquito Coast. These lands were devoted mostly to sugarcane, which at that time was a very profitable investment, and which resulted in the importation of large numbers of slaves from Africa. In almost all these areas, the indigenous people disappeared or became a very small portion of the population. Therefore, the main missionary challenge was the evangelization of the slaves—and later, when Christian conscience was aroused, their emancipation. Most of the work in this area was carried out at first by the Church of England, although with strong opposition on the part of many settlers who feared the consequences of the evangelization and particularly of the education of slaves. For this reason the Society for the Propagation of the Gospel in Foreign Parts began buying plantations with slaves in them and then evangelizing those who were thus placed under its tutelage. Obviously, this made it possible to reach only a small fraction of the slave population and, even worse, turned the church into a slave owner. It was in the second half of the eighteenth century, with the arrival of Moravians and Methodists, that an intense work of evangelization was undertaken in the British colonies in the Caribbean. Also the Quakers and the Schwenkfelders settled in the area, although they did not show as vibrant a missionary interest as did the Moravians and Methodists.

In general, British colonization in the Americas gave rise to communities comprised mostly of European and African immigrants, for the indigenous population tended to disappear in the areas colonized by the British much more than it did in those that had earlier been colonized by the Spanish. One of the reasons for this was that the native population in British territories had always been smaller. Another reason was that British colonizers were much more interested in native lands than in native labor and therefore did little to prevent the death of the original inhabitants or their flight into the interior of the land. Finally, one must remember that Protestant churches did not have the same power to curtail abuse as did the Catholic Church when supported by the Spanish crown.

One must point out that during this period the British also undertook trade with the Far East, although in that area British influence would be most notable at a later date.

(c) Danish expansion

Denmark began its expansion early in the seventeenth century, when its attention was directed mostly toward the east, but later in the same century the Danish settled in the West Indies and in Africa. The Danes seemed to be much less interested in missionary work than the Dutch or the British. It was a Danish king, Frederick IV, who first showed significant concern for the evangelization of non-Christians living in Danish colonies. Even then, when the king asked the court preacher to find people to send as missionaries to the Danish colonies, it was impossible to find anywhere in Denmark someone to take this responsibility, and therefore the Danish king had to turn to the nascent Pietist movement in Germany. This was the origin of the famous

Tranquebar mission in India. This mission, though financially supported by the Danish crown, was the work of German Pietist missionaries, and therefore we shall discuss it when we study the impact of Pietism. It is also important to point out that, although the first Danish settlers showed little interest in missionary work, their settlements themselves were later used by Moravian and Pietist missionaries for the proclamation of the gospel.

3. New Movements within Protestantism

Late in the seventeenth century and throughout the eighteenth, there was an awakening of personal piety within Protestantism, and this was closely related to a new interest in missions. The leaders of this movement protested against the rigidity of old-style Protestant orthodoxy, and even though they themselves were theologians with significant education, they tended to stress the importance of the practice of the Christian life above the affirmation of theological formulae. This practice of the Christian life was often understood mostly in individualistic terms, and therefore the personal experience of the believer and one's obedience to divine commands were stressed. In general, these movements did not pretend to create new churches or sects, but rather to serve as a leaven within the existent churches. Sometimes that was not the end result, but this was due not to a schismatic spirit within the founders of the movement as much as to the rigidity of the churches they sought to reform.

(a) Pietism and the University of Halle

The first of these movements, whose name is often applied to others, was German Pietism. The father of Pietism was Philipp Jakob Spener, who proposed the main principles of the movement in his work *Pia desideria*, published in 1675. He criticized the cold and rigid orthodoxy of the Lutheran church of his day. He disagreed with his church not in doctrinal matters, but rather in practical issues, for he deplored the manner in which insistence on doctrinal formulae tended to obscure the need for a personal Christian life. After long years working both as a pastor and as a professor, Spener founded the University of Halle in 1694. This university would be of enormous importance for the later history of missions. In all of this, Spener and his friends were staunchly opposed by some of the most distinguished theologians of their times, who often accused them of doctrinal error.

The successor of Spener in the leadership of the Pietist movement was August Hermann Francke, who taught at the University of Halle, and who also founded in that city a home where orphan children could reside and study. Like Spener before him, Francke was much interested in mission work, and he turned the University of Halle into a mission center.

It was to that university that Frederick IV of Denmark turned when he decided to begin missionary work in the Orient and did not find anywhere in his kingdom people able and ready to undertake this task. This was the beginning of the Danish mission of Tranquebar, whose first missionaries were Bartholomaeus Ziegenbalg and Heinrich Plutschau.

Ziegenbalg and Plutschau initially had much difficulty, for they were opposed first by the church authorities in Denmark and then by the colonial authorities in India. This opposition had to do mostly with their Pietist convictions, which were looked at askance by more traditional Lutherans. This did not stop their work, and they settled in 1706 in Tranquebar in India. Plutschau returned to Europe after five years of work in India, but Ziegenbalg lived the rest of his days in Tranquebar. Their work was varied, for besides ministering to Danish and German settlers they worked among the Portuguese-speaking Roman Catholics and among the Indians. Most of the work among the latter took place in Tamil-speaking areas, into which language they translated Luther's *Small Catechism.* In 1711, the translation of the New Testament into Tamil was published.

The Tranquebar mission eventually gained wide support in various European circles, for it drew its missionaries from German Pietism centered at the University of Halle, and its financial support came at first from Denmark and then also from the English Society for Promoting Christian Knowledge.

There were very able successors to Ziegenbalg, and these expanded the missionary work to other areas near Tranquebar, so that soon there was Christian literature not only in Tamil, but also in Telegu and Hindi. Outstanding among Ziegenbalg's successors is Christian Friedrich Schwartz, who began working in India in 1750 and remained there until his death forty-eight years later. His humble but firm spirit gained him the respect of the European settlers as well as of the Indians, so that he was repeatedly called to mediate in a number of conflicts and was able to prevent several wars.

Although German Pietism was so widespread and so varied that it is impossible to show all its ramifications, there is no question that it was related not only to the mission in Tranquebar and others stemming from it but also with the College of Missions that was founded in Copenhagen and from which eventually missionaries left for Lapland and Greenland. The mission in these areas did not have as far reaching results as did the work in Tranquebar, but the one in Greenland is important because of its impact on Count Zinzendorf.

(b) Zinzendorf and the Moravians

Count Nicolaus Ludwig von Zinzendorf was a man of sincere personal Christian piety who studied at the University of Halle and was profoundly influenced by its founders. In 1722, the Moravian Brothers, whose origins can be traced as far back as John Huss, were looking for a place to live where they could avoid persecution. Count Zinzendorf offered them lands in his territories in Saxony where they could settle. There they founded the village of Herrnhut. Zinzendorf had always been interested in missions as a result of his training in Halle, but this interest was aroused in 1731, when visiting Copenhagen he met two Eskimos from Greenland who had been baptized by the missionary Hans Egede. Upon returning to his lands he began turning the Herrnhut community into a missionary center. Thanks to his contagious enthusiasm and the depth of his religious convictions, Zinzendorf was able to inspire a similar spirit among the Moravians, and soon they began spreading throughout the world, carrying the message of the gospel.

As was to be expected, the first Moravian missionary endeavors were directed to Greenland, but at the same time, in 1732, Moravians also went to the Caribbean, settling on the island of St. Thomas, and three years later they were already in Dutch Guyana (Surinam). Shortly thereafter, they also began traveling to the Far East, where they worked in India and Ceylon, and to Africa, where they settled in Cape Town.

The missionary thrust of the Moravians could not continue growing at the same rate. Their limited numbers made it difficult for them to establish many lasting missions. But their influence would not be lost, for their work called many others in Europe to a missionary task.

(c) The Wesleys and Methodism

Among the thousands who were influenced by Zinzendorf and the Moravians, none is as important for the history of missions as John Wesley and the Methodist movement that developed out of his joint work with his brother, Charles. The two brothers were Anglican priests who sought to renew the life of their church rather than to create a new denomination. John was discontent with his own Christian experience and also frustrated in his attempts to serve as a priest in Georgia. As he traveled across the Atlantic to America, his ship was in danger of sinking, and Wesley was profoundly impressed by the unshakable faith of the Moravians who traveled with him. That experience awakened his interest in the Moravian movement and eventually led him to establish contact with Zinzendorf. It is commonly said that Methodism was born when Wesley had his famous religious experience at Aldersgate Street and felt his heart "strangely warmed." But there is no doubt that his relationship with Zinzendorf and the Moravians left a profound impact on Wesley and through him on Methodism.

Methodism did not intend to become a new church but intended instead simply to promote an awakening of personal piety within the Church of England and among other Protestants in the nation. Throughout his whole life, Wesley and his companions continued being members of the Church of England and sharing in its worship. It was only later events that led to the birth of the Methodist Church.

At any rate, Methodists represented a religious awakening both in the British Isles and in North America, and this would have far-reaching consequences for the missionary movement. The first Methodist society was founded in London in 1739, and by 1766, there was also a Methodist society in America. It was in 1771, with the arrival of Francis Asbury, that the vast Methodist expansion in North America began. Soon the movement would be much more numerous in the Western Hemisphere than in Great Britain. Although many Methodist preachers contributed to the growth of the movement in America, there is no doubt that the most outstanding was Asbury, who preached more than 16,500 sermons, ordained at least 4,000 preachers, and traveled half a million kilometers. Much of this work took place on the western frontier of the British colonies in North America, which was moving westward more rapidly than the more established churches were able to do. Thus the Methodists—jointly with the Baptists, who were also experiencing an awakening—contributed significantly to the persistence of an active Christian faith among people moving westward.

Methodism expanded mostly through simple preaching, often in open air, and by organizing small groups or "classes" for the nurture of the spiritual life of their members. As years went by, Methodism became a church in the more traditional fashion—first in the United States, and eventually in England—and the system of classes as well as public preaching in the open began receding into the background.

Although at first Methodism worked particularly in Great Britain and its colonies, its growth in those lands was such that by the nineteenth century it had become one of the main sources of Protestant missions.

(d) The Great Awakening

Toward the middle of the eighteenth century, and then again at the end of that century and early in the next, a series of movements arose in the British colonies in North America that is difficult to explain or even to describe in a few words. This was a general awakening in the religious life of the settlers, and it was parallel to European Pietism. The main figures in the first stages of the awakening were Jonathan Edwards and George Whitefield. The latter had been a close friend and collaborator of John Wesley, whom he had persuaded to preach in open air. Then, when at the end of the eighteenth century and early in the nineteenth, there was a new movement usually known as the Second Great Awakening, Methodist influence could once again be seen in the movement. Although these movements did not result in religious institutions, and therefore their history is difficult to follow, there is no doubt that the deepening of religious life that resulted from them was an important factor leading to the great missionary movement that began early in the nineteenth century. Thus, the influence of German Pietism, and particularly of Spener and Francke, may be followed through Zinzendorf, Wesley, and the Great Awakening. Since it was through these movements that the great missionary expansion of Protestantism in the nineteenth century took place, it is not surprising that the resulting churches in various parts of the world had many of the characteristics of Pietism and the various movements inspired by it. Thus, for instance, Protestant missionaries in the nineteenth century tended to underscore the need for a personal decision much more than had earlier missionaries. There is no doubt that this is partly due to the emphasis of Pietism on a personal religion.

African Americans had an important role in all these movements, particularly in the field of missions. John Marrant, a freedman from New York, was a distinguished missionary to Native Americans. As reported in *A Narrative of the Lord's Wonderful Doings with John Marrant, a Black*, he worked among the Cherokee, Creek, and other tribes. George Liele was among the early American missionaries overseas, for in 1782, he settled in Kingston, where, together with four other freedmen, he founded the First African Baptist Church of Kingston. It 1792, another group of freed slaves established in Africa the "Province of Freedom," which was the first such endeavor by African Americans.

It is also important to point out that, in spite of the common assertion that Pietism tended to withdraw from the realities of the world, it was precisely this movement that led the church to become involved in the global reality of the world. It is true that on occasion missions resulting from the Pietists and other similar movements tended to withdraw their converts from the surrounding world and culture; it is also true that Pietism itself served to call Protestants to the realization that the world was much wider than Europe.

D. General Considerations

The period we have just studied records the greatest process of territorial expansion in the entire history of Christianity. It was during this period that belief in Jesus, until then mostly the faith of a relatively small corner of the world, expanded throughout the globe. Up to that point, the geographical spread of Christianity had been limited to Europe, North Africa, the Near East, and some small portions of the Far East. During these 200 years, Christianity expanded throughout the Americas and entered almost every nation in the Far East, besides taking root in various places along the coast of Africa.

Most of this geographic expansion of Christianity was the result of conquests and colonization by European powers, particularly Spain and Portugal. Spain centered its efforts on the Americas and from there crossed the Pacific to the Philippines. Portugal focused on the Far East but also established colonies in Africa and South America. In general, and for reasons already stated, Spain was able to leave its cultural and religious imprint on its colonies to a greater degree than Portugal. Also France and Great Britain began establishing colonies that contributed to the expansion of Christianity—Catholic Christianity from France and Protestant Christianity from Great Britain.

Spanish and Portuguese missions were not under the direct jurisdiction of the pope but were directed by the Crown through the right of patronage that the Roman see had granted the rulers of Spain and Portugal. Although at the beginning of the conquests this arrangement was useful, for it forced the colonizing powers to invest in missionary work, later, when those powers began declining, that very system would become a thorn in the flesh of the Church of Rome.

Catholic missionary expansion was greatly aided by the friars, who were its main agents. Franciscans, Dominicans, Jesuits, and Mercedarians poured into the new colonies in a missionary avalanche without precedent. Although among them some were a hindrance rather than a help, most of them undertook their task quite seriously, and many died as missionaries in distant lands. Also, one must never forget that the friars played a significant role in their attempts to improve the condition of the conquered.

Finally, it is important to realize that in several areas, particularly in the Western Hemisphere and in Africa, conversions took place en masse rather than individually. However, in the Far East, where there were political structures and civilizations that would not collapse with the arrival of Europeans, the situation was quite different, with converts coming into the Christian faith individually.

Chapter 6

MISSIONS IN LATE MODERNITY

A. General Introduction

The nineteenth century brought both a serious challenge and a vast opportunity for Christian missions. Late in the eighteenth century and early in the nineteenth, there was a series of events in the West that undercut the support that the church had received from the state since the time of Constantine. The French Revolution was characterized by its anticlerical attitude, and all would seem to indicate that part of its outcome would be the loss of vitality in the European church—particularly the Roman Catholic Church. The Napoleonic Wars weakened Europe and particularly the two powers that had been until then the main source of missionary outreach, Spain and Portugal. In North America, the newly independent United States made the separation of church and state one of its constitutional principles. Given these new circumstances, one might surmise that Christianity, tied as it was to a dying order, would be hard-pressed to survive.

In the field of thought and ideas, the signs of the times also seemed to be unfavorable for Christianity. New discoveries in the fields of history, biology, and astronomy posed questions about the reliability of the Bible. The theory of evolution seemed to undercut the Genesis accounts. Traditional views of biblical cosmology were collapsing as new astronomical theories developed. Eventually, people would even doubt the historical existence of Jesus, while others sought to rediscover the historical truth that seemed to be hidden behind the accounts of the New Testament. In the main universities in Europe, including in their chairs of theology, many held that Christianity would soon become only a historical memory, left behind by the new discoveries. At the same time, some theologians undertook the task of reinterpreting Christianity in the light of the new discoveries and perspectives of the natural and social sciences. In this endeavor, while keeping their faith in conversation with the surrounding culture, some seemed to abandon what until then had been considered essential elements of that faith. Within Christianity itself there were divisions and dissensions that weakened its witness. These divisions were not only those along denominational lines but also those having to do with the manner in which Christians ought to respond to the new discoveries and scientific theories.

The history of the expansion of Christianity in the nineteenth century is therefore quite complex. Had such expansion depended completely on the inner unity of the church or its support on the part of the state, the nineteenth century would have seen the end of Christian missionary advance. Since the new ideals of the French and North American revolutions undercut state support for the church, one could have expected that as those ideals gathered strength and were spread throughout the world, Christian missions would suffer. And yet, what actually happened was that a multifaceted relationship developed between the imperialistic thrust of Western Europe, and then of the United States, on the one hand, and the missionary enterprise, on the other. In the pages that follow we shall see that European colonialism sometimes was an ally of the missionary task, that in other situations the missionaries were among the staunchest opponents of imperialism, and that in still other situations the missionaries occupied a difficult and often ambiguous position between the expansionist policies of the West and the interests of the inhabitants of other lands.

However, against all negative expectations, the nineteenth century became one of the high points of Christian missions from the North Atlantic—to the point that the historian of missions Kenneth Scott Latourette dubbed the period "the Great Century." Given the ambiguous position of missions in their relationship with civil authority, the church found the lack of official governmental support a challenge whose eventual result would be the spread of a profound missionary interest among more Christians than ever before. The questions posed by the nineteenth century regarding the truth of Scripture and of Christianity also led Christians to ask basic questions about the nature of their faith and what was essential to it, opening new paths for obedience to God. Also, the Pietistic impulse that was discussed in the last chapter would continue growing throughout the nineteenth century and play an important role in the missionary movement.

In general, the nineteenth century is the high point of Protestant North Atlantic expansion. Both the Roman Catholic Church and the Russian Orthodox Church continued their missionary work. But it was Protestantism that, thanks to its direct relationship with the European and North American nations that arose as new world powers and to the political and economic changes within those nations—industrialization, new political structures, and new views as to the nature and values of human existence—manifested a greater readiness to adapt to the new circumstances as well as greater vitality for entering into lands that until then had not heard the gospel. For reasons of clarity, however, in this chapter we shall discuss first the Roman Catholic Church and then the Orthodox communion in order finally to turn to the Protestant missionary movement.

It is important to point out, however, that the present chapter is only a general introduction to the missionary history of the nineteenth and twentieth centuries. Indeed, the expansion of Christianity during that time was so vast and complex that it would be practically impossible to summarize it in a single chapter. For that reason, after the present introduction there will be separate chapters discussing various regions of the globe.

B. The Roman Catholic Church

For Roman Catholic missions, the nineteenth century was not the new point of departure that it was for Protestant missions. The Roman Catholic Church—in contrast to Protestantism—had long been engaged in missionary work. But it was indeed a century of serious challenges for Catholicism. A long series of events leading to the French Revolution, the Napoleonic Wars, and the wars of independence in the Americas had resulted in the colonial and political decline of Spain and Portugal, which for centuries had been the main centers of Catholic mission. The other major Catholic land in Europe, France, had never laid as much stress on missions as had Spain and Portugal, and the possibility of it now becoming a center of missionary work was further hampered by the French Revolution and its aftermath. Such circumstances deeply challenged the Roman Catholic Church and its traditional view of its relationship with the state. However, in spite of such circumstances, the nineteenth century witnessed a number of developments within Roman Catholicism that in the long run would strengthen its missionary work.

First of all, the nineteenth century was the time when the Catholic Church developed a centralized system of government and consolidated the power of the papacy. In insisting on the separation between church and state, the nations of Europe and the Americas sought to avoid the intervention of the church in civil matters; but they also gave up the authority that governments had long had over the church.

Even in the case of those countries where there still was a close union between church and state, the latter was often so weakened that it could not oppose the direct control of the church by the Roman see. All of this was strengthened by Ultramontanism, a movement that sought to increase papal authority and that culminated when the First Vatican Council (1869–70) officially promulgated the doctrine of papal infallibility.

A second development within the life of Roman Catholicism in the nineteenth century was the revitalization of some of its already-existing instruments for missionary work, particularly the Society of Jesus and the *Sacra Congregatio de Propaganda Fide*. The Jesuits had been dissolved by papal decree in 1773, but beginning in 1801, their existence was authorized once again, and in 1814, all their ancient rights were restored. The *Propaganda* was used by Napoleon as an instrument of his policies, but after the Napoleonic Wars, it was reconstituted with new energy. That agency increasingly became the focus of Catholic missionary work until 1938, when its function was revamped and it began administering a vast project to promote the development of native clergy and the contextualization of Catholicism in various parts of the world.

Third, the nineteenth century forced the Catholic Church to begin developing new means to fund its missionary work, which until that time had been funded by the colonial powers. As these powers became unwilling or unable to cover the expenses of missionary work in their colonies and former colonies, the church had to seek new sources of financial support. These were mostly the many societies for the support of missions that appeared throughout Europe, particularly in France. Some of them, such as the Association for the Propagation of the Faith, collected money for missionary work. Others gathered clothes or other resources that could be used in missions. The net result was that the support for mission within Roman Catholicism was increasingly widespread among the laity.

Yet, it is still true that the nineteenth century was not a new beginning for Catholic missions, as it was for their Protestant counterparts. Most of the instruments and agencies that the Catholic Church employed in the nineteenth century were simply a continuation of what had already existed. Although the Napoleonic Wars and the independence of the various nations in the Americas were for Catholicism a parentheses, during which its missionary enterprise was put on hold, once that parentheses was closed, the missionary methods and theology that the Roman church employed were generally the same as before. Indeed, in the case of the Roman Catholic Church, the first years of the twentieth century mark more significant changes than the beginning of the nineteenth.

C. Eastern Orthodoxy

Of the various Orthodox bodies, it was the Russian church that most expanded during the nineteenth century. Most of that expansion took place in connection with the growth of the Russian Empire itself. The most extensive Russian missions during the nineteenth century took place in Siberia, where there were still large numbers who had not become Christian. The most remarkable missionary enterprise of the Russian church during that time took place in Altai, in western Siberia, and was mostly the work of Makarij Glucharev. There were also missions in Tobolsk, Irkutsk, and Transbaikal.

Beyond the borders of the Russian Empire, the most important Orthodox mission was in Japan, where the church flourished under the leadership of Father Nicolai, as we shall see in another chapter. There were also Orthodox missions in China, Korea, and the Caucasus. Finally, the Russian Orthodox Church extended to the northwestern regions of North America, particularly in Alaska (1784), although that mission came to an end when Russia sold Alaska to the United States in 1887. There were also large numbers of Russian immigrants to the Americas, particularly to the United States and the regions around São

Paulo and Buenos Aires. The first Russian Orthodox church in Latin America was organized in Buenos Aires late in the nineteenth century, and the first bishopric was founded in São Paulo in 1934.

As could be expected, the Russian Revolution opened a new period in the history of the church in that land. The church no longer received economic and political support, which was needed for missionary work. Russian missions declined rapidly, particularly in the early years after the revolution. Also, in the areas not under Bolshevik control, the varying attitudes of believers toward Russia and its political situation led to several schisms.

D. Protestantism

The nineteenth century was the high point of Protestant colonial and missionary expansion. Several Protestant countries, particularly Great Britain, extended their economic and political power over various areas of the globe. The British Empire became the largest the world had ever known, with millions of subjects—some of them belonging to cultures and traditions much older than the British. Meanwhile, the United States continued expanding westward, sometimes through colonization, sometimes through purchase of lands, and sometimes by armed conquest. The discoveries of Captain James Cook in the Pacific opened new horizons for the North Atlantic world, and particularly for Britain, which then ruled the seas. All of this would lead to a renewed missionary interest, first in Britain and then in other Protestant powers. However, it is important to note that this missionary expansion—particularly in the case of the United States—was much more independent from political and economic colonization than had been the Roman Catholic expansion in the preceding centuries. Although many missionaries settled in colonies established by the British and the Dutch, there were also vast missionary enterprises in areas where the colonial powers were not yet present. An example of this is the mission of Adoniram Judson in Burma, which will be discussed in the next chapter.

Another important factor in the development of Protestant missions was the agencies organized to support missionary work, which often were organized as what Philipp Jakob Spener would have called an *ecclesiola in ecclesia*—a small group of people within the church at large, which was more committed to mission than the larger community. The missionary movement of the nineteenth century was characterized by the development of groups of Christians with great missionary zeal who worked without the support of their own denominations—and sometimes against the wishes of those denominations. In the United States, missionary work became vigorous thanks to a spirit of voluntarism, which was an important aspect of the individualistic ideology that characterized both Europe and the United States toward the end of the nineteenth century and the beginning of the twentieth.

1. William Carey

One of the greatest missionaries of all times was William Carey. Carey was born in England in 1761, in a middle-class Anglican family. He was six years old when his father became a schoolteacher, and this allowed young William to attain an education that would normally have been beyond the reach of his family's limited resources.

It was while reading a newspaper that his father received as a teacher that Carey first learned of the voyages of Captain Cook, which awakened in him a passion for geography and for distant lands. He was also very much interested in natural science, and throughout his life he would continue showing that inclination. He was sixteen years old when his father sent him to a nearby town to apprentice as a cobbler. There, through his contact with an elder apprentice, he discovered depths in Christian commitment that he had not known before, and he decided to become a Baptist. When he needed further income in order to support his marriage, he widened his economic activities, teaching and also serving as a pastor, although always continuing his work as a cobbler. During this time, in order to teach geography, he constructed a globe out of leather, and on it drew a world map. For his own personal study, he designed a much more detailed map in which various areas were named, including a description of the culture and religion of their inhabitants. All of this gave him a worldwide perspective that would later enrich his work as a missionary. It was also during this time that he studied Latin, Greek, Hebrew, Dutch, and Italian, thus showing linguistic abilities that later would prove valuable.

Through his study of the Bible and of geography he came to the conclusion that Christians of all times had been entrusted with the missionary task. This led him to publish *An Inquiry into the Obligations of Christians to Use Means for the Conversion of the Heathens.* In May of 1792, he preached before the Baptist Ministers Association a famous sermon on Isaiah 54:2-3, the two main points of which were: "Expect great things of God" and "Attempt great things for God." In October of the same year, as a result of his efforts, the Particular Baptist Society for Propagating the Gospel Among the Heathen was organized. At the beginning, this society was composed of a very small number of other ministers and of Carey's friends, and its annual budget was less than fourteen pounds. In spite of such limitations, Carey began making arrangements to go to India with physician John Thomas, who had been there before.

From the very beginning there were seemingly insurmountable difficulties. Carey's wife, Dorothy, refused to go with him to India and finally agreed that only their eldest son would accompany him. Carey's response was that, were he to own the entire world, he would gladly give it up in order to be with her and his children but that this was not enough to abandon his missionary obligation. Then it was learned that Dr. Thomas had debts that would not allow him to leave England. Finally, it was well known that the British East India Company did not favor the presence of Christian missionaries in its colonies and would seek to avoid it. In spite of all these difficulties, Carey remained firm in his purpose. Eventually Dorothy agreed to accompany him, and, after many efforts, the arrangements were made so that Dr. Thomas and his wife could go with them. It should be noted that Dorothy Carey, who had at first refused to accompany her husband, now lent him her support—until, after burying her children, and within a context of isolation, she became insane and died.

It was late in 1793 that William Carey and his party landed in Calcutta—although without letting the authorities know of their purpose, for if they did so they would run the risk of being returned to England. Carey's plan was that he and Dr. Thomas would work for the support of their families, so as not to depend on the society that had covered the expenses for his trip. However, it soon became apparent that Dr. Thomas, although a good physician and a sincere Christian, was thoroughly incapable of managing his finances. The money that the missionaries had brought with them was quickly exhausted, and Dr. Thomas became increasingly entangled in debt, which did not do much for the prestige of the missionaries. Then there was the further difficulty that Carey and his party could not actually declare that they were missionaries, which would have led to their expulsion from India by the East India Company. Thus his case illustrates the complex situation in which missionaries lived: enjoying some of the benefits of an imperial presence, receiving from it some legitimization, while at the same time having to remain distant from imperial authorities and policies. This led Carey to try to settle in various places, working in a variety of occupations that seemed to offer a modest income. At the same time, he studied Bengali and presented the gospel to the Indians. Since this difficult period lasted several years, he also learned Sanskrit and began translating the Bible into Bengali. When circumstances seemed overwhelming, Carey wrote to England, declaring that his position was unbearable and that there were difficulties everywhere, and many more ahead, and that therefore there was no other option but to move ahead!

Even in the midst of all these difficulties, Carey requested that more missionaries be sent from England to share with him the vast task of the evangelization of India. His plan was to gather a number of families in a small community in which all would share income and expenses, and women as well as men would participate in various ways in the missionary task. In response to this request, other missionaries joined him.

When Carey's new colleagues arrived, the East India Company did not allow them to land in Calcutta, and therefore they had to go across the bay to Serampore. After some negotiations, and since the Danish governor in Serampore seemed favorable to missionary work, Carey decided to move his headquarters there. Serampore thus became the center for the missionary work of Carey and his party.

The work of the missionaries in Serampore was outstanding. One of the newly arrived missionaries, William Ward, was a printer by trade and printed the Bibles that Carey translated. Another, Joshua Marshman, showed to have as much mettle as Carey himself and became a professor. Carey continued his linguistic activities, to the point that he wrote grammars and dictionaries for several Indian languages. At the point of his death, he had translated the Bible or portions of it into no fewer than thirty-five different Indian languages. Today we know that his work in this respect did not have the linguistic rigor that one would desire; but there is no doubt that Carey had a passion for translating the Bible and making it accessible to Indians in their own languages.

When politics brought to Calcutta a new governor who sympathized with missionary work, this made it possible for Carey to work within the British colony. The new governor wished for the employees of the East India Company to be better prepared for their work, and therefore he established a school whose offerings included studies in the various languages of the area. Carey was invited to occupy the Bengali chair. After consulting with his colleagues, he accepted that invitation, although always bringing the income from his teaching to the common fund of the missionary community. This new activity helped him establish closer contacts with Indians from various parts of the country who would then help him translate parts of the Bible as well as other Christian literature into their various languages. Thus, the printing press in Serampore was eventually producing Christian literature in forty-two languages.

His work in India was complex. At first it would appear that the Serampore mission would be quite successful in attaining a large number of converts. In 1800, they baptized their first convert, a carpenter who had earlier heard the gospel from Moravians. The news of that conversion led to public riots and to the renewed opposition of colonial authorities who feared that the work of the missionaries would lead to riots and rebellion throughout the land and that these would undercut not only missionary work but also the entire colonial regime. In spite of this, the missionaries continued their work, and three years later they baptized their first Brahman convert. Their opposition to the caste system that was traditional in Indian culture resulted in serious difficulties; but on this point they would not change their attitude, which so undercut the caste system that in 1803, a Brahman convert married a carpenter's daughter.

Opposition to missionary work continued, and repeatedly new governors would lend an ear to those who objected to the missionary enterprise. This continued until 1813, when thanks to the work of Lord William Wilberforce and of the missionary society in England that supported Carey, Parliament demanded that the new charter of the East India Company include a clause to the effect that all British colonies would be open to missionary work. This was in part beneficial for missions, but it also could become a hindrance, for it tended to present Christianity as an imperialistic imposition on Hindus. Later, some Hindus would see in that charter and in the resulting missionary work the religious side of British imperialism.

From the very beginning, Carey and his companions had been convinced that eventually the task of preaching the gospel in India belonged to Indians themselves. Therefore they soon began establishing outposts from Serampore where they would place groups of converts who lived with their families in a community similar to that of the missionaries in Serampore—although for some time under the supervision of missionaries. The purpose of this plan of action was to develop throughout the entire area a network of evangelizing centers that would be in the hands of Christian Indians. As a foundation for that wider project, as well as in order to bring to India the technological knowledge of Western culture, Carey and Marshman established a center of higher education that would eventually serve as a model for many others in various mission fields. This school enrolled students of various religions. Its purpose was to offer to those students a wide knowledge both of Western technology and of their own traditional culture. In the case of Christian students, they were also to receive such knowledge of Christianity as well as of the sacred books and religions of India that it would be possible for them to present the gospel to other Indians approaching them, not as foreigners, but as truly Indian Christians. In the case of non-Christian students, the college in Serampore sought their conversion, but even if this did not take place, it was considered that by improving their education, something had been attained. As support for its educational task, the college began developing a vast library including printed books as well as manuscripts and Western texts as well as Indian. As a fundamental element in the policy of the school, education was offered in Sanskrit and in Arabic, and English was reserved for the more advanced students. Unfortunately, even though the purpose of the school was to give Christianity an Indian flavor, what often resulted was that its former students developed a sense of superiority over other Indians, thus contributing to the cultural and social isolation of Christianity. Once again, the life and work of Carey and his companions show how difficult it is to develop a community of faith within a complex cultural and religious context such as existed in India.

Besides these activities, the Serampore missionaries also undertook the task of countering what they considered the most serious evils of Indian society. They were particularly concerned over two practices: the offering of children as sacrifices and the burning of widows on the funeral pyres of their husbands—the practice of *satee*, which Roberto di Nobili had accepted earlier. When Governor Richard Wellesley learned of the practice of sacrificing children in the Ganges, he commissioned Carey to study the ancient sacred books of India in order to see if those practices were grounded in them. Carey came to the conclusion that those sacred books did not order such sacrifice. Strengthened by that argument, Lord Wellesley ordered that the practice of sacrificing infants should immediately cease and established a system to enforce that new law. After a few years, thanks to this and to a number of Hindus who themselves disagreed with infant sacrifice, the Hindus of the region had ceased in that practice. Something similar happened in the case of the burning of widows—although this custom was so deeply rooted in tradition that it was much more difficult to stamp out. Once again, Carey showed that what had become a traditional religious custom was not based on the sacred books of the Hindus. After long hesitations, British authorities finally decided to forbid the burning of widows on the funeral pyres of their husbands. When Carey received the edict, he suspended every other activity in order to translate it into Bengali, so that not one widow would die due to his negligence.

The work of Carey and his companions had far-reaching consequences. Some of his own children became missionaries, one to Burma—where he did not persevere as well as his father—and another to Java. In England, the news that arrived from Serampore awakened new interest in hundreds of Christians. The Particular Baptist Society for Propagating the Gospel sent younger missionaries—which also created conflicts and eventually led to a schism. Other societies also drew their inspiration from Carey's work. One of these was the British and Foreign Bible Society, which supported the work of translation that was taking place in Serampore, and soon it expanded its outreach throughout the world. Thanks mostly to Carey's work, but also to the favorable political, colonial, and economic circumstances, soon missionary enthusiasm would sweep through the church both in Great Britain and in the United States.

It is important to point out that Carey's theological motivation was not grounded in a sense of pity or condescension toward heathens who were being lost, as had earlier been the case with the Moravians. Carey did believe that those who did not know the gospel were lost, but what moved him was not so much a sense of pity toward them, as the obligation to the commandment of Jesus to go throughout the world placed on him. He saw missionary work more as an act of obedience than as one of compassion. Compassion is important, but it follows from obedience.

Finally, it is important to note that even though the circumstances of the time did not make this dream possible, Carey always believed that missionary work should be free of all sectarian inclination, in that the divisions that the church suffered in the land of the mission's origin should not be exported to the mission field. More than a hundred years before the historic World Missionary Conference met in Edinburgh in 1910, Carey was already dreaming of a great world assembly that would gather in Capetown and include missionaries from all parts of the world as well as representatives of the societies supporting them. In that dream, Carey was moving far ahead of his time, for history would eventually show that an ecumenical spirit, necessary as it is throughout the life of the church, becomes an urgent matter in missionary work.

2. Missionary Centers

To a great degree, as a consequence of the work of Carey and his companions, the last years of the eighteenth century and the early years of the nineteenth witnessed a growing missionary interest in Great Britain. Some of the societies that grew out of Carey's work have already been mentioned. His letters and other news from India led many people of deep Christian commitment to begin asking themselves how they could participate in the missionary efforts. The London Missionary Society was established in 1795, and four years later, the Church Missionary Society was founded. The former gathered people belonging to several denominations—mostly Congregationalists and Presbyterians—while the latter was formed by members of the evangelical wing of the Church of England. As was to be expected, and also as a result of a long-lasting interest that has already been discussed, the Methodists organized a missionary society, and the same was true of other smaller denominations. We should note that these societies were worldwide in scope and did not limit their interest to British possessions, as had those that had appeared before Carey. There is no doubt that much of this worldwide vision was the result of Carey's work and influence.

The founding of these societies was an unprecedented phenomenon in Protestant missions, which were now widened, not only in their geographic outreach, but also in the source of financial and other support, coming from an ever-increasing number of people. These societies were also the first Protestant attempt to organize mission work so that it would have a presence and a role both in other lands and in the nation where the mission originated. Yet, the existence of such missionary societies that were not an official part of the denomination, but rather a small group of greater commitment within the church at large, created a distance between "church" and "mission" that would later have to be bridged. However, the distance between missionary organizations and the denominations themselves provided room for missiological reflection that contributed to the contextualization of the church in other lands. For instance, the missiology of Henry Venn (a member of the Church Missionary Society) and then of Rufus Anderson (American Board of Commissioners for Foreign Missions) was able to develop precisely because these missiologists did not have to follow or express the interests of their own denominations. Anderson's main missiological contribution was the "three-self principle," which held that churches founded by missionary societies should move to the point where they would be self-governing, self-sustaining, and self-propagating.

In the nineteenth century, and as a result of both William Carey's work and its own growing maritime and colonial power, Great Britain was the main center of Protestant missions. However, other Protestant nations in Europe, as well as in the United States, also launched their own missionary enterprises. Eventually, the missionary work of North American Protestantism would be much greater than that of any other Protestant center.

In continental Europe the main Protestant missionary centers in the nineteenth century were Germany and Switzerland, where the influence of the British missionary movement joined the Pietist tradition in order to give rise to a greater missionary interest. A characteristic of mission work from those countries was that, following the example of the University of Halle, other schools were organized whose main concern was the training of missionaries. The most notable were those in Berlin and Basel. Also, a wide variety of missionary societies were founded, although later some of these merged for the sake of efficiency. The Dutch Missionary Society, closely related to the London Missionary Society, worked mostly in South Africa. Also, the Scandinavian countries saw the birth of mission societies during the nineteenth century. The Danish society was particularly noted for its work in Greenland and India, while its Swedish counterpart centered its attention on Lapland.

During the nineteenth century, and even more in the twentieth, the United States became one of the main centers of Protestant missions. As we have already seen, from an early date, there were missions among the Native Americans in the thirteen colonies. At the end of the eighteenth century, the Moravians founded a missionary society, and a group of Christians created another whose purpose was to train and send black North Americans as missionaries to Africa. But it was during the nineteenth century that the great American societies were founded. An important contributor to the new missionary interest was the Second Great Awakening, which began early in the nineteenth century. These various trends were reinforced by the news of the evangelizing work of the British in India and particularly of Carey and his companions.

The most important missionary society in the United States during the early nineteenth century was the American Board of Commissioners for Foreign Missions. This society gained root among a group of students at Andover Theological Seminary, particularly Adoniram Judson and Samuel J. Mills. It was centered in Connecticut and Massachusetts and represented mostly Congregationalists from that area. The American Board sent Adoniram Judson to India, but during the ocean-crossing, the prospective missionary decided to become a Baptist. We shall encounter him again as the outstanding Protestant missionary in Burma. His presence in the Far East led North American Baptists to organize the Baptist Society for the Propagation of the Gospel in India and Other Foreign Parts. Mills also continued promoting missionary interest in the United States; and thanks to his efforts, several new missionary societies were formed, as well as others for the production and distribution of Bibles and Christian literature.

In 1822, and under the support of the American Board of Commissioners, Betsey Stockton, a Presbyterian African American, was appointed as a missionary to Hawaii. She came as a missionary with the Stewart family, who were also appointed to do missionary work there. She worked as an educator, teaching the nationals languages, mathematics, and Latin. This was a new approach to missionary education, since most missionaries taught Christianity to the nationals but excluded them from other subjects. She trained nationals and contributed to the development of a Hawaiian educational system. Stockton is considered to be the first Protestant single woman to do overseas missionary work.

During the first half of the nineteenth century, all major Protestant denominations in the United States organized missionary societies and sent representatives to various regions of the globe, particularly the Far East. Since in the middle of that century almost all Protestant denominations were split as a consequence of the events leading to the Civil War, those divisions resulted in similar ones overseas and there came into being in various parts of the world both "Northern" and "Southern" Baptists, Methodists, and Presbyterians. In some cases, it was the mission field itself that first laid bare the futility of such divisions, and therefore in those areas, many divisions were healed earlier than in the United States. Repeatedly such unions in the mission field forced their mother churches to question the justification of divisions that were connected with a past war. Thus, even unconsciously, the younger churches were already contributing to the development of their mother churches.

In addition to the denominational divisions, there were ethnic divisions that also shaped denominational missionary efforts. The African Methodist Episcopal Church sent missionaries to different parts of the world. Amanda Smith, a missionary and evangelist, traveled England, India, Monrovia, Liberia, and West Africa, to later return and establish in Illinois the first and only orphanage for African American children.

The Protestant Christianity that North American missionaries took to the churches that they founded was strongly individualistic, stressing the need for an experience of personal conversion, often suspicious of all rationalistic study of revealed truth, and emphasizing whatever was pragmatic and efficient. Churches in the United States became entangled in the controversy between fundamentalists and liberals, and it was mostly the former that continued emphasizing foreign missions, with the result that many of the churches they planted were suspicious of the use of reason in matters related to faith. The North American missionary movement was closely connected to the Second Great Awakening, and therefore the individualism that characterized that awakening was also present in churches founded by North American missionaries. Likewise, the nineteenth century was a time when the United States was reaching ahead with technology and an emphasis on organization and efficiency, and the churches that resulted from American missions bore the same traits. As so often happens in the history of missions, even after the mother churches in the United States had surpassed their earlier divisions between liberals and fundamentalists and had begun moving away from extreme individualism, the churches founded out of the United States lagged far behind in these matters, reflecting conditions that were being surmounted in the United States.

It is also important to point out that, as elsewhere, the relationship between missions and the expansion of North American political and economic influence was complex and ambiguous. In many areas of the world, North American Protestant missionaries were present long before the United States developed any political or economic interests. Throughout the nineteenth century, most North American missionaries went to lands that had little contact with the United States. When the political and economic expansion of the United States took American diplomacy, industry, and trade to the Far East, Protestant missionaries had long preceded them. Yet, one must also point out that it was in the nineteenth century that a messianic ideology was developing in the United States. This saw the nation as a new Jerusalem and its inhabitants as the new chosen people who were to take throughout the world the truth of the gospel and the values of a "Christian culture."

Finally, one must remember that during the nineteenth century, Protestantism settled in some areas that would soon become new missionary centers. In the South Pacific, Australia and New Zealand began sending missionaries to neighboring islands, as well as to the Orient. In Africa, the British and Dutch who settled in the southern tip of the continent worked among their neighbors, although their work was soon undercut by the racism of many settlers. In the west coast of Africa, as a result of the antislavery movement in England and the United States, Sierra Leone and Liberia were established as places for the resettlement of freed slaves. Since many of the black settlers in these two lands were Christians, and also since the close connections with Britain and the United States opened the way for other missionaries, these two lands immediately became centers of missionary activity. Throughout the twentieth century, citizens of Liberia and Sierra Leone would continue the mission to other areas in Africa.

3. Missions and the Ecumenical Movement

As already stated, William Carey had the dream of a missionary enterprise that would go beyond the divisions that existed in the North Atlantic. This dream, albeit premature, took into account very real needs and challenges facing every missionary effort. The first need was for a united witness, so that missionary interests would not turn into an obstacle on the way to faith for those whom they sought to reach. Jealousy and strife among denominations and missionary endeavors would be greatly counterproductive. A missionary who went to India to proclaim the message of Christ should not at the same time proclaim the differences and distance between a Baptist and an Anglican. At least at the local level where they were most visible, both Hinduism and Islam at that time seemed to be monolithic religions with few or no inner divisions. Many people in India had no experience of diversity within a single religious tradition. Therefore, denominational divisions within Protestantism became a hindrance within the context of that subcontinent. Indeed, the same was the case with divisions within Buddhism, Confucianism, and other Asian religious traditions.

Another pressing need was for missionaries themselves to have an opportunity to share their dreams, their successes, and their frustrations with other Christians who would understand them. Then there was the need to avoid duplication of work when resources were relatively scarce and the task was enormous. Such duplication of work amounted to poor stewardship and would affect the interest in missions in the sending lands themselves.

The leaders and executives of the missionary movement in the sending lands also felt the need to work with their colleagues. If not, there would be reports from the mission field that would seem to be contradictory and that therefore would also affect support for the mission work. In order to avoid this, the various missionary societies began developing a network of communication that would eventually make a significant contribution to Christian unity.

All of this resulted in a cooperative spirit among Christians of various denominations. That spirit led them to leave aside much of the dissension that still existed in the older churches of Europe and the United States. Furthermore, since the original missionary societies were not organized by denominations, many of them included members from various churches, and this, too, contributed to bringing those churches closer to one another.

In brief, one may well say that the modern ecumenical movement is a child of missionary work. Although this movement gained impetus in the twentieth century, a hundred years earlier one could already see its first signs. Such signs could be seen in India, when beginning in 1825, a series of regional conferences was celebrated with the attendance of missionaries from various denominations. The first such conferences—such as the one held in Bombay in 1825 and the one in Madras in 1830—were limited to a city and its surroundings. But in 1855, a series of wider conferences began taking place in northern India and three years later also in south India. The year 1872 saw the gathering in Allahabad of the first all-India missionary conference, and from then on similar meetings took place every ten years. The same process took place in Japan and China, although later than in India—in Japan in 1872 and in China in 1877. With few exceptions, one of which was the conference that met in Mexico in 1888, Latin America did not have such interdenominational conferences until the twentieth century. The same is true of Africa, where the first missionary conference took place in 1904.

At the same time that the meetings already mentioned took place in the mission field, in the North Atlantic, there were other gatherings of organizations and individuals from various denominations committed to missionary work. Representatives of various European missionary societies gathered in Basel in 1837. The Evangelical Alliance was organized in Great Britain in 1846, with the purpose of promoting understanding and collaboration among Protestants from various denominations, and from its very beginning the Alliance was profoundly interested in missionary work. Due in part to this alliance, several missionary conferences took place in the Anglo-Saxon world: New York and London in 1854, Liverpool in 1860, again in London in 1878 and 1888, and finally, in New York in 1890. As a result of all this, directors of missionary work both in Europe and in North America began developing means of collaboration that would avoid conflicts in the mission field. However, there still was not a theology seeking to integrate the missionary task with the entire life of the church, and therefore these various meetings generally took for granted a division and even a tension between the mission—which was the task of missionary societies and agencies—and the church in the sending countries. It is also sad to note that quite often, particularly in the Anglo-Saxon world, these first attempts at unity did not take into account groups or movements not present at each gathering.

Among the forerunners of the ecumenical movement was the Student Christian movement. It is impossible to review here the history of that movement, which resulted in the founding of the World Student Christian Federation. Let it suffice to say that at the outset, the entire student movement—particularly the Student Volunteer movement—evinced a profound missionary interest. It was also this movement that produced some of the leading figures of the ecumenical movement during the first half of the twentieth century.

The importance of the missionary movement for the ecumenical movement that developed in the twentieth century is particularly noticeable in the history of the origins of the International Missionary Council and the World Council of Churches, both stemming from the missionary gathering that took place in Edinburgh in 1910.

All the main Protestant bodies were represented at the World Missionary Conference of Edinburgh. However, out of over 2,000 participants, only seventeen belonged to the younger churches that had resulted from the missionary work of the West. The rest were all European and North American. Also, in order for the Anglicans to participate, the agenda had to exclude all matters of faith and order as well as of missionary work in countries already deemed Christian—particularly Latin America. However, even in regard to these two great omissions, the meeting at Edinburgh yielded positive results, for many of those present at Edinburgh decided that these were matters of importance, which ought to be discussed. Thus, two by-products of the Edinburgh conference were the Faith and Order movement and, beginning in 1912, the Committee on Cooperation in Latin America. The latter led to the Congress of Panama in 1916, which provided for the continuation of the committee itself.

Although the Edinburgh Conference paved the way for the ecumenical movement of the twentieth century, it did have a severe limitation. As already stated, there were only seventeen representatives of the "younger churches." The reason for this was not prejudice or lack of interest, but rather the theological tendency already mentioned not to integrate church and mission. It was thought that missionary work was the responsibility of Western churches, and particularly of their missionary societies; but no consideration was given to the need for the younger churches to be themselves missionary in order to be true churches. Therefore, the conference dealt with the missionary responsibilities of the Western churches but omitted discussion of the same matters as they pertained to the younger churches.

In spite of such unavoidable limitations, the World Missionary Conference of Edinburgh gave the ecumenical movement an unexpected impetus. The conference itself named a continuation committee whose work resulted in the founding in 1921 of the International Missionary Council. By then a number of agencies of missionary collaboration had arisen in Europe, North America, and Australia, and these became the nucleus for the council. It was also determined that the "younger churches" in Africa, the Orient, and Latin America would be represented in the council. As had been the case with the earlier conferences, the purpose of the International Missionary Council was not to establish rules for the mission work of various churches, but rather to provide a forum for the discussion of common agendas.

The International Missionary Council held conferences in Jerusalem (1928), Madras (1938), Whitby, Canada (1947), Willingen, Germany (1952), and Ghana (1957–58). In 1961, in New Delhi, the International Missionary Council was merged with the World Council of Churches, which had been founded in 1948 and become the main vehicle for the ecumenical movement.

In 1928, the Jerusalem Assembly of the International Missionary Council took place on the Mount of Olives. Almost a quarter of those present belonged to the "younger churches," and this represented significant progress since Edinburgh. Meanwhile, in 1927, the Faith and Order movement, another by-product of Edinburgh, held its first international conference in Lausanne. Since many of those present in

Jerusalem had also been in Lausanne, the missionary conference began dealing more seriously with theological issues regarding mission and the unity of the church.

Beginning in Jerusalem, and increasingly, the International Missionary Council became aware of the indissoluble connection between church and mission. In Madras, the church was at the very center of discussion, but the impact of the gathering was weakened by the outbreak of the Second World War. In Willingen, in 1952, and in Ghana five years later, there was increasing emphasis on the unity between church and mission. It was this consciousness that led to the merger of the International Missionary Council with the World Council of Churches (in New Delhi in 1961), for there seemed to be no theological justification for the existence of two separate bodies. From that point on, the former concerns of the International Missionary Council were part of the tasks of the Division of World Mission and Evangelism of the World Council of Churches. This division continued celebrating meetings that may be seen as heirs of the Edinburgh tradition. Some of these meetings took place in Mexico (1963), Bangkok (1973), Melbourne (1980), San Antonio (1989), Salvador, Brazil (1996), and Athens (2005).

These gatherings also had an effect in Latin America, resulting in a series of Conferencias Evangélicas Latinoamericanas—Latin American Evangelical Conference—in the development of ecumenical bodies such as Iglesia y Sociedad en América Latina (ISAL, Church and Society in Latin America), the Comisión Evangélica Latinoamericana de Educación Cristiana (CELADEC, Latin American Commission on Christian Education), and eventually the Consejo Latinoamericano de Iglesias (CLAI, Latin American Evangelical Council of Churches) in 1979.

None of these agencies or organizations has power over its members, which remain autonomous and retain the right to make their own decisions. However, the opportunity to discuss and pose problems and issues of theology as well as of strategy has greatly strengthened Protestant missionary work.

Not all missionary societies and leaders embraced the missionary conferences or the International Missionary Council. Some, led by their expectation of the imminent return of Christ and by the bitter debate between fundamentalists and liberals, formed their own "interdenominational" organizations—for some rejected the word *ecumenical*—to discuss and plan missionary work. The most important of these is the International Foreign Missions Association founded in 1917. These organizations brought together evangelical missionary societies, many of them known as "faith missions." One of these was the Central American Mission founded by Cyrus I. Scofield in the mid-nineteenth century.

Many of these societies criticized the strategies, ideas, and proposals of the world missionary congresses. However, the ecumenical character and the spirit of collaboration, which Carey had proposed much earlier, could be seen even among these more conservative societies and faith missions.

The more conservative organizations—some of them fundamentalist—have also led to the creation of ecumenical organizations in Latin America, although they usually prefer to call themselves "interdenominational" rather than "ecumenical," such as the Fraternidad Teológica Latinoamericana (Latin American Theological Fraternity) and the Confraternidad Evangélica de Iglesias Latinoamericanas (CONELA, Evangelical Confraternity of Latin American Churches). The first of these was founded in 1969 and the latter shortly thereafter. This history will also be discussed in another chapter.

Since the subject of this book is the history of missions, and not particularly of the ecumenical movement, this is not the place to tell the story of how during the second half of the twentieth century, the ecumenical movement, born among Protestants, took hold also among Orthodox and Roman Catholics. Let it suffice to mention this fact, which in the future will undoubtedly have an effect on the entire world missionary enterprise.

E. General Considerations

The nineteenth century has been called "the Great Century" in the history of missions. At that time, the greatest expansion that any civilization has ever known was combined with a genuine missionary interest. There is no doubt that the political hegemony, first of Europe and then of the United States, contributed to the geographic expansion of Christianity during the nineteenth century. But the missionaries of the nineteenth and twentieth centuries were less at the service of the political and economic interests of their own nations than had been any other missionaries since the beginning of the Middle Ages. There certainly were missionaries who profited from the power and prestige of their homelands to take the message to other nations that were somehow under the influence of that power and prestige. But even in this case, most of them did not do this with a pragmatic attitude, seeking to benefit from their privileged position, but did it rather in the conviction that the interests of the West, even though sometimes at the hands of corrupt politicians or merchants who only sought to enrich themselves, were still a civilizing force.

What is most characteristic of the missionary movement of this time is not so much that it sometimes served as an instrument for Western expansion—an expansion that was inevitable given the technological development of the West—as the spirit of superiority and condescension that the missionaries shared with Western societies when relating to people of other races, cultures, and religions. In Western missionary circles, it was common to speak of "the white man's burden" to take to the rest of the world his own civilization and, as part of it, his faith. Such an attitude was by no means universal, and in the chapters that follow, we shall find many examples of missionaries whose attitudes were quite different. But still, this was the general mood of the period and of missions during it, and it was reflected in the manner in which missions were understood, not as a fundamental aspect of the life of the church, which properly belonged to all Christians, but rather as the exclusive responsibility of Western churches.

Given its close relationship with Western expansion, the missionary work of the nineteenth and twentieth centuries also suffered the vicissitudes of that expansion. Throughout most of the nineteenth century, Western powers were increasing their influence throughout the rest of the world. Although there were lands such as China and Japan that for a long time resisted that influence, in the end they failed. Therefore, the nineteenth century resulted in an almost-uninterrupted missionary expansion.

In the twentieth century, a nationalist reaction began to develop, in which ancient cultures, religions, and traditions became an instrument and symbol of opposition to Western culture. Even while repudiating the West, that reaction found itself needing to make use of the technology that it had learned from colonial powers as well as from missionaries. However, the attempt was made to separate those technological advances from the rest of Western civilization and to make use of them without embracing the rest of the culture that had produced them. This made missionary work more difficult, for soon the new nations began using and controlling some of the technological advancements—for instance, in medicine, education, and agriculture—that before had given prestige and influence to the missionaries.

Also, during the twentieth century, Christians began thinking no longer in terms of a Western church with missions throughout the world, but rather of a church represented in all nations of the earth and with a mission in each of them. Thus, Christianity began becoming a truly universal faith and not the possession of the white race. This may be seen, for instance, in the increasing participation of the previously called "younger churches"—which today some prefer to call "churches of the Southern Hemisphere"—in the worldwide ecumenical movement.

Finally, one must note that, since the majority of Protestant missionaries during the nineteenth century came from the Pietist tradition, their message tended to be individualistic. This does not mean that they were not concerned for the physical well-being of people, but simply that they did little to discover the implications of the gospel for the society in which they worked as a whole. Even this, however, must not be exaggerated, for there were cases, beginning with Carey himself in India, of missionaries who worked in order to have more just laws and practices. But even then they did little to communicate to the churches that they founded a sense of their own social responsibility in their particular context. It was in the twentieth century, thanks to new biblical studies and the renewal of theology that resulted from them, that the "younger churches" began thinking more in terms of their own social responsibility, although sometimes they did not seem to be wholly prepared to discover on their own what such responsibility could imply in their concrete situation.

Chapter 7

MISSIONS IN THE FAR EAST AND THE SOUTH PACIFIC

Since in the previous chapter we pointed out that one of the great factors leading to the missionary movement of the nineteenth century was the series of discoveries that were made in the South Pacific, and since we also pointed out that William Carey, the famous missionary who worked in India, may be seen as a forerunner of that movement, it seems natural to begin our study of modern missions precisely in the area where Carey worked and where the great discoveries of the eighteenth century had taken place.

At the beginning of the nineteenth century there were in this area many diverse nations with different cultures and living under a variety of conditions. In places such as India and China, there were ancient civilizations joined to religions of high moral concern, which therefore proved more resistant to missionary work. In areas such as Japan, those ancient cultures had experienced very little contact with the West, and their ancestral traditions tended to shy away from any such contact and certainly from accepting missionary work. Then, there were areas recently discovered by Western explorers whose inhabitants belonged to traditional religions and therefore were much more amenable to the preaching of the gospel.

Since the period we are studying is also that of the great imperial expansion of Great Britain, we shall repeatedly find the English and the Scots as main characters in our story.

As to the order of our exposition, we shall begin in India, one of the best known areas for Westerners, in order to move from there to Ceylon, Southeast Asia, Indonesia, the Philippines, Japan, China, and finally the recently "discovered" islands in the South Pacific, as well as Australia and New Zealand.

A. Missions in India

India was always a preferred territory for Christian missionaries. According to an ancient tradition, the apostle Thomas was the first to preach the gospel in India. We are also told that in the second century, the Alexandrian teacher Pantenus visited the subcontinent. Later Nestorian Persians and Syrian Jacobites settled in the land. With the arrival of the Portuguese Jesuits, the Catholic Church began work in India. From that time on, some of the most fruitful experiments in missionary work took place there, including the Danish mission of Tranquebar and the work of Carey and his companions.

In the present section, we shall follow a chronological order, beginning with the "Christians of St. Thomas," whose church appears to be the oldest, and then moving to Roman Catholicism in order to end our narrative with Protestantism.

1. The Christians of St. Thomas during the Nineteenth and Twentieth Centuries

The last years of the eighteenth century and the first of the nineteenth witnessed the penetration of British power in those areas where the "Christians of St. Thomas" had been most numerous: Travancore and Cochin. The first representatives of the British government in this area, Colonels Charles Edward Macaulay and George Munro, were persons of profound Christian conviction who were very much interested in the Jacobites who lived in the area. Through their efforts and with the presence of the Church Missionary Society (CMS, a missionary organization affiliated with the Anglican Communion of the Church of England) and the services of several missionaries, links were made between the ancient churches of India and the Church of England. The instructions given to these missionaries was that they were not to turn Jacobites into Anglicans. Their function was to serve the Jacobite church in whatever manner it would request and to teach and preach Christian doctrine among them. The purpose of these missionaries was that their teachings would serve as a leaven within the existing church, with the result that the Jacobites would gain a deeper understanding of the gospel. This work began in 1816, and at first it was quite successful. The Jacobite hierarchy showed itself open to receiving help from the Anglican missionaries—although always with some reservations—who began a far-reaching project of translating and printing books, organizing schools in the Syriac parishes, and even furthering theological education, for one of the missionaries became the director of the seminary where the Jacobite priesthood was trained.

Difficulties began in 1825. Although many of these difficulties had to do with passing conditions, there were several factors involved. One of them was tension between the "tradition" that the Jacobites cherished and the "innovations" of the Anglicans. Another was the paternalistic and condescending attitude of some of those missionaries whom the Jacobite Indians saw as representing a deficient tradition. In 1827, the first Anglican missionaries were followed by a younger generation that did not understand the subtleties of the situation, and therefore relations began souring, to the point that in 1836, there was a final rupture.

After the break, these Anglican missionaries continued their work, although now addressing mostly those who were not Christian. Even so, a number of congregations abandoned the ancient Jacobite Church and became Anglican. These churches are now part of the Church of South India to which we shall turn later.

At the same time, within the Jacobite Church itself, some of the seeds planted by the British missionaries persisted, for many of the Jacobites who had favored the reforms that the Anglicans had suggested did not leave their ancient church. For a time it seemed as if the reforming party would be able to carry with itself the majority of the church, particularly since it had the support of the government, but a visit from the Jacobite patriarch of Antioch resulted in the weakening of the reforming party. This was not enough to avoid the schism, which resulted from what is usually called "the Case of the Seminary." Those who sought a different church and a different sort of theological education gave birth to the Church of Mar Thoma in 1889, with the support of the Church Missionary Society. This was led at first by Thomas Mar Athanasius and later by Titus II.

The Church of Mar Thoma was at first a small minority among Jacobite Christians, but its evangelizing zeal soon gained for it a place among the main churches in India. Together with the church, the Evangelistic Association of Mar Thoma was organized, which resulted in many conversions. At present the Church of Mar Thoma is widely represented among Indians living in the West. Beginning in 1895, the Church of Mar Thoma has sponsored annual meetings, congregating thousands of Christians in order to hear preachers of various denominations. It now has more than 900,000 members in India, organized into eleven dioceses, and in other parts of the world, it has another 200,000 members. Its theology is similar to that of Western Protestantism, while its liturgy still retains its Eastern characteristics.

The other branch of the Jacobite church suffered another schism in 1910, although this time not so much for theological reasons as over matters of authority within the hierarchy.

Finally, one must mention that there are still a small number of Nestorians in the area of Cochin.

2. Roman Catholicism

The period we are now studying was a discouraging time for Catholic missions in India, as was also the case throughout the globe. The decline of Portuguese power, the Napoleonic Wars, and the suppression of the Jesuits had a profound effect in India. This was further complicated by an ongoing dispute between the ecclesiastical authorities that still depended on Portuguese *padroado* and the new apostolic vicars now sent directly from Rome.

The conflict between those Catholics who considered themselves under the jurisdiction of Portuguese padroado and those who depended directly on Rome began in 1831, when Gregory XVI, who had been prefect of De Propaganda Fide, became pope. In 1833, the Portuguese government, eager to assert its authority vis à vis the pope, broke with Rome. In response, the pope abolished some of the ancient Episcopal sees that had been created under Portuguese jurisdiction and intensified missionary work in India. Since by then the Society of Jesus had been reinstated, large numbers of Jesuits from throughout Catholic Europe reached India. The conflict became even more bitter, for missionaries sent by Rome declared that those who still supported the Portuguese padroado were schismatics, while the latter argued that they were simply following the earlier decrees of the papacy granting the crown of Portugal authority over India. After long controversies, a series of concordats was reached, beginning in 1857. But even after Indian independence in the middle of the twentieth century, Portugal and the Vatican continued debating the matter. As was to be expected, all of this was not beneficial to Catholic work in India.

In spite of this long and debilitating debate, Catholic missions in India did achieve a measure of success. In fact, it was precisely the events of Catholic missions not under Portuguese jurisdiction that set off the conflict with those who still defended the ancient Portuguese padroado. One of the most notable Catholic missionaries during this time was Flemish Jesuit Constant Lievens, whose health allowed him to remain in India for only six years, but who in spite of that set off a movement of mass conversion. Lievens settled in the area of Ranchi, where he became a champion for the oppressed against exploitative landowners and moneylenders. He repeatedly took cases to court and won many victories for the poor. This began a flow of conversions to Catholicism, first among Protestants in the area and later among the Hindus. Seventy-five years after Lievens had to leave India and settle in America, seeking help for the tuberculosis that he had contracted, the Diocese of Ranchi was established. At that time it had 190,000 members, and currently it has more than a million.

Although one cannot survey here all the various places where the Catholic Church conducted missions in India, nor all of its missionaries, it is important to mention Catholic work in education, medicine, and interreligious dialogue as well as Catholic attitudes toward the caste system. The Catholic Church in India has been noted for its educational work, establishing schools at all levels of education. These schools are financially supported by the government, as are all other schools in the nation. There are also Catholic universities such as St. Joseph in Trichinopoly, Loyola in Madras, and St. Francis Xavier in Bombay and Calcutta. The most remarkable work in the field of medicine has been done by nuns who, at a time when ancient traditions would not allow Hindu women to become nurses, took the position of nurse not only in Catholic hospitals but also in other hospitals run by the government. It is also important to note that Roman Catholic work included interreligious dialogue from a very early date and that there are in India Catholic monastic groups whose mission is continuous intercession for people of other religious traditions.

Regarding the caste system, the attitude of the Roman Catholic Church has not been as firm as that of Protestant bodies. The reader will remember that already in the time of di Nobili there were Roman Catholic missionaries who argued that castes were simply an aspect of Indian culture and therefore were not something that converts had to abandon before being baptized. This was, in general, the attitude of most Roman Catholics throughout the nineteenth century, although efforts were made to avoid caste distinctions within the church. At first there were divisions within church buildings, separating people from various castes. Slowly, such distinctions receded, although an awakening of Hinduism late in the twentieth century and early in the twenty-first brought about a resurgence of emphasis on caste. At present the Catholic priesthood is open to people coming from the lower castes, which was not true at an earlier time. Even so, there are many regions in India where those who do not belong to the church consider the Christians to be a separate caste.

The ancient churches of the Syro-Malabar rite that had joined Rome at an earlier time continued existing. But they were rent by a schism that gave rise to the Syro-Malankara Church. These two communities continued existing into the twenty-first century, each with its own hierarchy, and both subject to Rome.

3. Protestant Missions

Protestant missions in India received a boost when a political change in England let Parliament take the East India Company under its wing. As we have already seen, the East India Company opposed missionary work—or at best accepted it as a necessary evil. The charter by which Parliament authorized the work of the company was to expire in 1813, and several Christian leaders, concerned over the obstacles that the company placed before missionaries, decided to take action so that Parliament would force the company to follow a more positive policy toward missionary work. One of these leaders was William Wilberforce, the great British social reformer who was known for his profound Christian motivation. In 1813, Parliament renewed the charter of the East India Company, although stipulating that the company was to offer facilities to those wishing to go to India in order to promote technical and religious knowledge in that area. This began a process in which numerous British subjects went to India, many as missionaries. In 1833, Protestant missions to India were further encouraged when Parliament eliminated restrictions that had hampered non-British missionary societies. That date marks the beginning of a large influx into India of missionaries from Europe as well as from the United States.

Protestant missionary work in India was quite varied. Among its dimensions, one must underscore educational work, medical missions, work among women, and mass conversions in certain tribes or castes.

Protestant educational work in India took its lead from Scottish missionary Alexander Duff. When he arrived in India, there was already the Hindu College in Calcutta, but this school had been led by people deeply steeped in European rationalism, and therefore students tended to be led toward religious skepticism. The result was that both Hindus and Christians began doubting the value of a Western-style education in India. Duff understood this situation and decided to found a school in collaboration with Hindu reformer Ram Mohun Roy. This school would offer a liberal education similar to what was available in England or at the Hindu College but was closely tied to Christian faith. Following the lead of ancient theologians, Alexander Duff believed that secular education was a preparation for receiving the gospel—a *preparatio evangelica*—and it was with this in mind that he opened his school. At the beginning, there were only five students, but soon there were almost 200. By the end of the first year, Duff surprised the intelligentsia of the city by offering oral public examinations in which his students showed how much they had learned of both a liberal education and Christianity. From that time on, Duff's school gained ever-increasing support. At the same time, he also established links with those students or alumni from Hindu College who through their studies there had abandoned Hinduism as well as any other religion.

Duff's work was reflected not only in other Protestant missions in India but also in the government's educational policy, which supported this sort of missionary work as "civilizing." In 1835, the government decreed that most of its funds devoted to education were to be employed in offering students knowledge of British language, culture, and science. Beginning in 1832, several schools were founded following the same policies as Duff's institution. In that same year, a similar school was founded in Bombay, and slightly thereafter there were others in Madras, Nagpur, Agra, and elsewhere.

All of these schools gained converts among the higher castes of Indian society. Such converts were few, and quite often a conversion led to a riot and to threats against the school by some of the more radical Hindus. Converts were persecuted by their neighbors and usually cast out by their families. There were also laws placing converts at a disadvantage, such as one making it illegal for a convert to Christianity to receive an inheritance. In spite of all this, throughout the nineteenth century, there was a slow but constant flow of conversions to Christianity from among the higher castes and the intelligentsia. It was a time when Hinduism did not seem to meet the intellectual needs of the cultured among its ranks. Not surprising, the number of such conversions diminished as nationalist sentiment grew and as Hinduism went through a renewal, showing itself capable of reacting and being revitalized by the very presence of Christianity. The second half of the nineteenth century and the beginning of the twentieth witnessed the flourishing of several movements within Hinduism that made it easier for the intelligentsia to continue living within the framework of their ancestral religion.

Another important aspect of missions in India during the nineteenth and twentieth centuries is the presence of medical missions. Although earlier missionary ventures, such as the one in Tranquebar and Carey's in Serampore, did include medical work, it was only well into the nineteenth century that there was an attempt to organize missionary medical work in India. Beginning in 1836, the American Board of Commissioners for Foreign Missions began sending to India ordained physicians who were to work at the same time in medicine and in evangelization. Later in the same century, other missionary societies also undertook medical work, sending physicians to India. While in 1868, there were only seven medical missionaries in India and Pakistan, by 1905, there were 280.

Christian medical missionaries worked particularly among children and women. They also built hospitals for people with tuberculosis and leprosy. Several centers were founded for the training of nurses and other support personnel. This work continued throughout the nineteenth century and the first half of the twentieth, when the government began taking responsibility for the care of the ill, and the question was posed as to the continued need for medical missions, given the disparity between the resources available for these missions and those available to the state. However, at that time, the resources provided by the state were still insufficient to meet the needs of the nation, and therefore the question that was being posed was not yet as urgent as it would eventually become.

Another characteristic of missionary work in India is the mass conversion of people in villages and even tribes, particularly among the aboriginal tribes that inhabited the land before the arrival of the Aryans, and among some of the lower castes of Hindu society. The first mass conversion began in 1846, when a German Lutheran missionary society began working among the aboriginal people in the region of Nagpur, known as the Kols. After ten years of work, that mission had gained slightly more than 1,000 converts, but that number began growing exponentially to such a point that early in the twentieth century, there were some 60,000 Christians in the region. Although some of the converts there joined the Anglican Church and others became Roman Catholic, the vast majority remained within the Lutheran tradition and organized an autonomous Lutheran Church. This is only one example of many that could be cited, particularly in South India. Such mass conversions accelerated after 1876, when a period of scarcity set in. During that time, Christian missionaries did much to ameliorate the difficult conditions in which the poor lived. The result was that many Hindus asked to be baptized. Some missionaries hesitated to do so, for they feared that people were asking to be baptized for reasons of material gain; but eventually they did baptize those who requested the rite. This may be seen in the work of Baptist missionary J. E. Clough, who, thanks to his contacts with civil authorities, had the possibility of employing a large number of workers and therefore began receiving requests for baptism from people who apparently thought that this would help their chances of being employed by him. At first Clough refused to baptize such people, but he agreed to it when Roman Catholics said that they would baptize them if Clough continued refusing. There is no doubt that many of these supposed conversions were faked or at least superficial. But it is also important to note that even after the period of scarcity was passed, the conversions continued, and that four years later, the Christian community around Clough's work had 20,000 members.

Besides these mass conversions of certain villages and aboriginal tribes, there were also mass conversions among some Hindu castes. This usually took place within the lower castes, which saw in Christianity a way out of their condition. One must remember that mass conversions of people who are used to thinking in collective terms are not always insincere or superficial. To demand an individual decision from people who do not usually think in individualistic terms would be tantamount to demanding that they become socially maladjusted before becoming Christians.

Protestant missions to India during the nineteenth century also were marked by their contribution to the emancipation of women. In ancient India, it was thought that women were unworthy of an education, the infanticide of girls was common practice, and the custom of burning widows on the funeral pyres of their husbands was relatively common, particularly among the higher castes. Within such a context, there is no doubt that the work of the first missionaries—and especially missionary wives—on the education of women was revolutionary. At first, such education took place privately, in homes; but in 1857, Alexander Duff founded the first day school for girls. Many other missionary societies followed suit.

The most outstanding personality in the emancipation of women was herself an Indian woman, Pandita Ramabai. Her family was exceptional, for her mother had taught her Sanskrit, even though this was highly unusual. After many and prolonged vicissitudes that involved the death of most of her family, Ramabai decided to devote her life to helping girls and young women who were widowed quite early because of the custom of being betrothed and even married in childhood. She eventually made contact with some Christian missionaries who sent her to England so that she could train for the task to which she had devoted her life. In England, she was converted to Christianity. She then went to the United States, where she gathered support for the work that she planned in India. Having returned to her native land, Ramabai founded a home for widows. Although this was not her initial purpose, there soon were some conversions among her protégées. The result was that some Hindus who had sympathized with her work now distanced themselves from her. But Ramabai continued with her work. In 1896, after a serious famine that spread throughout central India, Ramabai gathered a large number of orphan girls whom she settled in the homes of missionaries throughout the area. When she discovered that such families were insufficient in number, she founded a home for orphan girls that eventually had more than 1,000 residents and that continued existing throughout the twentieth century. By 1898, Ramabai established the Mukti Mission, and through her work a Pentecostal network was established in India. Recent Pentecostal historical studies show connections between the Azusa Street Pentecostal movement in the United States and India. Perhaps some of the best-known Pentecostal missionaries were George E. Berg and Robert F. Cook, who arrived in India early in the twentieth century.

Missions in India have also worked in the fields of agriculture and industry. Both in order to improve the economic condition of some communities and in order to serve as a means to develop character and discipline, Protestant missionaries in the nineteenth and twentieth centuries established in India several industries and agricultural projects. Most of the industries founded by missionaries were labor intensive, so that many people could be employed with limited capital. As to agricultural work, Christian missionaries have established centers to improve both agriculture and livestock. Probably the most notable is the one at the University of Allahabad.

The work of Pentecostal and Charismatic missionaries is also significant and is notable for the high number of native missionaries who serve their own people, so that thousands of leaders organize small groups of prayer and Bible study. These small groups have developed in practically every city in India. There are also large gatherings organized by Pentecostals and Charismatics, making use of the freedom of religion provided by the state. These gatherings usually involve the lower castes, particularly the Dalits, among whom vast campaigns of evangelization and faith-healing take place. There is no doubt that Christianity is penetrating into the lower castes of India and that through them it is gaining its own creative face within India.

These Charismatic and Pentecostal groups also developed educational projects. While most of the educational projects during the nineteenth century promoted a Western-style education, often hoping to "civilize" people, many of the newer projects under the auspices of Indian Pentecostals and Charismatics affirm the values of Indian society and culture. There are Christian schools that offer better education than the public ones and that insert Christian traditions jointly with those of Hindu and Muslim origin. These national Christian projects promote the pacific coexistence among various religions, noting both their differences and their similarities, and enjoining their students to live together in harmony.

Another interesting development in India is the "churchless Christians," that is, a large number of Hindus from the higher castes accepting the gospel but not the traditional ecclesial structures. This movement, strongly promoted by Christian Hindus within the higher castes, challenges traditional Christianity, for it seems to be a syncretism between Hindu contemplative practices and a Christian faith centered on the person of Jesus.

Finally, it is important to note that the globalization process has had a significant effect on Indian cultures and religions and that this has resulted in new models of missionary work led by nationals and often supported by Western missionary societies and agencies. Early in the twenty-first century, Indian Christians were creating establishments and businesses such as restaurants, coffeehouses, and the like, where the gospel was presented quite apart from the traditional missionary structures, and therefore avoiding conflict among the various religious traditions. In such settings, there is often a religious dialogue with an apologetic function, presenting and defending the gospel within the context of Hindu religious traditions. Paradoxically, these new missionary models, which are quite distinct from those received from Western missionaries, are possible precisely because of the effect of globalization and capitalism on the urban centers of India.

In brief, an overview of the results of Protestant missionary work during the nineteenth and twentieth centuries shows that it has led to large numbers of converts, particularly among the aboriginal tribes and the lower castes, but also among the higher castes and the intelligentsia. Christian missions have also contributed and still contribute to the educational, social, and economic development of India. The vitality of the Christian faith and the mission work led by Indians show that mission is not the exclusive property or responsibility of foreign missionaries and demonstrate the creativity of Christian groups less subject to the traditions of the West. In general, there is no doubt that Christian missions in India have had positive results and that this is particularly noticeable in the high degree to which Indian Christianity now develops its own leaders and its own missional models.

4. The Ecumenical Movement and the United Churches of India

The presence of a large number of missions and denominations in India hampered missionary work. Those Europeans who worked in India did not at first see any difficulty in the existence of various denominations and missionary societies. However, the situation was quite different for those who were not Christian, for whom the diversity of names and practices among Christians was confusing, and who often were more interested in learning about the differences among Christians than about the core of their faith. The missionaries themselves, who in their lands of origin did not work closely with members of other denominations, in India tended to consult among themselves, for they were a small minority and felt the need to make use of the wisdom and advice of their colleagues. The net result of all this was a sense of Christian unity that was much deeper than any existing at the time in Europe or in the United States. Thus, the case of India is one more example of the degree to which the ecumenical movement is a product of mission and missionary circumstances.

After the World Missionary Conference held in Edinburgh in 1910, the various churches and missions in India organized the

National Missionary Council of India, which after 1923 took the name of National Christian Council. This body includes most of the non-Catholic Christians in India.

Furthermore, during the twentieth century, India saw important organic unions among different denominations. At first these were unions among churches belonging to the same tradition, such as the one in 1901, which brought together the various Presbyterian groups in South India, and its continuation in 1904, when the Presbyterians of various bodies in North India joined with those from South India. However, the demarcations among denominations or among traditions were soon overcome. Thus in 1908, the United Church of South India was formed, bringing together Presbyterians and Congregationalists. In 1924, similar developments in the north gave birth to the United Church of North India. But the most remarkable of all these unions was already proposed at Tranquebar in 1919, and twenty-eight years later, in 1947, the result was the birth of the Church of South India. This included the United Church of South India—formed, as has been stated, by Presbyterians and Congregationalists—the Anglican Church, and the Methodist Church. The success of this union was such that it soon became an example and norm for similar plans, particularly in North India, where the Church of North India joined the United Church of North India, the Anglicans, the Methodists—both American and British—the Baptists, the Brethren, and the Disciples of Christ.

For all these reasons, as well as for the manner in which it has been able to respond to the new conditions after the independence of the land, the church in India is a clear example of what is taking place and what may still take place in some of the most ancient missionary fields for Christianity. This ecumenical activity not only has contributed to the unity of the church but also has created a space for interreligious dialogue, for the discussion of the relationship between church and society, for programs of theological education and formation, and for projects of economic development. New challenges and opportunities are also provided by the very active Pentecostal and Charismatic presence, as well as by missionaries coming from other parts of the Third World. In India itself, the Friends Missionary Prayer Band supports national missionaries and is notable both for its success in evangelism and for its protection of marginalized tribes. All of this indicates new vitality in the Christian community.

B. Christianity in Ceylon

Late in the eighteenth century, the British took the Dutch possessions in Ceylon; and in 1815, they occupied the entire island (today's Sri Lanka). The first years of British rule showed how superficial the conversions were that had taken place under the Dutch. Many of the supposed converts had accepted the faith of their masters only because this would produce various economic and other advantages, and they had not abandoned their ancient traditions and customs. An eyewitness tells of the following interview between a British governor and one of the inhabitants of the island:

–What is your religion? asked the governor.
–I am a Christian.
–A Christian, yes, but, of what sect?
–I am a Dutch Christian.
–Then you worship the Buddha.
–I most certainly do!

The new situation was eventually advantageous for Catholicism, for the laws against it that the Dutch government had enacted were abolished in 1806, when the British granted freedom of worship and equal civil rights for Roman Catholics. At that point, many of the earlier "Dutch Christians" became Roman Catholics. Although the controversy regarding the Portuguese padroado did hinder its growth, by the beginning of the twentieth century, the Roman Catholic Church in Ceylon already had 300,000 members, and by 1933, it had surpassed 400,000.

During the second decade of the nineteenth century, British Protestant missionaries began arriving, and it was those of Wesleyan and Anglican extraction that had most success. As elsewhere, these missionaries founded schools and made use of the printing press to promote their ideas and their faith. The British Methodists were able to develop a cadre of able pastoral leaders from among their Ceylonese membership. But even so, Protestantism never approached the size of Roman Catholicism, for in 1936, they numbered less than 40,000. Thus, even though Protestantism was growing more rapidly than Roman Catholicism, the latter was by far the faith of most Christians.

As in India, the twentieth century brought a revival of nationalist sentiments. After a prolonged period of debate and negotiations, Ceylon became independent in 1948. The growing nationalist sentiment that led to independence also brought with it a revival of Buddhism. Much of this revival imitated Christian methods such as Sunday schools and a certain missionary interest. Catholics and other Christians complained that the constitution of Ceylon did not provide sufficient guarantees for religious and other minorities, which placed Catholics and other Christians at a disadvantage. At any rate, Protestantism continued growing throughout the twentieth century, and toward the end of that century it was joined by Pentecostals and Charismatics. The result was a church that was rapidly growing, not only in numbers, but also in its ability to provide an effective witness within the new conditions that were developing in the land early in the twenty-first century.

Also, as in the case of India, the missionary situation of the small Christian communities of Ceylon led them from a very early date to a profound ecumenical sense, resulting in a church into which several Protestant denominations merged. However, early in the twenty-first century, some independent Pentecostal and Charismatic groups challenged that ecumenical spirit.

C. Christianity in Southeast Asia

As in the rest of the world, the continuous advance of European domination characterized the nineteenth century in Southeast Asia. Of all the various kingdoms in the area, only Siam (today Thailand) was able to preserve its independence. West of Siam, Southeast Asia became the possession of the British, while the French dominated the lands east of Siam. Generally, the British presence and effect on the area under their aegis were greater than those of the French in their own areas, where they arrived much later than the British arrived in their areas. Throughout Southeast Asia, Roman Catholicism was weakened by the ongoing controversy on the Portuguese padroado, as well as by frequent persecutions in areas where Catholics were most numerous. In French Indochina, the nineteenth century was characterized by almost-constant persecutions by the kings of Cochinchina and Annam, who sought to eradicate Catholicism from their lands. In other areas, Catholic missionaries had preceded French power and therefore did not have the protection of a colonial government. Because of these persecutions, the Catholics asked France to act in their defense, and the result was that, after a protracted war, Cochinchina became a French possession. Apparently there were no Protestant missionaries in French Indochina before the beginning of the twentieth century.

The government of Siam was open to missionary work. It was particularly during the reign of Monghut, beginning in 1851, when the king was eager to introduce into his lands the technological advances of the West, that Christianity—both Catholic and Protestant—achieved its first success. Roman Catholicism had been present in Siam much longer, but during the reign of Monghut, the number of missionaries increased dramatically and schools, hospitals, and seminaries were founded. Often Christian converts would be brought together to live in a village in which all were Catholic and under the direct supervision of the church hierarchy. Thanks to the innovations brought by missionaries, such villages were often more prosperous than their neighbors. Although this led to many conversions, it also increased the animosity of others toward Christianity. Something similar happened in French Indochina, even though repeated persecutions hindered the work of missionaries there.

The first Protestants to show an interest in missionary work in Siam were Adoniram Judson and his wife, Anne Haseltine Judson, whose life will be discussed further on. But their interest was limited to the translation of some small portions of the Bible to the language of the land. It was Presbyterian missionaries from the United States who were most successful in Siam. At first their work was centered in Bangkok, but soon they moved northward where they found a more fertile field in Laos. As a result, to this day the Protestant population in Thailand is mostly in the north of the country. The Presbyterians, however, did not abandon the capital but continued working there, and eventually some of their missionaries were given positions of high responsibility within the Siamese government. In 1934, the Presbyterians and Baptists joined to form the Church of Christ in Siam—now the Church of Christ in Thailand.

As to the British territories, the area where Christianity gained most converts was Burma (now Myanmar). The Roman Catholic Church did not expand much in this area during the nineteenth century, particularly during its first fifty years. This was mostly due to the reasons already listed elsewhere: the French Revolution, the Napoleonic Wars, and the controversy regarding the Portuguese padroado. It was only after 1856 that the Société des Missions Étrangères was given responsibility for the work in Burma, and at that point Roman Catholicism began growing in the area. By the end of the nineteenth century, there were two seminaries, several schools, and a printing press to serve the Catholic missionary endeavor.

Although the first Protestant missionaries to reach Burma were the result of the renewed interest in missions produced by Carey and his companions, the most important of the early missionaries, and the first who attained permanent results, was Adoniram Judson. When he was still a student at Brown University, Judson had become interested in missionary work in the Orient. His work promoting missionary interest among the Congregationalists in Massachusetts led to the birth of the American Board of Commissioners for Foreign Missions. This board sent him to England to establish contact with the London Missionary Society in order to plan joint work. The project was not acceptable to the London society, and therefore Judson, fearful that the support that he could have from the American Board of Commissioners would be insufficient for his work, decided to offer his services to the London society and not continue working with the board that had been founded at his initiative.

A series of vicissitudes followed, taking him back to the United States and then to England after having been made a prisoner by a French privateer. Eventually he reached India, where he contacted William Carey and his companions. In the crossing toward India, Judson and his wife had studied the New Testament from a different perspective and had come to the conclusion that infant baptism was against the teachings of the New Testament. Therefore, when they arrived at Calcutta, they decided to become Baptists. There in India, new difficulties followed, for the British authorities wished to rid themselves of Judson and his North American companions, and there seemed to be no possibility of beginning missionary work anywhere in the region. Finally, more as a result of circumstances than out of a careful decision, Judson and his wife left for Burma. Once again the voyage was difficult, including the stillbirth of their first child. The missionaries hoped that in Rangoon they would be able to count on the support of Felix Carey, a son of the famous missionary, who had settled there. But young Carey was too busy serving the government as a physician to lend much support to missionary work. When his wife died in a shipwreck, Felix Carey decided to leave Burma. At that point, it would have seemed that there was no future for the mission of the Judsons.

But the Judsons were not people who would give up easily. While Judson and his wife, Anne Haseltine, served the small English-speaking congregation where Carey had worked before, they studied Burmese, a language in which they became fluent in spite of its great difficulty. While both studied Burmese, Anne also studied Thai, for she had met some Thai prisoners who had been taken to Burma, and he studied Pali, the language of the sacred Buddhist books. A few years after the Judsons arrived in Burma, the American Baptist Mission was organized in the United States, greatly as a result of the interest that the Judsons and their companions had awakened in America. This new agency sent a printer to Burma. The result was the publication of the first printed books in Burmese. The translation of the Gospel of Matthew, prepared by the Judsons, was published in 1817. At that time, a number of Buddhists gathered regularly in the missionaries' home in order to discuss religious matters. But the conversions that the Judsons had always sought did not seem to materialize. It was not until 1819 that Judson baptized the first Burmese convert to Protestant Christianity. In 1834, the Burmese translation of the Bible was completed. As a result of the harsh conditions of life in Burma, Judson was twice widowed and therefore was aided in his missionary work by three successive wives. He seems to have chosen well in all three cases, for all three wives contributed significantly to his work. When he died in 1850, he left behind a growing body of Christian literature in Burmese and the beginning of missionary work among the Karens, among whom in ensuing years missionary work would produce greater fruit than among the Burmese themselves.

It was through the work of Judson and his companion, George D. Boardman, that Ko Tha Byu, a Karen, became a Christian. Ko Tha Byu worked earnestly among his fellow Karens, gaining numerous converts. By the time of his death in 1840, there were already signs of a mass conversion among the Karens. Later the Karens themselves would conduct missionary work among the Chins and other tribes in Burma.

As throughout the rest of Asia, the twentieth century brought both a growing nationalist sentiment and a renaissance of ancient religions. All of Southeast Asia was involved in movements seeking independence and also declaring Buddhism to be the religious expression of their nationality. The struggle was particularly difficult in Southeast Asia, where in each of the emerging countries there were various tribes or linguistic groups that sought hegemony over the rest. The European powers withdrew from the area, sometimes peacefully, and sometimes after violent confrontations. In missionary work, national leadership assumed more responsibility and authority. The Second World War brought the Japanese invasion and further weakened European authority in Southeast Asia. Shortly after that war ended, Southeast Asia was already divided into several independent nations. However, two political elements remained that must be taken into account: on the one hand, in most of the newly born nations were strong minorities whose national origins and languages were different from those holding the power of government, and which were therefore a permanent opposing factor against the established government; on the other hand, the proximity of Communist China and the interest of the United States in stemming the spread of communism rendered the political situation even more unstable, eventually leading to the Vietnamese war. As we have seen, in some regions, Christians—particularly Roman Catholics—lived in their own Christian communities. This increased the tension between the Buddhist majority and the Christian minority, often resulting in violence.

Beginning in 1959, the non–Roman Catholic churches of Southeast Asia joined in the East Asia Christian Conference. This ecumenical organization has promoted missionary work along different lines, including interreligious dialogue, matters of church and society, the relationship between cultural identity and Christian identity, economic development, the struggle against the abuse of women and children, the problem of prostitution, migration, urban issues, poverty, and the contextualization of the gospel.

As in other areas, toward the end of the twentieth century and early in the twenty-first, various independent, Pentecostal, and Charismatic groups entered the area. Quite rapidly their work was placed in the hands of national leadership, and this work was mostly concerned with developing new churches. It is also important to underscore the growth of Christianity among some of the groups and tribes in remote areas. Since there is a constant migration from those areas to urban centers, Christian growth in many cities presents a complex reality. Part of this complexity is the tendency of some Christian bodies to ask for economic support and other forms of help from ecumenical organizations, while at the same time refraining from participating in the ecumenical movement.

D. Christianity in the Malay Archipelago

Given its position in the southeast corner of Asia, the Malay Archipelago was long the object of the colonial ambitions of the main European powers. During the nineteenth century, most of the archipelago was in Dutch hands, but there were also other colonies: Portuguese in East Timor, British in Borneo and the western section of New Guinea, and German in East New Guinea. There were also regions that were independent, such as the area in northern Borneo where English adventurer James Brooke became rajah and the sultanate of Brunei on the same island. Most of the population of the archipelago was centered—and still is—on the island of Java, a predominantly Muslim area. Islam reached the archipelago long before Christianity and took possession of most of it, although there were always regions inhabited by aboriginal, animistic tribes. These would be important in the history of Christianity on the archipelago in the nineteenth and twentieth centuries. Finally, there were also some remains of Brahmanism, which had been the predominant religion of most of the archipelago before the arrival of Islam.

Since most of the territory in the archipelago was in the hands of Protestant colonial powers, most conversions to Christianity that took place during the nineteenth century were to Protestantism. In the Dutch colonies, the Dutch East India Company did not have great interest in missionary work and on occasion opposed it for fear that it would create difficulties with the Muslim population. However, well into the nineteenth century, there was in the Netherlands a religious awakening, and this resulted in renewed missionary zeal. The Missionary Society of the Netherlands, founded in 1797, gathered new impetus during the nineteenth century, and there were several other missionary societies founded at that time. The result was greater missionary activity in the Malay Archipelago. Most of this work took place among the animistic population and resulted in the mass conversion of several tribes. In the region of Sarawak, in northern Borneo, the English adventurer James Brooke, in the well-being of his subjects, sought Protestant missionaries. Besides those missionaries coming from the Netherlands, Brooke made the arrangements necessary so that an entire colony of Chinese Methodists could move into his lands. Soon more than a third of the inhabitants of Sarawak were Christian.

Toward the middle of the nineteenth century, the Dutch crown, seeking to strengthen its position in its colonies, declared that all Protestant churches in the Dutch East Indies should merge into one. This was done in 1854, resulting in the Protestant Church of the Dutch Indies. Although this church included most of the Protestants in the area, its missionary zeal was much less than that of missionary societies from Europe and the United States.

Most converts in the East Indies came from animistic religions, but there were also a number of converts from Islam. This number, although small, was greater than in all the rest of the Muslim world.

As throughout Asia, the twentieth century brought to the East Indies a renewed nationalist sentiment, and this was often joined to the old Muslim religion. In order to compete with Christianity, Islam adopted some of the instruments and means introduced by Christian missionaries. On its part, the church, imbued with the same nationalism, became more independent and developed a native leadership, thus creating a legitimate place for Christianity on Malayan soil. Most of the missionaries had to withdraw when the Japanese invaded the area during the Second World War. After that, the constitution of the Independent Republic of Indonesia, which included most of the archipelago and whose policies were markedly anti-Western, placed foreign missionary work—sometimes also national work—in a difficult position. In spite of this, throughout the twentieth century and into the twenty-first, Christianity—Protestant, Catholic, Pentecostal, and Charismatic—continued growing, mostly among converts from animistic religions.

On the island of New Guinea, which was not part of the Independent Republic of Indonesia although it was subject to the ambitions of Indonesian rulers, a surprising mass conversion that had begun in the nineteenth century continued into the twentieth. This was mostly the result of British and Australian missionaries.

E. Christianity in the Philippines

During the early years of the nineteenth century the Philippines were not as shaken by the Napoleonic Wars as was the rest of the world. Not surprising, the independence of Mexico, the land through which contact was maintained between Spain and the Philippines, made that contact much more difficult. Later the Suez Canal made those contacts easier; but Spain was already in decline and was unable to provide the Philippines with the technical and political advances of the nineteenth century. Through a number of alternative means, the ideas associated with the French Revolution came to the Philippines. Fearing disorder, the Spanish authorities, who at first had tried to bring some of the technological and other advances of the West to the Philippines, became rigid, impeding most contact between the islands and the modern world. Increasingly there was criticism in the Philippines against the Spanish administration and particularly against the church. The Spanish friars, both out of patriotism and out of loyalty to their church, usually rejected those criticisms and claimed that they were groundless. When conspiracy and rebellion against Spain arose, the friars, believing it to be their duty, opposed the conspirators and revolutionaries. This may be seen in the following lines by an anonymous author who sought to defend the attitudes of the friars:

> Since the parish priest was in continuous contact with his flock, sooner or later he came to know what their opinions were on political matters and if any among them were promoting separatist ideas. When that happened, they would make the necessary inquiries and, convinced that Spain was threatened, let the Spanish authorities know what was afoot, accusing the troublemaker so that proper action would be taken. Now this behavior on the part of the parish priest, which no [Spanish] patriot would reprove, has become the true and only cause of Filipino animosity against their parish priests.
>
> Sometimes out of carelessness, sometimes out of impudence, and sometimes out of sheer malice on the part of the authorities in whom the priests confided, eventually all the Filipinos who were imprisoned or deported knew who had unveiled their machinations. What could happen then? What we have seen for the last twenty years: that the anti-Spanish began a defamation campaign against the friars, making them appear as enemies of all progress, oppressors of the peoples, in fact, monsters loaded with vices who had to be destroyed.
>
> And, oh Spanish blindness! Some out of self-interest, others out of sectarian hatred and all out of a want of patriotism, they repeated the calumnies of the separatists and turned their backs on the friar and rejected his loyal and patriotic advice, thus providing the opportunity for those who were conspiring to prepare the insurrection. (Quoted in J. R. Rodríguez, *Gregorio Aglipay y los orígenes de la Iglesia Filipina Independiente*, vol. 2, pp. 235-36)

The result of all this was that the separatist movement, following the advice of patriot leader Aguinaldo, began insisting on the need to have Filipino bishops. When Aguinaldo was able to do so, he appointed Filipino priest Gregorio Aglipay as head of the church in the Philippines and sent Isabelo de los Reyes to Spain and to Rome to gain papal approval. When de los Reyes returned to the Philippines after having failed in his mission, he advised Aguinaldo and Aglipay to organize an independent Filipino church. After some delays, this church was formed and broke with Rome, taking the name Independent Filipino Church. At first its doctrines and practices were very similar to those of the Roman church, but de los Reyes himself, who in Europe had been influenced by Protestantism, began moving the church toward Protestant positions. After the North American regime took over, and Protestant missionaries came with them, the Independent Filipino Church became increasingly Protestant. However, due to a lack of inner vitality, which was reflected in the scarcity of properly prepared ministerial leadership, and in part to the proselytizing by Protestants among its members, the Independent Filipino Church has greatly diminished in size. When it was created it counted 25 percent of the population, and early in the twenty-first century it had decreased to 10 percent—according to the statistics of the church itself, for the official national census gives a figure of 2.6 percent.

The year 1898 brought the war between the United States and Spain, one of whose consequences was that the Philippines were now under American rule. This brought about profound changes in the islands. From the beginning, the United States declared its intention of preparing the Filipinos for independence, but even so its rule was at best condescending, and there were quite a few North Americans who took the opportunity to exploit the land and its people as the Spanish had done before. In the field of religion, the new political situation brought religious freedom, which until then Spain had refused to grant. Many in the United States saw these new conditions as a call from God making them responsible for the evangelization of the Philippines. For this reason, early in the twentieth century, a vast number of religious movements from the United States entered the Philippines. Those Protestant churches that had most experience in missionary work elsewhere sought to apply from the very beginning some of what they had learned in other fields, particularly in matters having to do with collaboration among various denominations. As a result, a conference was held in which the area was divided among Methodists, Presbyterians, United Brethren, Disciples of Christ, Baptists, Congregationalists, and the Christian and Missionary Alliance. The city of Manila itself was left open to all the various missions.

This period of collaboration characterized Protestant missionary work in the Philippines throughout the twentieth century and into the twenty-first. In 1900, a ministerial alliance was founded, and in the following year the Evangelical Union of the Philippines was organized. Two denominations, to which others were added later, established in Manila the United Theological Seminary in 1907. The National Christian Council was organized in 1929, and ten years later took the name Filipino Federation of Christian Churches. Probably the most notable achievement of this collaboration was the merger in 1932 of eleven denominations, which joined to form the United Evangelical Church in the Philippine Islands. Another merger in 1948 led this church to take the name of United Church of Christ in the Philippines.

Any discussion of mission work in the Philippines must include the name Frank C. Laubach, who is known throughout the world for his work in literacy. It was in the Philippines, and as a means to reach Muslims, that Laubach developed his method for teaching people how to read. In later years, Laubach himself, as well as his many disciples, adapted his method to dozens of languages. This has been a significant contribution to missionary work throughout the world, at once giving it a dimension of social service and facilitating the penetration of Scriptures and Christian literature, which throughout the centuries has been one of the main and most effective missionary methods.

Though there were several setbacks resulting from Aguinaldo's rebellion and from the Spanish-American War, the Roman Catholic

Church enjoyed a new awakening in the Philippines. Perhaps as a result of the hard lesson of the birth of the Independent Filipino Church, the Roman church began placing more responsibility in Filipino hands, including the consecration of several Filipino bishops. In 1934, and for the first time in its entire history, a Filipino came to occupy the archdiocese of Manila. Thanks to these changes, many of those who had originally followed Aglipay and the Independent Filipino Church returned to the Roman Catholic Church.

The impact of the Japanese invasion in 1951 did not affect Filipino Christianity to the same degree it did Christianity in Southeast Asia. Most likely, the Japanese were seeking to avoid resentment among the Filipinos, who were mostly Christians. Thus, they were exceptionally tolerant not only with Filipino Christians but also toward some foreign missionaries.

Although the independence of the Philippines changed the political situation, it did not bring about any great upheaval among Christian churches. To this day the majority of the population remains Roman Catholic, but the Roman Catholic Church has never attained the degree of political power that it achieved in several countries in Latin America. After independence, as in many other lands, Pentecostals, Charismatics, and independent Christians began working in the Philippines. Some missionaries from these traditions worked mostly among Muslims, while others recruited their membership from among the other churches.

F. Christianity in Japan and Korea

From the Philippines, following the rim of Asia, we move to Japan, and to the Korean peninsula, whose history is indissolubly and tragically connected with the history of Japan.

1. Christianity in Japan

The situation in Japan during the first half of the nineteenth century was similar to that of China during the sixteenth and seventeenth centuries. The Tokugawa regime was opposed to any foreign influence, most particularly any Western influence. This policy was grounded in the fear that the history of Japan would follow the same route of other Asian lands where Western powers had begun establishing commercial ports and had eventually taken possession of the entire area. Responding to that danger, and basing their policy on a nationalist feeling that was closely bound to the national religion, the Tokugawa decided to close the country to any foreign influence. Western powers repeatedly tried to establish relations with the Japanese government, but they all failed. Even Japanese citizens who landed on the shores of another land as they fished could never return to their own native land. The result was that there was a small number of Japanese scattered throughout the neighboring islands, and it was among them that missionary work began, although this could not at first be used as a point of departure for missions in Japan itself.

In contrast with China—where, as the reader will remember, Christianity entered thanks to its cultural and intellectual adaptations through the work of Mateo Ricci and his companions—in Japan, Christianity managed to enter through the economic and military power of the nations supporting it. In 1854, the United States forced Japan to sign its first treaty with a Western power. Four years later, France did likewise. There is no doubt that the reason why the government decided to sign these commercial treaties was the fear that, were it to refuse, military power would be used. At any rate, the establishment of commercial and diplomatic relations with Western powers provided the occasion for the entrance of Christian missionaries. The order we shall follow in discussing missions in Japan, although not strictly chronological, will be similar to what we have followed in previous sections, discussing first Roman Catholic, then Orthodox, and finally Protestant and Pentecostal missions.

(a) Roman Catholic missions

As was to be expected, since Catholic missions began thanks to a treaty between Japan and France, such missions were placed under the supervision of the Société des Missions Étrangères de Paris. The first missionaries arrived in 1859 and settled in what is now Tokyo. Some years later, they discovered that there were still 100,000 Christians in the area around Nagasaki. These seem to have been a remnant of old Catholic missions from the time of Francis Xavier. The first French missionaries established contact with them and convinced about a tenth of them to rejoin the Catholic Church. The rest remained apart from any connection with Western churches, until slowly they joined the various churches entering the area.

Roman Catholicism, like all other branches of Christianity in Japan, gained most of its converts from among the higher middle class. This seems to have been partly the result of the insecurity of that class as it faced a number of changes within the land and also to the eagerness of people from the high middle class to absorb Western culture. Even so, soon the Roman Catholic Church had extensive missionary work among the lower echelons of society.

The Catholic hierarchy was organized in Japan in 1891 and was headed by an archbishop in Tokyo. This see was at first occupied by foreign missionaries, and it was only in 1937 that the first Japanese was named to it. This was partly due to the pressure of growing nationalism leading to the Second World War. During that conflict Catholicism did not suffer as much as did Protestantism, particularly since most of its missionaries came from lands that were not at war with Japan, while most Protestant missionaries came from the United States and England. But even so, during the first half of the twentieth century, Roman Catholicism did not gain as many followers as did Protestantism.

After the Second Vatican Council, Catholicism in Japan, already a fully Japanese church, was still suffering a scarcity of priests and other national leadership. Therefore, the Conference of Japanese Bishops affirmed the need for continued foreign missionary work given the context of a country that is still mostly not Christian, and where approximately half a million are Catholic, out of a total population of some 110 million.

(b) The Russian Orthodox mission

In 1861, the Russian Orthodox Church established a mission in Japan through the work of Father Nicolai. This priest arrived in Japan as a chaplain for the Russian consulate but soon began sharing his faith with the Japanese. Following the tradition of other Orthodox missions, Nicolai sought to create in Japan a church that would be truly Japanese. His work consisted above all in training people who would be able to spread Christianity and in supervising the general work of the church. In 1904, when Russia and Japan went to war, Nicolai followed his Orthodox principles, insisting that Japanese Christians should be loyal to their country. He established the center for his work in what eventually became the Cathedral of the Holy Resurrection. He worked on translating the Bible and the liturgy of the Orthodox Church and on establishing seminaries for the formation of national clergy. When he died in 1912, at that point serving as the Orthodox archbishop of Tokyo, Nicolai left behind a community of more than 30,000 believers. His successor, Sergius, who was also a Russian, ruled the church in Japan until the first Japanese archbishop was consecrated in 1941. Even so, this church did not show the same rate of growth as it had enjoyed under the leadership of Nicolai.

In 1970, the church was granted autonomy within the Orthodox community, and Metropolitan Theodosius led the church through a process of renewal whose consequences can still be seen early in the twenty-first century.

(c) Protestant missions

The first Protestant missions in Japan came from the United States. The first commercial treaty between Japan and the United States was signed in 1854, and another treaty followed four years later allowing North Americans to practice their religions freely and to build churches. This new treaty, although not actually granting permission for missionary work, did produce in the United States an interest in sending missionaries to Japan. It seemed to indicate that the Japanese government, although not quite ready to support or protect missionary work, at least would allow it.

The first Protestant missionaries to Japan, all coming from the United States, were Episcopalian, Presbyterian, and Dutch Reformed. The Free Baptists arrived slightly later. As in other cases in the history of missions, one important aspect of the work of these early missionaries was translating the Bible and some basic Christian literature. The Presbyterians established educational and medical work, particularly a school for girls that was a novelty in Japan and a school of medicine that trained the first Japanese in the medical technology of the West. Even so, by 1872, only twelve Japanese had been baptized by Protestant missionaries.

Beginning in that decade, the eagerness of many Japanese to adopt Western culture had an effect on missionary work. Although Japan had taken longer than any other Eastern land to open its doors to Western influence, when it did so, that influence penetrated much more rapidly than in the neighboring nations. The Japanese were eager to learn Western technology, and many understood that such technology was closely tied to Christian faith. For that reason, and also because it was Protestants who brought to Japan many of the Western techniques, Protestantism experienced great growth during the decade of the 1890s. This growth was such that many thought that Japan would soon become a totally Christian country, and there were even some

Japanese who, although they were not Christians, argued that Japan should adopt that faith officially.

These new conditions resulted in the entrance into Japan of a vast variety of denominations, mostly North American and British. Soon there were in the islands dozens of denominations, with the result that the immediate growth of Christianity was noticeable but also that some Japanese expressed doubts about the validity of a faith so divided.

Since most converts to Christianity embraced the new faith led by their intellectual quest, Protestantism gained great influence in the academic and intellectual circles of Japan, even though the number of converts itself was not large.

The last decade of the nineteenth century brought a nationalist reaction. As they came to understand Western culture better, the Japanese saw some of its faults and weaknesses and therefore became more critical of it. This, and the confusing number and variety of Christian movements present in Japan, slowed the growth of Christianity. Ever since that time, even though Christianity has continued gaining converts, its growth has never been as surprising as it had been in the previous decade.

Nationalism, which toward the end of the nineteenth century began hindering missionary work, continued developing during the first half of the twentieth century. War with Russia broke out in 1904, and there were some who tried to turn it into a religious conflict. This led some to begin mistrusting Christians. During the First World War, Japan invaded Siberia and remained there until 1922. Throughout the first half of that century, relationships between China and Japan were tense and led to frequent armed conflict. All of this contributed to a growing nationalist and militaristic mood in the nation, culminating in Japan's participation in the Second World War. Japan's expansionist interests were justified by means of an ideology promising a new order in East Asia. For this reason, most Japanese Protestant leaders supported the government in its expansionist policy and only began withdrawing their support when events proved that the high-sounding ideology that they had supported was no more than an excuse for Japanese expansionism. By then the government had turned many Christians into instruments of its imperialist policies and had employed its ideological stance to persecute those Christians who would not submit. It was only when the government sought to demand that Christians eliminate from their creed the article regarding the resurrection of Christ that the churches decided that the time had come to face outright persecution. Although there are no trustworthy statistics regarding the number of Japanese martyrs during this period, a sign of the extent of the persecution is the fact that at the end of the war there were only 483 church buildings, out of 1,468 that had existed before.

One of the characteristics of Christian missions in Japan, which was a great help for Christians resisting the growing nationalist sentiment, was that from a very early time the missionaries took care to train national leaders and give them responsibility over the work of the church. This was made easier in that many of the early converts belonged to the higher middle class and were therefore educated people. Furthermore, the general level of education was always relatively high in Japan. The national leaders who emerged helped allay the suspicion that the church was at the service of foreign powers, and thus they made Christian witness more effective within Japanese society.

As a remarkable example of the work of Japanese missionaries in communicating the gospel by word and deed, one must mention Toyohiko Kagawa. Kagawa was the illegitimate child of a Japanese man from the high middle class who eventually acknowledged him. His father's death placed him under the care of relatives who did not provide a happy childhood. From an early age he met Christian missionaries and embraced their faith, so that eventually he studied theology and was ordained. However, instead of following the common path of most pastors in the country, he settled in a slum and there sought to bring both the Christian message and social improvement to those whose life he shared. From a sick man whom he sheltered in his home, he contracted a disease that later left him blind. He also worked far beyond the limits of the slum where he lived, organizing consumer cooperatives and labor unions, and this soon cost him his freedom. His profound social consciousness and his social activism did not lessen his sense that Japan must hear the gospel of Christ. Kagawa was one of the main leaders of the "movement of the kingdom of God," whose purpose was the evangelization of Japan while promoting Christian principles of social action. In 1938, on the eve of Japan's entry into the Second World War, he began a national evangelization campaign that lasted two years and gained a large number of converts. For reasons of his social work, his zeal in Christian witness, his many books, and above all, his love of neighbor, Kagawa became a symbol of what the gospel is able to achieve in a person's life.

From the early days of missionary work in Japan, there were Japanese Christians who insisted on the need for a united witness, at least among Protestants. In 1911, a group of Japanese leaders organized a society whose purpose was to work for the unity of Christian churches. In 1923, the National Christian Council of Japan was formed. At first this included only Protestants, but Roman Catholics joined in 1943. During the Second World War, government pressure forced all Christian churches to join, thus giving birth to the Nipon Kirisuto Kyodan, or United Church of Christ in Japan, which was organized in June of 1941. Once the war was over, several denominations withdrew from this union, but even so, this church continued being the largest Protestant body in Japan. Even though the actual merger of churches was the result of pressure on the part of the government, for long before that time there were many Japanese Christians at work trying to lead the churches into a merger.

Born out of the missionary movement, the Japanese church itself became a point of departure for further missionary work. Beginning in 1931, a number of societies were organized whose main purpose was the evangelization of the islands of the Pacific and of China and Manchuria. Japanese churches also began missionary work among the Japanese in the Philippines, Brazil, and Perú. This is one more example of what we have found repeatedly in the history of Christian mission, in which a country that a few decades earlier had been almost ignorant of Christianity, soon becomes an instrument for Christian expansion to other lands.

Finally, toward the end of the twentieth century and early in the twenty-first, Pentecostal missionary work began in Japan. The Assemblies of God in Japan has published a history of its first fifty years, and in there one finds that Pentecostal roots in Japan go at least as far back as 1913. The history of Pentecostal mission in Japan is characterized by much volunteer work and great dedication and conviction. Churches such as the Apostolic movement, the Assemblies of God, and, from Europe, the Missionary Pentecostal Union made their way into Japan early in the twentieth century. In that history, difficult as it is to uncover, a number of names stand out, such as M. L. Ryan, C. F. Juergensuen, Estella Bernauer, William and Mary Taylor, and Tanimoto Yoshio—a Japanese who became an outstanding missionary in his own land. Both the Pentecostals and various Charismatic groups continue growing in Japan. It would seem that the effects of globalization and the development of a sophisticated sort of capitalism in Japan, jointly with the fact that some of these movements proclaim a gospel of prosperity, make Pentecostal and Charismatic groups attractive to a number of Japanese.

2. Christianity in Korea

During the nineteenth and twentieth centuries, Christianity faced in Korea much greater difficulties than it did in Japan. During most of the nineteenth century, the Korean government would not allow any foreigners to enter the land, particularly Westerners. In 1876, Japan forced Korea to sign a trade pact. This was followed by similar agreements with the United States and with the main European powers, and this in turn opened the way for Christian missionaries.

Even before the Korean government allowed foreign missionaries, there was already a Christian community in that land. Late in the eighteenth century, a number of Koreans, after reading some Christian books in Chinese, decided to accept that faith. Through many difficulties, some of them managed to establish contact with the Catholic bishop of Beijing, who gave them some instruction. For a while they were organized as a church, with their own bishop and several priests; but when the bishop of Beijing informed them that this was not correct, that they needed a bishop consecrated by other bishops, they limited their activities to those that the Roman Catholic Church considered legitimate for lay Christians. Both the Roman Catholic Church from outside the peninsula and those Christians who lived there repeatedly sought to have Western Catholic missionaries in Korea. A few managed to enter the land, but most were discovered and executed. Throughout the first half of the nineteenth century, Catholic missionaries in Korea, as well as Korean Christians, wrote one of the most remarkable pages in the entire history of Christianity with their own life and blood. Sometimes there were periods of relative tolerance, but these were followed by violent persecutions during which vast numbers of Christians died. Between 1866 and 1868, there were more than 2,000 Christian martyrs. Toward the end of the nineteenth century, as Korea became increasingly open to Western influence, the Roman Catholic Church grew rapidly. Large numbers of missionaries arrived, mostly from France. When the Japanese annexed Korea in 1910, there were already more than 77,000 Catholics in the peninsula. Since in Japan the Catholic Church followed the policy of allowing its members to participate in Shintoist ceremonies, claiming that these were not religious, but only acts of patriotic affirmation, the same policy was followed in Korea, and therefore the Japanese regime was not as harsh with Roman Catholics in the peninsula as it was with Protestants.

The Russian Orthodox Church also began working in Korea toward the end of the nineteenth century and early in the twentieth, although such work seems to have been an attempt to open the way for Russian power. Not surprising, after the war between Japan and Russia in 1904 and 1905, the Japanese saw this mission as an agency of the Russian government. Therefore, when Japan annexed Korea in 1910, the Russian Orthodox mission faced serious difficulties. These became even greater when the Bolshevik Revolution of 1917 led to the end of the subsidies that had supported the mission in Korea. Furthermore, the communist Russian government now ordered that those churches that had been created among Koreans in Russian territory be closed.

Early Protestant contacts began in 1832 under the sponsorship of the Netherlands Missionary Society. Later in 1865, the London Missionary Society sent Robert J. Thomas, another missionary originally assigned to China. In fact, many of the missionaries who first had contacts with Koreans were originally assigned to China and later went to Korea to continue their missionary endeavors.

The most successful missions in Korea were Protestant, particularly Presbyterian and Methodist. Both denominations arrived in 1885, both sent missionaries from their northern branches in the United States, and both paid particular attention to medical work. Thus, the first Presbyterian missionary was declared a physician by the Korean court and the director of the first hospital established by the government. Another remarkable Presbyterian missionary in Korea was Horace G. Underwood, whose brother became rich through the manufacturing of typewriters and dedicated a significant part of his income to the support of the Korean mission. After the first northern Presbyterian missionaries from the United States, other missionaries followed from the southern church, as well as from Reformed churches in Canada and Australia. Something similar happened with the Methodist Church, for missionaries from the Southern branch of that church also went to Korea.

Historians debate whether the first Protestant Korean was Yi Ungchan or Sang-yoon Suh. What is quite certain is that their conversion contributed to the translation of the Bible in Korean. At the same time the Bible was being translated into Korean in Japan. One of the leaders of this enterprise was a Korean refugee in Japan, Soo-jung Yi, who worked mostly on the Gospel of Mark. Therefore, when the first ordained missionaries arrived in Korea through Japan, they were able to bring with them the Gospel of Mark in Korean.

In 1893, the Presbyterian missionaries in Korea adopted what had become known as the "Nevius" method, advocated by John L. Nevius, who suggested, among other things: (1) centralizing all evangelizing effort on the working class; (2) the conversion of women and the education and formation of girls and young women; (3) the building and support of primary schools in rural areas; (4) the translation of the Bible and other Christian literature into the vernacular; and (5) the immediate development of national leaders and of the economic self-support of churches.

Another important development in Korean Protestant Christianity was the Great Revival of 1907. During the first two decades of the twentieth century, Protestant missionaries and Korean nationals experienced an outbreak of the Holy Spirit. Some Korean scholars trace the beginning of the revival to a group of Methodist missionaries at Wonsan, and particularly to Methodist medical missionary R. A. Hardie. The legacy of the revival is present in the charismatic forms of worship, the significant growth of Korean churches, and the development of Korean leadership. Early in the twentieth century, the various Presbyterian branches joined to form the Presbyterian Church of Korea, and the Methodists followed suit.

As was the case elsewhere, the first denominations were followed by a vast number of others, although in the particular case of Korea, that number was limited by the difficulties posed by Japanese domination.

That domination brought serious difficulties for Protestant Christianity. Most Protestants refused to participate in the ceremonies celebrated in Shinto sanctuaries, declaring that they were religious rites and not mere acts of patriotic affirmation. Since the Japanese government saw such ceremonies as the ideological basis for its expansion, it is not surprising that Protestant churches suffered the consequences. Most Protestant missionaries came from the United States and Great Britain, countries with which Japan was soon at war. Since this was not true of Roman Catholics, Protestant churches had to face great difficulties until the defeat of Japan at the end of the Second World War. During this process, Korean Protestantism was clearly developing a revolutionary spirit of resistance to Japanese occupation, and, later, a sense of affinity with North American Protestantism.

Since Protestant expansion had been greater in the northern section of the peninsula than in the southern, the division of the peninsula, with the north being controlled by a communist regime, greatly affected Protestantism in the land. One must also remember that almost immediately after the Second World War, Korea suffered a prolonged war that affected the entire land as well as its churches. Many of the northern Koreans who sought refuge in the south were Christians.

Beginning in 1960, there were a number of events and movements that are worthy of note. During a time of dictatorship, the Urban Industrial Mission supported workers who sought to defend their rights and protected them from government exploitation. By then, the National Council of Korean Churches had also issued a document in favor of human rights and political freedom—a document reminiscent of Korean Christians' resistance to Japanese domination. This is an indication of the profound spirit of dedication, cultural identity, and defense of human rights that is not typical of Christian movements in other areas. Many of the missional practices that began developing in the 1970s and 1980s came to be called *Minjung* theology, or a theology by those who suffer and seek liberation.

Finally, during the last decades of the twentieth century, there was a charismatic and contemplative awakening in Korean churches. The influence of Pentecostal and Charismatic missionaries has left its imprint in the missionary spirit of Korean Christianity. Elsewhere in this book, we shall once again meet Korean Christianity, now as a source of mission to other lands. Korea is no longer so much a "mission field" as it is a source of mission itself.

G. Christianity in China

The course of Christianity in China is one of the most complex and tragic chapters in the entire history of the Christian missionary movement. The first to take the name of Jesus Christ to that great nation in the East were the Nestorians whose traces disappear in the ninth century. Later, at the high point of the Middle Ages, Franciscans reintroduced Christianity in China; but once again it disappeared, a victim of political circumstances and of the enormous distance and lack of communication with its geographic center in Europe. Early in the Modern Age, Matteo Ricci and his companions were able finally to plant the Christian seed in China, but even their endeavors took centuries to bear fruit. The history of Christianity in China during the nineteenth century is similar to its history in the ancient Roman Empire, when popular prejudice and governmental action produced repeated local persecutions. Sometimes these were vast persecutions, and Christian martyrs numbered into the tens of thousands. In the twentieth century, the course of Christianity in China was interrupted by two world wars, and particularly by the Second World War, when Japan invaded much of the territory. Partly as a consequence of the Japanese invasion, the war had hardly ended when the communists took control of China, establishing a regime that was noted for its antipathy toward Christianity. Even at the beginning of the twenty-first century, the government was inconsistent in its attitude to the Christian church—an inconsistency that reflected a situation of a government that was communist in its ideology and neocapitalist in its actual policies.

During most of the nineteenth century, China kept its doors closed to any foreign influence. As we have seen, this was also the policy of other nations at the periphery of the great Chinese Empire, and there is no doubt that in this they were emulating the practices of their larger neighbor.

The inner coherence of the Chinese way of life was such that any foreign influence or Western idea seemed to be a threat to the established system. The Chinese Empire, which existed before the time of Jesus, felt that all that came from the West was an unnecessary and perhaps even dangerous innovation.

At the same time, the Western powers as well as Japan saw great commercial opportunities in China. This led to a series of wars between China and various other powers, usually leading to commercial treaties that allowed for the settlement of foreign traders and missionaries in some specific ports along the Chinese coast. The first and probably the most infamous of these wars, in this case between Great Britain and China, is known as the Opium War. Its result was that China was forced to sign a treaty with Great Britain opening its ports to a greater extent than before. Soon the United States, France, and other Western powers followed suit. After another war with Great Britain, China was forced to sign treaties in 1858 and 1860 allowing foreigners to visit the interior of the land and also guaranteeing tolerance for Christianity. It was under the wing of these treaties that Christianity expanded throughout China during the second half of the nineteenth century.

Toward the end of that century, the war between China and Japan, in which the latter used Western technology in order to achieve victory, convinced the Western powers that it was possible to conquer China and share the spoils. This brought about a period of ever-increasing foreign intervention in China, leading to the Boxer Rebellion at the very turn of the century. This rebellion spread throughout northern China, and, although its purpose was to expel all foreigners, its direct consequence was that the foreign powers, whose armies crushed it, gained even greater influence in China.

The result of all this was a growing sentiment among the Chinese that their ancient culture, as well as the political structure attached to it, lacked the necessary dynamism to face modern conditions. Beginning in the twentieth century, republican sentiment began growing, and in 1911, the Republic of China was founded. This republic was not able to bring political stability to the nation, which was divided among various territories whose governments followed different and even contradictory policies. Finally, after a prolonged struggle, Chiang Kai-shek's Kuomintang managed to establish its authority over almost the entirety of the national territory. The main focus of resistance remaining, which would eventually destroy the Kuomintang government, was the communist government in Chensi. At that point, however, Chiang Kai-shek's party seemed to crystallize the hopes of the vast majority of the Chinese people, and the communist regime did not seem to be a great threat.

It was the Japanese invasion, first of Manchuria in 1931, and then of China itself in 1937, that undermined and eventually destroyed the political position of Chiang Kai-shek. His government was forced to retreat toward the West in the face of the Japanese invasion, and in spite of China's valiant resistance, the Chinese people as well as much of the outside world came to the conclusion that the Kuomintang had shown itself incapable of ruling China. At the same time, the other focus of resistance against the Japanese, the communist regime in Chensi, shared with Chiang Kai-shek's government the glory of resistance but was not blamed for the invasion. Furthermore, administrative corruption undermined the nationalist government of the Kuomintang and would not allow it to reconstruct a land that had been devastated by war. The net result of all this was that, with Russia's support and in the face of the hesitation of the Western powers, which did not know whether or not to support Chiang Kai-shek, the communists came to rule the entire Chinese Empire except Formosa—now Taiwan. As was to be expected, this began a new chapter in the history of Christianity in China.

1. Roman Catholic Missions

The history of Roman Catholic missions during this period is a continuation of what we have seen before. The ancient Jesuit mission—later continued by the Lazarists—and the work of the Portuguese in Macao resulted in the birth of a Catholic community that by the beginning of the nineteenth century had several thousand members. Although in China, as in India, Ceylon, and other regions of the East, the Portuguese insisted on the ancient rights of padroado even after they had lost their political power, in China, the consequences were not as serious as elsewhere. Part of the reason for this is that Portugal was never able to exert its power in China or to have missionaries in the interior of the land.

During the second half of the nineteenth century, France became the protector of Catholic missions in China. French protection was also extended to Chinese Catholics. This was particularly important in the case of the courts, for it was fairly simple to turn a civil case into one of religious persecution, thus invoking the support of the French. This led many to seek baptism because of the advantages it represented, and it also led to a deep hatred of Christians in some Chinese circles.

Besides the French, there were also in China Catholic missionaries from Italy, Germany, Spain, and other European lands, as well as—during the twentieth century—from the United States and Canada. Most of these missionaries belonged to religious orders such as the Jesuits, Lazarists, Franciscans, and Dominicans. But many others were diocesan priests coming to China under the auspices of the Société des Missions Étrangères de Paris, which was in charge of missionary work in vast areas of China as well as in Tibet and Manchuria.

The missionary methods followed in China were questionable, for we have already seen that many converts came to Catholicism seeking only legal and other advantages. Furthermore, some missionaries established a custom of paying people who came to catechetical lessons, and in some cases loans were made to the needy with the condition that they allow the missionaries to teach them Christianity.

There were, however, other less dubious methods. Thus, for instance, Catholic missions were noted for having founded a large number of homes for orphans in a land in which the death of abandoned children was frequent. They also established schools, clinics, and centers for the rehabilitation of people addicted to opium. In general, the life of missionaries in China was full of sacrifices and hard labor, particularly traveling from one place to another. They often made every possible effort to establish Christians in separate communities or villages in which it would be easier for them to live according to their Catholic principles. They normally sought the conversion of entire families or social groups rather than of individuals, for experience had taught them that it was much more difficult for an isolated individual to face the obstacles that society placed before converts than it was for an entire family or community. During the twentieth century, some missionaries worked at rural reconstruction, particularly in Mongolia, where they did much to solve the problems resulting from long periods of drought. The Roman Catholic Church did not do as much as Protestants in the field of education. Its educational interests centered mostly on the training of Chinese who would become priests and church leaders in the future, and not so much on influencing the future of the ruling elite in China. Therefore, the Roman Catholic Church was able to have a large number of Chinese priests but few lay leaders within the Chinese community at large. Early in the twentieth century, in founding three major universities, the Roman Catholic Church was beginning to pay more attention to the general education of the land.

In spite of the interest of missionaries in developing a native clergy, during the entire nineteenth century, not a single Chinese was made bishop. This is even more remarkable since two centuries earlier there had been a Chinese bishop. What was happening was simply that the Catholic missionary enterprise in China reflected the general attitude of Europe during the nineteenth century, which looked down upon the lands where colonies and missions were established and considered their population inferior and incapable to bear the same responsibilities as the Europeans. Finally, it was in 1926, in St. Peter's Cathedral in Rome, that the first six Chinese bishops were consecrated.

The Catholic Church continued growing in China throughout the nineteenth century and the first half of the twentieth. However, communist rule complicated the life of that church. There were bishops and priests who supported the regime, even after there were major persecutions during the Cultural Revolution of Mao Tse Dung. By 1970, the Catholic Church was divided—as the Protestants also were. On the one hand, there was the official church, that branch of Catholicism that was tolerated and recognized by the communist government as a legitimate religion. On the other hand, there were also the "underground" or "subversive" churches, which the government would not acknowledge. Rome had to show great tact and diplomacy in order to maintain a balance in its relationships with these two churches, both claiming to be Catholic.

Even in spite of major debates and complex political situations, the Roman Catholic churches in China continued pursuing their mission of protecting and nourishing their laity and always seeking to find a space—acknowledged by the government or not—for the church to exercise its faithfulness. Also, the political situation in which these churches found themselves promoted the development of a Chinese leadership that now provides pastoral care and guidance to millions of Roman Catholics in China.

Finally, the political changes that took place in China late in the twentieth century and early in the twenty-first made it possible for missionary exchange. This has been a great help particularly to the official Catholic Church, for it is now able to have greater contacts with Roman Catholicism elsewhere. As a result, that church is experiencing missional renewal in its liturgy, its theology, its ministerial formation, and its support for development projects in rural areas.

2. Orthodox Missions

Ever since the seventeenth century, there had been a small Russian Orthodox community in Beijing. Throughout the nineteenth century, it remained quite small, for it made no effort at evangelizing its neighbors until a treaty between Russia and China in 1858 guaranteed religious tolerance for Christians. Some missionary efforts began at that point, but it was only after the Boxer Rebellion killed almost half of the Russian Orthodox in China that a real effort was made to reach the Chinese themselves. At that point, the Orthodox community began growing, and at the beginning of the First World War, it had slightly more than 5,000 members. The Russian Revolution in 1917 deprived it of its earlier economic support, but the influx of Russian refugees fleeing from the communist regime gave it a new impetus. Before the triumph of communism, the Russian Orthodox in China had an archbishop in Beijing and quite a few parishes in Manchuria, which was the area where most Russian exiles took refuge. Under the new regime, this small Orthodox Church was almost annihilated. However, late in the twentieth century, the Church of the Protection of Our Lady was opened as a place of prayer in Harbin, and the first service was held by a small group of Russian immigrants as well as some Chinese. Later, the Russian Orthodox patriarch visited Harbin, and the church there was reconstructed. These are small signs that there may be a renewal of life for the Russian Orthodox in China.

3. Protestant Missions

China was the main focus of Protestant missions during the second half of the nineteenth century and the first half of the twentieth. In the beginning of the period we are studying, there was in China a very small number of Protestants, and their interest was mostly in trade and not in spreading their faith. Furthermore, the laws of the land were such that any attempt to spread the gospel would have been ruthlessly stamped out. However, beginning in 1806, Joshua Marshman, a companion of Carey in the mission of Serampore in India, began translating the Bible into Chinese. This marked the beginning of a mission that would eventually be quite large.

Besides Marshman, who remained in India and whose work was limited to translating the Bible, the initiator of Protestant missionary work was Robert Morrison, a Scottish Presbyterian. After studying medicine, astronomy, and Chinese, Morrison persuaded the London Missionary Society to send him to China. Since the trading interests of the British did not support such a project, Morrison traveled to the United States and from there to Canton, where he settled. At that point, the law would not allow him to move into the interior of China, and therefore in Canton, Morrison devoted himself to the study of Chinese and to producing literature in that language. His work included the translation of the Bible and several of the most important Protestant books from England and Scotland. His efforts did not immediately result in a large number of converts, for it took seven years for Morrison to gain his first convert. But they did awaken in Europe a growing interest in Chinese missions, and therefore when the doors of China later became open to missionary work, there was a contingent of missionaries ready to respond to the new possibilities.

Another forerunner of missions in China was the German Karl Gutzlaff, although his project was more ambitious than Morrison's. He considered the best way to proceed in China was to train Chinese

Christians to move inland and there distribute literature and organize Christian communities. His plan did not succeed, and it was eventually discovered that many of the people that he thought had moved far inland carrying the gospel message were simply using the resources that Gutzlaff provided them in order to live comfortably. However, this was not always the case, and at any rate, Gutzlaff's plan and the reports that he sent back to Europe contributed to the growing missionary spirit among Protestant churches. Thanks to the work and reports from Morrison and Gutzlaff, other missionaries settled in Canton and also in areas outside of China where there were large numbers of Chinese residents, particularly Malacca.

The first opening of China to European missionary work was the result of the Opium War, a shameful episode in which Great Britain went to war against China in order to protect the opium trade. As has already been stated, that war resulted in the opening of five important Chinese ports to international residents. From that point on, and through a series of similar treaties, various Western powers gained ever-increasing rights of penetration for their citizens. This also widened the area where missionaries could settle.

At first the main missionary society working in China was the London Missionary Society, which after commissioning Morrison sent other colleagues to reinforce his work. The American Board of Commissioners for Foreign Missions sent the first North American missionary in 1829. Shortly thereafter the same agency sent other North American missionaries, including the first Protestant medical missionary to work in China. Besides these societies, the main British and North American denominations and missionary societies soon began sending missionaries. Foremost in this work were the American Baptists, Episcopalians, and Presbyterians.

Among the many Protestant missionaries in China during the second half of the nineteenth century, three are worthy of special note:

Timothy Richard, Samuel I. Schereschewsky, and J. Hudson Taylor. Timothy Richard was an English Baptist, and his missionary methods are reminiscent of Ricci's three centuries earlier. Richard focused his work on the scholarly and ruling class within Chinese society. He looked on Confucianism with greater sympathy than did other Christian missionaries of his time. Throughout his life he promoted the founding of Christian universities in the main cities of China as a means for Christianity to penetrate into Chinese society. His writings, seeking to bring the whole of Western culture into China, were very much read in Chinese scholarly circles.

Schereschewsky was a Lithuanian Jew who converted to Christianity in the United States, where he joined the Episcopal Church. This church sent him to China as a missionary, and there he worked on the translation of the Bible and the Book of Common Prayer. He was consecrated a bishop in 1887, but he gave up this position six years later, when he lost much of his physical mobility. In spite of his handicaps, he continued his translation work, and his literary production during the last years of his life, when he was precluded from more arduous work, was quite extensive and influential.

There is no doubt that the most remarkable Protestant missionary in China during the nineteenth century was J. Hudson Taylor. Although himself a Methodist, he left for China in 1853 under the auspices of the Chinese Evangelization Society. He soon separated from that organization due to differences on missionary strategy, and from then on he continued his work on his own account. When some years later he had to return to England for health reasons, it seemed that his Chinese work had come to an end. However, in England, he devoted himself to awakening interest in China and to contributing to Chinese Christian literature in a particular dialect in which he was fluent. Five years later, after a long spiritual struggle, he decided to return to active work in China and to organize a society that was called the China Inland Mission. Taylor did not believe in excessive organization, and the purpose of his society therefore was not so much to found churches as to preach the gospel throughout China. His dream did not consist in establishing Christian communities in various provinces, nor even in attaining a large number of converts, but only in making sure that every Chinese person had the opportunity to hear the preaching of the gospel. This would be the pattern later followed by most faith missions. In theory, the China Inland Mission was open to missionaries of all theological tendencies, but in fact it attracted only missionaries with views relatively similar to Taylor's. These missionaries lived frugally, without a fixed salary. Furthermore, Taylor himself and the China Inland Mission did no fund-raising but simply prayed and asked others to pray so that funds would be forthcoming. Thanks to the great movements of awakening of individual religion that for some time had been taking place in Great Britain and the United States, Taylor's project was widely embraced, and soon the China Inland Mission became the largest missionary enterprise in all of China. Although in theory its purpose was not to found churches similar to those that existed in Great Britain or the United States, but simply to preach the gospel and then let others organize Christian communities, in fact thousands of churches resulted from the work of the China Inland Mission. The mission itself was interdenominational, but missionaries of the same denomination tended to gather in particular areas, and thus a number of regional churches developed, each reflecting the practices of a mother denomination in the Western world.

Throughout the second half of the nineteenth century, the main Protestant missionary methods were the distribution of Christian literature—particularly the Bible—preaching, and establishing social service institutions such as schools and hospitals. At first, most of the schools were at the primary and secondary level of education, but slowly centers of higher learning were founded, as well as seminaries. As to medical work, besides general hospitals, there were other centers of specialized care, such as homes for the mentally infirm and rehabilitation programs for opium addicts. The work among such addicts was particularly impressive, for many of the Chinese converts, and some of the best Chinese pastors, were the product of these centers. Several British and North American universities established their presence in China—particularly Yale, which built a hospital to which were attached schools of medicine and of nursing.

In general, Protestant missionary effort during the second half of the nineteenth century focused on territorial expansion more than on the development of the institutions and programs necessary for the continued life of the church. This was particularly noticeable in the field of education, especially if one compares Protestant work in this field with its Roman Catholic counterpart. While Catholics focused on theological education and, to a lesser degree, on the general education of the people, Protestants became known for the degree to which they were able to train the future leaders of the land, but at the same time the training of their own ministers lagged behind Roman Catholics. Toward the end of the nineteenth century, the Protestant Chinese church was still completely in missionary hands and had not yet developed leaders able to take responsibility for the life of the church as a whole.

During the war between China and Japan in 1895 and the Boxer Rebellion five years later, China was completely open to Western influence. Many young people, seeing that Western technology had been able to crush Chinese power, were eager to learn that technology and to understand the culture that had produced it. Since for decades Protestant missionaries had become known for their interest in bringing to China the technological advances of the West, the new intellectual atmosphere of the land resulted in greater prestige for them. Therefore, during the early decades of the twentieth century, Protestantism grew exponentially, even though it was still a small minority. Just before the Second World War, there were more than half a million Protestants in China. However, as Chinese interest in what missionaries had to offer was based on a nationalist urge, it is not surprising that as soon as the Chinese felt they had gained a foothold in such technology there would be a new reaction against all matters Western. During the third and fourth decades of the twentieth century there was a growing anti-Western and anti-Christian movement that, although not fully supported by the majority of the population, did include many of the Chinese political leaders. This anti-Christian feeling was reflected in the growth of communism in China beginning in 1930, as well as in the appearance within the Kuomintang of a wing that opposed the excessive influence of Christians in China—an influence exerted particularly through Chiang Kai-shek and his wife, who had been raised in a Christian home.

As elsewhere in the mission field, during the first half of the twentieth century, there was in China a movement seeking Protestant unity. This resulted, in 1922, in the founding of the National Christian Council. Some years before that, the various branches of the Anglican community had joined into a single church, and the Lutherans had done likewise. Somewhat later, the China Baptist Alliance was organized. But the most remarkable ecumenical effort in China at that time was the founding of the Church of Christ in China, which included representatives of the Reformed, Congregational, Baptist, and Methodist traditions, an effort that at that point was setting precedent for the rest of the world.

It is also important to note that Protestant missionary work was not always based on a sense that Western civilization and traditions were better than those in China. There were some missionaries, as well as children of missionaries, who did not accept the traditional views and strategies. Among these whom one should mention are Edgard H. Hume, Frank J. Rawlinson, and Pearl S. Buck—winner of the Nobel Prize for Literature in 1938—whose lives attest to a conversion to Chinese culture and a profound sensitivity toward Confucianism, Buddhism, and other religious expressions in China. Many of these

Christians saw their missionary vocation as beginning to develop a more adequate model for mission, involving a true encounter with people of other cultures and religions.

The lot of Protestant missions in China was closely tied to the nationalist government. Sun-Yat-Sen, whose spiritual heir Chiang Kai-shek claimed to be, had been a Protestant. Chaing-Kai-Shek himself was a member of a Protestant church, and his wife certainly came from a home of profound Protestant convictions. Many missionaries saw in these circumstances an opportunity similar to what the Roman Empire had offered in the time of Constantine. Others were not quite as optimistic, pointing out the many cases of political corruption within the Kuomintang. At any rate, it is not necessary here to judge the character of Chiang Kai-shek but simply to note the fact that his expulsion from continental China by the communist armies brought a new period for Chinese Christianity, Protestant as well as Catholic.

The first consequence for missions after the communist victory of China was the withdrawal or expulsion of almost all foreign missionaries. Many Chinese abandoned Christianity for the sake of Marxism. Particularly those among the intelligentsia and younger students who had been trained in liberal theology found that theology unable to withstand the challenges of the new situation. Some Christian leaders thought that the only way to save the church was to place it at the service of the state. In 1950, a group of Christian leaders gathered in Shanghai were presented with a Christian manifesto for their approval. When they refused to agree to it, they were simply told that since Premier Chou En-Lai had already approved the document they were not allowed to reject it. Shortly thereafter a "campaign of denunciations" began, in which some Christian leaders defamed other Christians through the press and radio. Next was the "consolidation" of churches, so that in Beijing, for instance, where before the revolution there had been sixty-five churches, only four remained—the rest were given to the state as a "patriotic gesture."

For some time, Christians in China kept in touch with the rest of the church through their brothers and sisters in Russia. But when relationships between China and Russia became tense, this last line of communication was also broken. By 1961, it was impossible to know how many Christians there were in China, and it was even more difficult to know how many belonged to "clandestine" or subterranean churches, which had emerged as a reaction to the attitude of the churches acknowledged by the government.

Even so, mission work in China continued. As has just been stated, there was a division among Protestants between the official churches, which were acknowledged by the state and later known as the China Council of Churches and as the Three-Self Movement Church, and on the other side, the many churches that were considered clandestine, subterranean, or even subversive. Once again, the Chinese government declared that all Protestant churches were one religion, and a complex history of relationships began developing between the official church, with its ecumenical and educational organizations, and the clandestine churches. There were Chinese Christians and foreign missionaries who criticized the Western Protestant enterprise in China and wrote in favor of the Marxist Revolution. By the time the Cultural Revolution broke out in the 1960s, it became clear that Christianity—both official and unofficial—was under severe stress and even persecution and that the goal was the total extirpation of Christianity from Chinese soil.

However, toward the end of the 1970s and early in the next decade, a new attitude began developing within the Chinese government, allowing a certain measure of freedom of religion. Surprisingly, when churches were open, thousands of members returned to pray and praise God. Also, partially as a result of its earlier ecumenical initiatives and partially as a result of government pressure, denominations had disappeared, being merged into the Christian church in China, with various expressions testifying to the faithfulness of the Chinese Christian people and making it clear that all mission work in China must be supported and led by Chinese.

In the midst of those developments, various missionary groups joined Protestant Chinese in creating the Amity Foundation in 1985, an independent and volunteer Chinese organization whose purpose is to promote educational and social services and to support development projects in the rural communities of China. Under the leadership of Bishop K. H. Ting, lay leader Han Wenzao, and Presbyterian missionary Philip Wickeri, Amity became a link between Christians in China and their brothers and sisters elsewhere, promoting interchange and sponsoring ecumenical events.

H. Christianity in Australia and the Islands of the Pacific

Since one of the events leading to the great missionary movement of the nineteenth century was the series of travels in which, from 1768 to 1779, Captain Cook explored the lands of the Pacific, it is not surprising that Great Britain would soon establish its presence in those lands and that traders and colonists would be accompanied by missionaries. However, the process of colonization was slow because the ancient civilizations of the Far East offered better commercial prospects than the sparsely inhabited lands of Australia and the islands of the Pacific.

1. Australia

The first British subjects to settle in Australia were convicts, for Australia was originally a penal colony. The first contingent arrived in 1788, and this resulted in the founding of the colony of New South Wales. Throughout the first half of the nineteenth century, and even later although in smaller numbers, convicts continued settling in Australia and Tasmania. From the very beginning, chaplaincies were established in the penal colonies, partly as a result of the work in Great Britain of Wilberforce, an Anglican Christian whose convictions led him to seek penal reform as well as the abolition of slavery.

Since most early immigrants—the first convicts as well as the colonizers who went to Australia out of their own free will—came from the British Isles, the Church of England was always the largest in the area, and by the middle of the twentieth century, about a third of the population was Anglican. Next was the Roman Catholic Church, followed by the Methodists and Presbyterians, who had begun work quite early in the new colonies. Also, although in lesser numbers, there were Baptists, Congregationalists, Lutherans, Pentecostals, and others.

From its beginnings, Christianity in Australia was challenged by a missionary task. It is estimated that when the first British convicts arrived in Australia, there were more than a quarter million aborigines, living at a level of civilization corresponding to the Stone Age, and nourished by hunting and collecting fruits and other plant material. The arrival of the British colonizers placed them in serious disadvantage, for they were constantly pushed into the desert regions in the interior and the north of Australia. Many of the colonizers abused them and even hunted them down as if they were animals. In response to those conditions, the churches began missionary work among them and also made efforts to protect them. Given the nomadic customs of the aboriginal population, this missionary work was very difficult. Missionaries therefore decided it was best to try to get them to settle in a particular place—much like the ancient *reducciones* that the Spaniards had established in the Americas—in order to teach them the Christian faith as well as new agricultural methods and other Western advantages. The purpose of these missions was not only the conversion of the aboriginal people to Christianity but also helping them adapt to the conditions of modern life. Quite often people who had lived in one of these missions would abandon the sedentary life that they were forced to lead there and return to roaming in the desert.

Throughout the nineteenth century, most missions, Catholic as well as Protestant—which were the majority—failed. The aboriginal population continued diminishing, and many thought that it was destined to disappear. Also, quite often those who did accept and adapt to the sedentary life of the Christian missionary settlements had become so accustomed to having their needs met by missionaries, that it was difficult to get them to accept responsibility for their own lives.

There was some improvement during the twentieth century. Thanks to medical advances, infant mortality was reduced, so that the aboriginal population began growing anew. Schools were established, which by 1965 had enrolled 80 percent of all aboriginal children, and slightly later legislation was issued granting the aboriginal population the same rights as other Australians. The growing number of people of aboriginal blood began giving signs of being ready to take greater responsibilities. By 1970, there were in Australia only a few hundred nomads, and the rest of the descendants of the original inhabitants had adapted to modern life in one way or another.

Australia soon became a center from which missionary work developed toward New Zealand and the other islands of the Pacific. Some of its first pastors and chaplains, particularly among the Anglicans and Methodists, were very much interested in work among the Maoris of New Zealand and then among the inhabitants of the other islands.

Before turning to New Zealand, we must note that in Australia, as in so many other regions of the globe, the twentieth century was characterized, on the one hand, by movements seeking unity among Christians and, on the other, by the presence and growth of Pentecostal and Charismatic believers. There were several cases of organic unions among Protestant churches coming from the same tradition. The National Missionary Council of Australia was founded in 1927. From the very foundation of the World Council of Churches, two

Australian churches were members. There were also many mergers and conversations about merger among various denominations.

The list of churches and traditions of Pentecostal inclinations in Australia is impressive. The Apostolic Church, the Assemblies of God, the Church of the Foursquare Gospel, the Church of God (Cleveland), and other Pentecostal groups have made a significant contribution to mission work in Australia, particularly among immigrants, migrant workers, and people in the urban centers. A growing number of Australian Pentecostal churches resulting from the worldwide Pentecostal missionary movement became national churches, such as the United Pentecostal Church of Australia. Many of these Pentecostal and Charismatic bodies conduct mission work in other lands.

2. New Zealand

Christianity came to New Zealand from Australia. Well ahead of the first great waves of British immigrants, some Australian Christians had begun work among the Maoris, the original inhabitants of New Zealand. The Maoris were more advanced than their Australian counterparts, but their cannibalistic and warlike customs limited population growth. The first Christian missions to New Zealand were the work of Samuel Marsden, the second Anglican chaplain in Australia, who in 1814, after having worked among Australian aborigines, established missionary work among the Maoris. Shortly thereafter, and partly following Marsden's inspiration, Methodist missionary Samuel Leigh settled in the same area. Roman Catholicism arrived some twenty years after Anglicanism, but even then its work was mostly limited to the Irish colonists. The first Anglican and Methodist missionaries contributed to the decline of cannibalism among the Maoris, and already by the middle of the nineteenth century, most of them were inclined toward Christianity.

Then came the overwhelming wave of British settlers. Although some who had advocated settlements in New Zealand had done so for religious motives, the actual result was tragic for the Maoris. The firearms introduced by the settlers turned wars among the Maoris more deadly. Soon the exploitation and abuse by the settlers led the Maoris to a rebellion that was crushed by the British, but not before a vast number of Maoris died.

Even so, Christianity—particularly in its Anglican form—was able to take root among the Maoris. These roots were such that soon the Maoris began creating their own churches and religious movement, such as the Hau-Hau in the nineteenth century, and the Church of Ratana in the twentieth. The latter was named after its founder, and it combined highly emotional worship with an emphasis on divine healing and a political and economic dimension, for it promised that a total devotion to God would bring social justice to the Maoris.

By the end of the twentieth century, the vast majority of the country was Protestant, mostly Anglican, Presbyterian, and Methodist. The Catholic Church counted slightly over an eighth of the population. Within the Anglican tradition, the Maoris had insisted on the need to have their own diocese, and the result was the creation of such a judicatory, with a Maori at its head. Soon New Zealand, like Australia, had become a source of missionaries to other Pacific Islands.

3. The Islands of the Pacific

No chapter in the history of Christian missions is more inspiring than the expansion of Christianity in the islands of Polynesia, Melanesia, and Micronesia. There were thousands of these islands, most of them quite small and sometimes with enormous distances between them. Missionary work was not helped by the vast variety of languages in the area. Quite often traders and adventurers arrived before or at the same time as the missionaries, and their bad example and, in many cases, their active opposition became a hindrance for missionary work. Many of the inhabitants of the islands practiced cannibalism, and some were head-hunters. Wars among various tribes were endemic and became much more deadly as Europeans introduced firearms. The diseases brought by Westerners, against which the inhabitants of the islands had no immunity, decimated the population. Quite often the repeated epidemics were blamed on the missionaries, who had provoked the ire of the gods.

In spite of these difficulties, the evangelization of the islands of the Pacific continued without abating. Quite frequently, particularly in the case of Protestant work, those who were recently converted decided that they had the responsibility to take their faith to their neighbors and even to people on other islands. In several of the islands where Christianity had recently taken root, schools were created for training missionaries to other islands. This was particularly true of Christianity in Samoa, Tonga, and Fiji. Frequently these native missionaries were killed and devoured by the inhabitants of another island whose conversion they sought, and in such cases the usual result was the immediate volunteering of other Christians to continue the mission of the deceased.

Protestants performed most Christian work in these islands, and by the middle of the twentieth century, most of the population was Protestant, although Roman Catholics also were quite numerous. Missions to the islands of the South Pacific came originally from Australia and New Zealand, as well as directly from Great Britain under the auspices of the London Missionary Society. In the North Pacific, missionary work was mostly under the auspices of the American Board of Commissioners. Given these origins, the strongest denominations on the islands were the Congregationalists and the Methodists. There were also large numbers of Anglicans as well as some Baptists, Disciples of Christ, and others. Naturally, in those islands that were under Dutch or German rule, most missionaries came from those lands and represented the churches that were powerful there. But the missionary influence of the Netherlands and of Germany never reached the level of Great Britain, Australia, New Zealand, and the United States.

French priests headed most Catholic missionary work in this area. As was the case among Protestants, there were among them many examples of great dedication and heroism. The best known of these is Father Damian, who devoted his life to work among the lepers in Hawaii. Quite often French missionaries appealed to French military power to support their work. On more than one occasion, when a local king or chief who had converted to Protestantism would not allow Catholic work in his island, France forced him to do so by dint of arms. This was the case in Tahiti, which had been one of the first areas in which Protestant missionaries had worked, and which through a combination of Catholic missionary work and French naval power became both French and Catholic. In such cases, since French authorities would not allow the presence of foreign missionaries in those lands, Protestants began sending missionaries from the Société des Missions Évangéliques in France. However this was not enough to stem the tide of Roman Catholicism, which soon overcame Protestantism.

In general, the history of the penetration of Christianity was repeated from island to island. In some places, missionaries arrived ahead of other Westerners, while in others they arrived after traders and settlers had introduced the seed of physical and moral destruction. In the first case, the original inhabitants of the islands were able to adapt more rapidly and completely to the new conditions resulting from their contacts with the rest of the world. Usually, Christianity was taken to an island by missionaries who were recently converted Christians from a neighboring island. In other cases it was taken back to their own island by someone who had been shipwrecked in a place where Christianity was already present and who had thus come to know the new faith. In a few cases, white missionaries took it. Frequently those first missionaries, native as well as Western, were killed and eaten by the population of an island whom they hoped to convert. However, eventually small missionary centers were established, and these continually gained a slowly growing number of converts. Since most Protestant missionaries came from traditions that underscored the need for a personal religious experience, such conversions were frequently accompanied by emotional upheavals and a radical change of life. Occasionally converts would revert to their former religion and way of life, but eventually a small group of believers developed, often including some of the leading members of the community. Then, after long years of seemingly fruitless work, mass conversions occurred.

Such conversions took place during revivals in which people experienced profound emotions, feeling a conviction of sin, followed by general confessions. Once this happened, it took a few years for almost the entire population of an island to become Christian. Then the community would usually develop a communal life and a system of law reflecting Christian principles. Quite often, since an island whose population had been converted had greater knowledge of Western technology, that island attained hegemony over its neighbors, to which Christianity then expanded. A remarkable case is that of the king of Tonga, who, upon being baptized, took the name of George. Through George's military and diplomatic ventures, his power expanded to several islands, and Christianity reached even beyond his political power.

By the end of the nineteenth century, almost all the inhabitants of Polynesia were Christians, and there was missionary work on most islands of Melanesia and Micronesia. During the twentieth century, the conversion of these latter islands continued, and by the middle of that century, almost all their inhabitants declared themselves to be Christian. The main strongholds of the ancient religions were in the mountainous interior of some of the larger islands, particularly New Guinea where there were still mass conversions among various tribes. The Japanese invasion during the Second World War does not seem to have affected the advance of Christianity. The extension of New Zealand and

Australian protectorate over some islands in the South Pacific awakened a new missionary interest in those countries. Hawaii was annexed by the United States in 1898.

Thanks to Christian influence, and to the unceasing work of many missionaries, the various languages of the Pacific were reduced to writing, and the Bible and other Christian literature were translated into them. Cannibalism and head-hunting disappeared, as well as the custom of strangling widows—which had earlier prevailed in Fiji. In their sexual mores, the inhabitants of the islands of the Pacific also seemed to follow the teachings of Christian missionaries. In the field of education, from the very beginning, several missionaries had founded schools, and later they made strong efforts to train those converts who were to serve as missionaries to other islands. Thus a numerous native clergy arose. However, throughout the nineteenth century and the earlier decades of the twentieth, most Western missionaries seemed hesitant to trust native pastors with major responsibilities. Such tendencies began to disappear later, so that the churches in several of the islands became relatively autonomous and self-governing. This was particularly true of Samoa, Fiji, and Tonga.

I. General Considerations

During the entire period we are studying, Asia and the South Pacific were the focal point of missionary interest in Europe and the United States. It was to that region of the globe that William Carey turned his sights in his cobbler's workshop, and it was in Asia that he spent the best years of his life. From then on, the main missionary efforts from Europe were directed toward the Far East and, to a lesser degree, toward the South Pacific. In the United States, the American Board of Commissioners for Foreign Missions was also born out of the interest of believers in missions to the Orient, and it was to that area that it devoted its best efforts.

The enormous distance separating the Far East and the Pacific from that region where the missionaries proceeded—except, naturally, those from Australia and New Zealand—resulted in a certain natural selection that was quite advantageous for missionary work. Only those churches and institutions that had a good measure of resolve and permanence could send missionaries to Asia or to the South Pacific.

The combination of these two factors—the concentration of missionary effort and the selection of its personnel—resulted in the founding of remarkably mature churches. It was in India, and then in the rest of the area we are now considering, that native believers were first able to take control of the new churches—and to do so not in a spirit of bitterness or of emancipation from the guidance of missionaries, but simply as the natural consequence of their Christian faith. By the beginning of the twentieth century, there were many churches in the Far East whose native leadership was able to guide them through difficult times and to continue their work without Western support. Thus the mistaken notion that there is a difference between "church" and "mission" was beginning to disappear.

From a very early date, some of the churches of south Asia had an important place in the ecumenical movement. The national leadership to whom we have already referred began seeking more effective structures and means to witness, and this resulted in the formation of several united churches that then became an example for similar mergers elsewhere, including in the West. Besides such organic unions, there were councils of churches, interdenominational centers for theological education, and many other instruments of collaboration.

It is important to note that Charismatics and Pentecostals also contributed to the development of a national leadership. The presence and growth of these traditions soon became a challenge and an example to other churches, since many of the newly formed Pentecostal and Charismatic churches showed an ability to contextualize the faith and an affinity with the culture of the people themselves that is much to be commended and that has often been lacking in other churches.

On the age-old question of the degree and the manner in which missionary work ought to adapt to the surrounding culture, there were various positions. In general, Catholics were more willing to adapt than were Protestants—as may be seen for instance in the case of the Hindu caste system—but they also maintained the organization they had brought from Europe. On their part, Protestants attained various degrees of adaptation, and some simply refused to do so, resulting in small Protestant churches that were little more than cultural transplants. Similar ambiguities exist also among some Pentecostals. Although many of them take into the life of the church much of the ancient cultures of Asia, expressing an affinity that some critics consider syncretistic, others present an inflexible and uncompromising witness to Jesus Christ as they have learned about him from the West. At the same time, there is much evangelizing work following the patterns established by Hudson Taylor, whose purpose was not to found a church, but simply to share the gospel in all the realms of life, even though this may not result in the birth of a church.

At any rate, there is no doubt that by the early twenty-first century the Far East and the Pacific had become a center of vitality for Christian faith and mission.

Chapter 8

MISSIONS AND WITNESS IN THE MIDDLE EAST AND MUSLIM MAJORITY COUNTRIES

The most difficult field for Christian missions has always been the Arabic-speaking Muslim countries and Muslim majority countries. For centuries, the law in many Arabic-speaking countries punished conversion to Christianity with death. In some others, including Muslim majority countries outside of the Middle East, there has generally been a measure of tolerance and even protection for the religious rights of Christians. The movement of conversions between Islam and Christianity has always been controversial, for there is no set pattern that explains it. Usually, the two religions have lived in tension and ambivalence.

This resulted in the tendency of the ancient Christian churches that remained in the Middle East and North Africa to become small groups formed mostly by the descendants of earlier Christians and to hold staunchly to ancient tradition. Furthermore, in many

Arabic-speaking Muslim countries, Islam so involves the entire life of society that anyone who withdraws from it necessarily has to withdraw from that society, the only alternative being to join one of the ancient Christian traditions or one of the churches founded more recently. The existence of a sacred book, the Koran, which is similar to the Bible in many points, but in others radically different from it, does not make it possible for some evangelical Christians in the region to engage in mission as others have done elsewhere on the basis of the authority of the Bible. Yet, for many Christians, the Christian Scriptures provide a mission foundation to engage in other forms of mission practice such as peace, justice, social services, education, and interreligious dialogue. The Crusades and the long history of conflicts and tension between Christians and Muslims have contributed to an attitude not only of suspicion but also of hostility toward Christianity, for many have come to believe that conversion to Christianity results in abandoning the concerns of the community at large.

Relations between Christians and Muslims in the Middle East, in North Africa, and in Muslim majority countries, such as Indonesia and Malaysia, have also been framed within the history of Western colonization and expansionism. Both colonialism itself and the Westernization of these regions have left a resentment that in recent decades has resulted in violent attitudes and actions against anything that could seem to be the result of Western or Christian influence. It is difficult therefore to tell the story of Christianity in that area in a balanced way that does justice to the various positions and interests involved.

Many countries in the Middle East include some of the most ancient and venerated places in the history of Christianity, as well as some of the most ancient Christian churches: the area of Palestine and Syria, where Christianity first developed and expanded; Egypt, where the school of Alexandria flourished; North Africa, which was the cradle of Latin-speaking Christianity; and the areas of Mesopotamia and Persia, where Christian faith rapidly expanded during its earlier centuries.

The area therefore includes, besides the Eastern Orthodox Church, several churches that follow what are usually called the Monophysite and Nestorian traditions, some of them as old as the fifth century, for they resulted from the christological controversies and the political and ethnic tensions that existed toward the end of the ancient Roman Empire (see chapter 3). All of these churches still exist, some with large numbers of members and ecumenical vitality and participation, and others with very small remnants of what earlier were large congregations.

Throughout the Middle Ages, the Catholic Church sought the conversion of Muslims and the recovery of the lands they had conquered. This was one of the reasons—and certainly the main excuse—for the Crusades. We have also seen how St. Francis of Assisi and Ramond Lull, as well as a host of Franciscans, worked for the conversion of Muslims. Thus, one would expect that the Roman Catholic Church would keep alive its interest in the Arabic-speaking Muslim countries and would continue significant missionary work within it. However, the fact is that during the late Modern Age most of the effort of Catholic missionaries within the region was not addressed at Muslims themselves, but rather toward the conversion of other Christians to Roman Catholicism. This was done by bringing large sectors of the ancient Eastern church into obedience to Rome and turning them into "uniate" churches—also known as united churches of Oriental rites.

Protestantism has also worked in the Middle East and, like all other branches of Christianity, but perhaps not quite as much, it has experienced great difficulties in promoting the conversion of Muslims. More than once, particularly in the case of Anglican missions, the purpose of Protestant missionaries has not been primarily the creation of new churches of their own denominations, but rather the introduction of leavening elements into the ancient Eastern churches in order to awaken them to their missionary calling. But too often the result of such Protestant mission has been the development of tensions within those ancient Eastern and Oriental churches, usually leading to schisms resulting in the creation of new Protestant churches. Also, particularly during the nineteenth century, Protestant missionaries showed a particular interest in seeking the conversion of Jews living within the Arab-speaking Muslim countries.

During the last decades of the twentieth century and early in the twenty-first, two different evangelical missionary strategies shaped the life of Christians in the region. Many independent groups of evangelical and conservative convictions have entered the Arab-speaking Muslim countries in order to seek conversions, particularly through the use of mass media and social networking. Many of these groups also tend to support the foreign policies of Western powers—particularly of the United States—that protect the interests of Israel. In response, several evangelical organizations and conferences, such as Christians for Palestine, World Vision Middle East, Bethlehem Bible College, and the 2012 Christ at the Checkpoint Conference, were created to undo the stereotype, that is, that every evangelical must be pro-Israel, thus underscoring the social, historical, religious, and economic forces that shape the policy of nations and creating an awareness of the presence and feelings of millions of Arab Christians—as well as Christians of other ethnic groups who live in that area of the world. The tension between these two positions has been exacerbated by the presence of missionary endeavors, often supported with financial resources from the Western powers, but with personnel from the Third World—especially from Latin America, the Caribbean, and some countries in Asia—who under the cover of tourist and business visas conduct missionary work in very risky situations, often without the awareness that they are also promoting the interests of Western powers. Thus, the situation of Protestant Christianity in the Middle East early in the twenty-first century was complex and controversial.

From the early 1900s, Christian communities in this region have sought other expressions of Christian mission, broadening the concept of mission from conversion to church unity, education, dialogue, social justice, peace, reconciliation, and so on. This long and complex process came to an important point in 1974, when the Middle East Council of Churches had its first assembly. Currently, the MECC seeks to (1) strengthen the unity, trust, and continuity among Christians in the region, (2) encourage its member churches to help one another understand their traditions and faith witness, and (3) build bridges of understanding and mutual respect among people of other faiths.

A. The Ancient Eastern Churches

1. The Eastern Orthodox Church

Throughout the Middle East and in some Muslim majority countries, the Eastern Orthodox Family of Churches is a very small minority. Although it was in that area that strong Christian communities existed in the early centuries, the long years of Muslim rule have resulted in the stagnation of many churches in the area, so that now the majority of Eastern Orthodox churches are not within these regions, but rather in Greece, Russia, the former Yugoslavia, Romania, and Bulgaria. In the Middle East, Orthodoxy has four patriarchs: the patriarch of Constantinople, also known as the Ecumenical Patriarchate of Constantinople in Istanbul, and those of Alexandria and All Africa, Antioch and all the East, and Jerusalem. Although the patriarch of Constantinople has a certain primacy of honor, his authority is limited to Greek Orthodox Christians within Turkey, who are a small minority. His administration takes place through a Holy Synod, composed of a small group of bishops who manage the life of the church. He also has authority over some Greek Orthodox churches in the Americas, Western Europe, Australia, and New Zealand. As part of its mission, this ecumenical patriarchate participated in the early beginnings of the ecumenical movement and continues to promote relationships with Oriental Orthodox churches and the other Christian traditions.

The area under the jurisdiction of the patriarch of Alexandria and All Africa includes Egypt and the rest of North Africa and counts with slightly more than 100,000 believers. Although most of the Orthodox in Africa reside in Egypt, there are also churches in Kenya, eastern Congo, Zimbabwe, and South Africa. Liturgy is done in Arabic, Greek, and other African languages, and its mission is focused on unity and renewal of the churches, education, health services, and orphanages (also servicing Muslim children).

The patriarch of Antioch, who actually resides in Damascus, has under his care the largest number of Orthodox believers in the area, amounting to approximately 1.6 million members, most of them in Syria, where they are the largest Christian group. As is customary in Orthodoxy, the liturgy and prayers of this patriarch are in the language of the people—in this case Arabic. After the First World War, an exodus began from Syria to the New World, and this resulted in large Syrian Orthodox communities in North America, Brazil, and Argentina. These are also under the jurisdiction of the patriarch of Antioch.

Finally, the patriarch of Jerusalem rules over Arab Orthodox Christians in the surrounding area, including Israel, Lebanon, Jordan, and the Emirates. One of his main functions is to head the Brotherhood of the Holy Sepulcher, which is in charge of the care of the holiest sites of Christianity. The Greeks have profoundly influenced this patriarchate, and therefore its liturgy and prayers take place both in Arabic and Greek.

In that portion of the Middle East that formerly belonged to the Persian Empire, there are very few Orthodox Christians. The reason for this is that long before the Muslim invasion, the Persian rulers persecuted Orthodox Christianity because they suspected it to be an instrument of the Roman Empire. Therefore, Monophysite and Nestorian Christians are more numerous in those areas.

2. The Oriental or Non-Chalcedonian Orthodox Churches (also Known as the Monophysite Churches)

There are three major Oriental Orthodox churches within the Arab-speaking context: the Coptic Orthodox Church, the Apostolic Church of Armenia, and the Syriac Orthodox (Jacobite) Church of Syria. Before the twentieth century, due to the political and social conditions surrounding them, these churches were out of contact among themselves and with the rest of the Christian world. However, they later came to share in ecumenical organizations and to develop a variety of missionary projects both in their own lands and elsewhere.

The common characteristic of all these churches is that they reject the authority of the Council of Chalcedon and of Pope Leo's *Tome.* Although they are usually called "Monophysite," their Christology does not seem to be the same as that for which Eutyches was condemned, and their disagreement with the Council of Chalcedon entails political, ecclesial, cultural, and linguistic factors that are profoundly deep on both sides. At any rate, these Oriental Orthodox churches have a significant presence in this region.

The Coptic Church claims to have its religious origins in St. Mark the evangelist, and its ethnic origins in the Egypt of the Pharaohs. Theologically, this church draws mostly from the ancient School of Alexandria. Many of the monastic movements in Egypt that we have discussed earlier are historically connected to it.

The head of the Coptic Church is its patriarch of Alexandria—whose title is *Pope*—who resides in Cairo, and who must not be confused with the Orthodox patriarch that bears the same title. Although his authority extends to Ethiopia, this is mostly nominal, for the church in the latter land, besides being larger than the one in Egypt, is practically autonomous. The Coptic Christians of Egypt are mostly descendants of the ancient Christian church that existed there before the Muslim invasions. Due to the laws that have already been mentioned, conversions to Christianity among Egyptian Muslims have always been rare. Also, during the twentieth century, the growth of nationalistic political movements joined to Islam led a significant number of Coptic Christians to work with Muslims, some abandoning their ancient faith in order to embrace Islam and others claiming an Egyptian "Muslim" national identity, and yet, they were still deeply Christian. In fact, many Coptic Christians continue to claim a political space for their Egyptian Christian identity, particularly through the Coptic Lay Council. It is roughly estimated that the Coptic Church membership ranges between 10 and 12 percent of the current Egyptian population, and the church keeps communion with the other Oriental Orthodox traditions. Although at the beginning and toward the middle of the twentieth century, the Coptic Church did not do much missionary work, later, particularly under the leadership of Pope Shenouda III, in the decade of the 1970s, it began developing a missionary spirit based on the reading and study of Scripture. Pope Shenouda III's missional leadership extended to the World Council of Churches and the Middle East Council of Churches. His missional renewal work involved the Coptic Church in several projects of support for youth, particularly in Egypt itself. Also, new dioceses and congregations emerged beyond the confines of Egypt, particularly in Europe, the United States, and Canada.

The Syriac Orthodox Church has a significant presence in Syria, Iraq, and southeast Turkey, and it has slightly more than 1 million in India. In another chapter of this book we have already seen that the Monophysites from Syria expanded eastward, particularly thanks to the work of Jacob Baradacus, in whose memory they are called Jacobites. With the Muslim invasion, this church, like the other Eastern churches, lost much of its missionary character and devoted itself to the maintenance of its own inner life. Its main hierarch is the patriarch of Antioch, who lives not there but rather in Damascus, and its main representative is the Maphrian—a title that was earlier given to the head of the Jacobites beyond the confines of the Roman Empire. Their liturgy and prayer life takes place in ancient Syriac, a language closely connected to Aramaic, the language of Jesus and the earliest disciples. Early in the twentieth-first century, this church, like many others in the area, was undergoing a process of revitalization, creating programs for youth and promoting ministry of vocations in its newly built seminary in Syria. It did this with the support of the Evangelical Lutheran Church of America. With its sister churches, this church also serves a population of immigrants in Canada, the United States, and Latin America.

The membership of the Church of Armenia is scattered throughout the Middle East as well as throughout the world, particularly in France and North America. This church has two centers, one in Etchmiadzin in Armenia and the other in Antelias, Beirut, Lebanon. Its leaders receive the titles of patriarch and catholicos. During the twentieth century, this church faced many difficulties. Between 1915 and 1923, hundreds of thousands of Armenians suffered persecution and genocide in Turkey, which has resulted in a vast dispersion of Armenian Christians in various parts of the world. For most of that century, Armenia itself was politically divided so that many Armenians lived under Soviet rule. In spite of all these difficulties, the Armenian church continues its work both in the areas of its birth and throughout the various parts of the world where its membership is now scattered. This church has also been one of the most active in the ecumenical movement in the Middle East. Catholicos Kerekin II served during the end of the twentieth century as one of the presidents of the World Council of Churches and of the Middle East Council of Churches. Catholicos Aram I with his Catholicosate in Antelias, Lebanon, is known for his passionate ministry and revitalization of the church in the areas of theological formation, justice, peace, church restructuring, youth work, human rights issues, and ecumenical relationships. Both give witness to a new meaning of Christian mission work beyond conversion and grounded in their context.

The Armenian church is particularly strong in Syria and Lebanon, as well as in Iran and Iraq. During the first Gulf War between the United States and Iraq, the Armenian bishopric of Iraq directed humanitarian support for the thousands of people affected. Even after the war, this bishopric continued serving Iraqi and foreign residents in returning to normal life. The same policy continued during the second war in Iraq, early in the twenty-first century.

3. The Nestorians

In earlier chapters, we have seen how the Nestorian community expanded and gained followers throughout the Near and Middle East, and even as far as China. Given those beginnings, it is sad to see that today there are only about 50,000 Nestorians in the entire world. This is a result of a long and tragic history of being subjected to hostile powers and repeated massacres. The last such massacre took place early in the twentieth century, and its result was that the number of Nestorians, which at that time was 100,000, was reduced to half that much. Forced to move from one place to another by political circumstances and often by the hatred of their Muslim neighbors, today the small Nestorian remnants are to be found mostly in Iraq, Syria, Iran, and other countries in the Near East. At the time of the massacres early in the twentieth century, a large number of Nestorians fled to North America, but their ecclesiastical life has been feeble. Although they are generally known by the pejorative name "Nestorians," the truth is that most of them are not interested in the theological subtleties that early in the fifth century led to the Nestorian controversy. As a result of that controversy, they refuse to give Mary the title of "Mother of God," but in point of fact Nestorians' Christology does not seem to differ much from that of the Orthodox churches. In order not to call them by the pejorative name of "Nestorians," some Anglicans working among them began calling them "Assyrians," and they are thus known throughout the Western world. They also call themselves "Syrians."

As could be expected given such difficult circumstances, this church has not been very active in missionary work. The difficulties in Iraq early in the twentieth century led Catholicos Mar Simon XXI to take refuge in Cyprus, and from there to move to the United States in 1941, hoping to organize the ecclesiastical life of Nestorians exiled in that country. By the middle of the twentieth century, he had attained a limited measure of success in Chicago, which from then on became one of the main centers of this very small church.

B. Catholic Missions

Before turning to the missionary work of the Roman Catholic Church in the area we are studying, it is important to take note of something that is often forgotten in the West: the presence in the Near and Middle East of various faith communities that are part of the Catholic Church in that they accept the authority of the pope, but still retain their ecclesiastical order as well as their rites and ministerial practices in matters such as liturgy and clerical celibacy. Such churches were usually referred to as "uniates"—and now preferably as united Oriental churches.

The most ancient of these communities is the Maronite Church in Lebanon. This is the largest church in that country and is politically quite influential. According to tradition, the founder of the church was St. Maron, a priest who followed monastic life in the mountains of Syria back in the fourth or fifth century. His followers developed a deep sense of Christian identity, and it is recorded that they participated in the Council of Chalcedon (451). The Maronite Patriarchate was established after the Islamic conquest in the region. For many years this church has suffered and struggled to keep its identity and spiritual vitality. We do know, however, that its relationships with the Roman Catholic Church began in the twelfth century. Like many other churches in the area, the Maronite Church also has communities scattered throughout the Middle East, as well as in Europe, North

America, Latin America, and Africa. Its missionary work in Lebanon itself has centered in serving as a mediator and promoting peace during the many years of war and seeking to contribute to the establishment of a new political order in a land constantly wracked by conflicts among various religious traditions. In relation to the church, the Maronites have contributed to the spirituality and mission work of the region through their monastic orders—for both men and women—hospital work, schools and higher education, and appropriating new forms of communication such as the internet, social media, and others.

In 451, Jerusalem became a patriarchate of the church. Later after many political and religious conflicts between the church in the West and the East, the crusaders entered the Holy City and established the Latin Patriarchate of Jerusalem. It has been repeatedly shaken by the continuing conflicts in that area. Its relationship with Rome goes back to the twelfth century, and it has served as a center for Catholic missions in the region. Its membership is over 100,000, its liturgy is traditionally celebrated in Latin, and it serves expatriates in various cities in the Middle East, particularly Cairo and Beirut, as well as others in North Africa. There are many Palestinians among its membership, and it has sought to work for peace and reconciliation in the conflict between Palestinians and Israelis. Among its most recent prominent leaders is Patriarch H. B. Michel Sabbah, who was appointed by Pope John Paul II as the first Arab Latin Patriarch of Jerusalem. Patriarch Sabbah has contributed to the unity and mission of the church in the area, including improving the relationships between Catholic and Orthodox churches in the region. This patriarchate witnesses to interreligious dialogue and provides social services to Muslims as well as to Christians. The current patriarch, Fouad Twal, continues to lead the church in mission work focusing on schools, the youth, interreligious dialogue, and social services.

Next we must take note of the Chaldean Catholic Church, founded in the sixteenth century. Counting approximately a quarter of a million followers, this church is particularly strong in Iraq, where it is one of the largest churches. Like other churches in the area, its membership is scattered in other places, particularly in Canada and the United States. The Greek Catholic Church is the third oldest united Oriental church. It was begun in the eighteenth century by large contingents leaving the Greek Orthodox Church and joining the Roman communion. It is present mostly in Lebanon, Syria, and Palestine. Three other small Oriental churches under the authority of the pope are the Catholic Syriac Patriarchate of Antioch, the Coptic Catholic Patriarchate of Alexandria, and most recently, the Catholic Armenian Patriarchate. All of these churches have been part of the broader missionary work of the Roman Catholic Church.

However, most Catholic growth in the Middle East is the result of immigration of Catholics from Europe and the Christians' conversion to Roman Catholicism from other Oriental churches. The immigration of Catholic Europeans is not part of a conscious program for the expansion of Catholic Christianity but is simply the result of political and economic circumstances. It is one more aspect of the great expansion of the European peoples during the nineteenth and twentieth centuries. Since the nations of the Western Mediterranean are mostly Catholic, the vast majority of those who migrated to the region, and particularly to North Africa, were Catholics. This was somewhat counterbalanced by the growing power of Great Britain and the United States, both mostly Protestant. But at any rate, the period that we are now studying saw the establishment of strong French and Italian communities in North and northeast Africa. Priests and other ecclesiastical functionaries went to those lands in order to minister to the immigrant communities. Acknowledging this expansion throughout the Mediterranean, in 1884, the papacy reinstituted the ancient bishopric of Carthage, which had been occupied by some of the most illustrious Christians in antiquity.

The growth of the Catholic population in the Near East awakened among their fellow believers in Europe a new interest in the Arab-speaking countries. This resulted in the establishment in 1862, by Pope Pius IX, of the Congregatio pro Negotiis Ritus Orientalis, which was in charge of all the relations of the Church of Rome with the ancient Eastern churches, and whose main purpose was to bring the churches mentioned above under the authority of the pope. Thus, most Roman Catholic mission work in the Middle East was not so much seeking the conversion of non-Christians as bringing other Christians to obedience to Rome, forming "uniate" churches that kept their traditional rites and practices. In some cases such Christians were brought into the churches of the Latin rite that had been established in their lands, but in most cases new ecclesiastical bodies were founded that followed the ancient Eastern traditions but that at the same time accepted the authority of the pope. As we have seen, each of these bodies had its own patriarch and liturgy. It is evident that the effort on the part of Catholic missions to bring about unity through obedience to the pope has had a measure of success, and this very fact is constantly affecting ecumenical dialogue.

Among Muslims, Catholic conversions have not been very successful. Their mission work has consisted mostly in founding homes for orphans as well as schools, but the opposition of society at large, and quite often of governments, has made it difficult for them to offer religious teaching in those schools. The most remarkable effort was the founding of the White Fathers under the inspiration of Charles M. A. Lavigerie, bishop of Argel. The main purpose of this organization was the conversion of Muslims; but as a further indication of how difficult this work is, the greatest achievements of the White Fathers took place in equatorial Africa, and not among Muslims. Another important work of the Catholic Church was the founding of the University of St. Joseph in Beirut.

During the last decades of the twentieth century and early in the twenty-first, the Catholic Church was active in promoting interreligious dialogue, which had become of particular significance after the Second Vatican Council. Led mostly by priests from the area itself, this has resulted in significant dialogue and collaboration on issues such as the theology of religions, matters of peace and justice, refugee work, the reconstruction of communities destroyed by conflict, the search for common spirituality, and in general the protection of human life and the environment. One commonly known example of Roman Catholic missionary work during this period is the story of nine Trappist monks in Algeria who were kidnapped and assassinated during the civil war. The novel *Des hommes et des dieux* was turned into a movie by the same name illustrating the missional work of these men living in and serving a poor Muslim community. The Catholic Church in the region has also entered into dialogue with other Christian bodies seeking to heal the wounds left by ancient debates and conflicts. It participates actively in the work of the Middle East Council of Churches, particularly in justice issues and work with refugees.

C. Protestant Missions

The two main forerunners of Protestant missions in the Middle East and in Muslim majority countries were Henry Martyn (1781–1812) and Karl Gottlieb Pfander (1803–1865). Martyn's work as a missionary began in India, and four years later, he moved to the Middle East. There, with the help of national translators, he translated the Bible and held many theological debates with Muslim sages. His life of total dedication is best summarized in the words that he wrote in his diary upon beginning his missionary work: "Now let me burn out for God." This petition was answered, and he died in Armenia in 1812 as a result of his relentless missionary work. He is also well remembered for his ecumenical spirit, though often his peers were concerned for his polemical spirit with Muslims.

Pfander was sent to Central Asia by the Basel Mission in 1825. His ease in learning languages was astounding, and soon he knew

Arabic, Persian, Turkish, and Armenian. His work consisted mostly in penetrating the secrets of the Koran and then debating with the most cultured among the Muslims. Joining merchants' caravans, he traveled from one place to another. In 1937, when the authorities made it impossible for him to continue his work, Pfander moved to what was then North India—now Pakistan—in order to continue working among the Muslims there, now under the auspices of the Church Missionary Society. There is no doubt that sometimes his methods were offensive, for his crushing arguments against Islam seemed disrespectful to Muslims. But in spite of this, his life and dedication to the evangelization of the Muslim world contributed to awakening an interest in that work among Christians in England—and his descendants continued the work he had begun.

The first Protestant missions into the Arab-speaking Muslim regions—besides those undertaken in the East Indies, which were discussed in a previous chapter—were Anglican. The main purpose of these missions was not so much the conversion of Muslims as the introduction of new perspectives and activities within the ancient Eastern churches, so that they would in turn be called to renewed mission. This was extremely difficult work, and in spite of its good intentions, it tended to create tensions within the ancient Eastern churches that could only lead to schism. The center of this sort of missionary work was in Malta. Here literature was produced and sent to Arab-speaking regions and other Muslim majority countries. In 1840, the Church of England tacitly acknowledged that its work among the Eastern churches had not had the expected results when it established a bishopric in Jerusalem. In an effort not to alienate further those ancient churches, the Church of England made it clear that this was a bishop "in" and not "of" Jerusalem. Furthermore, the work of this bishop was directed mostly to the conversion of Muslims and Jews, and not of other Christians. Remarkably, the first occupant of this see was a converted Jew. In spite of these precautions, Anglo-Catholics severely criticized the founding of that bishopric, while the more evangelical-minded Anglicans affirmed that it was necessary. Later the bishop in Jerusalem was raised to the rank of an archbishop.

Besides Anglicanism, the Protestant church that has worked among Middle Eastern Muslims most extensively and with the greatest results is the Presbyterian Church, but extensive work was also done by Congregationalists and Lutherans. Their work began in Egypt in the mid-nineteenth century. Although the purpose was to renew the Coptic Church, the result was a schism within that communion and the ensuing birth of a Protestant church. This brought about difficulties and resentment on the part of the Coptic Church, so that collaboration between the two churches became difficult.

The American Samuel Zwemer (1867–1952) is known as the Apostle to Islam. He made his home in Arabia and Egypt and, in addition to his work as an evangelist, helped Christians understand the Islamic faith. Since he did not find a missionary agency to sponsor him, he and his friend James Cantime founded the American Arabian Mission. Later, the Reformed Church agreed to sponsor his work among Muslims. Zwemer was the founder and editor of the important journal *The Moslem World*, and in 1929, he was appointed Professor of History of Religions and Mission at Princeton Theological Seminary.

In Egypt, the Presbyterian Church founded many hospitals and schools and focused on the development of an Egyptian pastoral leadership. Although the majority of its members came from the Coptic Church, some were converts from Islam. Later, as Islamic governments began taking responsibility for health and education within their lands, this brought a crisis to educational and medical work, which the Presbyterian Church could not underwrite at the level to which the government subsidized its own institutions.

Presbyterian work has also been strong in Syria and Lebanon, resulting in the foundation of the National Evangelical Synod of the

Province of Syria and Lebanon. There is also important Presbyterian work in Pakistan.

Several other Protestant denominations have missionary work in the regions, although not quite as extensive as the Anglicans and Presbyterians. As in many other mission fields, there were also in the Arabic-speaking countries various groups that were not directly related to any particular church. One of these is the North Africa Mission, which is similar to the China Inland Mission discussed in a previous chapter, and whose work centers in Morocco. There are also many Pentecostal groups that seem to be growing, although it is difficult to determine to what extent that growth is the result of conversions of Muslims to Christianity or of the attraction that these groups have for other Christians.

Other important sources of missionary work among Muslims were the Bible societies, at first particularly the British Society, although in the twentieth century its work was taken over by the American Bible Society and eventually by the United Bible Societies. It is an understatement to emphasize the importance of printed materials for schools, universities, and churches and the way these materials contributed to the life of Protestant churches and other churches in the region.

In the twentieth century a powerful radio station was established in Ethiopia with the purpose of providing Christian broadcasting addressing the Arab-speaking countries and other Muslim majority countries in Asia while at the same time remaining free from the restrictions imposed by various Muslim governments and societies. Ironically, at a time when the government in Spain did not allow Protestant radio programming, Morocco became a base from which Protestants transmitted such programs into Spain.

During the last decades of the twentieth century and the beginning of the twenty-first, partly as a result of the war between the United States and Iraq and the ensuing occupation of the latter, Pentecostal and faith missions in the Near East have created a difficult and complex situation. On the one hand, many evangelical missionary agencies come to the area on the basis of an eschatological expectation that interprets the conflict between Palestinians and Israelis as the forerunner of the second coming of Christ. Therefore, many of these agencies have supported the foreign policy of the United States, leaning toward Israel. Furthermore, some of these groups completely ignore or ferociously attack the ancient churches of the area, claiming that they are not really Christian. Although early in the twenty-first century, some communication was established across these lines, long-standing conflicts remained between these evangelical groups and the ancient Eastern churches.

On the other hand, and as indicated earlier in the chapter, in 1986, a group of evangelicals taking the name of Evangelicals for Middle East Understanding began seeking more justice and openness both in their relations with the ancient churches of the Near East and in the policies of the United States and other Western powers. World Vision has also developed missionary work among the poor in the area, and much of this work shows greater intercultural and interreligious openness than do the various faith missions. World Vision has also published studies that seek to inform Western Christians regarding the ideological and political difficulties and complexities of the area and also to encourage them to seek peace.

After the events of September 11, 2001, and as a result of wars in Afghanistan and Iraq, missionary work in the entire area became more difficult. Ecumenical agencies and various missionary groups—national as well as international—moved in quite disparate directions: some are seeking to help refugees, work on social reconstruction, and promote justice, peace, and reconciliation, while others are eagerly seeking the conversion of Muslims, and still others are no more than reflections of the foreign policy of the United States. This latter attitude sometimes took the form of calls to martyrdom in defense of "democratic struggles" and Western interests.

Two other important figures in missionary work within the Arab-speaking and Muslim majority countries must be noted: one a foreigner and, another, a native of the area. The first is Anglican bishop Kenneth Cragg, whose work began in Lebanon under the auspices of the British Syria Mission. He also taught at the American University at Beirut and later became Professor of Islamic Studies at Hartford Seminary, where he was editor of the journal *The Moslem World*. He returned to the Middle East in the 1950s and continued to work on the theme of Christian-Muslim dialogue. To date, Cragg's *The Call of the Minaret* is one of the most important contributions to Muslim-Christian dialogue in the region. Cragg's work contributed to the development of the ecumenical movement among Protestants and with the ancient churches of the area. He also was a key person in helping the West understand the faith of Islam and the actual reality of Christianity in the Middle East. The second is Lutheran Palestinian minister Mitri Raheb, director of the Bethlehem International Center and of the Dar al-Kalima Academy of Health. Raheb has made a significant effect in helping the Christian world understand the struggles of Christians in the area—particularly Palestinian Christians. Likewise, the current bishop of the Evangelical Lutheran Church in Jordan and the Holy Land, Rev. Munib Youman, leads the church in mission as interreligious dialogue, education, social services, and a missiology shaped by justice and peace.

In the Arab gulf, the Arabian Mission, a mission group established by the Reformed Church in America, contributed to the formation of congregations, which served not only the Arabic-speaking community, but also the immigrant community from different regions in Asia who came to the region to work in the booming oil business. Also, this mission group helped more conservative evangelical groups, such as the Evangelical and Alliance Mission, to create interdenominational relationships with other Christians in the region, including Anglicans, Catholics, and Orthodox.

In Dubai, the Anglican Holy Trinity Church is an interesting model of Christian missions and witness. Offering hospitality to a great number of nationals and internationals, Holy Trinity Church is an ecumenical chaplaincy. With multiple hospitality and educational programs, it serves the needs of a growing community of professionals and very diverse people with the celebration of the sacraments, Bible studies, and preaching.

The most recent statistics indicate that the Middle East is still the area of the world with the least number of Christian missionaries. Although hard data is difficult to come by, there is no doubt that a large number of well-intentioned Christians from the Third World are moving to that area in order to do mission work among Muslims. Regretfully, with little or no training in mission work or understanding of the context of Arab-speaking and Muslim majority countries and Islam, many of these missionaries end up working among people who are already Christians; or, in the worst of cases, they are imprisoned or killed.

A word must be said about Protestant missionary work among the many Jews in the Near East. Most of this work was carried on by the London Society for Promoting Christianity amongst the Jews, founded in 1809 in order to seek the conversions of Jews in Abyssinia, but the society extended its work also to Morocco, Tunisia, Algeria, Arabia, and other Muslim lands. The Church of Scotland also established a mission among Jews in Alexandria, and the American Board of Commissioners for Foreign Missions reached out to Jews as well as to other faith groups in Turkey and elsewhere. Among Protestant missionaries to Jews, Joseph Wolff and Henry Aaron Stern—both of Jewish origin—deserve special mention.

More recently, mission work among Jews in this area reflects a wide variety of tendencies and goals. Some seek the conversion of Jews to historic Christianity, others seek their conversion to a messianic sort of Christianity, and still others promote interreligious dialogue, particularly in relation to the conflict between Palestinians and Israelis.

Finally, some Christian missiologists working in this region are proposing a theology and strategy of "Christian missions to folk Muslims." They distinguish between "formal Islam," which is more a comprehensive code of rituals and laws, and a "folk Islam," shaped by traditional tribal religions with beliefs in spirits, healing, and curses. Consequently, they argue, mission theology and strategy needs to address the worldview of the folk, rather than the codes of Islam. Without dismissing interreligious dialogue and debate between Muslims and Christians, this approach needs to include an appreciation for a traditional worldview. Notwithstanding the missionary concern, missions to Muslims who practice "folk Islam" face the challenges of three different levels of religious exchange and encounter: Islam and traditional religions, Christianity and traditional religions, and Islam and Christianity.

D. General Considerations

In summary, all the churches in this area carry forth their mission in a context of profound conflicts with Islam, with Islamic states, and even with other Christians who do not know or understand the history of the area. Christians in the Middle East not only struggle in their own land with questions of identity and mission but also suffer the indifference of many Christians both in the West and in the Far East who lack a spirit of solidarity with them. The negative effect of some extremist groups also sharpens conflicts and reinforces prejudices of Muslims against Christians, while ignoring the need to protect the rights, life, and hopes of the people in the area.

Nevertheless, Christians, both nationals and foreigners, who know the context and are well aware of the difficult situations involved provide an admirable witness to the gospel in the land where Jesus walked. Christian communities engage in missions and witness at the level of personal relationships and as the body of Christ gathered in ecumenical organizations. The Christian faith, though often accosted, continues to carry a message of hope and reconciliation. Thus, mission and witness in Arab-speaking and Muslim majority countries are also a mission and witness to us, who have much to learn from the persistent and costly witness of our sisters and brothers in the area.

Chapter 9

MISSIONS IN SUB-SAHARAN AFRICA

A. The Orthodox Tawahedo Church of Ethiopia

Before we turn to Protestant and then to Catholic missions in sub-Saharan Africa, it is important to remember the existence of a large Monophysite Church in Ethiopia. As we saw earlier, the origins of that church go back to the fourth century. Although some have thought that the conversion in Ethiopia was rather superficial, the fact remains that this church, completely severed from the rest of Christendom by Muslim invasions, was able to survive throughout the Middle Ages and to the present.

This church faced serious difficulties at the beginning of the nineteenth century. Its membership was declining. The immigration of Muslims from nearby countries presented new challenges, particularly in southern Ethiopia, where traditionally this church had been strongest. There was a lack of able leadership and of priests who could lead the church through the changes that were coming about.

However, toward the middle of the nineteenth century, there were significant improvements. One of them was the naming of an Ethiopian rather than an Egyptian "abuna"—head of the church. During the first half of the twentieth century, the Ethiopian church, under the leadership of Menelik II, played an important role in the struggle of Ethiopia to preserve its political freedom in the face of Italian invasion. This made it possible for Ethiopia to remain an independent nation even while various Western powers were occupying the rest of the continent. Thus, a theology and a parallel ideology were formed, affirming African Christian identity over against the imposition of a foreign European Christianity.

Early in the twentieth century Tarafi Makonen, also known as Halie Salassie (1892–1975), an Ethiopian Orthodox Christian, became emperor of Ethiopia. His rule lasted from 1930 to 1974, and under his leadership, Ethiopia received international attention. His nationalism supported a policy of resistance against the colonial powers in Ethiopia and influenced movements in other regions of Africa. However, some of his critics argue that his policies did not contribute to the modernization of the country. For the Rasta religion in Jamaica, Salassie is the messiah whose return will bring justice to the African people. His figure was crucial in the Pan-African movements that emerged in the Western Hemisphere in the early twentieth century.

During the last decades of the twentieth century, the Ethiopian church still faced serious inner struggles, besides having to face an important challenge with the development of a communist-leaning government in the decade of the seventies. It currently has more than 35 million believers, so that it is the second largest of all the Eastern churches. It is a member of the World Council of Churches and participates actively in ecumenical dialogue as well as in justice issues.

In terms of the history of missions, the Ethiopian church did not follow the traditional practice of sending many missionaries abroad;

although in more recent times, due to the migration of many Ethiopians to the west, that church has established roots in the United States, Europe, and Canada.

B. Protestant Missions in Sub-Saharan Africa

Early in the nineteenth century, the interior of Africa was mostly unknown to Western nations. Apart from the Muslim strip along the Mediterranean coast and the colonies that some Western powers had established along the coastline, Africa remained, as it was dubbed by the West, the "Dark Continent." Even the Portuguese colonies that were mentioned in an earlier chapter were almost abandoned, and there was practically no missionary work from their church. Although Portugal claimed the right to colonize the interior of Africa, it had never even begun to explore those lands. Even so, Africa would not be left outside the scope of the great missionary thrust of the nineteenth century. Campaigns in Great Britain against the slave trade, the colonizing interests of the great sea powers, the interest that churned among Westerners at that time to explore and to discover new lands, and above all the worldwide missionary thrust would not stop at the known edges of the African continent. If one leaves aside the small Catholic groups in Angola and Mozambique—which were almost completely abandoned by the church and lacking in priests—it was Protestants who first began the expansion of their faith into Africa. In the creation of Liberia and Sierra Leone, the movement seeking to repatriate freed slaves to the African continent was also imbued with the hope that they would become a beachhead for the expansion of Christianity. Religious goals were not dominant in the Dutch and British colonization in southern Africa, but there were soon societies that saw that colonization as an opportunity to enter into the Dark Continent. Throughout the nineteenth century, it was missionaries such as Robert Moffat and David Livingstone—and people inspired by them, such as Henry M. Stanley—who opened the way to Western trade and civilization, at the same time that they sought to stop the violence and cruelty connected with the slave trade. Later, in the twentieth century, there were also missionaries who worked on the physical and spiritual development of Africa. Foremost among them was Albert Schweitzer (1875–1965), whose name must be recorded, not because he was unique, but rather because he was a symbol of a vast movement repeated throughout the continent.

One should also note that in their work in Africa, many missionary societies made an effort to develop national leaders as soon as possible and to place the responsibility for mission in their hands. This led to the creation of hundreds of national missionary leaders. However, this story, too, is full of tension and struggles between foreign missionaries and national leaders. These struggles, hardly studied until recently, once again point to the complexity of the missionary movement.

1. The Foundation of Liberia and Sierra Leone and Missions in Western and West Central Equatorial Africa

It was in England, and mostly through the influence of the Christian faith, that the antislavery movement first gained momentum in Europe. As a consequence of that movement, Parliament approved laws and the nation followed policies that eventually forced other European powers to abolish the slave traffic. This was parallel to a movement to return to Africa those who had been forcefully uprooted from it. This effort, eventually expressed in the "Doctrine of Providential Design," began in 1787, when the British took to Sierra Leone the first contingent of freed slaves. Later, with the support of the American Colonization Society, other black settlers arrived from North America, where Britain's antislavery movement was having an effect. Due to Sierra Leone's close connection to Great Britain, it is not surprising that missionaries began arriving very early. This was at first the work of the Church Missionary Society, an Anglican agency whose first mission field was precisely Sierra Leone. The result of this venture was the Sierra Leone Pastorate Church, an independent church within the Anglican communion. The Methodists also had great success in Sierra Leone. Later, other Protestants arrived, as well as the Catholic Church, but they never had the effect of the pastorate church or of Methodism.

The work of the Church Missionary Society in Sierra Leone illustrates a frequent dilemma in the history of the missionary movement. By 1840, the society was facing a scarcity of missionaries as compared with the exponential growth of churches thanks to national leadership. This led to a double problem: the lack of financial resources, on the one hand, and the need to train and accredit national leadership, on the other. Missionary policies resulting from these conditions eventually led to what later became known as the Three-Self Movement Church—self-propagating, self-sustaining, and self-governing. Thus, the Church Missionary Society clearly affirmed that for its mission to be successful, it must be placed in African hands as soon as possible, and that from the beginning Africans themselves would have to be the protagonists of mission in their own land.

However, from 1880, European countries shifted their interest in Africa from trading to colonization. Consequently, European missionaries grew in numbers and tensions developed between those missionaries and the national leadership. Africans' leadership began to be questioned and they felt that their authority had been removed. One example of the growing tensions is the story of African missionary and bishop Samuel Ajayi Crowther (1807–91).

Crowther, ordained in 1843 in England and later consecrated the first African bishop of the Anglican Church in 1864, worked on translations of the Book of Common Prayer and the Scriptures. He received an honorary degree from University of Oxford for his accomplishments in translations and knowledge of African languages, particularly Yoruban. His responsibilities as bishop included all of West Africa. Yet, the Church Missionary Society missionaries accused him of incompetency and lack of orderly administration and constantly interfered in his pastoral and missionary work. They strongly suggested that Africans were not good enough to do the missionary and pastoral work needed.

Eventually Crowther, who was heading the Niger Mission, was removed from his office, and a European was appointed bishop. The irony was that Crowther was deeply appreciated by the nationals, but the missionaries did not like him, putting him in difficult positions. Some European scholars saw in the removal of Crowther a wise decision by the society. More recent studies, including African scholarship, point to a conspiracy: Crowther was set up to resign. Crowther's work was followed by Tomas Maxwell and George Nicol, both sons of freed slaves, who continued the struggle for equality with European missionaries.

The origin of Liberia was similar to that of Sierra Leone, although slightly later. Liberia was one of the results of the strong antislavery movement that swept through the United States during the first half of the nineteenth century, culminating in the emancipation of slaves and in the Civil War. In 1822, before slavery was abolished and as had been done earlier in Sierra Leone, the American Colonization Society took the first contingent of freed slaves to Liberia. This effort was inspired by Christians who thought that freed slaves should be given the opportunity to return to their native continent. Other settlers followed, thus creating the nucleus of a new nation. In 1847, the United States granted Liberia its independence after twenty-five years of dependency. Since many of the former slaves who settled in Liberia were Baptists, most of the immigrants in the new nation belonged to that tradition. Partly due to that connection, the various Baptist missionary societies in the United States began sending missionaries from a very early date. These missionaries included both blacks and whites.

Liberia also witnessed a clash among African American missionaries and settlers and African nationals. Some of the settlers from the United

States, already third- and fourth-generation African Americans, did not speak any of the African languages and tried to recreate the social and religious structures of black Christianity in the American South. There was deep mistrust between the new settlers and the nationals.

This cross-cultural situation hindered missionary work. History records that Lott Carey, a black Baptist pastor from Virginia, died when ammunition he was planning to use against local Africans exploded. There are historical records of African American missionaries who considered Africans "savages" and "backward."

Also, the Episcopal Church and the various Methodist churches in the United States had followers among the Liberian colonizers. Most notable was the work of the African Methodist Episcopal Church in the United States, which took place not only in Liberia but also in Sierra Leone and other coastal areas of western Africa. The African Methodist Episcopal Church Zion sent Andrew Cartwright as a missionary to Liberia. The AME and AMEZ also supported the education of African students in the United States. Various European and North American missionary societies also sent people from the Caribbean as missionaries to Africa.

The Liberian experiment awakened missionary interest in the United States. Thus, the first missionaries that the Methodist Episcopal Church and the Presbyterian Western Foreign Missionary Society sent to Africa went to Liberia. Yet the missionary work done by Euro-Americans had little success. Evidently, the most successful missionary work was born and developed as the result of the effort of African leaders.

One must not forget that when the freed slaves settled in western Africa, the area was already inhabited. Pushed by the presence of the colonizers, the original inhabitants of the region moved to the interior. From an early date efforts were made to reach them. The British and North American missionary societies as well as Africans—such as William Wade Harris (1865–1929), a "born Methodist" and a forerunner for churches initiated by Africans, and Garrick Sokari Braide (1880–1918), who would become one of the first Nigerian prophets and who embodied the Africanization of the Anglican tradition—worked assiduously at this task.

The result was that by the end of the twentieth century, Liberia was one of the nations in Africa with the highest proportion of Christians among its population, and it served as a center for sending missionaries—Europeans as well as Africans—to other African lands. Among the African missionaries who took Protestantism to equatorial lands was Simon Kimbangu (1887–1951), who would later found the Kimbanguist movement, which led to the Church of Jesus Christ on Earth—Kimbanguist Church of Zaire (later the Democratic Republic of Congo). Others are Lewis Bandawe, David Kaunda, and Harry Matecheta in Malawi and Apolo Kivebulaya and Victor Mukasa in Uganda.

The missionary enterprise set roots in Nigeria between 1838 and 1842. Thomas Birch Freeman (1809–90), a British Methodist of mixed blood—African and English—and William de Graft, a Fante national Christian, established a church in the region. Freeman and de Graft built strong relationships with Ashanti kings and other important chiefs. Freeman continued to visit the town of Kumasi and kept building relationships among the chiefs. Jointly with de Graft, he was able to establish missionary work in Yorubaland. Nevertheless, the work was fragile due to missionary mortality. Tensions between the Dahomey people and the colonial powers also hindered the missionary enterprise. After years of service, Freeman was dismissed as a missionary, though he later returned to ministry and continued his preaching and charismatic ministry in the region.

The Niger Mission of 1841 was similar to Livingstone's mission to the Zambezi River. The Church Missionary Society sent missionaries with the expectation of opening the interior of Africa to Christianity and commerce. Crowther, whom we have already met, headed the Niger Mission beginning in 1857, and it was there that his clashes with foreign missionaries led to his deposition. Opposition to him came mostly from young European missionaries who considered the churches that he had founded too worldly and superstitious and in desperate need of holiness. The entire mission was collapsing.

The Sixteen Years' War—in which the main contenders were the Ibadan Empire and the colonial powers in the region seeking to end slavery, supported by those tribes that had been subjected by the Ibadan—ended in 1886. During the war, many slaves became Christian, so that when they returned to their homelands, they became missionaries. Records show that Babamuboni and Shadrach Mogun from the Ekiti preached and established local Christian communities. Samuel Laseinde is another example of a freed slave doing missionary work, though his Christian community did not last.

Ghana is another country hosting a significant number of missionaries from Europe and the United States. Jacobus Elisha Capitein (1717–47), who had been captured as a slave and taken to the Netherlands, became the first African ordained by the Netherlands Reformed Church and was appointed to Elmina in the Gold Coast. Capitein studied theology at the University of Leiden, where his dissertation defended slavery, claiming that it was compatible with Christian freedom. Although his missionary work began with success, he later faced problems with the community. In Africa, Capitein had problems with both Africans and Europeans: the former did not accept him, and the latter would not accept him as their pastor. The support promised by the Netherlands Reformed Church never came.

The Basel Evangelical Missionary Society sent missionaries whose work resulted in the Presbyterian Church of the Gold Coast. The work of the Basel Evangelical Missionary Society gave birth to the Evangelical Presbyterian Church. This church in turn divided into the

Evangelical Presbyterian Church of Ghana and the Evangelical Presbyterian Church, Ghana.

Later in the twentieth century, Pentecostalism entered the area. Some Pentecostals came from Great Britain, such as from the Apostolic Church of the Faith, and others came from the United States, such as from the Church of Pentecost, founded by North American missionary James McKeown. These churches are now a permanent fixture within Christianity in Ghana.

Not all missionaries and evangelists were associated with missionary societies, nor were they all men. For instance, Anna Peters, who worked as a trader in Ondo from 1880 until her death in 1892, led a group of women in preaching campaigns throughout the area. Bribrina was an Afro-European woman who had been expelled from her village for having twins and then marrying an Isoko merchant and was a pioneer in mission among the Isoko population.

The Universities' Mission to Central Africa, an organization created on Livingstone's recommendation for missionary work in central Africa, particularly in Buganda (today in Uganda), was founded in 1857. With the financial support of Robert Arthington—perhaps the most important missionary philanthropist of the nineteenth century—Dallington "Scorpion" Maftaa, considered the apostle to the Ganda, established missionary work in the region. Since Christianity offered technological advances, it lured Ganda rulers, and many among the Ganda embraced the Christian religion. But when European powers became a threat to national leaders, European powers opted for Muslim alliances, and persecution and martyrdom befell many Christians. This history is the background for the current religious conflicts in the region.

The early twentieth century marked the growth of African leadership in the region. A network of African Christians that spread throughout western Africa challenged the legacy of Western missionary work and its domination. Among this cadre of leaders is J. E. Casely Hayford, a Methodist layman whose literature challenged the West in his book *Ethiopia Unbound* (1911). E. M. Lijadu funded a self-supporting group that evangelized Africans through trade. His most important contribution, however, was his theological proposal: Jesus Christ was already present in Yoruban religion.

These national and missional leaders integrated evangelization, mission work, human rights, and the quest for a true African identity. Those working within European denominations struggled against attempts of exclusion and removal of ministry. Some left and organized new Christian communities. Others became prophets.

A notable characteristic of the churches resulting from these various sources is the richness of the liturgy and music created by the diversity of churches, Protestant, Catholic, and Pentecostal. Churches in this region have also developed educational institutions, including universities and centers of education, which have attracted the attention of the politicians. In the midst of many difficulties, these churches continue to struggle with issues of church and state and to claim a space in the political future of the region.

2. Missions in East and East Central Africa

The background for missions in East Africa before the twentieth century includes the encounter and tensions with Islam, the effects of the slave trade, droughts in the region, and limited knowledge of African languages. Fairly recent scholarly work shows that many accounts of this history are dependent on European sources, and it also notes that nationals concealed information from European missionaries. African historian Elizabeth Isichei points out that the Paris Missionary Society confused languages among the tribal groups. For instance, they thought that seSotho was the language of the Ila, whose language actually was ciLa. Therefore, translations were inadequate, to say the least.

In contrast with the regions discussed above, many of the first converts in this area were deeply frustrated with traditional religions and sought in Christianity an alternative. They were people traditionally marginalized in their communities, and their conversion to Christianity further confirmed their exclusion. In the few places where leaders embraced the Christian religion, they were unable to make Christianity an appealing religious alternative.

The famous Christian villages created in the region also hindered missionary work. Former slaves, witches, and other "undesirables" lived with missionaries in these villages. By their very existence, such villages implied that Christianity could not survive in an African environment. Furthermore, some of them became places of abuse and exploitation. In 1879, one of those villages became an international scandal. Originally sponsored by the Church of Scotland in 1875, the missionaries exploited the Africans and even performed executions. Ironically, during the colonial period, these villages progressively disappeared.

The beginning of the missionary enterprise in East Africa dates back to 1873, when the Church Missionary Society recruited students at the Basel Mission Seminary (Switzerland) to be sent to the region—particularly to Kenya. Johann Ludwig Krapf (1810–81), who was originally sent to work in Ethiopia but was expelled from that land, moved to Mombasa in 1844. He proposed creating a series of missionary stations that would appeal to the nationals because they did not sponsor slavery, thus developing a chain of stations that would stretch across Africa. However, the hostility of the landscape, the tensions with Africans, and the lack of appropriate missionaries frustrated his vision.

Johannes Rebmann (1820–76), a German Lutheran trained in Basel Mission Seminary who became Krapf's colleague and a linguist, was one of the missionaries to draw the first map of Mount Kilimanjaro and its landscape. By identifying an inland sea between Mount Kilimanjaro and Mount Kenya, Rebmann's maps generated new interest in exploration, commerce, and missions. Through his maps, new routes were established to the kingdom of Buganda, where the first successful missionary work in East Africa took place. Rebmann's missionary legacy is not limited to cartography. He compiled many vocabularies and translated the Gospels of Luke and John to Swahili. Furthermore, the work of Krapf and Rebmann provided the conditions for Livingstone's later expeditions.

Robert Laws (1851–1934), a Scottish Presbyterian leader considered the "Bishop of Central Africa," traveled on Lake Malawi on the first mission steamer in 1875. He worked as a missionary leader and a medical doctor for the Livingstonia Mission in Malawi—a name recognizing the legacy of Livingstone, whose work is discussed below. Out of this mission, the people of northern Malawi and northeastern Zambia were reached. Laws's work included the establishment of schools, and Christian leaders from Livingstonia would extend their work as far as South Africa and what was then, the Rhodesias today Malawi and Zimbabwe.

In 1894, Laws also established the Overtoun Institution. Although its curriculum was essentially British, the institution trained civil servants for the emerging urban areas. Schools under the institution were linked to evangelists and pastors, most of them nationals, who had a significant effect in their communities. However, the growing number of European missionaries began to displace the national workers. African missionaries suffered from progressive discrimination and isolation for the benefit of European and some American missionaries. An example of this situation is found in the person of Charles Domingo. After years of waiting for ordination, he left the mission. Domingo was highly educated. His devastating critique to European presence in Africa is worth citing:

> There is too much failure among all Europeans in Nyassaland (today Malawi). The Three Combined Bodies: Missionaries, Government,

> and Companies or Gainers of money do form the same rule to look on a Native with mockery eyes. It sometimes startle us to see that the Three Combined Bodies are from Europe, and along with them is a title "CHRISTNDOM." And to compare or make comparison between the MASTER of the title and His Servants it pushes any African away from believing the Master of the title. If we had power enough to communicate ourselves to Europe, we would have advised them not to call themselves "CHRISTNDOM" but "Europeandom." We see that the title "CHRISTNDOM" does not belong to Europe but to future BRIDE. Therefore the life of the Three Combined Bodies is altogether too cheaty, too thefty, too mockery.[1]

Despite these conditions, African nationals continued to do missionary work. William Mtusane Koyi (1846–86), a Xhosa evangelist, worked with the Livinsgtonia Mission in Malawi. His missionary work extended to people in South Africa, particularly the Ngoni. His close relationship with the Ngoni paved the way for other missionaries and a grounding of Christianity among this tribal group. Koyi is one of the most important figures in the evangelization of northern Malawi.

Frustrated by the Livingstonian missionaries, Elliot Kenan Kamwana (1870–1956), an African independent preacher and founder of the Wacitawala churches in Central Africa, was inspired by revival movements of the late 1800s and early 1900s and established missionary work in Malawi and South Africa. Under his leadership, the Wacitawala became an independent and widely extended African church.

Missionary work in equatorial Africa met little success until the middle of the twentieth century. For instance, in Buganda and Madagascar (a land to be discussed later), Christians were a very small minority in 1900. By 1938, they were 8 percent of the population in Kenya, 10 percent in Tanganyika, and 25 percent in Uganda. During the second half of the twentieth century, Christian growth was exponential to the point that by the beginning of the twenty-first century, 60 percent of the population in Uganda and Kenya are Christians, as is a third of the population in Tanzania.

A new phenomenon in the twentieth century shows the degree to which missionary work in Africa is in African hands. Later on we shall discuss the birth of indigenous African churches in South Africa that resulted from Pentecostal work beginning in the twentieth century. Revivals in East Central and Central Africa in the early years of the century gave birth to indigenous African churches that began sending large groups of missionaries throughout the area, although calling them "prophets" rather than "missionaries." In Kenya, one of the revivals emerged in the Quaker work in Kaimosi. Early in the 1900s, a group of mission agencies had entered the area. Among them were the Church of God Mission (CGM) and the Friends' African Mission. Arthur Chilson and his wife, Edna, met with missionaries of the CGM for joint prayer. Chilson invited some nationals, and they received the Holy Spirit. The national participants spread the news of the experience. Young people took up the movement and began creating prayer groups. When they were expelled from the mission church they created the African Church of the Holy Spirit, which was recognized by the government in the late 1950s. The Kimbanguist Church of the Democratic Republic of Congo, with other African churches such as Church of the Lord Aladura—which is based in Nigeria with congregations all over the world—are examples of the dramatic change that Christianity experienced throughout the latter half of the twentieth century. Several of these churches are members of the World Council of Churches, infusing the movement with new life as well as worship styles and theologies.

Regretfully, missionary work has been hindered by internal conflict and competition. In addition, the region has suffered from ethnic and civil wars and corrupt governments. In these wars, quite often Christians fought against Christians. Yet prophetic voices such as that of Roman Catholic Cardinal Joseph Malula (1917–89) engaged in ministries of peace and reconciliation and have never been completely silenced.

Several of these native churches, as well as others of Pentecostal and Spiritualist origin, are joined in national interdenominational organizations, such as the Pentecostal Council of Ghana and the Association of Spiritual Churches in Ghana. Two particular Pentecostal bodies in the region deserve special attention: the Redeemed Christian Church of God and the Church of Deep Life. Although Pentecostalism was already present in Africa early in the twentieth century, it was only during the middle of that century, as it developed more autonomous expressions, that Pentecostalism attained spectacular growth in western Africa. It is impossible to name or even count the hundreds of African Christians who have served as Pentecostal missionaries in the area, but there is no doubt that the growth of Christianity in Africa is due to the missionary work of members of these churches. More recently, African missionaries have begun work among African immigrants in Europe, the United States, Canada, and the Caribbean. Thus, African Christianity has experienced significant growth even beyond the confines of that continent.

3. European Colonization and Missions in Southern Africa

Although their original motivation was not basically religious, the presence of a large contingent of Protestant European immigrants in the southern reaches of Africa is important for the history of missions. During the eighteenth century, most of these immigrants were Dutch, but afterward also came the British. In 1795, English and Scottish immigrants began arriving. There were also a number of French Huguenots among the early colonizers. The presence of these various groups led to tensions that occasionally broke out in armed conflict. Also, as in Australia, white settlers saw the native inhabitants as obstacles to their economic interests, and often they seemed to have no other goal than exterminating them. As in the colonization of the Americas by Spain, the church and various Christian organizations sought to ameliorate the situation of the original inhabitants of the land. However, in the twentieth century, the white population of the South African Union was known throughout the world for their inhumane practices with regard to the black population of the land, and there were even several ecclesiastical bodies supporting those practices—while others tacitly accepted them.

At first, the religious life of the white settlers in southern Africa was limited to preserving their faith and expressing it in worship. The two major traditions were the Church of England and the Dutch Reformed Church. Although most of their members had no missionary interest, there were soon within those churches those who took seriously their missionary responsibility and began preaching to the black inhabitants of the area. In this task, missionaries from other churches, particularly from Great Britain and the United States, joined them.

George Schmidt (1709–85) was one of the first Moravian missionaries to South Africa. He established a missionary station among the Khoikhoi in 1737 but clashed with the Dutch clergy over the political implications of baptizing the nationals under colonial rule. We have no evidence of Schmidt's knowledge of Khoi language. In fact, part of his missionary work was to teach the Dutch language to the Khoikhoi. It is said that when Moravians returned in 1792, they found one of his converts—Helena—who had a Dutch New Testament.

In the history of missions in this region, one critical factor was the mixing of races. Many displaced persons of mixed blood became Christians and took missionary leadership: To such communities, and people of mixed descent, Christianity offered a new mode of identity, a place on which to stand. In 1804, a man of mixed descent was asked to serve in the army. He replied "that he served Jesus Christ and none other."[2]

Internal political tensions also characterized missionary work and affiliation. Some European missionaries preferred British over Afrikaner control. This was the case of John MacKenzie (1835–99), a leader in the Church of Scotland, who went to South Africa in 1858 under the auspices of the London Missionary Society and served among the Tswana people. He proposed direct colonial rule so that settlers would not be allowed to take the lands of tribal groups. Although such a proposal was controversial, it was an attempt to protect the nationals.

Many churches in South Africa have a unique missionary history. Partly through the influence of Ethiopian Christians, from very early these churches fought European domination. In that struggle, Nehemiah Tile (1850?–1891) founded the Tembu National Church in 1884. In 1892, Mangane Mokome founded the Ethiopian church on the conviction that white and African missionaries could not discuss missionary work together. Both of these leaders broke with Methodism and understood that their missionary work must begin with justice and equality between the races. Later, in 1898, Pambani Mzimba founded the African Presbyterian Church. Many of these churches sought financial support from the African Methodist Episcopal Church in the United States. This new relationship helped the AME Church extend its missionary work in southern Africa. These churches became an important stepping stone for the development of African churches seeking to be truly African and Christian.

The name of many churches in South Africa includes the word *Zion.* This tradition was begun by the Apostolic Christian Catholic Church, whose headquarters were in "Zion City," near Chicago, and which was founded by John Alexander toward the end of the nineteenth century. Dutch missionary Petrous Louis Le Roux brought it to South Africa. Today these "Zion" churches represent an enormous body of indigenous African churches throughout sub-Saharan Africa. In many academic circles, these churches are seen as the very first contextual expressions of black theology. The work of women in these churches and in their mission work is astounding. For instance, the first woman bishop of the Swazi Zion movement was Jane Nxumalo, who came to occupy that post in 1913, and who did extensive work through faith healing.

As the colonization progressed and the new African nations were born, missionary work in Africa was characterized by an ecumenical spirit seeking reconciliation even in the midst of serious and complex political and military confrontations, such as in Zambia (former Northern Rhodesia), Zimbabwe (Southern Rhodesia), and other nations in southern Africa. The All Africa Conference of Churches became known for its work promoting peace, providing resources for refugees and people displaced by war, dealing with the emergency situations created by HIV-AIDS, and attending to ecological disasters. Many Western denominations and mission agencies have joined the All Africa Conference of Churches, whose headquarters are now located in Nairobi, to collaborate in mission work in the region.

The struggle of the African churches against apartheid is one of the most important events in the twentieth century. Community leaders and organizers, pastors, missionaries, prophets, and martyrs gave witness to justice and reconciliation. Figures such as Archbishop Desmond Tutu and many others engaged the struggle for a more equal South Africa. The *Kairos* document provided the missiological grounding for Christians to face the power of apartheid prophetically and to dismantle it.

Other mission agencies, such as World Vision and the Navigators, continue including social work as part of their mission responsibilities. Many independent groups working in villages and small communities in the interior of the land have attained large followings. Quite often their interest centers on attacking the traditional African worldview of spirits and of the power of ancestors, which is still present in many new converts, and which these churches consider an unacceptable and dangerous syncretism. This has led to doubts and questions about missionary methods, although it is clear that Christianity is engaged in a vigorous interaction with the traditional religions and cultures of the area.

Finally, there are several Korean evangelical groups with mission work in southern Africa. Although they have focused on the needs of Korean immigrants, they have also sought to evangelize the African population. However, this work has been characterized by seeking the conversion of those who are already members of other churches, rather than by missionary work among people of other religions or none.

4. An Example of the Connection between Colonization and the Missionary Legacy in Southern Africa: David Livingstone

The Dutch settlers in southern Africa were not interested in spreading their faith beyond the borders of their own colonies. Many did try to evangelize their own slaves, but few sought to do likewise for free Africans. Slowly, and partly due to the example of other Christians, the Dutch churches in southern Africa began to be interested in missionary work and eventually established missions in Rhodesia (now Zambia and Zimbabwe), Nyasaland, and Nigeria.

However, the most outstanding of Dutch missionaries in southern Africa, Johannes Theodorus van der Kemp (1747–1811), worked under the auspices not of the Dutch Reformed Church but of the London Missionary Society. He was the first missionary whom that society supported in Africa, and his example led to the recruitment of a large number of missionaries who went to Africa under the auspices of the London Missionary Society—David Livingstone among them. Van der Kemp had great appreciation for African culture and customs, which he often claimed were better than those of Europe. His example was followed by a number of missionaries who, like van der Kemp himself, took up African customs and married African women. Two other outstanding representatives of the London Missionary Society were John Philip (1775–1851) and Robert Moffat (1795–1883). Both became known for their staunch opposition to the slave trade and their sincere love of Africans. It was through Robert Moffat that David

Livingstone felt called as a missionary to Africa. Later, Livingstone married Moffat's daughter.

There is no doubt that David Livingstone was the most outstanding British missionary in Africa. He was born in a humble home in Scotland in 1813. His family's scarce means did not allow him a formal education as a child, and he had to begin working in a weaver's shop when he was ten years old. However, he was interested in reading, and he devised a means whereby he could place a book in front of his loom so he could read as he worked. In the evenings, after a long day's work, he would go to school. The basic education that he thus achieved allowed him to study medicine and theology when he decided to become a missionary. His original purpose was to go to China, but difficulties in achieving that purpose, and then the effect of Robert Moffat during one of the latter's visits to Great Britain, led Livingstone to Africa.

He arrived at Capetown early in 1841 and spent the first years of missionary work under the supervision of Robert Moffat, who had established a missionary center in Kuruman. Those early years in Africa were the most sedentary of Livingstone's long life in that continent. After working for some time with Moffat, he married Mary Moffat, his mentor's daughter, with whom he had four children. Already at that time, he began showing an interest in going constantly beyond the edges of the known world. Out of Kuruman, he undertook several expeditions of hundreds of kilometers, usually riding an ox; but it is said that his energy and his zeal for exploration were such that sometimes the ox would tire and he had to continue on foot. He was moved in these explorations both by his profound intellectual curiosity, seeking to know the unknown lands beyond the horizon, and by his desire to preach to the hundreds of villages that still had not heard the gospel. One of his great complaints was the tendency of many missionaries to remain near the centers of Western civilization without trying to penetrate Africa with the Christian message. After spending eleven years with Moffat, Livingstone decided to undertake more ambitious travels. By then he had repeatedly crossed the Kalahari Desert and reached Lake Ngami—which would later dry out and become an extensive field for grazing. In one of those crossings of the Kalahari, one of his children died, and in another, his entire family was put in grave danger. This made Livingstone and his wife decide that before he undertook the great trip across Africa that he planned, his family would move to Great Britain. Then, sometimes riding his ox, Simbad, and sometimes following the great African rivers in canoes, he undertook a trip that led him across the entire continent. It was then that he discovered the waterfalls that he named "Victoria" in honor of the queen of England. Twenty-seven different times he was racked by nearly fatal fevers. In every village in which he arrived, he was able to establish excellent relationships with the residents, partially due to his medical knowledge, but particularly because of his respectful and loving attitude. He thus left behind a wake of admirers. A clear example of his character and his respect for Africans was his attitude when he finally reached the coast. There he found a ship ready to take him to Great Britain; but he refused to sail in it because he had promised the chief of the Africans who had accompanied him that he would return them to their homes. In spite of the difficulties of the return trip, Livingstone resisted the temptation to go to Great Britain and to his family and returned with his bearers. Such gestures created a feeling of trust that became a legend, eventually reaching even places where he had never been.

When Livingstone returned for the first time to Great Britain after sixteen years of absence, the news of his travels had preceded him, and he was received as a national hero. His reports of the wondrous opportunities of Africa and his challenge to Christians led many others to offer themselves to continue and expand his work.

Thanks to Livingstone, during this visit to Great Britain, several groups with missionary purposes were organized—particularly the University Missions, which resulted from a speech he gave in

Cambridge and which later would be an important agent for the proclamation of the Christian message in Africa.

Furthermore, Livingstone's vivid descriptions of the slave trade and the suffering it produced in the interior of Africa provided great support for the antislavery movement, although the result was not immediately visible.

When Livingstone returned to Africa, he did so under the auspices of the British government and no longer of the London Missionary Society. He was to lead an expedition that would follow the Zambezi River, in order to establish trade routes toward the interior of Africa. Livingstone was convinced that the best way to stop the slave trade was to establish other kinds of trade that would be more humane as well as more lucrative. Livingstone did not completely share the attitude of van der Kemp, who thought that the primitive life of Africans was in most respects superior to that of the Europeans. He had seen much suffering that could be alleviated by his own medical knowledge, and therefore van der Kemp's romanticism was not for him. He was convinced that the technological and medical advances of the Western world should be taken to Africa, although at the same time he did not believe in the implicit superiority of all things Western. On the contrary, he appreciated and even admired many of the customs and virtues of the Africans. He was seeking ways whereby Africans could establish cordial relationships with Western people, in sharp contrast with those resulting from the slave trade. He therefore saw his expedition on the Zambezi under government auspices as part of his missionary work.

The Zambezi expedition was a failure. The river was not as easily navigable as he had been led to believe. The steamship that the government made available for the expedition was completely inadequate and often needed repairs that were very difficult in the interior of the continent. Relationships became increasingly tense between Livingstone and his companions. Finally, the entire expedition was abandoned, and Livingstone, in another memorable voyage, took the ship all the way to India, where he sold it. Meanwhile, in Great Britain, his wife had died. Finally, in 1864, Livingstone returned to Great Britain in order, once more, to tell of the inhuman suffering produced by the slave trade and to create among the British population the consciousness that would eventually lead to its abolition.

Throughout his entire life, Livingstone had been almost obsessed with discovering the sources of the Nile. He was convinced that by doing so, he would understand the entire fluvial system of Africa and would be able to establish new means of communication between the Mediterranean and the heartland of the continent. Therefore, in 1866, he returned to Africa to undertake a new expedition in search of the sources of the Nile. On this occasion, as in most others, he had no European companions and traveled with a faithful group of African bearers and supporters. He once again found many villages that had been destroyed as a consequence of the slave trade, and once again he wrote back home describing the tragedies of that trade. After two years with no contact with the exterior, he reached the town of Ujiji, by Lake Tanganyika, when the rest of the world thought that he had died. There Henry M. Stanley, a North American newspaper reporter who had been sent to Africa in order to discover what had become of Livingstone, met him a few days later. It was then that Stanley was said to have offered the memorable greeting: "Dr. Livingstone, I presume." Stanley and Livingstone spent several months together, and the impression that the old missionary made on the young newspaperman was such that the latter decided to devote the rest of his life to the exploration of Africa.

Although Stanley sought to persuade Livingstone to return to England, the latter remained firm in his decision of remaining in Africa and spending the rest of his life preaching the gospel to those who had not yet heard it. It was thus that he undertook his final trip, and after ten months of hardships, he was so weakened that he had to be carried by his faithful African friends. These friends found him dead on May 1, 1873, while kneeling by his bed. Following his instructions, they buried his heart in African soil and carried his body to the coast, from whence it was taken to Great Britain in order to be interred in Westminster Abbey. At present, by the Victoria Falls that he reached and named, there is a statue of Livingstone on the march as a reminder of the manner in which his indefatigable spirit left its imprint on African soil. His memory still lives in many villages and tribes, and even the growing nationalism of the entire continent and the often-justified rejection of things Western have not been able to erase it. The multifaceted interests of Livingstone as a missionary and explorer and, above all, a benefactor of the African population may be seen in the following lines from a letter he wrote to his brother-in-law, John Smith Moffat, who had followed in his father's footsteps and also become a remarkable missionary in Africa:

> Are ostriches monogamists or polygamists? Try to count their paces with your watch when at full speed and measure the length of their stride. Try and discover the root and plant by which the Hottentots make their mead to ferment. Is there anything religious in the Boguera [an initiation ceremony]? Or is it anything more than a political rite? Is there anything besides wool growing that would be a profitable investment for the Bechuanas, that would turn their land to the best account and establish them in them?[3]

Besides Livingstone's direct effect on Africa, the reports of his expeditions and missionary work created a great wave of interest toward Africa in Europe as well as in the United States. Partly in response to Livingstone's death and to the task to which he had devoted his life, Great Britain began to use its naval power to put an end to the slave trade. Although the Moravians, Methodists, and Baptists had been working in Africa long before Livingstone, the reports of his work, and particularly the drama of his death, gave new impetus to missionary ventures. Also several new denominations began projecting missionary work in Africa in response to these reports.

A contemporary of Livingstone who was also influential in the penetration of Christianity into Africa was Cecil Rhodes—who gave to Zambia and Zimbabwe the name of Rhodesia, by which the area was once known. Like Livingstone, Rhodes expressed a profound sense of Christian responsibility and of compassion toward the African population and was instrumental in opening the African continent to missions as well as to trade. However, he was inclined to think in terms of Western superiority, believing that since whites were superior, they had the responsibility of leading Africans along the paths of progress. In this he differed greatly from Livingstone, for the latter, after having seen the horrors of the slave trade, could not think of the white race in terms quite as positive as did Rhodes. Furthermore, Rhodes was a traditional colonizer, building what became his own empire. But even so, he was also moved by Christian convictions and sought to counteract the cruelty and brutality of other colonizers.

Livingstone was only one of the many missionaries who contributed to the penetration of the Christian message into central Africa. Naturally, colonizers and traders whose interests were not always as humanitarian or Christian often followed these missionaries. But it is necessary to point out that the presence of the missionary venture contributed to alleviate the consequences of the effect of the Western world on Africa—an effect that would have taken place inevitably and that would have been much more devastating were it not for the missionaries and their work.

C. Catholic Missions in Africa

Although Catholics had settled in Africa long before Protestants—in the Portuguese colonies of Angola and Mozambique—their missionary work in that continent had been practically abandoned, and it was only after the exploration and work of the first Protestants, and partly as a reaction to Protestant presence, that the Catholic Church took an active interest in Africa.

At that point, Catholic incursions into Africa came mostly from the West, East, and North, in sharp contrast with Protestant missions, which came mostly from the South, even though there were also strong Protestant centers in Liberia and Sierra Leone. In the west of the continent, in 1842, the Catholic Church established the Apostolic Vicariate of the Two Guineas, which worked mostly in Gabon, Angola, and the Congo. These missions did not penetrate very far into the interior of the continent, reaching mostly as far as Landana, in the Congo.

On the eastern side of the continent, in 1860, the Catholic Church established the Apostolic Prefecture of Zanzibar, whose purpose was to use that island as a center from which to launch missions into Africa.

From the North, the project was to move into central Africa through a series of missions going up the Nile. This project is closely bound with the name and the life of Father Daniel Anthony Comboni (1831–81), who had a profound passion for the evangelization of central Africa. Since previous efforts had failed because large numbers of missionaries died as a result of various fevers and climatic difficulties, a first project was to take Africans to Europe in order to be trained there as missionaries. This plan failed, for Africans who had adapted to European life found it difficult to adapt once again to their native lands. Therefore, Comboni decided to establish a number of centers on the continent, in areas where conditions were not too harsh for Europeans, that would serve to train Africans without completely taking them out of their context. Comboni received moral support from Rome and the approval of the Sacra Congregatio de Propaganda Fide, but he never had the material support necessary for establishing the various centers he had planned, and he had to settle for a single center under his personal direction. Throughout his life, Comboni worked there, although his results were not as great as he had hoped.

It was when Rome and other Catholic capitals in Europe learned of the expeditions of Livingstone and the work of other Protestants, that the Roman Catholic Church began actively and seriously supporting missionary work in Africa. Even then, the Sacra Congregatio de Propaganda Fide worked independently from the other major supporter of Catholic missions, King Leopold II of Belgium. Inspired by the discoveries of Livingstone, Stanley, and others, Leopold II convoked the International Conference on Geography, which gathered in Brussels in 1876. The result of this meeting was the birth of the International African Association, whose purpose was to enter more deeply into that continent, taking to it the supposed advantages of Western civilization. Although the association thought that the preaching of the gospel was one of the necessary foundations for its task, it affirmed its lay character, declaring that missionary work was most properly left to the churches and that the association itself should not undertake it. With a realistic reading of the situation, and seeing that most exploration into Africa was being led by Protestants, King Leopold II, who personally was very committed to missionary work, agreed to the creation of this lay association and agreed to serve as its president. The Sacra Congregatio de Propaganda Fide, rather than cooperating with the International African Association, was suspicious of it, particularly after Bishop Lavigerie—whom we have already met in previous chapters as the founder of the White Fathers—presented a report in which he claimed that the association was merely a front by which Protestants were trying to gain the support of trusting Roman Catholics—the king of Belgium among them.

Throughout the nineteenth century, Catholic missions in the Congo were mostly a response to the presence of Protestant missionaries, or at least to the fear of such presence. The reason why Lavigerie disliked the International African Association was that it was ready to allow the entry of Protestant missionaries in its lands. His White Fathers was one of the main Catholic missionary agencies in Africa. But quite often, they seemed to be more interested in competing with Protestant missionaries than in evangelizing the many tribes that still followed traditional African religions. The same may be said about the Fathers of the Holy Spirit, one of the main orders working in African missions. Although these missionaries had settled in Landana before the Protestants entered that area, when in 1877, Stanley opened the way to the interior of Africa through the Congo River, the main motivation of that missionary order to follow that route was to stop what they considered the virulent doctrine of Protestantism, which threatened to infect the area. Before Catholic missionaries followed Stanley's route, there were already missions along it founded by the British Baptists and by the Livingstone Inland Mission—an agency that had resulted from the joint inspiration of Livingstone and of the China Inland Mission. As Catholics followed the steps of Protestant missionaries, much of the work in the area was one of competition rather than of evangelization.

During the second half of the nineteenth century, Catholic missions in Africa were hindered and weakened by conflicts over issues of jurisdiction. When the Sacra Congregatio de Propaganda Fide decided to grant the White Fathers the right to settle in what, up to that point, had been territory nominally under the jurisdiction of Comboni's vicariate, the latter claimed that this decision was "a strong toothache" and continued opposing it until Comboni's death. There were also conflicts between the Fathers of the Holy Spirit and the White Fathers as to which areas fell under the jurisdiction of each of these two orders.

To complicate matters further, various European powers were trying to settle in Africa and feared that the presence of missions from rival powers would serve as a beachhead to the political interests of those other nations. Portugal was still claiming its ancient rights of padroado that had been granted at the time of the discoveries and conquests of the sixteenth century, but in the nineteenth, given the decline of Portuguese power, they were an impediment rather than an aid to Catholic missions. France and Belgium vied for rule over the Congo Valley. Portugal itself, in spite of its political, military, and economic weakness, insisted on territorial demands. Great Britain was willing to cede its colonial claims in equatorial Africa in favor of Portugal, as long as the Portuguese were willing to forbid the slave trade—an attitude in which one could see the influence of David Livingstone, but that the Portuguese resisted. Finally, in 1884, the various European powers vying for African lands gathered in Berlin. This led to a political partition of Africa, with King Leopold II of Belgium receiving authority over the "Independent State of the Congo." Leopold then stressed the need to send Belgian missionaries to the Congo, for he feared—apparently justifiably—that French missionaries would serve as a beachhead for French interests. Since the Belgian Catholic Church was much committed to missions in Mongolia and other areas of the Far East, for a long time it was impossible to find a sufficient number of Belgian missionaries to work in the Congo. All of these tensions and competitions presented before Africans some of the worst sides of European culture, and this hindered Catholic penetration into that continent.

During the twentieth century, Roman Catholicism in central Africa grew much more rapidly than it had in the nineteenth. This was generally a continuation of the efforts begun in the previous century, although now better organized, with more personnel and financial resources. During the first half of the twentieth century, the growth of Catholicism in Belgian colonies was amazing, particularly in the Belgian Congo.

However, the growing nationalist sentiment in the latter half of the twentieth century soon began having its effects on Catholic missions. Since many of these were closely tied to colonial powers—more so than their Protestant counterparts—they suffered severely when African sentiment turned against European colonialism. In places such as the Congo, the close connection between colonial interests and the missionary enterprise resulted in the destruction of much church work, as well as the violent and often cruel deaths of many missionaries—although it is important to point out that many of those who died in the hands of African extremists were paying for the sins of others.

Toward the end of the twentieth century and early in the twenty-first, the Catholic Church began to focus its work also in providing social services and health support, particularly for people suffering from HIV-AIDS. Catholics created a large number of homes for children or youth affected directly by this disease and developed extensive programs of education on it, as well as on other health matters. They also provided resources for refugees from wars and natural disasters.

The Catholic Church in Africa is also undergoing a thorough process of enculturation. Early in the twentieth-first century in Zaire, now the Democratic Republic of Congo, it produced a document on liturgy and its connection with culture that for many years was studied and debated in the Vatican, finally being approved with some modifications. As part of that process of identifying with African culture, the Catholic Church also promotes interreligious dialogues with traditional African religions as well as with Islam.

Finally, it is important to note that a growing number of African clergy are serving the Catholic Church in Europe and the United States. For many of these African priests, this work is a missionary vocation, for they not only are in charge of immigrant communities but also serve as priests in those countries where, due to the crisis in Western Christianity, there are not sufficient pastoral resources.

D. Christianity in Madagascar

Although geographically very close to Africa, Madagascar is populated by people who are more closely related racially and culturally to the islands of the Pacific than to the Africans. However, through long-standing contacts with Arabs and with others in the Indian Ocean, the

Malagasy culture developed in its own directions. Early in the twentieth century, the Hova tribe controlled the island, for one of its kings, making use of Western weapons that he obtained in exchange for slaves, was able to subject the other inhabitants. Later the British, moved by their antislavery zeal, signed a treaty with the king of Madagascar in which the latter committed to forbidding the slave traffic in exchange for an annual shipment of Western weapons and other products.

The French had unsuccessfully attempted to settle on the island, but the first Christian missionary who was able to work there arrived in Tananarive, the capital, in 1820. His name was David Jones, and the London Missionary Society, to which we have repeatedly referred, had sent him. Jones and those who followed him were able to found a church that proved to be sufficiently strong to resist twenty-five years of persecution when a queen who opposed Christianity decreed that severe penalties should be applied to Christians—including death and being sold as slaves.

When political change on the island once again opened it to missionary work, the London Missionary Society sent new representatives, and their number grew after Queen Ranavalona II and her husband accepted baptism. From that point on, Protestant work in Madagascar enjoyed uninterrupted progress.

At the request of the London Missionary Society, which understood that the opportunities and needs of Madagascar presented a challenge much greater than it could meet by itself, other missionary agents entered the island. Among them were the Anglican Church Missionary Society, the Society for the Propagation of the Gospel in Foreign Parts, the Quakers, and a large number of Norwegian Lutherans. All of these organizations worked in close collaboration and established schools, clinics, and other centers of social service.

Roman Catholicism made its entry into Madagascar precisely during the time of persecutions that has already been noted. During its early years, these difficult political situations impeded its growth. Later, however, supported by French power, it was able to outgrow Protestantism. After repeated conflict, Great Britain acknowledged French protectorate over Madagascar. Five years later, in 1897, the French overturned the ruling house of Madagascar and turned the island into a French colony. This naturally tended to strengthen Catholic missions and to hinder Protestant work. Since the Catholics accused Protestants of opposing French rule, the latter decided to turn much of their work to the Société des Missions Évangéliques de Paris, which, being French, could not be accused of favoring British interests. Although at first Catholic missions profited from French action and power in Madagascar, eventually they suffered from that connection, for the French government, reflecting the growing anticlericalism in France, began hindering the work of all missionaries. Furthermore, when Malagasy nationalist sentiment grew in response to colonial domination, much of that sentiment was directed against missions, particularly Catholic ones. In the rebellion that took place at the end of the nineteenth century, the ire of the people against missions and against all foreign influence was vented.

Throughout the twentieth century, both Protestantism and Roman Catholicism continued growing in Madagascar, although by the middle of the century, most of the island's inhabitants were still not Christian. This growth continued, as the ancient religions gave way to various forms of Christianity. Eventually, roughly two-thirds of Christians were Roman Catholic.

As in other mission fields, Protestant churches in Madagascar had discovered the need to collaborate. In 1934, almost all the Protestant bodies present on the island joined in the United Protestant Church of Madagascar, although this was not a total merger. After that time, conversations regarding union and mergers have taken place, although the growing number of faith missions and similar movements has also resulted in a greater variety of denominational affiliation.

Finally, one must note that the Orthodox Church is also present in Madagascar. In 1997, with the approval of the patriarch of Alexandria, an Orthodox bishop for Madagascar was named. Early in the twenty-first century, the Orthodox Church in Madagascar had twelve parishes, seven churches, and twelve native priests. The government recognized this body as a legitimate Christian church.

E. General Considerations

In 1850, Africa was a continent unknown to the West, lacking practically all contact with the outside world—except that prompted by the slave trade—and having few of the advantages and disadvantages of modern technology. A hundred years later, the African continent had joined the world of nations, and it included several independent states. This process had been joined to a growing nationalist sentiment justifiably rebelling against the abuses and the paternalistic attitude of Westerners, although often also ignoring the spirit of sacrifice that led many Westerners, particularly missionaries, to Africa. Today Christianity in Africa celebrates the result of missionary work, although internally it still struggles with the legacy of colonialism. In Africa, many churches resulting from missionary work have to negotiate a number of hurdles as they seek to participate in the new cultural awakening of their nations without thereby forsaking "the deposit of the faith." There are also many churches and Christian movements born on African soil that seek to be faithful to the gospel within their very complex situation. Although some of these have contacts with churches elsewhere, others have little or no such contact.

As elsewhere, the African churches face issues of nationalism, ethnic and religious struggles, deterioration of the environment, development, human rights issues, and the effects of globalization. But overall they face two closely connected issues: first, the degree to which Christianity is to become African; second, the presence and expansion of Islam.

In ancient African cultures, there were a number of practices that traditionally Christians have considered incompatible with their faith. Two of these are ancestor worship and polygamy. The first Christian missionaries and almost all of their successors insisted on the need to abandon such customs before embracing Christianity. Livingstone refused communion to those who practiced polygamy. But the problem is quite complex, for the total abolition of polygamy would imply that many women and children would be repudiated and therefore become homeless. Something similar is true in the case of ancestor worship, which is closely tied to a sense of social loyalty to tradition and is at once a religious practice and a social and political custom. There are in Africa several Christian groups that allow polygamy and some that insist that the veneration of ancestors is not idolatry but a cultural tradition of family loyalty. These churches rebel against the attempt of other churches and of foreign missionaries who impose on Africa what from their perspective is not Christianity itself, but rather European customs dressed as Christianity.

All of this aids the advance of Islam, which allows polygamy and which also, perhaps due to its long-standing contacts with sub-Saharan Africa, seems to be able to adapt better to social conditions. Also, since in the minds of many, Christianity is joined with Western colonial powers, African nationalism often turns to Islam as an ally. Furthermore, the advance of Islam receives the silent support from the government of Egypt and other Muslim nations that seek to expand their influence southwardly. Therefore, during the early twenty-first century the encounter with Islam was a major issue for Christian churches in Africa.

The church in Africa cannot ignore the problem of HIV-AIDS. Early in the twenty-first century, millions of people were dying annually as a result of this disease. The rate of contagion was alarming, partially due to lack of education, partially to ancient myths and cultural traditions, and partially to sheer poverty. While many churches are seeking to respond to this situation, they hardly seem adequate to the task. At the same time, Christianity is enjoying in Africa an unprecedented and even surprising rate of growth and vitality. For all these reasons, the future of sub-Saharan Africa, and of Christianity within it, remains uncertain, but full of promise and perils.

Chapter 10

MISSIONS IN LATIN AMERICA

As throughout most of the world, the nineteenth century in Latin America was characterized by profound changes that would greatly affect the history of Christianity in the area. In the field of civil and political life, the most important of these changes was the independence of new nations. In the history of missions, the most notable event was the introduction of Protestant Christianity, which was made possible by new political and intellectual circumstances.

A. New Circumstances

Throughout the eighteenth century, Spanish power and prestige in Latin America had been declining. With the exception of Charles III, the Spanish throne had been occupied by an almost-uninterrupted succession of weak and inept rulers. The court constantly demanded more income from colonies that, partially due to their bad administration, were unable to supply the requirements of the Peninsula. In the Americas, the Indian population, excluded from the benefits of a society in which they were the main source of wealth, had no attachment to European rule. The condition of most *mestizos*—those of mixed blood—was not much better. Blacks, most of them still living in slavery, were considered of no account. The *criollos*—people of European descent born in the Americas—carried the heaviest load of trade and social administration but were excluded from the highest honors in the lands where they had been born. The *peninsulares*—people born in Spain—were privileged with those honors and with easy loads and were therefore the only ones who were truly interested in the survival of the existing order and in unconditional obedience to the government in Spain. But they were only a small fraction of the population and could not counteract the feelings of the rest. Finally, ideas arriving from France and news from the recently born United States produced a general state of dissatisfaction with Spanish rule.

The independence of the Spanish, Portuguese, and even French colonies was a result of the Napoleonic Wars. The process began with the establishment of governments that would not acknowledge the authority of Napoleon and his brother Joseph, who had been placed on the Spanish throne. Eventually, however, most Spanish colonies declared their independence, mostly due to the ineptness of Ferdinand VII, who upon his return to the Spanish throne sought to restore the old order and ignored the changes that had taken place during his absence. In a space of fifteen years, between 1810 and 1825, Spain lost almost all its American colonies. In the Portuguese colony of Brazil, the process of independence began before it did in the rest of Latin America. In 1807, the ruling house of Braganza was forced to leave Lisbon, fleeing from Bonapartist invaders. Fifteen years later, one of its members refused to return to Lisbon, declared independence, and created the Empire of Brazil. France itself suffered territorial losses in the Americas as a consequence of Napoleonic Wars. Although Toussaint L'Ouverture's adventure for the independence of Haiti led to his death, a year later, in 1804, Haiti became the first independent nation in all of Latin America and the Caribbean. It was clear that Spain, Portugal, and France had to abandon their territorial pretensions in the Americas. This geopolitical reality was reaffirmed in 1823 by the

Monroe Doctrine, by which the United States declared itself against any new European colonial ventures in the Western Hemisphere.

The new conditions created serious difficulties for the Catholic Church and opened the way for Protestantism. As to the former, the salient event of the last two centuries has been a movement from a time of stagnation and conservatism in the nineteenth century to new vitality and creativity in the twenty-first. As to the latter, growth has been enormous, fueled at first by immigration and by missionary efforts from abroad and then by the explosive growth of Pentecostalism.

Although in some circles the legend has become common that Latin American revolutions were directed against the abuses of the Catholic Church, such an interpretation is generally contrary to fact. Miranda, Hidalgo, Morelos, Moreno, and San Martín—all of them revolutionary leaders—favored the continuation of the ancient privileges of the church. Bolívar was the only one among the main leaders who advocated for the separation between church and state. What did actually happen was, the peninsulares held the higher ecclesiastical positions; the hierarchy—including the popes, whose policies favored Spain—opposed independence. The natural consequence was that soon a strong anticlerical minority appeared who opposed not so much the doctrines of the church as its excessive influence.

The triumph of independence resulted in the return to Spain of most of the priests who were peninsulares. Although these were the most conservative among the clergy, they were also the best trained. This brought greater difficulties to the Catholic Church. Even before this time it had been incapable of erasing the vestiges of ancient religions among Indians and blacks. Nor had it been able to eliminate or even restrain the abuses of white colonists. Now, after independence, facing radically new circumstances, such tasks would become even more difficult.

The Catholic Church in Latin America took over a century to recover. However, by 1955, with the creation of the Latin American

Bishops Conference, the Catholic Church began exploring new paths in its own inner life, creating various departments dealing with issues such as mission and spirituality, social justice and solidarity, and family faith and culture. These were signs of renewal.

As for Protestantism, its first gains came through the support of liberal governments that sought to use it as a source of support against the conservatism and even obscurantism of the Catholic leadership. Such governments promoted immigration from Northern Europe and encouraged the work of the first Protestant missionaries. Thus, early Protestant growth was the result of both immigration and missions. But explosive growth began in the twentieth century, with the Pentecostal movement.

It was immediately after independence that Protestant missions began developing in Latin America. In the World Missionary Conference in Edinburgh in 1910, Latin America was declared to be Christian territory and therefore was excluded from discussion as a mission field for Protestants. This led Protestant denominations and missionary societies to organize three important conferences on missions in Latin America: Panama (1916), Montevideo (1925), and Havana (1929). These would be landmarks in the development of ecumenical Protestantism in the area.

Early in the twentieth century, some evangelical missionaries who had contact with the birth of Pentecostalism in the United States promoted their new charismatic experiences within the more traditional Protestant churches, thus leading to divisions from which new Pentecostal churches emerged. There were also large numbers of Pentecostal missionaries—both foreigners and Latin Americans—who built new congregations. Thus, as elsewhere, the history of missions in Latin America is complex. In order to simplify our discussion, we shall organize the rest of this chapter by dividing Latin America into various regions.

B. Christianity in the Southern Cone

1. Roman Catholicism

Throughout the nineteenth century, the Catholic Church continued its missionary work. The Salesians and the Lazarists settled in Patagonia, while Franciscans took charge of several Indian missionary settlements and established mission schools, particularly in Tarija and Salta.

Since most of the population in Uruguay was of European descent, and therefore traditionally Christian, the great challenge in that country throughout the twentieth century and even into the twenty-first was how to witness in the "dechristianized" areas of national life. It took the Roman Catholic Church several decades and radical political and ecclesiastical shifts to begin responding to this challenge.

During the "Dirty War" in Argentina (1976–86), there was severe dissension within the Catholic ranks. Grassroots groups directly affected by the war took action in defense of human rights and supported movements opposing the military regime. Quite often, the official position of the church was to remain silent before the oppressive policies of the government. In time, international Catholic organizations from Europe, and later a number of ecumenical agencies, supported those who promoted human rights and who eventually managed to overthrow the military regime and return to democracy.

On April 30, 1977, reacting to the disappearance of thousands since the beginning of the Dirty War, a group of women gathered in the Plaza de Mayo in Buenos Aires in order to demand the return of those who had disappeared, or at least news about them. The support of Catholic groups both in Argentina itself and abroad resulted in the movement of the Women of Plaza de Mayo, who continued raising a symbolic but powerful voice against the atrocities being committed.

Grassroots Catholicism became engaged in theological and critical reflection on the political and economic order, and how it affected the poor and other marginalized people. This provided a vital space for development of Latin American liberation theology. Finally, toward the end of the twenty-first century and as part of its task in the face of the growth of "New Age" and of various Eastern religions, the Catholic Church in Argentina developed an extensive program to evangelize the masses by means of radio, television, and printed material. Also, as people migrated toward cities, various missional organizations, including both national and foreign missionaries, sought to provide health, education, and shelter in the slums.

As in the rest of Latin America, the history of the Roman Catholic Church in Chile during the nineteenth century was closely connected to the political vicissitudes of the country. The first years were difficult, for the church's attitude during the struggle for independence had led to a great loss both in its prestige and in its power. The national government claimed the right of national patronage over the church that had earlier belonged to the Spanish crown. It was only in 1925 that the separation of church and state as well as freedom of worship were officially enacted as law. But much earlier, particularly under the direction of José Manuel Balmaceda, the Chilean government had issued laws guaranteeing freedom of worship and eliminating all official privileges of the Catholic Church.

By the beginning of the twentieth century, there were signs of a new Catholic generation that was conscious of the new situation in which it was living, and it was ready to work within that context. From that point on, there was a growing sector within the leadership of the Catholic Church, arguing that the church should be more cognizant of the real needs of the country. Catholic Rural Action was organized in 1952, and it became a very significant agent in agricultural reconstruction and rural reformation in Chile.

Perhaps the most remarkable missionary effort among the native population was the mission of the Bavarian Capuchins in the region of Araucania, begun in 1898. Also, even before the time of the Second Vatican Council, there was a movement advocating for liturgical reformation, support to women's organizations, evangelization on the basis of small groups, and the creation and support of Comunidades Eclesiales de Base—or, Basic Ecclesial Communities, also known as CEBs. At the same time, there was a strong movement seeking donations to poor peasants of lands held by the Catholic Church. During the gatherings of the council, the Chilean representatives became known for their progressive and open attitude. Between 1966 and 1969, the archdiocese of Santiago held postconciliar synods that included grassroots representatives and that discussed issues such as ecumenism, Jewish-Christian dialogue, ecclesiology, and the renewed participation of laity within the life of the church.

The last three decades of the twentieth century were marked by controversy and conflict. In 1970, Socialist candidate Salvador Allende won election with a minuscule margin against the opposition conservative Catholics led by the *Opus Dei*. By 1971, as a result of the work of Catholic priests and lay leaders working among Marxist laborers, the organization Christians for Socialism was founded, mostly to promote dialogue between Christians and Marxists. But then a coup overthrew Allende and brought to power Augusto Pinochet, under whose dictatorship thousands of Christians associated with Christians for Socialism as well as other popular movements suffered persecution and death. The thousands of people who disappeared during the dictatorship placed the Chilean Catholic Church in a difficult situation. The declarations of its bishops were profoundly ambivalent, on the one hand supporting "political order," and on the other claiming justice and transparency in the military and political processes of the country.

Toward the end of the twentieth century, the Chilean people voted in favor of democracy and the inner tensions and conflicts within the church were alleviated. Early in the twenty-first century, Catholic mission took various directions. Given the economic crisis that all of Latin

America was undergoing, the region experienced a large and constant migration from rural areas to cities. In that setting, priests, monastics, and laypeople worked assiduously in order to provide at least minimal resources in education and in other social needs. Following the tradition of the CEBs, some leaders began providing opportunities for biblical and social reflection. On the more conservative side, there were movements such as Catholic charismatics and others who insisted that the center of the mission was in the supporting of movements such as the Tradition, Family, and Property movement. These groups and movements favored a Catholicism more clearly subject to the hierarchy and impinging on all dimensions of life, public and private. For this reason they were often called *integristas.*

Responding to the papal encyclical *Redemptoris Missio*, the Catholic Church also sent missionaries, both men and women, to North Africa and to Asia, thus illustrating the increasing significance of missionary activity from one Third World country to another.

2. Protestantism

The first Protestants to settle in the area were immigrants from European nations where Protestantism was strong. Even before independence, there were Scots and English in Argentina. But it was Rivadavia that first developed an official and active policy to promote immigration. In order to facilitate the settlement of Scottish colonists, they were guaranteed freedom of worship, and in 1825, under government contract, the first large contingent of immigrants arrived from Scotland. Similar processes that continued until the twentieth century brought large numbers of German Lutherans to Chile, Italian Waldensians to Uruguay, and Mennonites to Paraguay. All these immigrant groups have left their mark on their host nations, and the churches they brought with them eventually became integrated into the fiber of society.

However, already by 1820, even before freedom of worship was guaranteed to foreigners, the first Protestant service had taken place in Argentina. Those who participated in this service were nine British immigrants, led by James (Diego) Thomson. Thomson, a Baptist, had studied at the University of Glasgow. After serving as a pastor in Scotland, he began studying Spanish and the Lancaster educational method. He then requested the British and Foreign Bible Society to appoint him their agent in Latin America. This was done, and on October 6, 1818, carrying reference letters from the British crown, Thomson landed in Buenos Aires as the promoter of a new educational method and an ancient book. There was a close connection between these two functions, for the Bible was the main text employed in the Lancastrian method. Furthermore, both that educational system and the freedom to read the Scripture were matters of interest to the more progressive elements in Latin America. James Thomson's work in Argentina was so remarkable that when he decided to move to other lands, he was awarded honorary citizenship.

In 1821, after a brief visit to Uruguay, Thomson went on to Chile. His success there was no less than it had been in Argentina—and the same eventually was true in Perú, Ecuador, Colombia, Mexico, and Cuba. In those countries he had the support of leaders as distinguished as Bernardo O'Higgins, José de San Martín, and Simón Bolívar.

For a long time, preaching was limited to immigrants and always took place in their native language, for the authorities opposed any Protestant preaching in Spanish. The first person to preach a Protestant sermon in Spanish, both in Argentina and Uruguay, was John Francis Thomson, better known throughout Latin America as Juan Francisco Thomson. Perhaps more important, it was through his work that Francisco Penzotti established his first contacts with the American Bible Society, whose most famous agent in Latin America he would become.

Anglican leadership had long held that missionary work among the Catholic population of Latin America was not appropriate, and therefore had shown little interest in missions in Latin America. At first, this interest was limited to a small circle and focused mostly on the native inhabitants of the area who were still unchurched. This was actually the reason why Latin America was excluded from consideration as a mission field in the World Missionary Conference of Edinburgh in 1910. The first Anglican who worked as a missionary in Latin America was Allen Gardiner. As a captain in the British navy, he had visited Chile in 1822 and developed an interest in missionary work there. He began working among the Araucanians in 1838, but four years later, he decided to focus his attention on Tierra del Fuego. His plan was to settle on the Malvinas (the Falkland Islands) and to make this the center for missions into the continent. His plan never succeeded, and first he and later his son died in the attempt.

Paul (Pablo) Besson, a Baptist missionary, worked among French Baptists who had settled in the area of Santa Fe in Argentina. He was a valiant defender of religious freedom and of the separation between church and state, and he published his views in newspapers in the main cities of Argentina.

Pastor David Trumbull, who had studied at Yale and Princeton, was sent to Chile by the Foreign Evangelical Union in the United States. He arrived at Valparaiso in 1846, with the task of seeing to the religious needs of the immigrant community and of the many British sailors who would visit the port. In 1855, the first Protestant church in Chile was built. Due to the opposition of the Catholic clergy, the building had to be surrounded by a high wall so it could not be seen from the outside, and singing could not be such that people passing by could be attracted by it. Since the law prohibited any other but Roman Catholic worship, Trumbull joined the growing liberal intelligentsia in efforts for legal reform. In 1876, the Foreign Evangelical Union ceded its work to the Presbyterian Church, and eleven years later, the communities that Trumbull and his companions had founded organized themselves into a presbytery.

The conversion of Juan Canut de Bon, a Spanish ex-Jesuit, became an important turning point in the growth of Protestantism. In 1890, he was made a pastor, and he spent the remaining six years of his life preaching the gospel and founding Methodist churches. His notoriety was such that people began calling all Protestants "canutos," a pejorative term by which they were known well into the twentieth century.

In 1897, the Christian and Missionary Alliance began working in Chile, mostly among German settlers, but soon extended its outreach to native Chileans. An important aspect of its work was its printing press, through which material was produced supporting its evangelistic task. Baptist presence in Chile also began at the end of the nineteenth century, although the first Baptist church with Chilean members was organized in 1908. In the decade of the 1880s, at least three churches were organized among German immigrants. But the true birth of the Baptist Church of Chile took place when a missionary originally working with the Christian and Missionary Alliance withdrew from it with four pastors and some 300 members. They asked for support from the Baptist Convention of Brazil, and after some time they became associated with the Southern Baptist Convention in the United States.

One of the most remarkable phenomena in the history of Protestantism in Chile is the growth of the Pentecostal movement. This movement began in 1902 in the Methodist church of Valparaiso, whose pastor was missionary Willis C. Hoover. Between 1902 and 1909, Pentecostal manifestations and experiences were limited to the Methodist church of Valparaiso, but by 1909, they began appearing in other churches. In 1910, the Chile Annual Conference of the Methodist Church condemned the movement, and as a result, people with Pentecostal tendencies withdrew and formed the Methodist Pentecostal Church.

The newly born Methodist Pentecostal Church was directed by Hoover, until he was forced to resign by a group led by Pastor Umaña, a former colleague. Together with Víctor Pavez and others, Hoover then formed the Evangelical Pentecostal Church. Umaña's group continued calling itself the Methodist Pentecostal Church. By mid-century, the Evangelical Pentecostal Church was also conducting missions in Argentina, Bolivia, Perú, and Uruguay.

Montevideo was the venue for the Second Congress on Christian Work in Latin America, which gathered there in 1925. Argentina also provided the setting for two important meetings on Christianity and Protestant missions in Latin America. One was the First Latin American Evangelical Conference, held in 1949, and the other was the Third Latin American Evangelical Conference, in 1969. These gatherings—particularly the one in 1969—showed that Latin American Protestants were taking a more active role in the leadership of their churches.

The churches in this region contributed significantly to the development of the Latin American Council of Churches—Consejo Latinoamericano de Iglesias (CLAI). Under the guidance of Methodist bishop Federico Pagura, Emilio Castro, Mortimer Arias, and other Protestant leaders, Latin American ecumenism became an agent of peace, justice, and reconciliation in many of the areas deeply affected by war or by ideological persecution.

The Facultad Evangélica de Teología de Buenos Aires (now the Instituto Superior de Estudios Teológicos [ISEDET] was founded in 1884, partly at the insistence of laity who requested that native Argentinians be trained to occupy positions of leadership in the church. Directed at first by North American missionary Dr. B. Foster Stockwell, it soon became one of the most prestigious academic institutions in the Río de la Plata area.

Hundreds of Protestant groups throughout the nation, including some with origins in South Korea and other Asian nations, are part of the religious landscape in the region. The latter half of the twentieth century and the early years of the twenty-first were marked by significant Pentecostal growth while most of the immigrant churches and the older denominations seemed to cease growing. Among some of these other churches there was what many called the "Pentecostalization of Protestantism," which developed an ecclesial life joining the particular tradition of a church and the charismatic spirit and forms of worship. Although when they began in the twentieth century, Pentecostal churches generally refrained from ecumenical or interdenominational relations, by the beginning of the twenty-first century, not only had they organized interdenominational ministerial associations and networks among congregations, but also many had joined the Latin American Council of Churches. Under the leadership of people such as Bishop Gabriel Vaccaro from Argentina, Pentecostalism made a significant contribution to the development of the Pentecostal Ecumenical Conference in Latin America, an organization bringing together many Pentecostal churches open to interdenominational relations.

Another significant denomination in Chile is the Pentecostal Church of Chile, led by Pastor Enrique Chávez. This denomination was born in 1942 (although some historians place its birth around 1945) as the result of a schism within the Methodist Pentecostal Church. It also contributed to the creation and development of the Pentecostal Ecumenical Conference in Latin America and is a member of the World Council of Churches.

During the decade of the 1990s, there was explosive growth among Pentecostal denominations in Chile. Statistics indicated that there were approximately 5.6 million members in the various Charismatic, Pentecostal, and independent groups. The Church of God (Cleveland) did begin work in Chile, seeking to support national Pentecostal groups, but national churches and leaders often resisted the presence of foreign Pentecostal missions.

The enormous growth of Protestantism in this region is a landmark in the history of missions in Latin America. Protestants make significant contributions to different ecumenical movements. From the Latin American Council of Churches to mission organizations such as Cooperación Misionera Iberoamericana (COMIBAM), Protestants and Pentecostals engaged in Christian missionary work, though they were frequently at odds among themselves.

C. Christianity in the Andean Region

1. Roman Catholicism

Andean popular Catholicism, particularly in rural areas, was strongly rooted in ancient cosmic beliefs. In the cities, it was much more formal and conservative, although there were also some charismatic expressions. As elsewhere in Latin America, Roman Catholicism moved from extreme conservatism in the early nineteenth century to creative renewal in the twenty-first. One should also note that the region is marked by frequent movement from one religious expression to another: ecumenical Protestantism, Pentecostalism, Catholicism, indigenous religions, and new-age religions—a reality present in several countries in Latin America.

Throughout the nineteenth century and well into the twentieth, the Bolivian government continued claiming the right of national patronage over the church; and although Rome did not expressly accept such claims, it did in fact respect them. In 1871, immigrant colonies were granted freedom of worship, and in 1905, this was extended to everyone in the nation. In Perú, too, the government claimed the patronage over the church that the Crown had enjoyed. Pope Pius IX acknowledged this claim with some limitations. It was not until 1915 that freedom of worship was the law of the land. In Ecuador, under the iron-fisted ultraconservative government of Gabriel García Moreno, a concordat was signed with Rome in 1862. This gave Rome more authority over the church in Ecuador than during the colonial period. This continued until the liberal revolution of 1895, when measures were taken that infringed on what the Catholic Church thought were its rights. Debates and battles continued until 1946, when the constitution established the separation between church and state and granted freedom of thought and worship.

As to missions, in Bolivia, the Franciscans, led by Father Andrés Herrero, were the first to restore their missionary work among the indigenous people. This consisted mainly in the establishment of "apostolic schools" such as the ones in Tarija, San José de la Paz, Santa Ana de Sucre, and Potosí. Most of the clergy to serve in these schools came from Europe, for the Bolivian church was not able to produce sufficient priests. In Ecuador, the Franciscans, Salesians, Jesuits, and Dominicans had significant missionary work among the tribes in the eastern jungles, seeking to bring the Amerindian population into full participation in the life of the church at large. In Perú, the Dominican missions in the region of Urubamba abounded with cases of self-denial and sacrifice. The French Redemptorists worked in Huanta and Caracora. Even so, the situation of Catholicism in Perú was precarious, for the lack of national clergy pastoral work. The diocese of Riobamba, also in Perú, led a vast awakening in Catholic missional studies in Latin America. Bishop Leonidas Proaño underscored the right of Amerindians to the land and led radical changes in the manner in which pastoral work was conducted among them. Missionary work in that diocese included agricultural and rural education, radio programs for the peasants, grassroots communities for consciousness raising, and several changes in the liturgy that brought it more in line with indigenous cultures.

The Second Vatican Council brought significant change to missionary work among the native peoples in the region, as missionaries began stressing the need for contextualization. Taking into account the long history of abuse and exploitation that the native peoples had suffered, missionary work centered on accompaniment, particularly in the struggles for land rights. It also affirmed popular religiosity and supported political and cultural resistance to globalization and economic exploitation. Given the migration of many of Indian descent to the cities, the church began offering services of health and education and other forms of support as people went through harsh geographical and cultural transitions.

In 1971, the Peruvian episcopate published the declaration "Justice in the World." This was based on the encyclical *Populorum Progressio*, issued by Paul VI in 1967, as well as on the documents of the Second Assembly of the Latin American Episcopal Conference (CELAM), in Medellin. It responded to the grave political and economic crisis through which the continent was going. Based on a Christian Marxist reading of the situation in Latin America, the document "Justice in the World" was a radical declaration contrasting with what other bishops and Catholic agencies in Latin America were saying and doing. In that document, the Peruvian bishops called for the cessation of a sort of evangelization that destroyed Amerindian cultures, and denounced the power of absent capitalists. It was at the same time that the seminal book by Gustavo Gutiérrez, *Theology of Liberation*, was published, thus giving new impetus to revolutionary Christian endeavors.

As a result of this renewal and of the growing Pentecostal presence, some Catholic parishes joined the Catholic charismatic movement, affirming both their traditional faith and their renewing experience of the presence of the Holy Spirit. This sort of Catholicism emphasizes missionary work in both evangelization and justice, although it tends to stress the former. In this process of renewal, the Maryknoll Fathers, present in Bolivia since the second half of the twentieth century, have played an important role. Although the outcome of all these developments is still unknown, there is no doubt that the Catholic Church among the indigenous peoples is helping believers practice the Christian faith in new ways.

2. Protestantism

The Andean region did not have large numbers of Protestant immigrants, and therefore most of the early growth of Protestantism in the area was the result of missionary work. James (Diego) Thomson (1788–1854) arrived in Perú in 1822 at the invitation of José de San Martín. There he distributed Bibles and, with the help a Catholic priest, organized two schools. His work was generally well received by the population and by most of the clergy, who were not opposed to the public sale of Scripture. Thanks to Thomson's prompting, the Gospel of St. Luke was translated into Quechua. In 1833, the Reverend Lino Abeledo was sent by the British and Foreign Bible Society to take Bibles into Bolivia. At the border, the authorities confiscated their Bibles, and then health reasons seem to have kept them from going far into the country. Eventually the courts declared that the laws of the land did not forbid the importation of Bibles. Also in 1883, there was a visit to Bolivia by agents of the American Bible Society. They managed to traverse the entire country and eventually reach Chile, selling and distributing Bibles along the way. Among this group were Andrew Milne (1838–54)—who would later disappear while on a missionary journey—Francisco Penzotti (1851–1925), and a Bible distributor by the name of Gandolfo. The following year, Penzotti returned with two other Bible distributors. Under the leadership of Lucas Mathews, translations of the Bible into Quechua and Aymara were produced but were not immediately published. In spite of all these efforts, and mostly due to political vicissitudes and to the resistance of conservative governments, it was only in 1901 that the British and Foreign Bible Society established its first permanent agency in Perú.

After those early years, various Protestant denominations were able to establish a foothold in the area. The first Protestant church to settle permanently in Perú was the Methodist Church, thanks to the zeal and perseverance of Francisco Penzotti, who was convinced that it was necessary to begin preaching in Spanish. He was granted permission to use an old Anglican church that had been built by immigrants, but he had to leave this site when the Catholic clergy threatened to bomb it. He then continued his work in an old warehouse. Since the law did not allow the celebration of public Protestant worship, he distributed admission tickets beforehand to those who wished to participate, thus legally turning the service into a private meeting. He had to face staunch opposition from the clergy and from the ultraconservative elements that at that point ruled the nation. Constantly persecuted, he was jailed twice. In response to international media pressure headed by the *New York Herald*, Penzotti was released and thereafter had a limited measure of freedom to preach the gospel. In 1890, his congregation was organized as a Methodist church.

Beginning in 1921, the South American Indian Mission centered its missionary effort in the interior of Perú. The same is true of the Wycliffe Bible Translators, often known in Latin America as the Summer Language Institute. This latter organization had the largest number of missionaries in Perú, conducting work among more than forty different tribes, mostly on the eastern slopes of the Andes.

The history of the beginnings of Protestantism in Ecuador is parallel to that in other countries, and it also includes the same names as in Argentina, Uruguay, Chile, and Perú—names such as Penzotti and Milne, who made unsuccessful attempts to introduce Bibles into Ecuador. President Eloy Alfaro supported North American missionary W. E. Reed, who arrived in 1896 as a representative of the Missionary Union of the Gospel. Reed and his work later joined the Christian Missionary Alliance.

The first to establish permanent work in Bolivia were Canadian Baptists, whose first missionary was Archibald Brownlee Reekie (1867–1942). After a short visit to Bolivia in 1896, Reekie began his permanent work three years later. The church he established in Oruro is the oldest Protestant church in the country. Though they focused on preaching and founding churches, the Canadian Baptists did open several centers for education and medical services, as well as one devoted to agriculture. They also contributed to land-reform policies in the country.

Methodist work in Bolivia began before the Baptists arrived, when William (Guillermo) Taylor undertook the evangelization of the Pacific Coast. But, since the areas where Taylor worked later became part of Chile, it is fair to say that the first Methodist to preach in what today is Bolivia was Juan Francisco Thomson, whom we have already met in the Southern Cone, and who in 1890 and 1891 preached in La Paz. For many years, the Methodist church there centered its attention on the creation of schools and on medical work rather than on developing congregations. Its main educational centers were the Institutos Americanos in La Paz (1907) and Cochabamba (1912). In the medical field, the Methodists founded the Pfeiffer Memorial Hospital and the American Clinic.

The twentieth century saw the beginning of new missionary enterprises. The Bolivian Indian Mission was patterned after the China Inland Mission. It was organized in 1907, and fifty years later it still had fewer than 1,000 members. As elsewhere throughout the globe, the need for church union and collaboration was also felt in Bolivia. The ecumenical organization United Evangelical Churches was organized in 1951 and included most Protestant bodies.

Missionary work in Ecuador received new energies in 1945, when the Presbyterian Church in the United States, the Reformed Evangelical Church, the United Presbyterian Church, and the Church of the Brethren joined to create the United Andean Indian Mission. Its attention centered on projects of education, health, and agricultural development rather than on evangelization. Toward the end of the twentieth century and early in the twenty-first, a number of evangelical conservative missions such as the Summer Linguistic Institute, the South American Mission, and the New Tribes Mission began working both in the translation of the Bible and in the founding of independent congregations. Many of these groups clashed with Catholics and other Protestants of more ecumenical inclination, who accused them of cultural imposition and even cultural genocide. There was also a wide network of radio programming into the interior of Ecuador, trying to reach the native population. Foremost among these was the Voice of the Andes, a pioneer radio station transmitting educational and Christian programs in several languages. In more recent times, due to violence related to cocaine as well as to a growing resentment against the United States, Protestant missionaries have often found themselves in situations of violence.

In the second half of the twentieth century, Pentecostal churches had active work evangelizing and organizing churches both in the cities and in the interior of the region. The network of Pentecostals and other charismatic groups was growing rapidly. Many of these churches and ecclesial networks created a new religious fervor that was often joined with a spirit of unity and of community work. An example was the Puerto Rican Movimiento Misionero Mundial, which focused on Bolivia and was engaged both in organizing new congregations and in supporting mineworkers in their struggles. Several Pentecostal denominations began work in Perú. Eventually the Assemblies of God would become the largest of the Protestant churches in the nation. Other churches that broke away from the Assemblies were also growing. Foremost among these was the Autonomous Pentecostal Church of Perú, with slightly over eighty congregations. At the same time, several independent movements, as well as others connected with nondenominational missionary agencies in the United States and Europe, continued growing, particularly among the Amerindian population. Two of these were the Christian Community of Living Water and the Evangelical Peruvian Church. The latter was originally the result of a Scottish Presbyterian mission.

Early in the twenty-first century, the Assemblies of God, as well as other Pentecostal denominations and independent charismatic groups, were growing quite rapidly. Missionaries from Korea came to work among Koreans and other Asian immigrants and among Amerindians who had migrated to the cities. At the same time, Quechuas were conducting work of evangelization throughout the region.

Various groups promoting the "gospel of prosperity" flourished in an area plagued by poverty. The theology of these neo-Pentecostal groups often connects with the conditions and the traditions of the indigenous population and of those of African descent. Foremost among these is the Universal Church of the Kingdom of God, originally from Brazil, which has large congregations in all urban centers in the area. It is clear that in the midst of poverty, Pentecostal churches—those that are part of worldwide movements such as the Assemblies of God and the Church of the Foursquare Gospel, those belonging to national organizations, and even those proclaiming God-given prosperity—will have an important effect in the future.

This region has played an important role in the ecumenical movement. Perú hosted a series of ecumenical and missionary gatherings that have been significant for the entire continent. The Second Evangelical Latin American Conference (CELA II) was held there in 1961. Part of what was discussed was the need to redefine evangelization as having to do with the entire human situation in the continent. This gathering began to establish closer connections between Latin American theology and its social and economic environment. It was partly as a result of that conference, as well as of various developments in ecumenical Protestantism throughout the world, that in the same year of 1961, two important ecumenical movements were organized at a gathering in Huampaní. They are both characterized by lay participation and by their strong criticism of the attitude of the church regarding social matters. These two organizations are the Latin American Board for Church and Society (ISAL) and the Latin American Evangelical Commission on Christian Education (CELADEC). Both would play an important role at the Third Latin American Conference (CELA III, celebrated in Buenos Aires), and later in the birth of the Latin American Council of Churches (CLAI) in 1978, as well as in its second assembly in Lima in 1982.

Perú was also the host for the Second Latin American Conference on Evangelization (CLADE II)—the first congress had been held in Bogota in 1969 and led to the creation of the Latin American Theological Fraternity. This gathering took place in Huampaní in 1979, where the attendance of more than 200 delegates represented more than thirty-five denominations. Their main agenda was to discuss the challenge of evangelization in Latin America. Taking the contextual reality of Latin America quite seriously, as well as the outcome of the meeting of the Latin American Council of Churches in Oaxtepec in 1978 and the third gathering of the Latin American Episcopal Conference (CELAM, 1979), this congress led to a critical evaluation of evangelization in Latin America and joined the voices of the worldwide ecumenical movement as well as of the Latin American Catholic Church regarding the difficult conditions of life in the continent and the mission of the church in that context. In the midst of political conflicts, this congress sought to rediscover the meaning of the gospel and of Christian hope for the people of Latin America.

Quito has also hosted several continent-wide mission conferences. The Third and Fourth Latin American Congress on Evangelization (CLADE III in 1992, and CLADE IV in 2000) revealed the growing consciousness among Protestants on issues regarding the relationship between the gospel and indigenous cultures. Both congresses sought new models and strategies for mission and evangelization in various contexts in Latin America. Quito also became the headquarters for the Latin American Council of Churches (CLAI) as well as for a number of regional and national ecumenical organizations, such as the Ecuadorian Evangelical Confraternity.

D. Christianity in Colombia, Panama, and Venezuela

Since throughout the nineteenth century, Panama was part of Colombia both politically and ecclesiastically, it is discussed in this section, rather than under Central America.

1. Roman Catholicism

During the second half of the nineteenth century and the first half of the twentieth, religion became a source of political conflict in Colombia, for one of the main differences between liberals and conservatives had to do with their varying positions regarding the relationship between church and state. Naturally, throughout the nineteenth century, Panama followed the religious policies established by Colombia, of which it was part. But at the time of its independence in 1904, freedom of worship was guaranteed. Even so, Colombia witnessed periods of religious violence and persecution to which we shall return.

No country in Latin America has been more subjected to organized Catholic influence in political matters than Colombia. As a reminder of its traditional religion, the nation has repeatedly been officially dedicated to the Sacred Heart of Jesus. Except in some isolated instances, which have become more common after the Second Vatican Council, most of the clergy do not seem to be aware of being out of step with the times.

Early in the nineteenth century and as a consequence of Spanish decline and the wars of independence, most missionary work in the interior of Colombia and in the jungles of Panama was abandoned. However, by the middle of that century, the Catholic missionary effort was gaining impetus, particularly after the concordat of 1887 determined that missions would be subsidized by the government. In 1953, out of forty-one ecclesiastical jurisdictions in Colombia, eighteen were considered mission territories. In those territories, covering some

845,000 square kilometers, there were 250 priests working, but most of them were foreigners.

During the second half of the twentieth century, the life of the Catholic Church in Colombia was full of contradictions. On the one hand, a series of eucharistic and Marian congresses reinforced the conservatism of the church. These congresses made much of opposition to communism and to any form of revolution and emphasized traditional Catholic doctrine, particularly social doctrine. On the other hand, it was in Medellin, Colombia, in 1968 that the CELAM held its second general conference. That event is a landmark in the growing commitment of the Catholic Church in Latin America to solidarity with the poor, affirming and promoting CEBs, denouncing oppression as well as the effects of colonialism, and favoring the liberation of the poor. In Medellin itself, a unique pastoral institute produced and promoted much of the missional strategy and theology for all of Latin America. It was only in 1970 that the first Colombian Amerindian—a member of the Paez tribe—was ordained as a priest.

Venezuela pursued a policy of close union between church and state, the latter claiming the right of patronage over the former. Given the scarcity of bishops and priests, as well as its subjection to the government, the church lost prestige and power. At the end of the nineteenth century, under the dictatorship of Antonio Guzmán Blanco, there was an attempt to create a national Catholic Church independent of Rome. Throughout this period, missionary efforts were few and weak.

Catholic missionary work among the original inhabitants of Venezuela, who were concentrated in the south of the country, began anew in 1891, when the government invited the Capuchin Fathers to take charge of missions among the Indians. This work has been quite fruitful, and throughout the twentieth century it continued reaching areas where Christian preaching had not been heard before. Other religious orders had come to support the work of the Capuchins. Catholic growth in Venezuela was due mostly to charismatic Catholics and to work among indigenous peoples both in the interior and in the major cities.

2. Protestantism

The first Protestants to settle in what is now Colombia were immigrants—mostly Anglo-Saxons and English-speaking blacks from the Caribbean—who began arriving in the seventeenth century and settled on the islands of San Andres, Providencia, and Santa Catalina. While these islands are closer to Nicaragua than to Colombia, and although English is the dominant language, in 1803, they were placed under the jurisdiction of the vicariate of Santa Fe in Colombia, and they eventually became part of the present Republic of Colombia. Most of the inhabitants of these islands are Protestant, and their culture is quite different from that of the rest of Colombia or of Latin America as a whole.

James (Diego) Thomson, whom we have already met in several other countries, was the first Protestant missionary in Colombia. In 1825, he visited Bogota, where liberal members of the government and of the clergy received him well. There he had one of the greatest successes of his career, for he was able to found a Colombian Bible society with the support of both the government and the Roman Catholic hierarchy.

In 1855, Catalonian ex-friar Ramon Montsalvatge (1815– ?), who had been ordained as a Protestant minister in Geneva, was shipwrecked near Cartagena. His welcome there was such that rather than continuing to Venezuela, which was his original plan, he decided to remain in Cartagena. There he preached for more than twelve years and was able to gather a small nucleus of Protestant believers. Unfortunately, not much more is known about the rest of his life nor about the congregation that he founded.

Apart from these forerunners, the founder of Protestantism in Colombia was Presbyterian missionary Henry Barrington Pratt (1809–1925). While he was a student at Princeton Theological Seminary, Pratt had decided to serve as a missionary in western Africa, but a series of events led him to accept a call from the Board of Foreign Missions of the Presbyterian Church to work in Colombia, and he set to the task of learning Spanish in preparation for his mission. Pratt worked in Colombia from 1856 to 1859 and then again from 1869 until 1878. During that time, with the help of other missionaries who joined him, he produced a large quantity of Protestant literature—including the Bible translation known as the *Versión Moderna*. The first Protestant church was organized in Bogota in 1861, at a time when Pratt was absent due to the Civil War in the United States. At that point, all of its members were foreigners. The first two Colombians joined the church in 1865.

The Presbyterian Church has continued work in Colombia ever since. In 1877, it founded the Colegio Americano in Bogota, and shortly thereafter similar institutions were founded in other cities. The Synod of Colombia was organized in 1937, and this eventually developed into an independent church—although with rather difficult frictions and clashes between foreigners and nationals in the decades of 1960 and 1970. The Presbyterian Church in Colombia has been noted for its work in education and for the excellent training of many of its pastors. Early in the twenty-first century, it had some 26,000 members in slightly over 70 congregations and kept close ties with the Presbyterian Church in the United States.

The Missionary Evangelical Union began working in Colombia in 1908. Its first missionary was Charles Chapman, who had previously worked in the Ecuadorian jungles. Chapman and other missionaries who joined him began their work as Bible distributors, traveling throughout the country. He finally settled in Cali, and from there he expanded the work to Palmira, which became a center for missions to the indigenous population in the interior of the country. Chapman died in Palmira in 1952, but by then he had organized several congregations and schools and had also established a printing press and a clinic that he named Maranatha. When violence broke out in 1948, the area where Chapman had been working was one of the most affected, and therefore members of the Missionary Evangelical Union suffered and witnessed some of the worst atrocities of that time. Even so, the movement continued growing, although at a moderate rate. At the beginning of the twenty-first century, it had some 207 congregations and more than 15,000 members.

Other denominations working in Colombia are the Christian Missionary Alliance, the Assemblies of God, the Seventh-day Adventists, the Church of the Foursquare Gospel, the United Pentecostal Church of Colombia, and the Baptists. The Christian Missionary Alliance began work in Colombia in the third decade of the twentieth century. It is one of the denominations that has experienced the most rapid growth, for in 1957, it had 1,145 members and 71 places of worship, and half a century later these figures had risen to 24,000 and more than 340. The Assemblies of God reached Colombia in 1930 and by the end of that century had a membership of more than 140,000, as well as a bookstore that served most Protestant groups in the country. The Adventists arrived at Colombia in 1921 and worked mostly in the islands of San Andres and Providencia, although later they began working also on the mainland. In 1970, it was estimated that they had 60,000 members, and by the year 2000, they had more than 200,000. The Church of the Foursquare Gospel began working in Colombia in 1942, and sixty years later it had 95,000 members. Its missionary work centered on people marginalized and in the slums of the major cities. The United Pentecostal Church of Colombia was the result of a schism within the Presbyterian Church of Colombia in 1969, mostly over the matter of control by North American missionaries. By 2004, it had 230,000 members and more than 1,000 congregations. The

Southern Baptists reached Colombia in 1941 and worked mostly in the cities, particularly Barranquilla, where they had a hospital and a small seminary. They founded in Cali the Seminario Bautista Teológico Internacional, one of the most prestigious institutions of that nature in Colombia. This group eventually became independent from the Southern Baptists in the United States, and it made a significant contribution to the training of pastors, not only for Baptist congregations, but also for several other denominations, both in Colombia and beyond. Some of the leaders of the Baptist Church in Colombia raised a prophetic voice in the midst of the violence reigning in the country and were active participants in the ecumenical movement, including the CLAI.

During the latter third of the twentieth century, Protestant growth in Colombia was hindered by violence and other factors—although by the beginning of the twenty-first century, the situation had changed and growth had accelerated. The violence generated a need for unity, and in 1950, the Evangelical Confederation of Colombia was created.

The violence of the early second half of the twentieth century is certainly one of the most tragic chapters in the history of the church in the twentieth century—more so since it was persecution of Christians against other Christians. Roman Catholics claim—with some justification—that what happened was due not only to religious differences but also to the liberal political convictions of many. On their side, Protestants affirm—and can prove—that repeatedly it was Catholic authorities who incited the masses to violence.

CLADE I gathered in Bogota in 1969. The agenda for this gathering was closely tied to the Third Latin American Evangelical Conference, which had gathered in Buenos Aires, and to the Second Conference of the CELAM, which gathered in Medellin the year before. This was probably the most widely represented gathering of Protestants that had taken place in Latin America. The conference recognized the strong evangelizing work of Pentecostal churches and, at the same time, the need for missionary work to take into account the political and social conditions of Latin America. As a result of this meeting, the Latin American Theological Fraternity was organized in 1970 in Cochabamba, Bolivia. This is a body devoted to theological reflection on the mission of the church in Latin America.

Unfortunately, Colombia is still in the grip of violence. During the last decades of the twentieth century and the first years of the twenty-first, Protestant churches found themselves in an ambivalent situation. Church growth was significant among many denominations, particularly those of Pentecostal, neo-Pentecostal, or Charismatic origins or inclinations. At the same time, however, churches had to find ways to live and witness in a context of violence related to guerillas, drug traffic, and battles between the government and large cartels of drug traffickers.

In 2001, the CLAI held its fifth assembly in Barranquilla. Items discussed in that assembly included the explosive growth of movements preaching the gospel of prosperity, the crisis of liberation theology, the challenge posed by the traffic in drugs, and the North American "Colombia Plan" to stop the production of drugs and to interdict traffic in them—a plan that seemed to be the centerpiece of North American policy in Colombia.

The first Protestants in Panama were Methodists who had emigrated from the British Caribbean as early as 1815. Between 1855 and 1900, more than 30,000 Caribbean blacks moved to Panama in order to work in agriculture; this flow of population increased as the canal was being built. The Methodist Synod of Jamaica sent missionaries to tend to the needs of these immigrants, and the Baptist Missionary Society of Jamaica did likewise. The first Methodist missionary from the United States arrived in 1877. Apparently Penzotti preached in Panama in 1886. But this was the limit of North American Methodist presence until 1905, when J. C. Elkins was appointed as a missionary to Panama. Methodist work developed slowly.

Other groups and traditions present in Panama are the Episcopal Church, the Baptists—particularly the Southern Baptists—the Salvation Army, the International Church of the Foursquare Gospel, and the Assemblies of God. As in many countries in Latin America, some denominations have grown very little, while there has been significant growth among Pentecostals, who surpassed half a million. In 1916, the First Congress on Christian Work in Latin America was held in Panama. This meeting was the reaction to the exclusion of Latin America from Edinburgh 1910.

Venezuela is one of the two Latin American countries where Protestantism has enjoyed less numeric success—the other being Ecuador. The first missionary efforts were the work of Bible societies. In 1886, Milne and Penzotti visited the country, which began an uninterrupted presence of Bible distributors in Venezuela. Most missionary work in Venezuela began toward the end of the nineteenth century. The first to arrive seem to have been the Southern Methodists, who began their work in 1890 and in 1900 ceded it to the Presbyterians. Presbyterian work has continued in Venezuela since that time, but its numeric growth has not been spectacular. At roughly the same time as the Methodists, the Canadian Brethren began work in Venezuela. Later came the Evangelical Alliance Missions, the Plymouth Brethren, the Southern Baptists, the Assemblies of God, the New Tribes Mission, and the Orinoco River Mission. After almost a century of work in Venezuela, the Brethren, who arrived in the country in 1910 and focused on traditional evangelization as well as on education and economic development projects, were one of the major denominations of the country. However, the largest Protestant church in Venezuela is the Assemblies of God, whose work began in 1916. The Assemblies of God soon established Bible institutes for the formation of national clerical and lay leadership and did extensive work among the Guajiro natives.

As in other countries of Latin America, several autochthonous churches have emerged with national leadership. The oldest of these, the Iglesia Aleluya, was founded toward the end of the nineteenth century. Another is the Native Venezuelan Church, also known as the Iglesia Bethel. These are small denominations whose effect on the country is minimal. The Evangelical Pentecostal Union Church, which was founded in the middle of the twentieth century, is both Pentecostal and profoundly ecumenical. Its missionary projects—mostly among the Guajiros—seek a Pentecostal identity deeply rooted in Venezuelan history and culture. Its many projects include evangelization, economic development cooperatives, the training of national leadership, and work among impoverished communities in urban centers. In 1970, it had 10,000 members, and 14,000 in 1995. Its ecumenical commitment is shown in its active participation in the Evangelical Council of Venezuela, which was founded in 1967, as well as in the CLAI and the Ecumenical Pentecostal Conference in Latin America.

Finally, one must note that other religious movements in the area present a significant challenge for all Christian churches. One of these is the rebirth and growth of spiritism and of Afro-Caribbean religious traditions. Another challenge is the Bahai, which claims that all religions are parallel roads to God; therefore, the Bahai faith, which includes all of them, is superior to the rest. Since these religions are rather flexible, there are believers who attend Christian churches and also partake of the religious ceremonies of these various groups.

E. Christianity in Brazil

1. Roman Catholicism

The general weakness of the church in Brazil after independence was due not to conflicts over national patronage or the freedom of Mendicant Orders, but rather to the weakness of the church itself during the colonial period. This is reflected in the slowness with which the ecclesiastical hierarchy of Brazil was established, both before and after independence. A hundred years into the colonial period, Brazil only had one bishopric, in San Salvador; a hundred years later, Brazil had seven. It took another century for the number of bishoprics to reach ten. Clearly, the development of the hierarchy did not keep pace with the development of the country in general.

During the empire, which was proclaimed in 1822, the Brazilian government progressively took over some of the ancient rights of the church. Pedro II proscribed religious orders owing their allegiance to others not in Brazil. By then, the few missions that had existed earlier had been almost completely abandoned. During the last twenty years of Pedro II's government, the Franciscans worked in the interior of the country, the Capuchins along the coast, and the Dominicans in the region of Alto Araguay—although all this work was supervised by the state. In 1883, the Salesians entered the country, working particularly in Matto Grosso, and the Redemptorists came in 1894, to work mostly in Minas and Goias.

The Brazilian Republic was proclaimed in 1889. Two years later, in 1891, the constitution established the separation of church and state, freedom of worship and religious gatherings, and the right of all confessions to official governmental recognition.

Toward the end of the nineteenth century and the beginning of the twentieth, missionaries from various European countries once again undertook the evangelization of the indigenous population. By 1956, there were thirty-two vast territories that the church still considered mission fields. Moreover, the greatest missionary task was no longer among the tribes of the interior as much as it was among the large, purely nominally Catholic population.

In 1964, a coup d'état turned the government over to a military junta. Conservative groups such as the Opus Dei, the Crusade for the Family Rosary, and the Group for the Restoration of the Rosary contributed to the fall of the democratic government. However, this was not the attitude of the entire church, and by 1967, tensions between the military regime and the church were such that the church claimed it was being persecuted, and therefore it broke with the government. This led to a series of confrontations and conflicts between the church hierarchy and the government, as well as within the membership of the church itself, for the hierarchy had to face inner dissension supported by Catholic conservative agencies that favored the military government.

Pressure and persecution from the government almost led to the disappearance of progressive movements such as Catholic Action and the various efforts of popular education that had been taking place before. Priests, nuns, and bishops supporting these groups and other similar Catholic organizations were killed.

By 1980, the conflict had reached such a point that the government expelled from the country a large number of missionaries involved in agrarian reform and the protection of peasants' rights. Even within that context, the church developed an impressive missionary work that would eventually lead to the fall of the military dictatorship.

During the latter half of the twentieth century, Brazilian Catholicism went through a profound renewal through the work of the grassroots ecclesial communities (CEBs). The people themselves took Scripture and interpreted it from a political perspective as they sought justice for the millions impoverished in the country. The pedagogical methodology of Paulo Freire created in the people a new sense that they were protagonists in the history of Brazil, and the church played an important role in that process. Missionary work turned toward liberation, justice, and resistance against oppression, pointing out that the gospel had much to say about problems such as military dictatorship, class struggle, the right of peasants to the land, the right to work, injustice in the distribution of wealth, and the lack of education and other basic resources.

This new missionary vitality was also reflected in profound changes in the structure of the church itself. Centers of pastoral formation were created for training a laity profoundly committed to the church and to its quest for justice. The participation of women—nuns as well as laywomen—in CEBs created new space for reflection on the role of women in the church. The church began acknowledging the importance of the indigenous and black population in the contextualization of the gospel, promoting and supporting the development of new liturgical forms incarnate in the cultures of these marginalized people who had often been ignored.

An outstanding example of this attitude on the part of the church was Bishop Dom Hélder Câmara, a champion for the poor and the marginalized. As bishop of Recife, and a key leader in the formation of the Latin American Episcopal Conference (CELAM), as well as of several other Catholic organizations in the continent and of the national and international network that contributed to overthrowing the dictatorship, Câmara not only promoted Latin American liberation theology but also encouraged what would later be called the "new evangelization"—a phrase that was taken up at the meeting of CELAM in Santo Domingo in 1992. This new evangelization acknowledges the violent history of earlier evangelization in Latin America and the manner in which such evangelization affects the poor and marginalized. At the same time, it calls for a new attempt to evangelize the continent within the context of the actual life of marginalized people and cultures. It was under the leadership of Dom Hélder Câmara that the Quilombos mass was developed. This is a liturgy rooted in the experience of Brazilian blacks in Recife and Bahia, and in the history of slavery as well as of continued Afro-Brazilian religious practices.

Toward the end of the twentieth century and early in the twenty-first, missionary work focused on ecology. National as well as foreign missionaries began working jointly with peasants and Amerindians in the protection of the Amazon basin. This mission moves in two directions: on the one hand, it stresses the integrity of creation and its right to justice and freedom from the exploitation of its resources; on the other hand, it also protects the rights of the ancient cultures still surviving in the jungles of the Amazon.

While all of this was taking place late in the twentieth century and early in the twenty-first, one must also acknowledge the more conservative elements within the Catholic Church. The Opus Dei, various charismatic movements, family-oriented programs, and other similar groups worked mostly in the cities and through mass media in order to produce what they understood to be a holistic evangelization. They agreed with the more progressive wing of the church on the need to go beyond a nominal Catholic religiosity. But they were also in tension with the more socially oriented proposals of the new evangelization. One of their emphases was purifying Catholic faith from the influence of Kardec-style spiritism, as well as from Afro-Brazilian practices such as Candomble and Umbanda, while at the same time opposing the rampant secularization and individualism that are a result of the rapid development of capitalism in the nation.

It is also significant to note that the Japanese community of Brazil amounted to 1.3 million people. Since these were mostly Roman Catholics, there were twice as many Catholic-Japanese in Brazil as there were in Japan.

2. Protestantism

The most notable early missionary to Brazil was the Scotsman Robert Reid Kalley (1809–88). It was he who in 1858 baptized the first Brazilian Protestant. This brought about the opposition of the Catholic clergy, but Kalley defended himself with both wisdom and tact. Through his work, and through a series of cases that were taken before the courts, Protestantism was legally acknowledged, and even

Protestant marriages were granted civil validity. In Rio de Janeiro, Kalley founded the Igreja Evangelica Fluminense.

In 1859, the Presbyterian Church in the United States began working in Brazil. Its founder was A. G. Simonton (1831–67), a young North American minister. At first Presbyterian work centered in Rio and then extended to São Paulo. Simonton died in 1867, but two years earlier, the presbytery of Rio de Janeiro had been organized and had ordained ex-Catholic priest José Manuel da Conceiçâo, who would be one of the most remarkable figures in the early years of Protestantism in Brazil.

José Manuel da Conceiçâo was born in São Paulo in 1822 and was ordained a priest when he was twenty-three years old. At forty years of age, he went through a profound spiritual crisis similar to Luther's, precisely on the matter of justification by faith and how this relates to the sale of indulgences and the salvific value of meritorious works. In 1864, he was baptized in the Presbyterian Church of Rio de Janeiro. After his baptism, he wrote "Evangelical Profession of Faith," in which he told of his spiritual crisis and the reasons why he had embraced Protestantism. He then went to Brotas, the last parish where he served as a priest. There he began preaching his new message and founded a Presbyterian church that grew rapidly and that eventually became a missionary center from which other churches were founded. After organizing the Presbyterian Church in Brotas, Conceiçâo began an itinerant life, preaching in various places, but particularly where he had previously served as a priest. Soon the missionaries began opposing Conceiçâo's strategy, for he did not seem capable of moving from evangelization to the actual organization of a church. Conceiçâo was not totally anti-Catholic, but rather tried to present a message that was the culmination and purification of what his hearers had previously heard from their ancestors.

Brazilian Presbyterianism continued developing. But this development was not painless. Conflicts between Brazilians and missionaries began toward the end of the nineteenth century. The main figure among the proponents of an autonomous church was Eduardo Carlos Pereira, with the able support of his close friend Remigio de Cerqueira Leite. Although Brazilian pastors were still a minority, Pereira was able to increase their influence by taking into account and making use of divisions within missionary ranks between those from the North and those from the South of the United States. Placing themselves between the two groups, and therefore having a deciding effect, the small Brazilian nucleus had to be taken into account. At the time there was a great outburst of nationalist sentiment, and this also awakened interest in the formation of an autonomous Presbyterian church.

At first Pereira and his followers simply founded the Brazilian Society for Evangelical Tracts, which published small pamphlets written almost exclusively by national pastors. Then he issued "Plan for National Missions." Most of the missionaries from the North of the United States believed that the best method for evangelizing Brazil was to establish schools that would put Brazilian children in contact with North American culture and Protestantism. Pereira, Cerqueira Leite, and their followers urged that the funds employed in this sort of educational work be employed more directly in evangelization, and particularly in the training of Brazilian pastors. His main opponent was Dr. Horace Lane, director of the Mackenzie Institute. Although Pereira had a request sent to the United States suggesting that funds be employed in more direct evangelization, this was not done thanks to the opposition of the northern missionaries. The outcome was the first of a long series of schisms within Brazilian Presbyterianism.

The Episcopal Church in the United States began missionary work in 1888. This mission was established with the consent of Presbyterians, who agreed that the Episcopalians would work in the state of Rio Grande do Sul. The Presbyterian missionary who was working there was withdrawn in order to leave the field open for the Episcopal Church. The first Episcopal service took place in Porto Alegre in 1890. Soon more missionaries followed, and by 1898, there was a resident bishop in Brazil.

The second half of the nineteenth century saw the beginning of several missionary efforts in Brazil. After the Civil War in the United States, many Southerners migrated to Brazil, and the churches from which they came began considering the possibility of sending missionaries to that land. Thus, the Methodist Episcopal Church, South, settled in Brazil in 1870—for the work that other Methodists had begun before had not continued. The same was true of Southern Presbyterians, who came to Brazil in 1871, as well as of Southern Baptists, who began working there in 1881. Toward the end of the century, in 1893, North American Congregationalists organized an agency that they called Help for Brazil.

Protestantism has enjoyed surprising growth in Brazil in part because of national pastors and laity. There are numerous reports of spontaneous conversions resulting from reading the Bible. Immigration has also contributed significantly to the numerical growth of Protestantism in Brazil. Although such migration was not the result of missionary motivations, some of the churches that resulted from it, after developing roots within the people and culture of Brazil, began undertaking missionary work.

In a similar fashion to the Presbyterian Church, but usually in lesser degree, most denominations in Brazil had growth pains having to do with the relationships between foreign missionaries and nationals. Besides the Presbyterian Church, the body that most suffered from this process were the Baptists. The main leader of the nationalist party among the Baptists was Antonio Pereira, who abandoned his denomination and created an independent Baptist organization. But this movement lost much of its impetus when Antonio Pereira returned to the Catholic Church. Shortly thereafter, under the leadership of Adrião Bernandes, a similar movement for ecclesiastical independence began in the north of Brazil, and this led to a much more serious schism than Pereira's. However, the effect of these movements among the Baptist community did not have the same results as among Presbyterians. This was mostly due to the congregational structure of Baptist government, so that Bernandes and his followers developed an extreme Congregationalist stance that they employed to counteract the centralization of power in the hands of foreign missionaries and agencies.

The Pentecostals followed a different method of establishing an autonomous church. Pentecostalism arrived in Brazil in 1911, when some Swedish missionaries began working in Belem. By 2005, the two largest Pentecostal groups were the Assemblies of God and Christian Congregations of Brazil. The first were particularly numerous in the northern sections of the country, while the latter were stronger in the south, particularly in the state of São Paulo and other neighboring areas.

A third group of churches resulted from the arrival of conservative missionaries from the United States after the Second World War. Many of these churches, although certainly growing, did not do so at the same rate as the earlier Pentecostal and Charismatic churches and movements.

Due to repeated divisions, there is an enormous number of different Protestant and Pentecostal churches in Brazil. For instance, the Presbyterian tradition has undergone more than three important schisms—due both to theological and to ideological reasons. The Evangelical Lutheran Church also divided, creating the Evangelical Lutheran Church of Brazil, which related more closely in the United States with the Lutheran Church, Missouri Synod. Many of the smaller Pentecostal churches are the result of divisions within Pentecostalism having to do with doctrinal and ecclesial differences as well as with personality clashes.

The more traditional Protestant churches, as well as many Pentecostal bodies, suffered under the military regime in like manner to the sufferings of the Catholic Church. There were tensions and divisions resulting from the contrast between an understanding of the gospel as having profound justice and social implications and a different understanding that saw the gospel only as a promise of life eternal, with little concern for the present situation of the people. Many Protestant churches did give a strong witness of solidarity and justice in the face of military dictatorship. Such was the witness of the Third Assembly of the CLAI, which was held in Brazil in 1988. Protestant Brazilians, men as well as women, have made significant contributions to a number of ecumenical and evangelical organizations such as the Latin American Council of Churches and the Latin American Theological Fraternity. They have also contributed to international organizations such as the Lausanne movement and the World Council of Churches.

An example of this contribution within the field of mission thought was the theological work of Presbyterian missionary Richard Shaull (1919–2002), who was an important forerunner to Protestant Latin American liberation theology and who saw in Pentecostalism a "new reformation," which the historical churches ought to heed, and a model of mission that took very seriously the preferential option for the poor.

Pentecostalism has grown in Brazil at a surprising rate. There are hundreds of Pentecostal and Charismatic churches in every city as well as in rural areas. As a result of the spread of traditional Pentecostalism, new movements have co-opted the style of classic Pentecostalism, joining it with a spiritualist worldview that is quite common in Brazil, and with a theology of prosperity. The largest national church in Brazil is the Universal Church of the Kingdom of God. This is a clear example of this neo-Pentecostal phenomenon, which promotes itself by promising prosperity and happiness to its members. It is said that this particular church is the largest international corporation with headquarters in Brazil.

Finally, one must note that beginning late in the twentieth century, several Brazilian Protestant churches, traditional as well as Pentecostal, were sending missionaries throughout the world. Brazilian Protestant missionaries were particularly numerous in the United States and Europe, working mostly with Brazilian immigrants in those lands but also seeking to strengthen Christianity in the areas from which they had first received it but where it seemed to be in decline.

F. Christianity in Mesoamerica

1. Central America

This region declared its independence from Mexico in 1823. In 1824 the Federal States of Central America were established until civil war (1838–1840) destroyed the Federation, leading to the present five republics—Guatemala, El Salvador, Honduras, Nicaragua, and Costa Rica. In general, Roman Catholicism followed a process of adjustment and renewal similar to that in the rest of Latin America, and Protestantism entered with the new encouragement and sometimes the support of liberal governments that wished to use it against Catholic conservatism. Also, during the times of the Federal States, the issue of patronage over the church was complicated by debates as to whether such patronage should now belong to the federation or to each particular state.

(a) Roman Catholicism

Mission work in Guatemala centered in two areas: one an "apostolic administration," and the other a "*nullius* prelature." The Maryknoll Fathers and the Franciscans were noted for their work among the poor. However, the situation of Catholicism in Guatemala remained difficult, particularly due to the large proportion of the population completely lacking in pastoral services. At the beginning of the twenty-first century, this situation was improved thanks to a large influx of priests from abroad, although there was some doubt as to how permanent such improvement would be. More permanent solutions were also being sought by promoting lay ministries.

Under the inspiration of the Second Vatican Council and the second meeting of the CELAM, which took place in Medellin in 1968, the liturgy began to be celebrated in Spanish. However, this change was not very useful to the Amerindian population in rural areas. Even before that time, missionary agents had already taken note of the grave crisis produced by poverty among indigenous and mestizo people and had begun to develop cooperatives in order to try to alleviate their situation. This was done mostly under the initiative of the Maryknoll Fathers and the Fathers of the Sacred Heart in the area of Quiche, of Canadian priests in Oriente and Solola, and of Benedictines in Solola.

In the last decades of the twentieth century, mission agents were under attack by dictatorial governments. This was part of a general persecution of grassroots and Amerindian elements struggling for respect of life, human rights, and the right to land. The episcopacy of the country was divided in its response to such conditions, although occasionally a voice was raised demanding integrity and transparency from the government. The earthquakes of 1976 aggravated the crisis with thousands of deaths and over a million refugees. Therefore, mission work now included also the protection and care of Indian refugees, the provision of resources for the needy in Guatemala City, and eventually the return and resettlement of Amerindians in their communities. Poet Julia Esquivel and Amerindian Rigoberta Menchú raised their voices in demanding justice and peace for the Amerindian people as well as for all the oppressed and uprooted.

In El Salvador, responding to a request from the newly born republic, the pope created the diocese of San Salvador in 1842. During the early years of the republic, the conservative party was in power and protected the privileges of the church and the clergy. But in 1871, a liberal reaction took place. This revolution—and the constitution that it produced in 1886—stressed the separation between church and state. From then on, the Salvadoran constitution has guaranteed freedom of worship, public education free from church control, and the legality of civil matrimony.

Late in the 1960s, a new cohort of ministers and missionaries arrived who had been formed by the theology of the Second Vatican Council. Their missional work was focused on grassroots movements, seeking to contribute to the economic and social development of poor and marginalized communities. The church also turned to Bible study, and the Basic Ecclesial Communities (CEBs) became a place for reflection and common work toward liberation. The first CEB in the archdiocese of San Salvador was organized in Suchitoto, and in ten years, there were CEBs scattered all over the city. Missionaries—both men and women—were killed in retaliation for their community work. Among them were four nuns who were murdered in 1984. Archbishop Oscar Arnulfo Romero, who developed a pastoral practice of accompaniment with the poor and the oppressed, was murdered in 1980 as he was celebrating Mass. In 1989, even after the peace process had begun, four Jesuit priests were murdered together with their housekeeper and her daughter.

Roman Catholicism seemed to be divided into three main sectors: a traditional Catholicism favored mostly by the middle and higher classes; a second, grassroots Catholicism emphasizing the memory of a period of political militancy, but still living in a political vacuum; and a third sort-of Catholicism that included ancient indigenous traditions. While most of the diocesan clergy was Salvadoran, the majority of the regular clergy, who were the ones entrusted with most of the mission work, were foreigners, and this resulted in greater tensions in missionary work.

The condition of the church in Honduras was depressing. Mission work took place mostly in the apostolic vicariate of San Pedro Sula and in the *nullius* prelature of the Immaculate Conception of Olancho. All the priests working in these judicatories were foreigners. However, after the decade of the 1960s, the church became more active in mission. This has taken the form of social community projects, lay apostolates, economic and educational development projects, the integration of the liturgy into the life and culture of parishes and communities, a quest for a pastoral practice that is more contextual, and greater participation of the laity in the ministry of the church.

In Nicaragua, it was in 1894, during José Santos Zelaya's dictatorship, that laws were issued against the traditional privileges of the church and its clergy. Most mission work was carried on in the area of Bluefields, which was still an apostolic vicariate and had not been raised to the category of a diocese. Although mission work was valuable, most of the mission agents in Bluefields were foreigners.

Under the dictatorship of Somoza, toward the end of the decade of the 1960s and early in the next, the Capuchins began CEBs. In these a lay leadership was formed that understood the reality of poverty and supported various community projects in the interior of the country. It was at that time that Ernesto Cardenal conducted his work in Solentiname. The discussions of biblical texts that took place there have been published, and they clearly show the manner in which CEBs understood the relationship among religion and social and political change.

Relationships between church and state in Costa Rica were more cordial than in the rest of Central America. Even so, church life in Costa Rica has not been much better than in its neighboring countries, and by 1962, the church was in worse condition than it had been fifty years earlier.

Because of its political stability, Costa Rica became the seat for a number of ecumenical organizations such as the Ecumenical Department of Research (DEI), whose publications and grassroots workshops have contributed to the political and religious formation of hundreds of Catholic leaders as well as some Protestants. During the latter half of the twentieth century, the church in Costa Rica, enjoying a situation of peace that was unique in Central America, played an important role in solidarity with the peace processes in neighboring countries, in the defense of human rights, and in support for refugees coming to Costa Rica as a result of widespread violence in the area.

(b) Protestantism

The first permanent Protestant presence in Guatemala was the result of a visit to New York by liberal president Justo Rufino Barrios. At the invitation of Barrios, the Presbyterian Board of Missions sent missionary John C. Hill, who organized the first Protestant church in the country in 1884. When Hill was forced to return to the United States for health reasons, Edward M. Haymaker succeeded him. From the beginning, Presbyterians in Guatemala were active in education. The same is true of medical work, although the first hospital was not built until 1913.

Having worked both among the Spanish-speaking population or "Ladinos" and the Amerindians—particularly the Quiches and the Mam—the Presbyterians experienced conflicts between the Ladino and the Amerindian presbyteries. The latter have developed educational programs seeking to discover connections between Amerindian culture and Reformed theology. These new theological explorations, and some of the liturgical practices that go with them, have increased the tensions between the two branches of the church.

During the decade of 1960, the Presbyterian Church in Guatemala gave rise to theological education by extension, a model that was soon replicated throughout the world, including in some areas of the United States. This method proposes that ministerial and theological formation emerges and takes place in the context in which ministry takes place. Therefore, rather than taking the student to an educational center, education "goes" to the students. Quite rapidly, with a number of modifications according to different contexts, this became one of the most common methods for ministerial formation throughout Central America.

The Central American Mission began working in Guatemala in 1899, and its pattern was replicated in the region. This was an organization founded in Texas in 1890 by Congregationalist and Dispensationalist Cyrus Scofield (1843–1921) and was first located in Costa Rica. Its principles and organization were patterned after those of the China Inland Mission: it was a mission of faith including workers from different denominations and without the support of a board or budget. One of its institutions was the Robinson Bible Institute established in 1923. The Central America Mission also worked closely with the Wycliffe Bible Translators, making the Bible available in various Indian languages.

The growth of Pentecostal and independent churches in Guatemala has been impressive. By the year 2000, the largest Protestant denomination in Guatemala was the Assemblies of God, with more than a quarter million adherents. The largest national group was the Iglesia Evangélica del Príncipe de Paz, established in 1945. Most of these groups focused on evangelization and on personal holiness, although in varying degrees some of them were also engaged in community services.

The CLAI and the Aboriginal Pastoral Coordinator (COPA) have provided opportunities for dialogue among indigenous people of various Protestant traditions—although Guatemala, which has the largest Amerindian population in the area, has not been consistent in its participation in such meetings.

The American Baptists began working in El Salvador in 1911. They have important schools in San Salvador and Santa Ana, besides missionary work among the Pipil people on the coast. Their initial success was remarkable, with a vibrant church up to 1934. After that time, growth has slowed but still continues.

The Assemblies of God were the fastest-growing denomination in El Salvador. They began work there between 1920 and 1922. Their mission work centers on evangelization and planting of churches. During the times of civil war, and in response to the earthquakes of 1986, the Baptist Association of El Salvador, the Lutheran Church of El Salvador, and the Episcopal Church of El Salvador, together with the CLAI, worked extensively with refugees and other people displaced by war and natural disasters. The martyrs that these churches produced during those times are an eloquent witness to a missionary work that is prophetic and takes risks in solidarity with the needy in difficult times.

The pioneers in mission work in Honduras were the representatives of the Central American Mission. They began working in that country in 1896. When the first missionaries arrived at the village of El Paraíso, they found a group of believers ready to support them. El Paraíso became a center from which many Hondurans set out to evangelize the rest of the nation. As a result, the Central American Mission became one of the largest Protestant denominations in Honduras.

The largest Protestant churches in Honduras are the various Pentecostal denominations—those resulting from foreign missions as well as those that originated in Honduras itself. The largest Protestant denominations in the country are the Assemblies of God and the Iglesia del Príncipe de Paz, which entered Honduras from Guatemala in 1960.

The first Protestant mission in Nicaragua was begun by the Moravian Brothers in 1849, among the Miskitos on the east coast. Protestant work was well received, especially after a princess by the name of Matilda was baptized. From Misquitia, the missionaries entered the lands of the Sumus, whose first converts were baptized in 1878. In both tribes, Moravian work did much to improve education and living conditions in general. The production of Miskito grammars and dictionaries was part of the work of translating the New Testament into that language.

The American Baptists began working in Nicaragua in 1917. Their work centered in Managua, where there are several churches, besides a hospital, schools, and a seminary. From Managua, the movement entered the rest of the country. While their membership has grown significantly, their effect on the country has been out of proportion to their number.

Nicaragua has been marked by ecumenical collaboration among denominations. The Comité Evangélico para Ayuda al Desarrollo (CEPAD), which arose as a response to a devastating earthquake, works in agricultural and economic cooperatives, health and education programs, consciousness raising, mediating among conflicting parties, and support for the needy and the marginalized. During the last years of the Somoza regime and the beginnings of the Sandinista revolution, CEPAD played an important role alleviating and resolving some of the growing tensions among Protestants, thus safeguarding a unity that was quite fragile in the midst of the polarization of the entire country. More recently, and with the support of the Baptist Church, the Martin Luther King University was founded in Managua—the first Protestant university in the country.

In the 1970s, Costa Rica's Protestants accounted for less than one percent of the total population. Much earlier, in 1891, the Central American Mission responded to a call from Costa Rica by sending there its first missionaries. However, the activity of the Central American Mission in Costa Rica has fluctuated. The church resulting from this mission is now called the Asociación de Iglesias Evangélicas Centroamericanas.

The Latin American Mission, organized in 1921, also settled in San José. Its two great figures in the early years were Susan and Henry Strachan (1872–1946/1874–1950). In 1922, this missionary agency founded the Instituto Bíblico, which at first also enjoyed the support and collaboration of the Methodists and of the Central American Mission. This institute eventually became Seminario Bíblico Latinoamericano and later the Universidad Bíblica Latinoamericana.

Thanks to a relatively stable and democratic political tradition, Costa Rica has also served as the seat for ecumenical organizations. In the face of civil war and revolutionary struggles in the region, in 1988, churches and ecumenical organizations produced the document "KAIROS," which called Christian churches to act jointly in supporting struggles for justice, in offering a prophetic voice, and in commitment to the poor and the oppressed.

In short, the Protestant churches in Central America—including Pentecostal churches—have a fragile history that bears the stamp of the many struggles as well as economic and political ambiguities of their context. Although today the polarization of earlier decades seems to be receding, all the churches face the challenge of rebuilding community in the midst of the overwhelming poverty of most of the region.

2. Mexico

(a) Catholicism

In no other country in Latin America has the history of Roman Catholicism been as turbulent as in Mexico. This is due mostly to the fluid relationship between church and state, which at times has been cordial, at other times, practically nonexistent, and on occasion, openly hostile. Mexican independence received decided support from the clergy, which saw in the Spanish constitution of 1812, profoundly influenced by the liberalism of the time, the removal of rights and the privileges of the church. Consequently, by 1829, there were no bishops in Mexico! In 1831, Pope Gregory XVI appointed six bishops for the Mexican church, although at the same time he made it clear that he was doing this *motu propio*, and not as an act of acquiescence to the Mexican claims for national patronage over the church.

By 1883, when Gómez Farías began urging a reformation of the entire nation, relations between church and state became tense. However, the next year, the church regained the privileges it had lost. Such fluctuations continued throughout the first half of the nineteenth century, until the revolution of Ayutla overthrew the dictator Antonio López de Santa Ana. These political vicissitudes during the first half of the nineteenth century resulted in the almost complete disappearance of missionary work within Mexico.

After the Ayutla revolution in 1854, the liberal and anticlerical party began paying more attention to the dispossessed, who were mostly Indians and mestizos and were by far the majority of the population. Liberals saw the dispossessed as exploited by the economic power of the conservatives, and particularly of the church, whose influence was due both to its vast possessions and to the authority it had acquired during the many centuries in which the spiritual life of the people had been under its control. As anticlerical sentiment grew among the less fortunate, ecclesiastical authorities found themselves in an increasingly unsustainable position.

In the second half of the nineteenth century and the beginning of the twentieth, church authorities repeatedly sought alliances with unpopular conservative governments. A violent anticlericalism merged with demands for a constitutional government. This led to revolution and to many acts of violence against the church. When Venustiano Carranza deposed the dictator Hurtas in 1914, a new constitution was drafted that forbid religious institutions from holding profit-making property. Those writing the constitution went beyond his suggestions, declaring that even church buildings were now the property of the state. However, neither Carranza nor later Alvaro Obregón applied the religious laws in all their rigor, for they wished to avoid a prolonged conflict with the clergy and were also aware that the latter had an important role that the government was not yet ready to fulfill, particularly in education.

Although Carranza and Obregón did not apply all the rigor of the constitution of 1917, the Catholic Church always saw that document as a threat. In 1926, when Plutarco Elías Calles became president, the threat became a reality. Reacting to declarations on the part of the Catholic hierarchy that the constitution and the laws regarding religion were unjust, President Calles decided to apply such laws. There followed a series of measures increasingly limiting the freedom and authority of priests. In response, the hierarchy ordered the suspension of all church services. This led to the rebellion of the *cristeros*—rebels who fought against the anti-Catholic laws—and to the attempt on the part of some Roman Catholics to have the United States intervene in Mexican affairs. This seemed to confirm the suspicion on the part of the government that Catholic opposition led to rebellion and perhaps even to treason. In 1929, a sort of armistice was reached. But this only lasted for two years. The precipitating cause of the new conflict was the decision on the part of several state governments—with the support of the federal government—to limit the number of priests who could work within their borders.

However, such constant hostility between church and state could not last in a nation in which the vast majority of the population was Roman Catholic. Although there were many Mexicans who reacted strongly against the excessive power of the church and its hierarchy, there were also many who felt the need for the support of the church in the faith that it had taught them. Thus, very slowly, the conflict between church and state was set aside. The Mexican clergy learned to accept the authority of the government in secular matters. Early in the twenty-first century, churches—both Catholic and Protestant—were once again granted the right to own property. Thus, through a lengthy process that lasted 200 years, Mexican religious history was forever changed. Roman Catholicism—and, to a certain extent, Protestantism—has had to learn how to exist in a context that is deeply religious and at the same time constantly suspicious of organized religion.

Roman Catholicism in Mexico has three important dimensions. The first of these is its expression of devotion to the Virgin of Guadalupe, shared by the vast majority of Roman Catholics, and even by some Protestants and nonbelievers. The second is a Catholicism that includes many elements taken from indigenous traditions, such as may be found in the region of Chiapas. And the third is the more traditional Catholicism of the urban higher and middle classes.

The Roman Catholic Church has also played a role in the defense of native rights, particularly in the state of Chiapas. Archbishop Samuel Ruiz promoted ecumenical work with Protestants, as well as development projects and the protection of the rights of indigenous people to their land. In the midst of serious confrontations with the government, the church has often served as a mediator seeking to alleviate conflict and at the same time maintain its position of solidarity with the native peoples.

Finally, the Roman Catholic Church has also experienced a sort of renewal in some of its sectors through the influence of charismatic groups as well as of more conservative programs for the support of families and traditional family life. There is a growing number of Mexican Catholic missionaries serving elsewhere in the world, particularly in other parts of Latin America, the United States, the Muslim world, and Asia.

(b) Protestantism

The forerunner of Protestantism in Mexico—as in so many other countries in Latin America—was Diego Thomson. He took Bibles to Guanajuato, Guadalajara, Aguascalientes, and Zacatecas. Despite resistance from the government, Thomson was able to continue much of his work on the basis of his acquaintance with some of the most educated people in the city, and also as a representative of the Lancastrian method of education—for in this latter capacity, he had the support of the government.

The penetration of the Bible in Mexico continued even after Thomson's departure through the constant contact between Mexicans and North Americans from 1846 to 1848. In 1873, the American Bible Society was established in Mexico.

The Protestant Episcopal Church in the United States began its work in 1853—that is, four years before Benito Juarez proclaimed freedom of worship. Missionary E. C. Nicholson organized in Chihuahua the Sociedad Apostólica Mexicana. Separately, in 1861, Ramón Lozano and Aguilar Bermúdez founded the Iglesia Mexicana. Eventually these groups came together and became the Iglesia Protestante Episcopal en Mexico.

A forerunner to Presbyterian work, Melinda Rankin (1811–88), an independent missionary, settled at first on the American side of the border, but in 1866, she moved to Monterrey. Six years later, she bequeathed her work to the Congregationalists and Northern Presbyterians from the United States. Her remarkable success was partly due to her ability in organizing and mobilizing Mexicans for the evangelization of their own land.

Northern Presbyterians from the United States began work in Mexico in 1871 in the state of Zacatecas, when a congregation that had resulted from Rankin's missionary work asked for a pastor. Since the Congregationalists could not respond to that request, they asked for help from the Presbyterian Board of Missions in New York. Ten Mexican ministers were ordained in 1883, and at the same time, the first Mexican presbytery was organized. Meanwhile, Southern Presbyterians from the United States had also begun work in Mexico, and in 1888, they organized their first presbytery. As was the case with other denominations, Presbyterian membership grew rapidly until 1910 and declined during the revolutionary period—although not as markedly as the Congregationalists and Quakers. The presbyteries of Chiapas and the Yucatan have also grown rapidly.

The Iglesia Nacional Presbiteriana and the Presbyterian Church in the USA (PCUSA) continued joint mission work along the border between the two nations. The Mexican church worked aggressively on evangelization, while its North American counterpart would train leaders and work on projects for the development of communities as well as for the protection of immigrants to the United States. The Iglesia Nacional Presbiteriana also related to the Presbyterian Church in America (PCA). The conservative tendencies of the PCA produced clashes with those within the church in Mexico of different theological inclinations, particularly in the seminaries, and eventually led the Iglesia Nacional to break ties with the Presbyterian Church USA as well as with most Reformed churches throughout the world—particularly over the ordination of women.

The mission of the Methodist Episcopal Church, South, developed out of the earlier work of Sóstenes Juárez, who had been converted to Protestantism by reading the Bible. In 1865, he had already preached the first Protestant sermon in Mexico City. He was ordained a Methodist minister in 1873, and his followers joined that church. At the time of the Mexican Revolution, early in the twentieth century, many Methodists—as well as other Protestants—took an active role in the revolution. In 1930, various groups resulting from different North American Methodist missionary enterprises joined to form the Iglesia Metodista de México.

The Southern Baptists, the American Baptists, and the Disciples of Christ also began working in Mexico during the nineteenth century. The American Baptists established their first permanent work in 1881. The first services in Mexico City took place two years later, and in

1887, they built their first church. As a result of this work, there are in Mexico several Baptist denominations, with a number of seminaries, Bible institutes, and schools. The Disciples of Christ began work in Mexico in 1894, but their growth has been extremely slow. Internal conflicts divided the church and limited its growth.

Much of the numerical growth of Protestantism during the twentieth century is the result of Pentecostal movements, many of them autonomous, whose history is difficult to discover and even more difficult to describe. Since it is impossible to tell the story of the origins of all of these movements, we will take as an example the case of Venancio Hernández and his Otomi people. While working in the United States, Hernández was converted in a Pentecostal church. Upon returning to Mexico, he decided to seek the conversion of Otomi Indians. He began by spending an entire year simply living in solidarity among the people, and only after that time did he preach the gospel to them. The response was almost instantaneous, with the result that he and his followers were evicted from the hacienda where they worked. With his small group of converts, he settled on a piece of arid land and, through continuous efforts, was able to make it productive. By repeating that process, and through the constant witness of all converts, the movement spread among the Otomi. This had enormous social and economic consequences for the entire community, including the construction of roads connecting the various population centers and the organization of a health insurance system allowing even the poorest in the community to receive medical services.

By the end of the twentieth century and early in the twenty-first, many Pentecostal movements—both those resulting from missionary work and those originating in Mexico itself—became much more visible. The Iglesia La Luz del Mundo—which preaches a gospel of prosperity—has almost 400,000 members, and the Assemblies of God have half a million. These various denominations emphasize evangelistic work, and in the last decades they have begun missionary work across the border into the United States. Even so, Protestantism remains a minority within the total population of Mexico.

G. Christianity in the Latin Caribbean

1. Roman Catholicism

Haiti was the first independent nation in Latin America, for in 1803, it expelled the French from its land. This movement for independence was marked by race considerations, so that almost all the white population was forced to leave the country. The main exception was a number of French priests who were allowed to remain on the island so they could administer the sacraments. The resulting scarcity of priests was ever more acute, and a population that had long retained many of their African rites and religious traditions once again turned to them. Ever since, in spite of every effort on the part of the clergy, it has not been possible to develop a strong Catholic Church in Haiti. Voodoo, a syncretistic system of African religions under a Catholic facade, is still the main religion of the land, which has thus become a vast missionary territory for the Catholic Church. Most of the clergy are foreigners, and in general, national priests do not occupy the most important positions. It is mostly in the fields of education and public welfare that Roman Catholicism has had an effect on Haitian life, for the public system of schools and hospitals is grossly inadequate, and therefore the parallel Catholic institutions become important instruments for the education and the well-being of the people. This situation has become even more marked after the devastating earthquake of 2010. According to statistics, 90 percent of the population in Haiti is Roman Catholic, although it is generally known that most Catholics also practice voodoo.

The area that is now the Dominican Republic was under Haitian rule from 1822 to 1844. Since that time, the Haitian government had severed its relations with the Holy See over the question of national patronage, and the Dominican Spanish-speaking population found itself in a schism for which it was not responsible. It was for this reason that the Dominicans' struggle for independence from Haiti took as its motto "God, Country, and Freedom." In 1844, and even well into the twentieth century, the various constitutions of the Dominican Republic declared Roman Catholicism to be the religion of the state although religious freedom was also guaranteed. In contrast with the rest of Latin America, and even though Catholicism was declared to be the official religion of the land, the matter of national patronage never became a serious issue, and in 1884, the government reached an agreement with the Holy See on this matter. According to this agreement, the pope would select the archbishop of Santo Domingo from among a list submitted by the Dominican congress. One should also note that some prelates have held high office in government—including the presidency—but that they have done this not as representatives of the church, but rather as private citizens and through an electoral process.

The scarcity of priests, already critical, continues to increase. In response, the church has taken a number of measures. First, it created the Instituto de Adaptación Pastoral, which offers courses for both national and foreign missionaries. Second, it organized and trained volunteers approved by the bishop to preach, distribute communion, and celebrate weddings, thus keeping a connection between the church and the daily life of people. Finally, "Councils of Ministries" were organized in order to aid in missionary work.

In 1992, the CELAM celebrated its fourth assembly in Santo Domingo. Its theme was "The New Evangelization." The government was harshly criticized for its expenses in connection with this gathering, contrasting with the extreme poverty of the people. Many also questioned the ideology and theology behind the celebration of 500 years of colonization after the "discovery" of America. Apparently responding to such criticism, the gathering of bishops acknowledged the complicity of the church in the genocide of the indigenous populations and in the practice of a violent form of evangelization. At the same time, it emphasized the "new evangelization," which was to promote justice and to turn the marginalized populations of Latin America into active agents of their own mission. These included groups such as women, blacks, and Indians. This gathering also discussed the enormous growth of Protestantism, particularly in its Pentecostal variety, throughout the continent.

When Cuba became independent in 1902, its constitution affirmed the separation of church and state and freedom of worship. Thus, the conflicts that characterized the early years of independence in other Latin American countries were not reproduced in Cuba.

Already in the last decades of Spanish rule it had become apparent that the Catholic Church in Cuba was in rapid decline, and this situation continued during the early years of the newly formed republic. However, in the third decade of the twentieth century, and due mostly to the work of Catholic Action, there were signs of new life: the number of Cuban priests increased; they were given greater responsibility; new religious orders were introduced into the country; and several schools and charitable institutions were organized. The result was that by 1956, there were almost 300 Catholic schools in the nation, besides several service-oriented institutions. By then, all the leading positions in the hierarchy were in Cuban hands, and the archbishop of Havana, who was also a Cuban, was a cardinal.

The revolution of 1959 brought enormous changes for the Catholic Church. Conflicts with the government increased rapidly—first on the matter of religious education, then on ecclesiastical property, and finally on ideological issues. A year after Fidel Castro came to power, a mass exodus of priests began. Eventually the government itself decided to expel hundreds of priests and prelates—both Cubans and foreigners. Given the circumstances, by the end of 1965, there were very few priests left in the country. Although the church was still free to continue its purely religious work, this was almost entirely limited to offering Mass and other sacraments.

Matters of relationships between church and state are normally under the jurisdiction of the Office of Religious Matters of the Cuban Communist Party. After the dismembering of the Soviet Union and the visit of Pope John Paul II, Catholics, as well as Protestants, have more freedom in church affairs. Another visit by Benedict XVI in 2012 did not seem to have much of an effect. Moreover, there are numerous reports that during the period beginning with the revolution of 1959, there has been an increase in church attendance as well as in the number of practicing Catholics, even though the number of nominal believers has declined drastically.

One of the most important challenges facing the Catholic Church in Cuba has to do with Afro-Cuban culture and religiosity. As Afro-Cuban traditions were affirmed by the revolution, their ancient religious practices came to the foreground, thus forcing the Catholic Church—as well as others, particularly the Episcopal Church—to struggle with an overt syncretism that clashes with traditional Catholic identity.

Puerto Rico became a North American possession in 1898 as a result of the Spanish-American War. Immediately there was separation between church and state, and freedom of worship was proclaimed. The matters of church patronage and properties that had so plagued other Latin American lands were more easily solved in Puerto Rico—the first by the separation of church and state, and the second through a negotiated agreement between the church and the new government.

When Spanish rule came to an end, the number of priests in Puerto Rico rapidly declined. This continued until 1930, when the number of priests began to increase, although slowly. To address this, large numbers of priests have been imported from other lands, to the point that in 1960, 80 percent of the clergy were not diocesan, but regular priests—and most of these were foreigners. Nevertheless, Puerto Rican and foreign priests have created Puerto Rican liturgies and missional ministries grounded in the Puerto Rican reality.

Early in the twenty-first century Puerto Rico confronted the United States, demanding that the U.S. Navy abandon the island of Vieques. The Catholic Church, together with many Protestant and Pentecostal bodies, joined in an ecumenical front in order to support the right of the people of Vieques to live without a constant military presence. The result of this ecumenical effort at solidarity led to the departure of the U.S. Navy.

Organizationally, there are in Puerto Rico no territories that the Catholic Church considers missionary jurisdictions. Rather, the entire island is under the jurisdiction of the diocesan hierarchy.

2. Protestantism

Protestant missionary work in Haiti began in 1807, when the British Methodists sent pastors to care for the Protestant immigrants arriving there from the British colonies in the Caribbean. The Baptists entered Haiti in 1823, when the Baptist Missionary Society of Massachusetts sent its first missionary, but this work was discontinued. Shortly thereafter, the Free Baptists and the London Baptist Missionary Society became interested in Haiti, but eventually the latter agency transferred its interests there to its counterpart in Jamaica. Finally, in 1923—a century after the arrival of the first missionary—the American Baptist Home Missionary Society began work in Haiti. The resulting church is one of the most remarkable aspects of Protestant growth in Haiti, for there have been mass conversions. Therefore, the Baptist community is an important sector of Haitian Protestantism.

The origins of the Episcopal Church of Haiti go back to 1861, when 110 black North Americans, in the hope of finding better living conditions than existed in the United States, migrated to the island republic under the leadership of James Theodore Holly. In spite of innumerable hardships and deaths, the remnants of the group conducted evangelism among their neighbors, and in 1874, the General Convention of the Episcopal Church granted independence to the new Haitian Orthodox Apostolic Church. Two years later, Holly was consecrated as bishop of Haiti and head of this church. When Holly died in 1911, at the request of the Haitian clergy, the church in Haiti become a missionary district of the Protestant Episcopal Church in the United States.

Other denominations working in Haiti are the Church of God (Cleveland), the Seventh-day Adventists, and the African Methodist Episcopal Church, whose work began in 1823. As in the rest of Latin America, the majority of Protestants are Pentecostal.

Protestantism entered what is now the Dominican Republic during the period of Haitian occupation, when Haitian president Jean Pierre Boyer decided that it would be advantageous to promote the immigration of North American blacks. The first immigrant contingent settled in Samana and Puerto Plata in 1824. From there they expanded throughout the entire peninsula of Samana, taking their faith with them.

Intentional missionary Protestant work in the Dominican Republic was the result of the initiative of Protestants in Puerto Rico and of the missionaries working with them. In 1920, Protestants in Puerto Rico formed the Board for Christian Service in Santo Domingo, with the participation of Methodists, Presbyterians, and United Brethren. At that point, such a board was a missionary experiment without precedent in the entire history of the church. Never before had several denominational mission agencies come together in order to establish a single united church in another land. The result of this effort was the Iglesia Evangélica Dominicana, which became independent in 1955.

There were a number of Episcopalians among the immigrants who settled in the Dominican Republic in the nineteenth century. They were interested in retaining their faith, and in 1898, they were able to have Bishop Holly, from Haiti, ordain their first pastor. However, the Protestant Episcopal Church of the United States did not show great interest in the Dominican Republic until the time when North American troops occupied it, and at that point it was interested only in ministry to foreigners living in that country. Work among West Indian immigrants was relegated to the background, and work in Spanish was completely abandoned. Work in Spanish was not begun in earnest until 1952.

The largest Pentecostal church in the Dominican Republic is the Assemblies of God. The Seventh-day Adventists are also quite numerous. As in the rest of Latin America, Pentecostal churches—both those resulting from foreign missionary work and those that originated in the country itself—were showing the most growth at the beginning of the twenty-first century.

Protestantism entered Cuba thanks to the efforts of Cubans who had been exiled during the struggles for independence and who had become Protestant in the United States. The leaders in these efforts were mostly Episcopalians, particularly a man by the name of Pedro Duarte, who finally decided that it was not enough to distribute the Bible. In 1884, Duarte gathered in Matanzas a congregation that he named "Fieles a Jesús"—that is, faithful to Jesus. After the war of 1898, interest in Cuba grew in the United States, and the Episcopal Church sent its first missionaries to support and extend Duarte's work. After the revolution of 1959, the political polarization of the church was such that for a long time it was unable to come together in the election of a bishop. However, even in the midst of these difficulties, this church has presented an ecumenical witness, participating actively in the Cuban Ecumenical Council, the Latin American Council of Churches, and the Caribbean Conference of Churches.

The origins of the Presbyterian Church in Cuba are similar to those of the Episcopal Church. The first Cuban exile was Evaristo Collazo, who, in 1890, wrote to the Southern Presbyterian Church in the United States letting it know of the existence of three congregations and a school for young girls that he and his wife had created and supported after that time. In response to Collazo's letter, a Presbyterian missionary working in Mexico was sent to Cuba, where he organized Collazo's congregations as Presbyterian churches. But all of this was interrupted during the War of Independence when the North American missionaries returned to their country and Collazo joined the rebel armies. After the war, Southern Presbyterian missionaries returned to Cuba, and Northern Presbyterians joined them. The latter worked mostly in Havana with the collaboration of Collazo and of Pedro Rioseco, another Cuban Presbyterian leader. The Southern Presbyterians made a significant contribution in education through the work of their missionaries Margaret E. Craig and Robert L. Wharton, who began in Cardenas the school that was eventually known as La Progresiva. In 1909, the Congregationalists bequeathed to the Northern Presbyterians the work they had begun in Cuba. In 1918, the Disciples of Christ followed suit with the three congregations and one pastor whom they had in Cuba. In 1947, the Seminario Evangélico de Teología was founded in Matanzas, Cuba. This was a joint enterprise of Methodists and Presbyterians, to which the Episcopal Church was added later.

Of all the churches in Cuba, it would seem that the Presbyterians were least affected by the revolution of 1959. This is particularly remarkable since before that revolution, this denomination limited its work almost exclusively to major cities and the higher middle classes. The Iglesia Presbiteriana Reformada en Cuba—the official name of the Presbyterian Church—has been at the vanguard of the ecumenical movement, not only in Cuba, but also throughout the Caribbean, Latin America, and the entire world, as part of the larger family of Reformed churches. It has produced national pastoral leadership with a high level of theological education, and it still serves a highly educated sector of the Cuban population.

Methodism, too, entered Cuba through the work of Cuban expatriots in the United States. In 1883, the Florida Conference sent two Cuban missionaries to their native land: Enrique B. Someillán and Aurelio Silvera. In December of 1898, after sending two representatives to explore the possibilities that the island offered, the Florida Conference of the Methodist Episcopal Church, South, organized a missionary district in Cuba.

As a result of the revolution, the Methodist Church, like others, suffered great losses. However, a charismatic awakening took place, which became quite apparent after the dissolution of the Soviet Union. The Methodist Church in Cuba is vibrant in growth and discipline, for one of the characteristics of this church has been that membership normally requires a very serious commitment and a long period of preparation. Partly as a result of this charismatic renewal, and partly due to different understandings of the role of the church in Communist Cuba, in 2007, the Methodist Church withdrew from the united seminary it had helped found in 1947 and created its own program of theological education. The Methodist Church continues participating in the Cuban Ecumenical Council as well as in other ecumenical agencies.

The Southern Baptist Convention, as well as the American Baptists and other Baptist bodies, have long had work in Cuba. This began in 1883, when Alberto J. Díaz, a Cuban who had been converted in New York, returned to his country in order to distribute Bibles. There are three main Baptist bodies in Cuba: the Convención Bautista de Cuba Oriental, the Asociación de la Convención Bautista de Cuba Occidental, and the Convención Bautista Libre de Cuba. The first of these three relates mostly with the American Baptists, the second with the Southern Baptists, and the third with the Free Baptists.

The most significant numerical growth in Cuba has taken place in the Pentecostal churches, both those founded by missionaries and those that originated in Cuba. The Iglesia Cristiana Pentecostal de Cuba—begun as a result of the work by Luis M. Ortiz, founder of the Movimiento Misionero Mundial in Puerto Rico—continues to grow and is an active participant in the Cuban Ecumenical movement and in the Latin American Council of Churches. The Iglesia Evangélica Pentecostal Cubana is one of the largest Protestant churches in the country, with a markedly national and independent character.

The pastoral leadership of all Protestant and Pentecostal churches is almost completely Cuban. Relations with other churches are generally limited to exchange of professors in theological institutions, small construction projects, visiting leaders, and participation in international ecumenical events.

The Cuban Ecumenical Council—which includes the Jewish community as an affiliate member—has served as a mediator between the churches and the state, often facilitating processes that are highly bureaucratic and political. It has also sponsored gatherings and consultations on Cuban history and theology. Finally, it serves as an important link among churches in Cuba and elsewhere.

The government has limited the activities of churches to an evangelizing effort generally isolated from social and cultural matters. Even so, after the dismemberment of the Soviet Union, and as a result of the ensuing economic crisis in Cuba, the churches began to rediscover dimensions of their mission on social and economic matters, as well as seeking to support the daily life of people living under very difficult conditions. While this rediscovery is going on, church growth seems to proceed apace. Since many of the new members have grown up for more than a generation under a communist regime that provided little or no exposure to Christian traditions, the churches have begun a process of Christian formation for membership that is in many ways similar to some of the practices of the very early Christian church—for instance, gathering in people's homes since it is impossible to build churches for new congregations, and the development of a careful process of preparation for baptism, which in some churches takes more than a year.

The first Protestant service in Puerto Rico was held in Ponce in 1869 in the home of a certain Otilio Salomons. The preacher was the pastor on the nearby island of St. Thomas. In 1870, the Dutch missionary Johannes Waldemar Zechune was granted permission to found a school in Vieques. In 1882, the first Anglican church in Vieques was organized. In 1902, James Heartt Van Buren, rector of the Episcopal parish of San Juan, was elected to serve as the first missionary bishop of Puerto Rico. From then on, this church continued building its Puerto Rican roots, and in 1964, the Right Reverend Francisco Reus Froilán became its first Puerto Rican bishop.

Puerto Rican Presbyterianism has its background in the earlier work of Antonio Badillo Hernández. During a visit to the neighboring island of St. Thomas in 1868, Badillo Hernández acquired an English translation of the Bible. His study of this Bible led him to embrace Protestant doctrines that he then shared with his family and friends. When a Protestant missionary arrived at Aguadilla in 1900, he found there a group of "believers in the Word" whose teaching coincided with Protestantism. This became the first nucleus for the Presbyterian Church in Puerto Rico.

Apart from the earlier work of Antonio Badillo Hernández, Presbyterianism has been present in Puerto Rico since 1899, when the first missionaries arrived. According to a comity agreement that divided the island among Protestant missionaries to evade competition, Presbyterians were to work in the western section of the island. There they organized an educational center that eventually became the Interamerican University of Puerto Rico. In San Juan itself, besides founding churches, this denomination also established the Presbyterian Hospital—a very prestigious institution that later was ceded to a private corporation. In 1919, jointly with several other denominations, they founded the Evangelical Seminary of Puerto Rico, which ever since has been the main training center for Presbyterian pastors and others. Eventually the Presbyterian Church in Puerto Rico was organized as a synod within the Presbyterian Church USA—the Sínodo Boriquén.

The Lutheran pioneer in Puerto Rico was a young seminarian, G. S. Swensson, who in 1898 began missionary work on his own account. As a result of his efforts and success, the General Lutheran Council sent other missionaries to the island, thus formally establishing Lutheranism there.

The first Baptist missionary in Puerto Rico, Hugh P. McCormick, reached the island in 1899 and centered his work in the city of Rio Piedras. There he held the first worship service in 1899, and the success of his work was such that the Baptist church of Rio Piedras was long one of the main Protestant churches on the island. One must also point out that as early as 1928, Puerto Rican Baptists were sending missionaries to El Salvador.

The Iglesia Evangélica Unida de Puerto Rico (United Evangelical Church of Puerto Rico) is the result of a union, in 1931, of the United Brethren, the Christian Church, and the Congregationalists. The United Brethren began working in Puerto Rico in 1899 and enjoyed great success in the south of the island. The denomination was just over twenty years old when it began sending Puerto Rican missionaries to the Dominican Republic. The Christian Church began working in Puerto Rico in 1901, also in Ponce. The Christian Congregational Church began work in Puerto Rico at approximately the same time, settling on the eastern region of the island.

Methodist work in Puerto Rico began in March 1900, when North American missionary Charles W. Drees arrived. He settled in San Juan, and from there expanded his work westward to Arecibo and southward to Guayama. From its very beginnings, Methodism showed its concern for education. It immediately opened a school in San Juan and shortly thereafter opened a home for orphan girls. This eventually resulted in the Robinson School, which still exists. After a long process culminating in 1992, the Methodist Church of Puerto Rico became autonomous. It also was an important participant in the ecumenical activities leading to the departure of the U.S. Navy from Vieques.

In 1901, the Disciples' Missionary Society sent William M. Taylor. In seven years, Taylor and those who later joined him organized two churches and five missions. But a revival in 1933 made the Disciples the largest non-Pentecostal Protestant church in the country. The Christian Church (Disciples of Christ) of Puerto Rico is an autonomous church, with missionaries in several Latin American countries, and has made significant contributions by providing leaders for the ecumenical movement as well as for theological education in Latin America and the United States.

Early in the twentieth century, a group of Puerto Rican laborers was moving to Hawaii in quest of better living conditions. Almost all of them were Roman Catholics, but several joined Protestant churches in Hawaii. It was there that Juan L. Lugo and Salomón Feliciano had their Pentecostal experiences. In 1916, while he was living in San Francisco, Lugo had a vision that he interpreted as a call from the Lord, and he decided to return to his native land to preach the gospel. Feliciano then joined Lugo and collaborated with him in Ponce. This was the beginning of the Assemblies of God in Puerto Rico. Lugo's work also lies at the foundation of other Pentecostal churches. This is particularly true of the Church of God (Cleveland), which in Puerto Rico is known as the Iglesia de Dios "Mission Board."

Most denominations showed interest in coordinating their work with others. This led in 1905 to the founding of the Federación de

Iglesias Evangélicas en Puerto Rico, which included Baptists, Congregationalists, the Christian Church, the Disciples of Christ, Methodists, Presbyterians, and United Brethren. In 1916, seeking to implement the resolutions of the congress held in Panama in that year, the federation became the Unión Evangélica en Puerto Rico. The union was at the very foundation of the Evangelical Seminary of Puerto Rico in 1919. In 1934, the Unión Evangélica became the Asociación de Iglesias Evangélicas de Puerto Rico, later the Concilio Evangélico, and finally the Concilio de Iglesias de Puerto Rico. In this entire process, the membership of this body was widened, coming to include Lutherans and Episcopalians as well as Pentecostals and independent churches.

While the "historical" denominations were losing their missional imperative, the Pentecostal and neo-Pentecostal movements continued to grow. By the middle of the twentieth century, Puerto Rico had become a center out of which Pentecostal missionaries were sent. The Movimiento Misionero Mundial is an example of a Puerto Rican Pentecostal church that has missions throughout the world.

H. General Considerations

As we look at the development of Christianity in Latin America some general considerations are in order.

Regarding the Roman Catholic Church, the independence of various Latin American countries was followed by a difficult period. These were sometimes due to the extremely conservative attitude of the higher clergy. To this was added the issue of patronage over the church, which placed the pope in the position of having to choose between acknowledging the still-insecure sovereignty of the new nations, and thereby alienating the Spanish crown, and leaving churches in Latin America without bishops and other leaders. Since initially Rome chose the latter option, Latin American Catholicism weakened considerably.

As the issue of patronage was solved, a slow reawakening of Roman Catholicism took place. This was aided by the presence of priests from Europe and North America. Slowly, a native clergy was developed, and the hierarchy was placed in the hands of native bishops.

The consequences of the Second Vatican Council for Latin America could be seen immediately after the closing of the council. The various sessions of the CELAM show both the vitality of the renewal movement and the many inner conflicts resulting from it.

Regarding Protestantism, the first important point to be made is that much of its early development was the result of the presence of immigrants from various Protestant countries. For a long time—in some cases, for entire generations—Protestant immigrants paid little attention to the task of communicating their faith to their Latin American neighbors. But eventually some of them felt compelled to witness to their faith. Early in the twenty-first century, there were still in Latin America significant pockets of Protestants speaking foreign languages, although trying to establish greater contact with the surrounding culture.

Another factor contributing to the growth of Protestantism in its early years was the political and philosophical liberalism that accompanied the struggle for independence. Leaders such as Bernardo O'Higgins, Domingo Faustino Sarmiento—President of Argentina—and Benito Juárez saw in Protestantism an ally against the excessive power of the Catholic clergy and the widespread ignorance among the people. This gave Protestantism access to the highest circles in a number of countries. Eventually, however, the very liberalism that had initially supported Protestantism became an obstacle. Liberalism itself, with its opposition to all religious authority and its emphasis on human power and dignity, conflicted with Protestant principles such as the authority of Scripture and the need for salvation in which all stand.

In general, the form of Protestantism that has developed most profound roots in Latin America is Pentecostalism. The reasons for this are not difficult to find. It suffices to remember the Pentecostal attitude of constant witness. To what extent this impulse will continue as new Pentecostal generations ascend in the social and intellectual scale is still to be seen. At present, however, it is necessary for the more traditional "historic" churches to ask themselves what is the nature of their own mission as a minority in Latin American Protestantism.

At the time of the Cold War, Latin American Protestantism was deeply divided. There are still wounds that hinder the work of all churches, traditional as well as Pentecostal, and that result in an attitude of competition rather than collaboration and solidarity. Overcoming such barriers is an urgent task facing Latin American Protestantism. It is also clear that the history of Protestantism in Latin American is actually the separate histories of Protestantism in different countries. There are some cases where the history of Protestantism in a particular country is entwined with another. But there are exceptions within a history of unconnected and sometimes mutually contradictory undertakings.

Despite the above, Protestantism and Pentecostalism, in their great diversity, continue to search for a missional identity that will bring healing to their Latin American context.

Chapter 11

FROM ALL THE NATIONS: MISSION IN A POSTMODERN AND POSTCOLONIAL WORLD

This history of missions concludes with a brief reflection on Christian missions in a postmodern and postcolonial era. It is important to note that both terms are included in this chapter because both "conditions" shape the global context and the interactions of Christian missionary work. While there are regions in the world that have not experienced modernity or have experienced it as human and natural devastation, many regions have gone beyond the late modern to a postmodern worldview. Although for many in the world the colonial era is gone, there are regions that continue to experience a neocolonial political configuration characterized by domination of economic powers. Yet, the postcolonial condition recognizes that the people in those regions claim their rights and are increasingly involved in resisting domination and changing their political and social condition.

As we look at Christian missions in a postmodern and postcolonial context, the history of missions helps us discern some of the challenges that Christian missionary work faces around the world.

A. A Complex History with Lessons for the Future

It is important to understand that the transmission of the Christian faith is not simply a matter of some nations sending and others receiving. Such distinctions were common in academic circles discussing missiology until well into the twentieth century, and they still remain in the thought and language of many believers. But this way of looking at things tends to disempower native agents, presenting them as passive and meek receptors who are being transformed through the work of foreign missionaries.

The truth is very different, for history shows that the missionary movement and action are multidirectional, multinational, multiethnic, intercultural, and interreligious. There is no doubt that many histories of mission written during the nineteenth century and early in the twentieth seem to take for granted that mission is a task undertaken by missionaries from Europe and North America. However, as we have seen, most missionary work has always been conducted by believers in each nation. Therefore, one must insist that the missionary movement is not a one-way street but is rather a network with multiple intersections and crossings, so that one cannot point to a particular center or to an established pattern of lineal, cumulative, and progressive movement. The fuller picture presents a much freer and fragile movement with success and failure, enthusiasm, frustrations, ambiguities, and perplexities.

1. Missions Depend on Context

Missionary work is affected by many factors, both internal and external to the missionary endeavor itself. Intense missionary work among certain groups never succeeded. Yet, an isolated historical event would trigger the growth and vitality of the spread of the gospel. Once the gospel takes root among the nationals, the continuity between the original missionary enterprise and its result becomes fragile and is often limited to ritual practices.

We also have examples of missionary work that resulted from the initiative of Christian leaders with very little or no ecclesial support. In such cases, missionary work had no expectations of duplicating a church organization. Yet, with time, missionary work created its own ecclesial structure with a new expression of church order, roles in ministry, sacramental practice, ethical demands, and character of witness.

Another lesson on the dependency of missionary work is that a successful missionary theology and strategy used in one context could not be replicated in another context. It is equally surprising to discover that missionary methods designed for a context were a disaster, yet when employed in another context, they were successful. It is quite obvious from this history of missions that any universal missionary recipe and structure falls short when tested in different contexts and that the genius of missionary work lies in the creativity of those involved in mission as they engage their context.

2. Translations and Cross-cultural Dynamics in Christian Missions

The Christian missionary movement shows that the gospel cannot be transmitted and received apart from the cultures of those transmitting and receiving it—their language, religion, symbols, rituals, ethical practices, and so on. Depending on how different the receiving cultures are from those transmitting the gospel, the levels of translation and cross-cultural dynamics vary. The principle of translation and cross-cultural dynamics in missionary work is based on the Christian experience of incarnation, for in Jesus Christ, God is present in translation within our human reality so that humanity may receive God not as a stranger but as one of us. The history of the Christian missionary movement shows how missionary activity was shaped by social, political, cultural, economic, and religious conditions of both the missionaries and their context, on the one hand, and the people and context where their missionary work took place, on the other hand.

This translation and cross-cultural dynamic in Christian missions points to the collapse of privilege in interpreting and living the gospel. Christians involved in missionary work discover what it means to live the gospel on other people's terms, hence becoming receptors of the gospel from those with whom they work. The cross-cultural dynamic of Christian missions always reverses the roles of missionaries and receptors. With time, the receptors become missionaries, the nationals become missionaries, and missionary work undergoes different cross-cultural engagements.

One must note that by far, most missionaries sought to live within the terms and requirements of the cultures in which they were working and to live with the people. Within this history there are two realities. On the one hand, one sees missionary work as distant, not rooted in the culture, and even exploitative; on the other hand, one sees mission work that is well set within its context and protective of the life of the people among whom it serves. These two realities appear constantly entwined in our history, so that the former is not easily or chronologically supplanted by the latter.

Another consequence of cross-cultural dynamics in Christian missions is the way in which people of other religions respond to missions. Christian missions in India resulted in what has been called the "Renaissance of Hinduism." In Africa, missionary work has revitalized traditional African religions and worldviews, producing different forms of syncretism between Christianity and traditional religious cultures. Some Buddhist schools find affinities and vitality with certain Christian expressions. Afro-Caribbean and Amerindian religions find in Christian missionary work a grounding for the consolidation of their faith. Yet, we also find significant tensions with and divisions against Christianity as a result of missionary work.

3. Motivations and Outcomes

There are many motivations for missions. This history not only shows how Christianity spread but also provides a window into what kind of Christianity spread and why. One important lesson from this history is that "the road to hell is paved with good intentions." Throughout this history, one can observe a variety of motivations and outcomes. Although motivations and outcomes did not always follow a cause-and-effect process, they continue to be interpreted under this rubric. Today, many missionaries return home on furlough in order to interpret to local congregations the missionary work they are doing. Despite the language of interpretation, many local congregations continue to understand these missionary interpretative visits as ways of keeping the congregation motivated in world missions. With that understanding in place, many congregations find deep disappointment in missions because the motivation is not coherent with the outcome *(How many new converts do we have in Africa, Asia, or Latin America?)*.

Motivations and outcomes in Christian missions stir profound religious sentiments that can either polarize people or bring them together. The present history shows many cases in which missions founded, motivated, and nourished a spirit of unity leading to what today we know as the ecumenical movement. Even those who did not join in or rejected that movement found in mission a spirit of unity and commonality of purpose. At the same time, missions also have resulted in severe conflict and division. Many of these divisions led to new denominations, and sometimes communication within such divided families has become very difficult. Motivational factors as well as the character of a particular expression of Christianity shape the way in which Christianity is received and appropriated. It takes generations to discern that the message transmitted through a particular missionary endeavor is not the normative standard for living and witnessing to the gospel in their own context.

The missionary task, even when it did not propose to create a new church or an organized Christian community—as in the cases of the China Inland Mission and of some of the more conservative evangelical denominations—normally gives birth to a church; and this church in turn becomes missionary. The history of missions underscores this symbiotic relationship between mission and church.

4. Breaking Christendom; Recovering Christianity

Missions have contributed to the dissolution of Christendom—the fusion of territoriality, a particular way of life, and certain values of the Christian religion that in fact have little to do with the gospel of Jesus Christ. Missions, by creating different forms of Christianity incarnate in various contexts, have brought into question the very notion of Christendom. This very diverse Christianity—not limited by territorial boundaries, fluid and prophetic, and particularly strong in the Third World—is the leaven within Christianity in the twenty-first century and a sign of the future of Christianity in a postmodern and postcolonial world.

B. Can an Old Center of Christianity Be a New Mission Field?

This history of missions points to a growing awareness: the old centers of missionary sending—North America (excluding Mexico) and Europe—are experiencing a significant decline in Christian population. In fact, Christianity is not declining at a faster rate in these old centers because immigrant Christian groups—from Africa, Asia, Latin America, and the Pacific—keep the vitality of the faith.

What makes the old centers new mission fields? The answer demands a brief historical account of the United States as a mission field.

1. Christianity to the Native Americans: Mission as Cultural Genocide

The conquest of the land and people in the Americas went hand in hand with the evangelization and Christianization of the continent. According to George Tinker, Professor of Native American Christianity and Religion, Catholic and Protestant missionaries evangelized under the paradigm of the *reducción,* which was a social and religious arrangement in which converts were under the very strict supervision, governance, and spiritual guidance of missionaries. From John Eliot (1604–90), a Congregational minister in New England, to Junípero Sierra (1713–84), a Franciscan priest in the Southwest and California, to Marcus and Narcissa Whitman (late 1840s), congregational missionaries of the American Board of Foreign Missions on the Oregon frontier, most missionaries removed the Native Americans from their cultural and social contexts as a method of evangelization and civilization.

Native Americans were considered to be either small children needing guidance and education or savages ready to be civilized. In many cases, to civilize the Native Americans became equally or even more important than evangelizing them. This mission principle is best illustrated in the now well-known words of John Eliot: Native Americans need to "have visible civility before they can rightly enjoy visible sanctity in ecclesiastical communion" (Rick Cogley, *John Eliot's Mission to the Indians before King Philip's War* [Cambridge: President and Fellows of Harvard College, 1999], p. 7).

Native Americans did not take this evangelization and civilization lightly. For every historical account of mass and individual conversions and the establishment of "missions," "prayer towns," and communities for farming, there are accounts of rebellions, massacres, and the fleeing of Native Americans from the missionaries and their compounds. Native Americans preferred to put their lives at risk with the government, the military, and the wilderness rather than undergo the cultural genocide and economic exploitation imposed by missionaries.

The result of this mission practice was devastating. Gustavo Gutierrez's term, "demographic collapse," referring to the genocide of the Amerindian peoples in Mesoamerica and South America, fits the North American experience of evangelization. Although missionaries were inspired to proclaim and teach the Native Americans about Christianity, the indigenous people of the United States experienced physical displacement, land theft, cultural humiliation, and genocide. Today, the Native American community continues to struggle against the historical and emotional baggage of this model of mission. Ironically, the Christian faith has become a source of hope for these communities in their struggle.

In summary, from the mid-seventeenth century to practically the turn of this century, mission to Native Americans was characterized by the following understanding: to the missionaries, conversion to Christianity meant conversion to Euro-American economic and political structures. These structures entailed the long-term subjugation of tribal peoples to a conquering people. To Native Americans, it meant conversion to new and destructively alien social structures, patterns of behavior, and concepts of morality. This more often than not resulted in the erosion of native cultural values and community structures. Missions to Native Americans left the people even weaker in their struggle for parity with the conqueror.

2. Christianity to the African American Slaves: An Unexpected Outcome

The first century and a half of evangelization of the African slaves represents a sad irony in the history of missions in the United States.

Albert Raboteau, Professor of Religion at Princeton University, points out that, although "preaching the gospel to all nations" usually meant that the Christian disciple was sent out with the gospel to the "pagan" nations, when a pagan slave was brought to a Christian disciple, the latter was frequently reluctant to evangelize the former.

This first attempt of evangelization was characterized by the objection of masters to evangelize slaves, the "lack of witness" of white people to slaves, and the linguistic and cultural barriers faced by the missionaries with their catechetical method of evangelism. Mission to the African slaves became more of a burden than a responsibility. It not only threatened the social, economic, and political structures of the colonies, but also represented a crossing of cultural and religious boundaries that few were willing to make.

The Awakenings became turning points in the acceptance of Christianity among African American slaves. Affinities between the revivals and the African religious culture were strong. The Awakenings also provided significant levels of inclusiveness that created conditions for a more genuine missionary work. Emphasis on the conversion experience rather than on catechesis became an additional factor in the acceptance of Christianity by slaves. The conversion of slaves to Christianity and the emergence of African American churches with their own leadership contributed to an increasing connection among redemption, liberation, and the awareness of human dignity as part of the Christian experience and life.

The role of black preachers cannot be underestimated when reflecting on the United States as a mission field. Though only considered lay preachers or exhorters by most white Christian leaders, black preachers were bridges between Christian theology and practice and the world of the slaves. Black preachers—including black women—were the epitome of the cultural synthesis "Afro-American" and a new stage in mission work to African slaves. From then on, American Christianity has had an African American flavor.

Between 1800 and 1865, the United States experienced what historians have called "Christian America." The United States was considered a "promised land" with a mission to the world. As this sentiment grew stronger, African American marginal voices began to question such interpretation and to propose a new understanding of North America as a mission field.

African Americans constructed, within their prophetic denunciation, an alternate understanding of mission for "Christian America." The African American Christian metaphor replaced the self-satisfying paradigm of "promised land" with a challenging paradigm of liberation, hope, and peace. It was both a prophetic voice for the white establishment, blinded by its greed, and a paradigm rooted in history and in evangelical experience.

Who would have known that these African American slaves and their descendants would appropriate the Christian faith in such a way as to disrupt the tranquility, optimism, and Manifest Destiny of the white establishment? For some, this has been a curse, for others, a wonderful development in the African American religious experience. For all, it should be a witness of Christian discernment and a revision of existing models for missions.

3. Volunteer Organizations and Women's Groups

The Second Great Awakening produced a number of voluntary organizations whose purpose was to do mission in the United States. The American Bible Society, whose purpose was to spread and make known the gospel, and the American Society for the Promotion of Temperance, which led the battle against alcohol, were some of the best-known voluntary organizations of this period.

Volunteer societies proved to be a driving force for defining and engaging in mission. These societies provided the opportunity for groups of people to come together for a particular purpose and objective without the need of official endorsement or support. Voluntary groups were organized to do mission to immigrants, Native Americans, African Americans, and people in other lands. The character of their mission activity and approach varied greatly. Some encouraged social and political transformation, while others were mainly preoccupied with "soul saving," civilizing, and education.

Women's groups had an important role in social and political work, contributing to defining mission in the U.S. context. Women such as Sarah and Angelica Grimké in the abolition movement, Dorothea Dix in the treatment of the mentally ill, Catherine Beecher in educational opportunities for women, Frances Willard in the temperance crusade, and Jane Addams in urban social work held leadership positions with an important political and social voice. They contributed not only to these causes but also to women's rights and suffrage.

The revivals provided a new social and religious space where women were able to have public participation and recognition. Roots of the modern feminist movement are found in the women's participation and changing roles that resulted from the Second Great Awakening.

4. A Contemporary Example: The United States Is a Mission Field!

The evangelical/liberal debate gives further insight into the question, "Can an old center of Christianity be a new mission field?" In many ways the debate is not over. However, the controversy over the meaning of the gospel produced interesting and long-term innovative responses that could be considered missionary in their character. Some examples are in order.

One of these innovative responses was the Holiness movement. In addition to their emphasis on the work of the Holy Spirit "as a second blessing," many appreciated and participated in social mission. The strong call for a simple lifestyle and the commitment to help the urban poor were intrinsic to conversion and discipleship. Many of these groups not only were involved in social and economic relief but also had a political engagement unique to their conservative character. In fact, American scholars agree that by 1910, there were signs of a progressive evangelical understanding of politics. The Holiness movement supported labor legislation, advocated for justice regarding women and children's labor, and promoted better treatment of immigrants. It also worked for peace in the world. While the Holiness movement's foreign missionary work was often fueled by dispensationalism, it did integrate social concerns and justice to its theology of missions and of the end of time.

Pentecostals still consider the United States to be a mission field. Their involvement in missions focused on the home front, extending congregations all over the United States and Canada. Their mission work, not limited to planting churches, also provided members and nonmembers with a deep and broad experience of love and care. Their work included practices such as visiting and caring for the ill, pastoral care and counseling, emergency financial aid, and help for the new arrivals in their process of getting acquainted with their new community. Drug rehabilitation programs and rehabilitating programs for prostitutes and other outcasts of the community were common, not only in separate congregations, but also in networks of Pentecostal Christian churches.

Many of these groups have entered the media culture with an emphasis on the United States as a mission field. Their programs, focused on the issues people face day to day, are having a great effect on the religious configuration of the country. Many of these programs, televised from megachurches or on living room stages, reveal the commitment of Pentecostals, neo-Pentecostals, and other groups "to bring the United States to the hands of God."

Finally, more recently, historic mainline, Evangelical, Pentecostal, and neo-Pentecostal Christian communities are engaging in different forms of missions. From evangelistic work to interreligious dialogue and hospitality events, Christian communities offer an interpretation of the gospel guided by some of the current expressions of world missionary work.

Regretfully, in many Christian communities, the old "sending" framework—to reach the pagans—continues to shape missionary work. In some circles the assumption is masked by expressions of hospitality, while in orders, Christian missionary encounters and engagement assume that people of color, immigrants, and women are children who need to be evangelized and civilized.

5. The Need for a New Mind-Set

Perhaps one of the biggest challenges our question poses is at the level of mind-set: can we Christians in the United States see ourselves as fresh receptors of the Christian gospel? Based on the lessons discussed above, can Christians in the United States rediscover the gospel as we receive it from those whom we rarely considered agents of God's missionary activity?

We have inherited a "sending" and "resolving" mentality that creates resistance to learning from those whom we believe have no true faith because they do not live like we do or have the religious structures that we have. We also carry the history of manifest destiny. Hence, how could we, the elected of God, now be receptors of the Christian gospel?

Yet, our local Christian communities are surprised and refreshed by the passion and zeal of Christians from the new centers of growth and vitality—many of them immigrants. Music, new rhythms, new language about God's care and presence with creation, and the passion that goes beyond a privatized Christian experience energize people in the pews and generate questions about the character of their faith. When those questions challenge our own structures of organized Christianity, we tend to suppress and domesticate the questions, the energy, and the passion generated by cross-cultural missional encounters—foreign or national. We seem to go back and quote Scripture: "Can anything good come out of Nazareth?" (John 1:46b). And the answer is yes!

C. Christianity at the Beginning of the Twenty-First Century: Missionary Challenges

Let us look at some of the statistics illustrating the results of the missionary movement in the twentieth century. At the beginning of that century, there were approximately 381 million Christians in Europe, 79 million in North America, 62 million in Latin America, 10 million in Africa, and 22 million in Asia. In 1950, the countries with the greatest proportion of Christian population were the United Kingdom, France, Spain, and Italy. Thus, it is evident that until the middle of the twentieth century, the majority of Christians were living in the Northern Hemisphere. By the year 2000, there were 481 million Christians in Latin America, 360 million in Africa, and 313 million in Asia. Out of 2 billion Christians in the world, 820 million were in the North Atlantic, and the rest (1.2 billion) were elsewhere on the planet. More concretely, approximately 58 percent of all Christians live in the Third World, while 42 percent live in North America (excluding Mexico) and Western Europe. This demographic change will probably become even more marked in the coming fifty years. It is projected that by the year 2050, 68 percent of Christians will live in the Southern Hemisphere. Furthermore, out of the remaining 32 percent, a fourth will be immigrants to the North from countries in the South where Christianity shows great vitality. As historian Philip Jenkins points out, soon the time will come when to speak of a "white Christian" will seem as strange as speaking today of a "Swedish Buddhist."

Thus, it is evident that Christianity is undergoing a process of transition that forces us to reinterpret history. Demographic change brings with it the challenge to reevaluate and reorient our understanding of Christian mission. This in itself has several facets: first, although this history of the Christian missionary movement stresses the activity of transmitting the faith, the task still remains of looking at the entire enterprise underscoring the process of reception. The new demographic order forces us, as African Lamin Sanneh has suggested, to study Christianity's relationship with indigenous people and the indigenous people's reception and appropriation of the gospel of Jesus Christ. The discovery is on the part of the people receiving the gospel. Agency and activity in mission belong to the people who discover the gospel, and this has to be narrated, recorded, evaluated, and celebrated.

A missiological corollary of the demographic shift is that we must reaffirm and study the mutuality involved in the process of transmission and reception of Christianity—the cross-cultural dynamic of Christian missions. This mutuality is like the two sides of a single coin, integrating the history of missions with the whole of church history. If mission and the life of the church are entwined, it follows that we must integrate our interpretation of what is already a single historical and religious phenomenon.

Second, within the present demographic change, it is clear that it is mostly poor nonwhite women belonging to traditional cultures who are the main transmitting and receiving agents for Christianity in the twenty-first century. When the protagonist of a drama changes, we actually have a different drama. Until very recently, the main protagonist of mission was the white man. There is a new protagonist, and we can therefore be certain that the drama itself will not be the same and that the presence of the spirit of Christ will show itself in different ways in this new drama. This drama points to the contextual constellation of sources that inform and shape the daily life experience of Christians in Africa, Asia, Latin America, and the Pacific. From Christianized ancient rhythms, cultural and religious linguistic expressions, to new testimonies of God's grace and power, this demographic shift offers a new grammar, a new musical score, a new configuration of power in the theology and practice of missions. What may seem superstitious, magical, and traditional for Euro-American Christians may be expressions of the gospel of Jesus Christ, embodied among poor traditional women of color. Such expressions generate meaning, challenge evil and injustice, and offer hope in a context of uncertainty and poverty.

Another implication in this new drama is the discovery of Jesus' activity in the daily life experience and expectations of Christians from the Third World, including immigrants in the Euro-Atlantic regions. Christianity's new space of vitality is a context of extreme poverty. Pentecostal and independent Christian communities abound in favelas and poor urban communities. Christian communities also grow in villages and in the rural areas. Poverty and faith have a synergy that challenges assumptions of faith and wealth typical of many Christians in Europe, Canada, and the United States. The daily life experience of being poor and Christian translates into the public domain, not as philanthropy or benevolence, but as a pillar of survival. For example, the confession "Jesus is my healer" takes a very different connotation in a context in which there are no medical resources. "Jesus is my healer" is not just a statement of confession or an assertion of biblical faith. It is an expectation of faith, framed in an eschatological lifestyle in which the intervention of Jesus as healer is expected. Jesus as healer is tested through the healing of a person who was ill. In this confession, the community participates in and embodies the power of Jesus' healing. Paradoxically, when healing fails, faith is not lost, but rather failure is usually explained as the battle of good against evil. Faith is not always about winning but is always being tested. In such testing, theology becomes generative!

Third, the current demographic change requires historical sensitivity for religions, for the history of their encounters with Christianity, and for the social and cultural dimensions of the process of conversion from another religion to Christianity. For many years, missionary work in various non-Christian lands provided resources so that new converts could face the struggles and conflicts resulting from their conversion to "Western religion." As the peoples of the Southern Hemisphere discover their Christianity is no longer a Western religion (just as technology is no longer merely Western), but has become a legitimate option among many religious alternatives, the dynamics between Christianity and other religions will be transformed. In addition, the quest for truth in ancient esoteric religions—what is often called "new-age" religions—will be part of the picture. This will lead to conversations that will be similar to those of early Christians with Greek philosophical and various religious traditions.

Fourth, the new demographics result in a missionary movement that is no longer the exclusive responsibility of the West toward the South, but rather it moves in all directions yet with a major protagonist role coming from the South. Thus, there are Korean missionaries working in Africa, Latin America, and the Caribbean. Hundreds of missionaries from Brazil are working in Muslim lands, although often without sufficient training. African missionaries work in Europe and the United States, with both immigrant groups and other people of African descent. Missionary families from Korea are developing congregations for Korean immigrants in Germany, but they are also beginning to develop a national ecumenical movement in which they become part of the tapestry of Christianity in Germany. This is not merely the result of churches from the developed world inviting their partners in mission to share with them. It is also an intentional decision on the part of many in the underdeveloped world to serve as missionaries in the northern countries that seem mired in moral decadence and "neopaganism."

Short-term mission trips have become an enterprise—financial and ministerial. To give an example, among United Methodists in the United States, over 100,000 people participated in some kind of short-term missionary trip in 2012. What mission framework shapes our short-term missionary trips? Are our Christian mission leaders helping congregations for their role in this new drama of the Christian faith and mission? Are Christian missionary leaders leaving in the hands of missionary entrepreneurs the crucial vocation of engaging in missionary work with cross-cultural awareness, including reinterpreting the gospel back home?

Fifth, this demographic change is taking place at a time of great global uncertainty—of wars, violence, death, and disasters whose effect is very significant in the southern regions. In Southern Africa, where Christianity is growing at a faster rate than anywhere else in the world, the rate of deaths from AIDS is also the highest in the world. The problems of poverty in Africa, Asia, and Latin America have resulted in the exploitation of children, particularly girls who are denied access to health care and education and are victims of human trafficking. More than 46 percent of the world's population lives in poverty, and more than a third of that population lives in extreme poverty, while 9 percent is extremely rich (and .05 percent are considered "super rich"). This demographic change in Christianity is not accompanied by a parallel political or economic shift. While Christianity grows in the South, poverty is also growing in the same lands. Therefore, the new conditions will require political and economic solidarity between the churches in the richer North and those in the South.

Sixth, these demographic changes, joined to the failure of economic globalization, have resulted in an unprecedented movement of people—paralleled by a similar movement of money and resources. Within this context there are three situations that have a profound effect on the life and mission of the church. The first of these is that there are millions of migrating Christians who expect that the churches in their lands of origin will meet their spiritual needs and who are thus forcing those churches to move beyond their traditional contexts to face new challenges. Another is that many of these Christians join other Christian traditions—for instance, Caribbean Pentecostals may become Methodists in the United States or might join the Reformed Church in Spain—thus creating cultural and religious dislocation both for them and for the traditions receiving them with open arms but without a full understanding of the changes that their presence will bring. Finally, the conversion of many of these immigrants to Pentecostal and Charismatic churches—which tend to be closer to the cultural and economic realities of the poor—continues changing the face of Christianity, which in turn causes confusion in some ecclesiastical circles and chaos in strategic and theological missionary circles still working with the old paradigm of mission from the West.

Seventh, the twenty-first century is also witnessing the growth of fundamentalist movements promoting violence at both the national and international levels, which results in an antagonism toward religion not only in the Western world but also among others who have been influenced by modernity. Therefore, very often many see the growth of Christianity within the context of traditional cultures as a step backward.

At the same time, conservative and fundamentalist groups in the North find some parallelism between their interests and those of believers in the South whom they consider their political allies. As a result, the latter are often subject to ideological and political manipulation by Christians in the North. A recent example is the debate taking place among the more traditional denominations in the North regarding the ordination of homosexuals. As a means to strengthen their position, conservative groups in these denominations have argued that agreeing to the ordination of homosexuals would lead to conflicts and division with sister churches in the South, which tend to be more conservative on such issues. In those southern churches, some allow themselves to be involved in this ideological maneuver, while most ask why their opinion is important in this matter but was not requested when it came to financial issues or to the distribution of economic resources.

Eighth, we are facing a new configuration in the manner in which churches are organized. For instance, in 1970, 41 percent of

Christian churches called themselves denominational, while 58 percent declared themselves to be postdenominational. By 2000, the statistics had changed, leaving only 35 percent in the first category and 65 percent in the latter. From the point of view of mission, this implies that the spirit of volunteerism that was so characteristic of the Christian missionary movement in the nineteenth and twentieth centuries will continue to grow. Many postdenominational groups do not have the structures of responsibility that are characteristic of denominations and their boards of missions. The absence of such structures—and even of a parallel bureaucracy—results in greater freedom in the missionary movement, coupled with the lack of training and of support for many who are engaged in mission.

Finally, the present changes will also affect the theological and ministerial tasks. Theology is now born out of the daily experience of millions of Christians who live in constant contact with poverty, with other religious traditions, with war, violence, uncertainty, lack of health services, and with many other evils related to the process of economic globalization. Refugees today will find hope and faith in the sermons of John Calvin, who was himself a refugee. Those traditions that have known and claimed John Calvin for generations, but that have not experienced human displacement for a long time, will discover a new interpretation of the reformer that may well serve as a power to revitalize the church. Poor women whom the structure of the church marginalizes will find in women missionaries of the past—both international as well as national and local—a voice affirming their spirituality above any religious establishment or bureaucracy. As a result, perhaps the church will awaken and do justice to the role that women have had throughout the life and development of the entire church.

In short, mission will not come to an end. Christianity lives today in spectacular times, full of tensions and paradoxes that demand faith, love, and hope. Christianity is no longer a Western religion; in fact, it never was, even though we may have thought otherwise. Christianity has reached every nation. It may have more vitality and experience greater growth in some nations than in others. But there is no doubt that its face has become more diverse, including various races and colors. The world Christian missionary movement has reached the point at which women and men of every race and culture, *from all the nations*, go *to all the nations* to discover and proclaim the message of salvation and of hope for the kingdom of God.

FOR FURTHER READING

This list provides the following: (1) some of the most current scholarship on the field of mission studies, particularly history and missiology; (2) some examples of past mission histories—general and based on geographical regions; and (3) some reference resources and journals on history of the missionary movement, missiology, and mission studies.

General Readings on History and Christian Mission

Bevans, Stephen, and Roger Schroeder. *Constants in Context: A Theology of Mission for Today.* Maryknoll, NY: Orbis Books, 2004.

Briggs, John, Merci Amba Oduyoye, and George Tsetsis. *A History of the Ecumenical Movement.* Vol. 3, *1968–2000.* Geneva: World Council of Churches, 2004.

Hunt, Robert. *The Gospel among the Nations.* Maryknoll, NY: Orbis Books, 2010.

Isichei, Elizabeth. *A History of Christianity in Africa.* Lawrenceville, NJ: Africa World Press; Grand Rapids: William B. Eerdmans, 1995.

Jenkins, Philip. *The Lost History of Christianity: The Thousand-Year Golden Age of the Church in the Middle East, Africa, and Asia—and How It Died.* New York: HarperOne, 2008.

Latourette, Kenneth Scott. *A History of the Expansion of Christianity.* 9 vols. New York: Harper, 1944.

Lindenfeld, David, and Miles Richardson. *Beyond Conversion and Syncretism: Indigenous Encounters with Missionary Christianity, 1800–2000.* New York: Berhahn Books, 2012.

Neill, Stephen. *A History of Missions.* Baltimore: Penguin Press, 1964.

Park, Hyung-jin. "The Journey of the Gospel: A Study in the Emergence of World Christianity and the Shift of Christian Historiography in the Last Half of the Twentieth Century." Diss., Princeton University, 2009.

Robert, Dana. *Christian Mission: How Christianity Became a World Religion.* Chichester, UK, and Malden, MA: Wiley-Blackwell, 2009.

Rouse, Ruth, and Stephen Neill. *A History of the Ecumenical Movement.* Vol. 1, *1517–1948.* Geneva: World Council of Churches, 1954.

———. *A History of the Ecumenical Movement.* Vol. 2, *1948–1968.* Geneva: World Council of Churches, 1967.

Tucker, Ruth. *From Jerusalem to Irian Jaya: A Biographical History of Christian Missions.* Grand Rapids: Zondervan, 2004.

Warneck, Gustav. *Outline of a History of Protestant Missions from the Reformation to the Present Time: A Contribution to Modern Church History.* New York: Fleming Revell, 1901.

Winter, Ralph, and Steven Hawthorne, eds. *Perspectives on the World Christian Movement: A Reader.* Pasadena, CA: William Carey Library, 2009.

Missions in Antiquity

Drijvers, Hans J. W. *East of Antioch: Studies in Early Syriac Christianity.* London: Variorum Reprints, 1984.

Ehrman, Bart D. *After the New Testament: A Reader in Early Christianity.* New York: Oxford University Press, 1999.

Harnack, Adolf von. *The Mission and Expansion of Christianity in the First Three Centuries.* London: Williams and Norgate, 1908.

Stark, Rodney. *The Rise of Christianity.* New York: Harper Collins, 1996.

Thurston, Bonnie Bowman. *The Widows: A Women's Ministry in the Early Church.* Philadelphia: Fortress Press, 1989.

Trevett, Christian. *Montanism: Gender, Authority, and the New Prophecy.* Cambridge: Cambridge University Press, 1996.

Missions in the Middle Ages

Abou-el-Haj, Barbara. *The Medieval Cults of Saints: Formations and Transformations.* New York: Oxford University Press, 1994.

Gervers, Michael, and Jibran Bikhazi. *Indigenous Christian Communities in Islamic Lands: Eighth to Eighteenth Centuries.* Ontario, Canada: Pontifical Institute of Medieval Studies, 1990.

Mingana, Alphonse. *The Early Spread of Christianity in Central Asia and the Far East: A New Document.* Manchester: University Press, 1925.

Papadakis, Aristeides. *The Christian East and the Rise of the Papacy: The Church AD 1071–1453.* Crestwood, NY: Vladimir's Seminary Press, 1994.

Russell, James C. *The Germanization of Early Medieval Christianity: A Sociohistorical Approach to Religious Transformation.* New York: Oxford University Press, 1994.

Sullivan, Richard Eugene. *Christian Missionary Activity in the Early Middle Ages.* Great Britain: Variorum, 1994.

Wemple, Suzanne Fonay. *Women in Frankish Society: Marriage and the Cloister, 500–900.* Philadelphia: University of Pennsylvania Press, 1991.

Winkler, Dietmar W., and Li Tang. *Hidden Treasures and Intercultural Encounters: Studies on East Syriac Christianity in China and Central Asia.* Berlin: Lit Verlag, 2009.

Missions in the Modern Era and by Geographical Regions

Far East and South Pacific

Bergunder, Michael. *The South Indian Pentecostal Movement in the Twentieth Century.* Grand Rapids: William B. Eerdmans, 2008.

Elia, Pasquale M. *The Catholic Missions in China.* Shanghai, China: The Commercial Press, 1941.

Firth, Cyril Bruce. *An Introduction to Indian Church History.* Delhi, India: Published for the Senate of Serampore College by ISPCK, 2008.

Frykenberg, Robert Eric. *Christianity in India.* New York: Oxford University Press, 2009.

Lee, Young-Hoon. *The Holy Spirit Movement in Korea.* Oregon: Wipf & Stock, 2009.

Lian, Xi. *The Conversion of Missionaries: Liberalism in American Protestant Missions in China, 1907–1932.* University Park: Pennsylvania State University Press, 1997.

Lyon, D. Willard. *Sketch of the History of Protestant Missions in China.* New York: Fleming H. Revell, 1895.

Moffett, Samuel Hugh. *A History of Christianity in Asia.* Vol. 1, *Beginnings to 1500.* Harper: San Francisco, 1992.

The Muslim World

Badr, Habib, ed. *Christianity: A History in the Middle East.* Beirut, Lebanon: Middle East Council of Churches, 2005.

Bailey, Betty Jane, and J. Martin Bailey. *Who Are the Christians in the Middle East?* Grand Rapids: William B. Eerdmans, 2003.

Cragg, Kenneth. *The Arab Christian: A History in the Middle East.* Louisville, KY: Westminster/John Knox Press, 1991.

———. *The Call of the Minaret.* New York: Oxford University Press, 1956.

Friedrich, Norbert, Uwe Kaminsky, and Roland Löffler. *The Social Dimension of Christian Missions in the Middle East: Historical Studies of the 19th and 20th Centuries.* Stuttgart: Steiner, 2010.

Makdisi, Ussama Samir. *Artillery of Heaven: American Missionaries and the Failed Conversion of the Middle East*. Ithaca, NY : Cornell University Press, 2008.

Richter, Julius. *A History of Protestant Missions in the Near East*. New York: Fleming H. Revell, 1910.

Sub-Saharan Africa

Du Plessis, Johannes Christiaan. *A History of Christian Missions in South Africa*. New York: Longmans, Green, 1911.

Fields, Karen Elise. *Revival and Rebellion in Colonial Central Africa: Revisions to the Theory of Indirect Rule*. Princeton, NJ: Princeton University Press, 1985.

Hanciles, Jehu. *Euthanasia of a Mission: African Church Autonomy in a Colonial Context*. London: Praeger, 2002.

Kalu, Ogbu. *African Pentecostalism: An Introduction*. New York: Oxford University Press, 2008.

MacMaster, Richard Kerwin. *A Gentle Wind of God: The Influence of the East Africa Revival*. Scottdale, PA: Herald Press, 2006.

Sanneh, Lamin. *Disciples of All Nations*. New York: Oxford University Press, 2008.

Sill, Ulrike. *Encounters in Quest of Christian Womanhood: The Basel Mission in Pre and Early Colonial Ghana*. Boston: Brill, 2010.

Sundkler, Bengt. *A History of the Church in Africa*. New York: Cambridge University Press, 2000.

Wallis, John Peter Richard, ed. *The Matabele Mission: A Selection from the Correspondence of John and Emily Moffat, David Livingstone and Others, 1858–1878*. London: Chatto & Windus, 1945.

Williams, Walter W. *Black Americans and the Evangelization of Africa, 1877–1900*. Madison: University of Wisconsin Press, 1982.

Latin America

Bailey, Gauvin A. *Art on the Jesuit Missions in Asia and Latin America, 1542–1773*. Toronto: University of Toronto Press, 1999.

Cardoza-Orlandi, Carlos F. *From Christian Continent to Mission Field: The Missional Discourse of the Committee on Operation in Latin America and Protestant Latin Americans Concerning the Missional Needs of Latin America (1910–1938)*. Michigan: UMI Dissertation Services, 1999.

Committee on Cooperation in Latin America. *Regional Conferences in Latin America: The Reports of a Series of Seven Conferences Following the Panama Congress in 1916, Which Were Held at Lima, Santiago, Buenos Aires, Rio de Janeiro, Baranquilla, Havana, and San Juan*. New York City: Latin America Education Missionary Movement, 1917.

Cook, Guillermo, ed. *New Face of the Church in Latin America*. Maryknoll, NY: Orbis Books, 1994.

Dussel, Enrique. *A History of the Church in Latin America: Colonialism to Liberation, 1492–1979*. Translated by Alan Neely. Grand Rapids: William B, Eerdmans, 1981.

González, Ondina E., and Justo González. *Christianity in Latin America*. New York: Cambridge University Press, 2008.

Goodpasture, H. MacKennie, ed. *Cross and Sword: An Eyewitness History of Christianity in Latin America*. Maryknoll, NY: Orbis Books, 1989.

Grose, Howard B. *Advance in the Antilles*. New York: Presbyterian Home Missions, 1910.

Irarrazával, Diego. *Inculturation: A New Dawn of the Church in Latin America*. Maryknoll, NY: Orbis Books, 2000.

Smith, Dennis, and Benjamín Gutiérrez. *In the Power of the Spirit: The Pentecostal Challenge to Historic Churches in Latin America*. Louisville, KY: Geneva Press, 1996.

Post-colonial Missions

Fox, Frampton F. *Edinburgh 1910 Revisited: Give Us Friends: An Indian Prospective on One Hundred Years of Mission*. Bangalore, India: CMS/ATC, Asian Trading Corporation, 2010.

Pui-lan, Kwok. *Hope Abundant: Third World and Indigenous Women's Theology*. Maryknoll, NY: Orbis Books, 2010.

Tinker, George E. *Missionary Conquest: The Gospel and Native American Cultural Genocide*. Minneapolis, MN: Fortress Press, 1993.

References and Journals

Anderson, Gerhard, ed. *Biographical Dictionary of Christian Missions*. Grand Rapids: William B. Eerdmans, 1998.

Moreau, A. Scott. *Evangelical Dictionary of Missions*. Grand Rapids: Baker Books, 2000.

Neill, Stephen, Gerhard Anderson, and John Goodwin. *Concise Dictionary of the Christian World Mission*. Nashville: Abingdon Press, 1971.

Note: The following list provides the reader with journal titles that address issues of history and theology of Christian mission.

International Bulletin of Missionary Research
International Review of Mission
Mission Studies: Journal of the International Association of Mission Studies
Missionalia (South Africa)
Missiology: An International Review
Exchange: Journal of Missiological and Ecumenical Research

NOTES

Chapter 4. Medieval Missions

1. In this chapter, the term *Catholic* is not used in its contemporary meaning, as opposed to Protestant, but rather as it was used then, as not being Arian.

2. Bede, *Ecclesiastical History of the English Nation*, 1.30, trans. David Knowles (London: J. M. Dent & Sons, 1910), 52–53.

3. Patrick, *Confession*, iii.23, in *The Life and Writings of the Historical Saint Patrick*, trans. R. P. C. Hanson (New York: Seabury Press, 1983), 92.

Chapter 9. Missions in Sub-Saharan Africa

1. Cited in Elizabeth Isichei, *A History of Christianity in Africa* (London: Africa World Press, 1995), 142.

2. Ibid., 106.

3. Quoted in Cecil Northcott, *Livingstone in Africa* (London: United Society for Christian Literature, 1957), p. 48.

INDEX